The Classic 1000 Dessert Recipes

Everyday Eating made more exciting

		QUANTITY	AMOUNT
Classic 1000 Recipes	0-572-01671-9 £5.99		
Classic 1000 Chinese	0-572-01783-9 £5.99		
Classic 1000 Indian	0-572-01863-0 £5.99		
Classic 1000 Italian	0-572-01940-8 £5.99		
Classic 1000 Pasta & Rice	0-572-02300-6 £5.99		
Classic 1000 Vegetarian	0-572-02375-8 £5.99		
Classic 1000 Quick and Easy	0-572-02330-8 £5.99		
Classic 1000 Cakes & Bakes	0-572-02387-1 £5.99		
Classic 1000 Calorie-counted Recipes	0-572-02405-3 £5.99		
Classic 1000 Microwave Recipes	0-572-01945-9 £5.99		

Please allow 75p per book for post & packing in UK • POST & PACKING
Overseas customers £1 per book.   **TOTAL**

Foulsham books are available from local bookshops. Should you have any difficulty
obtaining supplies please send Cheque/Eurocheque/Postal Order (£ sterling only) made out
to BSBP or debit my credit card:

☐ ACCESS ☐ VISA ☐ MASTER CARD ☐☐☐☐☐☐☐☐☐☐☐☐☐☐☐☐

EXPIRY DATE   SIGNATURE

ALL ORDERS TO:
Foulsham Books, PO Box 29, Douglas, Isle of Man IM99 1BQ
Telephone 01624 675137, Fax 01624 670923, Internet http://www.bookpost.co.uk.

NAME

ADDRESS

Please allow 28 days for delivery.
Please tick box if you do not wish to receive any additional information ☐
Prices and availability subject to change without notice.

The Classic 1000 Dessert Recipes

Carolyn Humphries

foulsham
LONDON . NEW YORK . TORONTO . SYDNEY

foulsham

The Publishing House, Bennetts Close, Cippenham,
Berkshire SL1 5AP, England

ISBN 0-572-02542-4

Printed in Great Britain by St. Edmundsbury Press, Bury St. Edmunds, Suffolk

Contents

Introduction

Eating desserts has to be one of life's greatest pleasures. Instead of delving through many cookery books to find a particular recipe, I thought it was about time I put everyone's favourites together in one massive, indulgent tome.

In *The Classic 1000 Dessert Recipes* you will find every pudding you've ever tasted and hundreds more you may only have dreamed of! A light, fluffy lemon soufflé or a dark, sinful devil's food cake, an elegant crème brûlée or a simple strawberry trifle – there is everything from steaming nursery puds to refreshing ice-cold sorbets. I guarantee you'll find the most decadent and delicious desserts for every occasion, or every day of the week for that matter! So cosset yourself and your family and friends with the most sensational recipes to round off any meal, any time.

Notes on the Recipes

- When following a recipe, use either metric, imperial or American measures, never a combination.

- All spoon measures are level: 15 ml =1 tbsp, 5 ml =1 tsp.

- Eggs are medium unless otherwise stated.

- Always preheat the oven, unless using a fan-assisted model. Cook on the shelf just above the centre unless otherwise stated.

- Always wash, dry, peel and core fruit when necessary before use.

- All cooking times are approximate and should be used only as a guide.

Basic Food Hygiene

- Always wash your hands before preparing food.

- Tie back long hair and don't wear rings or nail varnish.

- Wear an apron.

- Keep work surfaces clean and tidy.

- Never lick your fingers or dip the same spoon back in the food once tasted.

- If using eggs, make sure you buy them from a reputable source, store them in a cool place and use by the sell-by date.

- Some of the most sensational desserts are made with raw eggs. As there is a minimal risk of them containing Salmonella bacteria, we do not recommend you give them to infants or toddlers, people who are very old or infirm, or pregnant women. If you are in any doubt, consult your doctor.

- When leaving food to cool, cover loosely with foil, a clean tea towel (dish cloth) or clingfilm (plastic wrap) to protect from flies, dust etc.

- Always make sure food is completely cold before placing it in the fridge.

- Always transfer leftovers to a clean container and cover with a lid, clingfilm (plastic wrap) or foil before storing in the fridge.

- If reheating a pudding, make sure it is piping hot right through, not just lukewarm.

Steamy Sensations

Most steamed puds are wonderful winter warmers – ideal to fill up on and warm the cockles of your heart. They don't have to be heavy and stodgy either, though Chocolate Stodge with Mint Custard (my favourite from school days) is definitely a rib-sticker! You'll find every classic from Christmas Pudding to Spotted Dick in this chapter and some stunning new ideas too, such as Tropical Steamer.

Steaming Ahead

Any of these recipes can be steamed in several different ways:

- In a steamer over a pan of simmering water.

- In a metal colander, covered firmly with a saucepan lid or foil, over a saucepan of simmering water.

- On an old saucer or trivet in a large saucepan or flameproof casserole (Dutch oven) with enough boiling water to come half-way up the sides of the dish.

Whichever way you choose, make sure the water is boiling before you add the pudding and keep the water at boiling point (but not boiling rapidly) all the time. Top up with boiling water several times during cooking so it does not boil dry.

Jam Roly Poly

SERVES 4

Butter, for greasing
175 g/6 oz/1½ cups self-raising (self-
* rising) flour*
A pinch of salt
75 g/3 oz/¾ cup shredded (chopped)
* vegetable suet*
1 egg, beaten
60 ml/4 tbsp raspberry jam (conserve)
A little milk
Sifted icing (confectioners') sugar, to
* decorate*
A jam sauce (see pages 347–8) and any
* custard (see pages 354–5), to serve*

Grease the shiny side of a double thickness 30 cm/12 in square of foil with butter. Sift the flour and salt into a bowl. Add the suet and mix lightly. Stir in the egg and enough milk to form a soft but not sticky dough. Knead gently on a lightly floured surface.

Roll out to a rectangle about 20 × 25 cm/8 × 10 in. Spread the jam over, leaving a narrow border about 1 cm/½ in all round. Brush the border with a little milk. Roll up, starting at a short end. Place on the buttered foil and wrap loosely to allow for expansion. Make sure the edges are sealed well to prevent moisture getting into the parcel. Steam for 1½ hours. Unwrap, transfer to a warmed serving dish, dust with icing sugar and serve with a hot jam sauce and custard.

Marmalade and Ginger Roll

SERVES 8

350 g/12 oz/3 cups self-raising (self-
* rising) flour*
10 ml/2 tsp baking powder
2.5 ml/½ tsp salt
10 ml/2 tsp ground ginger
175 g/6 oz/1½ cups shredded (chopped)
* vegetable suet*
300 ml/½ pt/1¼ cups water
90 ml/6 tbsp orange marmalade
100 g/4 oz/⅔ cup raisins
45 ml/3 tbsp light brown sugar
Butter, for greasing
Thick cream, to serve

Sift the flour, baking powder, salt and ginger into a bowl. Stir in the suet and mix with enough of the water to form a soft but not sticky dough. Knead gently on a lightly floured surface.

Roll out to a rectangle and spread with the marmalade to within 1 cm/½ in of the edge all round. Sprinkle with the raisins and sugar. Brush the edges with water. Turn in the side edges, then roll up. Wrap in a double thickness of buttered foil, sealing the ends well. Steam for 2–2½ hours. Unwrap and serve with thick cream.

Spotted Dick

SERVES 4–6

*100 g/4 oz/1 cup plain (all-purpose)
  flour
10 ml/2 tsp baking powder
100 g/4 oz/2 cups fresh white
  breadcrumbs
100 g/4 oz/1 cup shredded (chopped)
  vegetable suet
100 g/4 oz/⅔ cup currants, or half
  currants and half sultanas (golden
  raisins)
75 ml/5 tbsp milk
Classic Custard Sauce (see page 354), to
  serve*

Sift the flour and baking powder into a bowl. Stir in the breadcrumbs, suet and fruit. Mix with enough of the milk to form a soft, dropping consistency. Shape into a roll on a double thickness of greased greaseproof (waxed) paper. Wrap up loosely and tie the ends with twist ties or string. Steam in a steamer or colander over hot water for 2½ hours. Serve sliced with Classic Custard Sauce.

Spotted Dog

SERVES 6

*225 g/8 oz/2 cups self-raising (self-
  rising) flour
100 g/4 oz/1 cup shredded (chopped)
  vegetable suet
A pinch of salt
40 g/1½ oz/3 tbsp caster (superfine)
  sugar
100 g/4 oz/⅔ cup sultanas (golden
  raisins)
135 ml/4½ fl oz/generous ½ cup milk
Plain (all-purpose) flour, for dusting
Syrup Sauce (see page 347), to serve*

Mix together all the ingredients to form a soft but not sticky dough. Place on a double thickness of greaseproof (waxed) paper, dusted with a little plain flour, and shape into a roll Roll up in the paper and tuck in the ends. Wrap in a double thickness of foil, twisting and folding the ends to secure completely. Steam for 2 hours. Unwrap and transfer to a serving plate. Serve sliced with Syrup Sauce.

Christmas Puddings

Make at least 6 weeks before Christmas, if possible, to allow the flavours to develop.

MAKES THREE 900 ML/1½ PT/3¾ CUP PUDDINGS

350 g/12 oz/3 cups plain (all-purpose) flour
350 g/12 oz/6 cups fresh breadcrumbs
5 ml/1 tsp salt
15 ml/1 tbsp mixed (apple-pie) spice
350 g/12 oz/3 cups shredded (chopped) vegetable suet
450 g/1 lb/2 cups dark brown sugar
1.5 kg/3 lb/8 cups dried mixed fruit (fruit cake mix)
2 carrots, grated
1 large cooking (tart) apple, grated
3 large eggs, beaten
300 ml/½ pt/1¼ cups stout or brown ale
Butter, for greasing
Brandy Butter (see page 359) or Brandy Sauce (see page 356) and cream, to serve

Mix together all the ingredients except the eggs and stout in a large bowl. When thoroughly blended, stir in the eggs and stout to form a moist mixture. Let the family stir and make a wish, then cover with a clean cloth and leave to stand for 24 hours.

Grease three 900 ml/1½ pt/3¾ cup pudding basins and line the bases with circles of greased greaseproof (waxed) paper. Divide the mixture between the basins. Cover each with a circle of greaseproof paper, then an old saucer, rounded side up. Tie in pudding cloths or cover with a double thickness of foil, twisting and folding under the rims to secure. Steam for 6–7 hours until their colour is really dark. Cool, then re-cover with clean cloths or foil. Store in their basins in a cool dark place. To serve, steam again for 2½ hours. Serve hot with Brandy Butter or Brandy Sauce and cream.

Extra-light Fruit Pudding

SERVES 6

100 g/4 oz/1 cup self-raising (self-rising) flour
2.5 ml/½ tsp baking powder
A pinch of salt
75 g/3 oz/⅓ cup hard block margarine, diced, plus extra for greasing
100 g/4 oz/2 cups fresh white breadcrumbs
25 g/1 oz/3 tbsp currants
25 g/1 oz/3 tbsp sultanas (golden raisins)
25 g/1 oz/3 tbsp raisins
75 g/3 oz/⅓ cup caster (superfine) sugar
1 egg, beaten
120 ml/4 fl oz/½ cup milk
Apricot Jam Sauce (see page 347), to serve

Sift the flour, baking powder and salt into a bowl. Add the margarine and rub in with the fingertips until the mixture resembles breadcrumbs. Stir in the breadcrumbs, fruit and sugar. Add the egg and enough of the milk to form a soft, dropping consistency. Turn into a greased 1.2 litre/2 pt/5 cup pudding basin. Cover with a double thickness of foil or greaseproof (waxed) paper, twisting and folding under the rim to secure. Steam for 2½ hours. Turn out on to a warmed plate and serve with hot Apricot Jam Sauce.

Alternative Christmas Pudding

SERVES 8

2 oranges
200 g/7 oz/generous 1 cup chopped
   cooking dates
2 cooking (tart) apples, quartered
3 carrots
175 g/6 oz/1½ cups plain (all-purpose)
   flour
175 g/6 oz/3 cups fresh wholemeal
   breadcrumbs
100 g/4 oz/½ cup light brown sugar
175 g/6 oz/1½ cups shredded (chopped)
   vegetable suet
75 g/3 oz/½ cup currants
75 g/3 oz/½ cup raisins
2.5 ml/½ tsp ground cinnamon
2.5 ml/½ tsp grated nutmeg
2 eggs, beaten
Butter, for greasing
St Clement's Butter Sauce (see page
   346), to serve

Finely grate the rind from the oranges. Cut away all the pith and peel and quarter the flesh, discarding any pips. Pass the oranges, dates, apples and carrots through a mincer (grinder) or finely chop in a food processor. Stir in the remaining ingredients until well mixed.

Butter a 1.75 litre/3 pt/7½ cup pudding basin and line the base with a circle of greased greaseproof (waxed) paper. Spoon in the mixture and cover with a double thickness of foil, twisting and folding under the rim to secure. Steam for 3 hours. Turn out and serve hot with St Clement's Butter Sauce.

Light Christmas Pudding

MAKES ONE 1.2 LITRE/2 PT/5 CUP PUDDING

Oil, for greasing
100 g/4 oz/1 cup plain (all-purpose)
   flour
5 ml/1 tsp baking powder
100 g/4 oz/½ cup hard block margarine,
   diced
100 g/4 oz/⅔ cup raisins
100 g/4 oz/⅔ cup sultanas (golden
   raisins)
100 g/4 oz/⅔ cup currants
100 g/4 oz/½ cup caster (superfine)
   sugar
100 g/4 oz/2 cups fresh breadcrumbs
5 ml/1 tsp mixed (apple-pie) spice
1 egg
150 ml/¼ pt/⅔ cup milk
30 ml/2 tbsp brandy or rum
Brandy Sauce (see page 356), to serve

Grease a 1.2 litre/2 pt/5 cup pudding basin. Sift the flour and baking powder into a bowl. Add the margarine and rub in with the fingertips until the mixture resembles fine breadcrumbs. Stir in the fruit, sugar, breadcrumbs and mixed spice. Mix in the egg, milk and brandy or rum. Turn into the basin and level the surface. Cover with a double thickness of greased greaseproof (waxed) paper with a pleat in the middle to allow for rising. Twist and fold under the rim to secure. Steam for 3 hours. Re-cover with clean paper, allow to cool and store in the fridge for up to 3 weeks. To serve, steam again for 1½ hours. Serve hot with Brandy Sauce.

Golden Christmas Pudding

MAKES TWO 1.2 LITRE/2 PT/5 CUP PUDDINGS

450 g/1 lb/2⅔ cups ready-to-eat dried apricots, chopped
450 g/1 lb/2⅔ cups sultanas (golden raisins)
175 g/6 oz/1½ cups chopped mixed (candied) peel
350 g/12 oz/3 cups chopped mixed nuts
Finely grated rind and juice of 2 oranges
Finely grated rind and juice of 1 lemon
225 g/8 oz/1 cup light brown sugar
5 ml/1 tsp ground mace
225 g/8 oz/4 cups fresh white breadcrumbs
50 g/2 oz/½ cup plain (all-purpose) flour
100 g/4 oz/1 cup shredded (chopped) vegetable suet
4 eggs, beaten
30 ml/2 tbsp apricot or orange liqueur
Butter, for greasing

Put all the ingredients in a large bowl and mix well. Grease two 1.2 litre/ 2 pt/5 cup pudding basins and line the bases with a circle of greased greaseproof (waxed) paper. Spoon in the mixture and level the surfaces. Cover with a double thickness of greaseproof (waxed) paper, then foil, twisting and folding under the rim. Steam for 5 hours. Leave to cool, then re-wrap in clean greaseproof paper and foil. Make up to 2 weeks before Christmas. Store in a cool, dark place. Steam for a further 3 hours on the day.

Mincemeat Layer

SERVES 6

Oil, for greasing
45 ml/3 tbsp mincemeat
100 g/4 oz/½ cup soft tub margarine
100 g/4 oz/½ cup caster (superfine) sugar
150 g/5 oz/1¼ cups self-raising (self-rising) flour
5 ml/1 tsp baking powder
25 g/1 oz/¼ cup ground almonds
A few drops of almond essence (extract)
2 eggs
Cream, to serve

Grease a 900 ml/1½ pt/3¾ cup pudding basin. Place 15 ml/1 tbsp of the mincemeat in the base. Put all the remaining ingredients except the remaining mincemeat in a large mixing bowl and beat well until smooth. Spoon half the sponge mixture into the pudding basin. Spread the remaining mincemeat over, then top with the remaining sponge mixture. Make a pleat in the centre of a double thickness of oiled greaseproof (waxed) paper or foil to allow for rising. Lay over the pudding and twist and fold under the rim of the basin to secure. Steam for 2 hours. Turn out and serve warm with cream.

Dried Fruit Dome

SERVES 6

Butter, for greasing
225 g/8 oz/2 cups self-raising (self-
    rising) flour
5 ml/1 tsp baking powder
100 g/4 oz/½ cup margarine, cut into
    small pieces
75 g/3 oz/⅓ cup caster (superfine) sugar
50 g/2 oz/⅓ cup ready-to-eat dried
    apricots, chopped
50 g/2 oz/⅓ cup chopped cooking dates
50 g/2 oz/⅓ cup dried pears, chopped
1 egg, beaten
Milk
45 ml/3 tbsp apricot jam (conserve)
5 ml/1 tsp lemon juice
Cream, to serve

Grease a 900 ml/1½ pt/3¾ cup
pudding basin and line the base
with a circle of greased greaseproof
(waxed) paper. Sift the flour and baking
powder into a bowl. Add the margarine
and rub in with the fingertips until the
mixture resembles breadcrumbs. Stir in
the sugar and dried fruit, then mix in
the egg and enough milk to form a soft,
dropping consistency. Turn into the
prepared basin. Cover with a double
thickness of greased greaseproof paper
or foil with a pleat in the centre to allow
for rising. Twist and fold under the rim
of the basin to secure. Steam for 1½
hours. Just before serving, warm the
jam and lemon juice in a saucepan.
Turn the pudding out on to a warmed
serving dish, spoon the warm jam over
and serve with cream.

Syrup Sponge Pudding

SERVES 6

Butter, for greasing
45 ml/3 tbsp golden (light corn) syrup
100 g/4 oz/½ cup soft tub margarine
100 g/4 oz/½ cup caster (superfine)
    sugar
2 eggs
175 g/6 oz/1½ cups self-raising (self-
    rising) flour
5 ml/1 tsp baking powder
30 ml/2 tbsp milk
Extra syrup and custard or cream, to
    serve

Grease a 1.2 litre/2 pt/5 cup pudding
basin. Put the syrup in the base.
Put the margarine, sugar, eggs, flour,
baking powder and milk in a large
mixing bowl and beat well until
smooth. Spoon into the basin and level
the surface. Cover with a double
thickness of greased greaseproof
(waxed) paper or foil with a pleat in the
centre to allow for rising. Twist and fold
under the rim of the basin to secure.
Steam for 2 hours. Turn out and serve
with extra golden syrup and custard or
cream.

Syrup and Ginger Pudding

SERVES 6

Prepare as for Syrup Sponge Pudding,
but add 7.5 ml/1½ tsp ground ginger
to the sponge mixture.

Syrup and Lemon Pudding

SERVES 6

Prepare as for Syrup Sponge Pudding (see page 15), but add the grated rind and juice of ½ lemon to the sponge mix and omit 15 ml/1 tbsp of the milk.

Steamed Jam Sponge

SERVES 6

Prepare as for Syrup Sponge Pudding (see page 15), but substitute any flavour jam (conserve) in the base for the syrup. Serve with a jam sauce (see pages 347–8) (the same flavour as used in the base) and Classic Custard Sauce (see page 354).

Marmalade Sponge Pudding

SERVES 6

Prepare as for Syrup and Lemon Pudding, but substitute marmalade in the base for the syrup, add the finely grated rind of ½ orange instead of the lemon rind and serve with Marmalade Sauce (see page 347) and cream.

Light Orange Pudding

SERVES 6

Prepare as for Syrup and Lemon Pudding, but substitute the finely grated rind and juice of 1 small orange for the lemon and put orange curd in the base instead of syrup. Serve with Sweet Orange Custard (see page 354).

Steamed Plum Sponge

SERVES 6

Prepare as for Syrup Sponge Pudding (see page 15), but substitute 30 ml/2 tbsp plum jam (conserve) in the base for the syrup and top with 3–4 halved and stoned (pitted) plums, skin-sides down. Serve with Plum Jam Sauce (see page 348).

Light Lemon Pudding

SERVES 6

Prepare as for Syrup and Lemon Pudding, but substitute lemon curd in the base for the syrup and serve with Sweet Lemon Custard (see page 355).

Steamed Apple Sponge

SERVES 6

Prepare as for Syrup Sponge Pudding (see page 15), but put 2 peeled, cored and chopped cooking (tart) apples in the base of the basin and use 30 ml/2 tbsp sugar instead of the 45 ml/3 tbsp golden syrup.

Steamed Cherry Pudding

SERVES 6

Prepare as for Syrup Sponge Pudding (see page 15), but put half a 410 g/14½ oz/large can of cherry pie filling in the base of the basin instead of the syrup. Flavour the sponge mixture with a few drops of almond essence (extract). Purée the remaining pie filling, then thin with a little apple juice, warm and serve with the pudding.

Traditional Sussex Pond Pudding

SERVES 6

Butter, for greasing
For the pastry (paste):
275 g/10 oz/2½ cups self-raising (self-rising) flour
5 ml/1 tsp baking powder
1.5 ml/¼ tsp salt
150 g/5 oz/1¼ cups shredded (chopped) vegetable suet
Cold water, to mix
For the filling:
175 g/6 oz/¾ cup butter, cut into pieces
175 g/6 oz/¾ cup granulated sugar
1 large lemon, scrubbed and pricked all over with a skewer

Grease a 1.2 litre/2 pt/5 cup pudding basin. To make the pastry, sift the flour, baking powder and salt into a bowl. Stir in the suet. Mix with enough cold water to form a soft but not sticky dough. Knead gently on a lightly floured surface. Cut off a quarter, roll out to the size of the top of the basin and reserve for a lid. Roll out the remainder and use to line the basin.

To make the filling, put half the butter and sugar in the basin and top with the lemon. Add the remaining sugar and butter around and on top of the lemon. Dampen the edges of the pastry and press the lid into position. Cover with a double thickness of greased greaseproof (waxed) paper or foil, with a pleat in the centre to allow for rising. Twist and fold under the rim of the basin to secure. Steam for 3 hours. Remove the paper or foil and loosen the edge with a round-bladed knife. Turn out into a serving dish. As you cut the pudding the sauce will flow out. Cut everyone a slice of lemon with the pudding.

Fruity Sussex Pond Pudding

SERVES 6

225 g/8 oz/2 cups self-raising (self-rising) flour
A pinch of salt
100 g/4 oz/1 cup shredded (chopped) vegetable suet
100 g/4 oz/⅔ cup currants
150 g/5 oz/⅔ cup light brown sugar
Grated rind and juice of 1 lemon
Cold water, to mix
100 g/4 oz/½ cup butter, plus extra for greasing
Single (light) cream, to serve

Sift the flour and salt into a bowl. Add the suet, currants and 25 g/1 oz/ 2 tbsp of the sugar. Mix with the lemon juice and enough water to form a soft but not sticky dough. Knead the pastry (paste) gently on a lightly floured surface. Cut off a quarter, roll out to the size of the top of the basin and reserve for a lid. Roll out the remainder and use to line a greased 900 ml/1½ pt/3¾ cup pudding basin.

Beat together the remaining sugar, the butter and the lemon rind until smooth. Place in the basin, brush the edges of the pastry with water and cover with the lid. Press the edges well together to seal. Cover with a double thickness of greased greaseproof (waxed) paper or foil, with a pleat in the centre to allow for rising. Twist and fold under the rim of the basin to secure. Steam for 2½ hours. Turn out and serve with single (light) cream.

Real Treacle Pudding

SERVES 6

*175 g/6 oz/1½ cups plain (all-purpose)
    flour*
2.5 ml/½ tsp ground ginger
175 g/6 oz/3 cups fresh breadcrumbs
*100 g/4 oz/1 cup shredded (chopped)
    vegetable suet*
1 egg, beaten
*175 g/6 oz/½ cup black treacle
    (molasses)*
45 ml/3 tbsp milk
*2.5 ml/½ tsp bicarbonate of soda
    (baking soda)*
Butter, for greasing
*Sweet White Sauce (see page 355), to
    serve*

Sift the flour and ginger into a bowl.
Stir in the breadcrumbs and suet.
Add the egg. Warm the treacle and milk
in a saucepan. Stir in the bicarbonate of
soda. Stir into the dry ingredients to
form a soft, dropping consistency. Turn
into a 1.25 litre/2¼ pt/5½ cup greased
pudding basin. Cover with a double
thickness of greased greaseproof
(waxed) paper or foil, twisting and
folding under the rim to secure. Steam
for 2½ hours. Turn out and serve with
Sweet White Sauce.

Gran's Apple Pudding

SERVES 4–6

*225 g/8 oz/2 cups plain (all-purpose)
    flour*
A pinch of salt
15 ml/1 tbsp baking powder
*75 ml/3 oz/¾ cup shredded (chopped)
    vegetable suet*
Cold water, to mix
Butter, for greasing
750 g/1½ lb cooking (tart) apples, sliced
50 g/2 oz/¼ cup granulated sugar
1.5 ml/¼ tsp ground cloves
15 ml/1 tbsp water
Clotted Cream (see page 359), to serve

Sift the flour, salt and baking powder
into a bowl. Stir in the suet and mix
with enough cold water to form a soft
but not sticky dough. Knead gently on
a lightly floured surface. Cut off a
quarter of the dough, roll out to the size
of the top of the basin and reserve for a
lid. Roll out the remaining dough and
use to line a buttered 900 ml/1½ pt/
3¾ cup pudding basin.
    Mix together the apples, sugar and
cloves and use to fill the basin. Add the
measured water. Dampen the dough
edges with a little water and place the
lid in position. Press the edges well
together to seal. Cover with a double
thickness of greased greaseproof
(waxed) paper or foil, with a pleat in
the centre to allow for rising. Twist and
fold under the rim of the basin to
secure. Steam for 2½–3 hours. Remove
the greaseproof paper or foil. Tie a clean
napkin around the basin and serve
straight from the basin with Clotted
Cream.

Vienna Pudding

SERVES 4–6

150 g/5 oz stale white bread
75 g/3 oz/½ cup sultanas (golden
raisins)
150 ml/¼ pt/⅔ cup sherry
100 g/4 oz/½ cup light brown sugar
50 g/2 oz/½ cup chopped mixed peel
Finely grated rind of 1 lemon
3 eggs
300 ml/½ pt/1¼ cups milk
Butter, for greasing
Classic Custard Sauce (see page 354),
to serve

Break the bread into small pieces.
Add the sultanas. Pour the sherry
over and leave to soak for 30 minutes.
Beat with a fork to break up. Add the
sugar, peel and lemon rind. Beat the
eggs and milk together and mix into the
bread mixture. Turn into a greased
1.2 litre/2 pt/5 cup pudding basin.
Cover with a double thickness of
greased greaseproof (waxed) paper or
foil, twisting and folding under the rim
to secure. Steam for 2 hours. Serve with
Classic Custard Sauce.

Brigade Pudding

SERVES 6

225 g/8 oz/2 cups self-raising (self-
rising) flour
A pinch of salt
100 g/4 oz/1 cup shredded (chopped)
vegetable suet
Cold water, to mix
Butter, for greasing
2 cooking (tart) apples, coarsely grated
100 g/4 oz/2 cups fresh wholemeal
breadcrumbs
50 g/2 oz/⅓ cup raisins
25 ml/1½ tbsp orange marmalade
45 ml/3 tbsp golden (light corn) syrup
Syrup Sauce (see page 347), to serve

Sift the flour and salt into a bowl. Stir
in the suet. Mix with enough cold
water to form a soft but not sticky
dough. Knead into a ball. Cut off a
quarter and reserve for a lid. Roll out
the remainder and use to line a greased
900 ml/1½ pt/3¾ cup pudding basin.
Mix together the remaining
ingredients. Spoon into the dough-lined
basin. Brush the edge with water. Roll
out the remaining dough to a round the
size of the top of the basin and press
gently into position. Cover with a
double thickness of greased greaseproof
(waxed) paper or foil, twisting and
folding under the rim to secure. Steam
for 2½ hours. Serve with Syrup Sauce.

Brown Betty

SERVES 6

*50 g/2 oz/¼ cup butter, plus extra for
    greasing*
*100 g/4 oz/2 cups fresh wholemeal
    breadcrumbs*
2.5 ml/½ tsp ground cinnamon
25 g/1 oz/2 tbsp light brown sugar
*450 g/1 lb cooking (tart) apples, thinly
    sliced*
*50 g/2 oz/⅓ cup sultanas (golden
    raisins)*
30 ml/2 tbsp golden (light corn) syrup
15 ml/1 tbsp water
Clotted Cream (see page 359), to serve

Butter a 900 ml/1½ pt/3¾ cup pudding basin. Add a few of the breadcrumbs and swirl round the basin to coat. Mix together the cinnamon and sugar. Put layers of apple, breadcrumbs, sultanas, and the cinnamon mixture in the basin. Dot with butter. Blend the syrup and water and pour over. Cover with a double thickness of foil or greaseproof (waxed) paper and steam for 2 hours. Serve warm with Clotted Cream.

Steamed Rhubarb Pudding

SERVES 8

100 g/4 oz/½ cup soft tub margarine
100 g/4 oz/½ cup light brown sugar
2 eggs, beaten
*50 g/2 oz/½ cup self-raising (self-rising)
    flour*
*50 g/2 oz/½ cup wholemeal self-raising
    flour*
2.5 ml/½ tsp baking powder
50 g/2 oz/1 cup fresh breadcrumbs
175 g/6 oz rhubarb, finely chopped
Butter, for greasing
*2 quantities of Orange Sauce (see page
    350), to serve*

Cream together the margarine and sugar until light and fluffy. Beat in the eggs, one at a time. Fold in the flours and baking powder with the breadcrumbs, then gently mix in the rhubarb. Turn into a greased 900 ml/ 1½ pt/3¾ cup pudding basin. Cover with a double thickness of greased greaseproof (waxed) paper or foil, twisting and folding under the rim to secure. Steam for 1½ hours. Turn out on to a warmed serving plate and serve with hot Orange Sauce.

Walnut and Sultana Pudding

SERVES 6

---

175 g/6 oz/1½ cups self-raising (self-rising) flour
75 g/3 oz/⅓ cup unsalted (sweet) butter
75 g/3 oz/⅓ cup caster (superfine) sugar
75 g/3 oz/½ cup sultanas (golden raisins)
40 g/1½ oz/⅓ cup walnuts, finely chopped
2 eggs, beaten
Cold milk
Burnt Almond Cream (see page 357), to serve

Sift the flour into a bowl. Add the butter and rub in with the fingertips. Stir in the sugar, sultanas and walnuts Mix in the eggs and enough milk to form a soft, dropping consistency. Turn into a greased 1.5 litre/2½ pt/6 cup pudding basin. Cover with a double thickness of greased foil or greaseproof (waxed) paper, twisting and folding under the rim to secure. Steam for 1¾ hours. Turn out and serve with Burnt Almond Cream.

Figgy Pudding

SERVES 6

---

225 g/8 oz/1⅓ cups dried figs, chopped
100 g/4 oz/1 cup shredded (chopped) vegetable suet
225 g/8 oz/4 cups fresh white or half white, half brown breadcrumbs
30 ml/2 tbsp caster (superfine) sugar
2 eggs, beaten
150 ml/¼ pt/⅔ cup milk
Butter, for greasing
Classic Custard Sauce (see page 354), to serve

Mix the figs, suet, breadcrumbs and sugar in a bowl. Add the eggs and milk and mix to form a soft, dropping consistency. Turn into a greased 1.2 litre/2 pt/5 cup pudding basin. Cover with a double thickness of greased greaseproof (waxed) paper or foil, twisting and folding under the rim to secure. Steam for 4 hours. Turn out and serve with Classic Custard Sauce.

Chocolate Hazelnut Pudding

SERVES 6

---

150 g/5 oz/⅔ cup soft tub margarine
100 g/4 oz/½ cup caster (superfine) sugar
100 g/4 oz/1 cup plain (semi-sweet) chocolate
3 eggs
150 g/5 oz/1¼ cups self-raising (self-rising) flour
2.5 ml/½ tsp vanilla essence (extract)
75 g/3 oz/½ cup chopped hazelnuts (filberts)
Butter, for greasing
Amaretto Sauce (see page 353), to serve

Beat together the margarine and sugar until light and fluffy. Melt the chocolate in a basin over a pan of hot water or in the microwave. Beat into the margarine and sugar. Beat in the eggs, one at a time, beating well after each addition. Add the flour, vanilla and nuts and fold in with a metal spoon. Turn into a greased 1.25 litre/2¼ pt/5½ cup pudding basin. Cover with a double thickness of greased foil or greaseproof (waxed) paper, twisting and folding under the rim to secure. Steam for 1½ hours. Serve warm with Amaretto Sauce.

Steamed Raisin Pudding

SERVES 6

225 g/8 oz/2 cups plain (all-purpose) flour
A pinch of salt
5 ml/1 tsp ground cinnamon
90 g/3½ oz/scant ½ cup hard block margarine, diced
50 g/2 oz/¼ cup light brown sugar
100 g/4 oz/⅔ cup raisins
5 ml/1 tsp bicarbonate of soda (baking soda)
150 ml/¼ pt/⅔ cup milk
Butter, for greasing
Caster (superfine) sugar, for dusting
Syrup Sauce (see page 347), to serve

Sift flour, salt and cinnamon into a bowl. Add the margarine and rub in with the fingertips until the mixture resembles breadcrumbs. Stir in the sugar and raisins. Blend the bicarbonate of soda with the milk and stir into the mixture to form a soft, dropping consistency. Turn into a greased 900 ml/1½ pt/3¾ cup pudding basin and cover with a double thickness of greased greaseproof (waxed) paper or foil, twisting and folding under the rim to secure. Steam for 1½ hours. Remove the paper, loosen the edge and turn the pudding out on to a warmed serving dish. Dust with caster sugar and serve with Syrup Sauce.

Baroness Pudding

SERVES 6–8

450 g/1 lb/4 cups self-raising (self-rising) flour
450 g/1 lb/4 cups shredded (chopped) vegetable suet
350 g/12 oz/2 cups large stoned (pitted) (not seedless) raisins
Cold milk, to mix
Caster (superfine) sugar, for dusting
Thick cream, to serve

Mix together the flour, suet and raisins with enough milk to form a dough. Shape into a sausage on a floured pudding cloth. Tie up well and boil or steam for 4 hours. Unwrap and dust with caster sugar before serving with thick cream.

Collegiate Puddings

SERVES 6

100 g/4 oz/2 cups fresh breadcrumbs
100 g/4 oz/⅔ cup dried mixed fruit (fruit cake mix)
50 g/2 oz/¼ cup caster (superfine) sugar
2.5 ml/½ tsp baking powder
100 g/4 oz/1 cup shredded (chopped) vegetable suet
2.5 ml/½ tsp mixed (apple-pie) spice
2 eggs, beaten
Oil for greasing
Syrup Sauce (see page 347), to serve

Mix together all the dry ingredients, then add the eggs to bind. Turn into six greased individual moulds. Cover with a double thickness of foil or greaseproof (waxed) paper, twisting and folding under the rims to secure. Steam for 35 minutes. Serve with Syrup Sauce.

Steamed Fruit Loaf

SERVES 8

*100 g/4 oz/1 cup self-raising (self-
    rising) flour*
A pinch of salt
5 ml/1 tsp mixed (apple-pie) spice
*100 g/4 oz/½ cup caster (superfine)
    sugar*
*175 g/6 oz/3 cups fresh white
    breadcrumbs*
*175 g/6 oz/1½ cups shredded (chopped)
    vegetable suet*
100 g/4 oz/⅔ cup currants
100 g/4 oz/⅔ cup raisins
100 g/4 oz/⅔ cup chopped cooking dates
A little milk
Butter or oil, for greasing
*Lemon Honey Sauce (see page 346), to
    serve*

Mix together all the ingredients in a
bowl, adding enough milk to form
a soft but not sticky consistency. Turn
into a 750 g/1½ lb greased loaf tin
(pan). Cover with a double thickness of
foil, twisting and folding under the rim
to secure. Steam for 2 hours. Turn out
on to a serving plate and serve sliced
with Lemon Honey Sauce.

Sinful Chocolate Pudding

SERVES 6

175 g/6 oz/¾ cup butter
150 g/5 oz/⅔ cup light brown sugar
5 ml/1 tsp vanilla essence (extract)
3 eggs
*45 ml/3 tbsp cocoa (unsweetened
    chocolate) powder*
25 ml/1½ tbsp potato flour
*100 g/4 oz/1 cup self-raising (self-
    rising) flour*
*75 g/3 oz/¾ cup plain (semi-sweet)
    chocolate, coarsely grated*
*Chocolate Custard, (see page 355), to
    serve*

Grease a 1.25 litre/2¼ pt/5½ cup
pudding basin with a little of the
butter. Beat the remaining butter with
the sugar and vanilla until light and
fluffy. Gradually beat in the eggs,
beating well after each addition. Sift the
cocoa, potato flour and self-raising flour
over the surface and fold in with a
metal spoon. Fold in the chocolate. Turn
into the prepared basin. Cover with a
double thickness of greased foil or
greaseproof (waxed) paper and steam
for 1½ hours. Turn out and serve with
Chocolate Custard.

Chocolate Stodge

SERVES 4–6

*50 g/2 oz/½ cup self-raising (self-rising)
flour*
*30 ml/2 tbsp cocoa (unsweetened
chocolate) powder*
*50 g/2 oz/1 cup fresh white
breadcrumbs*
*50 g/2 oz/½ cup shredded (chopped)
vegetable suet*
50 g/2 oz/¼ cup caster (superfine) sugar
1 egg, beaten
Cold milk, to mix
Butter, for greasing
A little flour
Mint Custard (see page 355), to serve

Sift the flour and cocoa into a bowl.
Stir in the remaining dry ingredients,
then mix in the egg and enough cold
milk to form a very soft, dropping
consistency. Grease and flour a 900 ml/
1½ pt/3¾ cup pudding basin. Spoon in
the chocolate mixture. Cover with a
double thickness of foil or greaseproof
(waxed) paper. Twist and fold under the
rim to secure. Steam for 2 hours. Turn
out and serve with Mint Custard.

Chocolate Chip Pudding

SERVES 6

*175 g/6 oz/1½ cups self-raising (self-
rising) flour*
2.5 ml/½ tsp baking powder
75 g/3 oz/1½ cups fresh breadcrumbs
*100 g/4 oz/1 cup shredded (chopped)
vegetable suet*
*100 g/4 oz/½ cup caster (superfine)
sugar*
2 eggs, lightly beaten
5 ml/1 tsp vanilla essence (extract)
100 g/4 oz/1 cup chocolate chips
150 ml/¼ pt/⅔ cup milk
Butter, for greasing
*Chocolate Custard (see page 355), to
serve*

Sift the flour and baking powder into a
bowl. Add the breadcrumbs, suet and
sugar and mix well. Stir in the eggs and
vanilla essence. Add the chocolate chips
and mix with enough of the cold milk to
form a soft, dropping consistency. Turn
into a greased 1.2 litre/2 pt/5 cup
pudding basin. Cover with a double
thickness of greaseproof (waxed) paper
or foil, twisting and folding under the
rim to secure. Steam for 1½ hours. Turn
out on to a serving dish and serve with
Chocolate Custard.

Orange Sponge

SERVES 6

75 g/3 oz/⅓ cup unsalted (sweet) butter,
plus extra for greasing
75 g/3 oz/⅓ cup caster (superfine) sugar
45 ml/3 tbsp sultanas (golden raisins)
2 eggs
Grated rind and juice of 1 orange
100 g/4 oz/1 cup self-raising (self-
rising) flour
Cointreau Custard (see page 355), to
serve

Grease a 1.2 litre/2 pt/5 cup pudding basin. Beat the remaining butter and the sugar until light and fluffy. Add the sultanas, then gradually add the eggs, beating well after each addition. Stir in the orange rind, then sift the flour over the surface and fold in with a metal spoon, adding enough of the orange juice to give a soft, dropping consistency. Turn into the prepared basin. Cover with a double thickness of greased foil or greaseproof (waxed) paper and steam for 1½ hours. Turn out and pour a little hot Cointreau Custard over. Serve the remaining sauce separately.

Rothschild Pudding

SERVES 6

100 g/4 oz/½ cup soft tub margarine
100 g/4 oz/1 cup self-raising (self-
rising) flour
225 g/8 oz/⅔ cup raspberry jam
(conserve)
2 eggs, lightly beaten
2.5 ml/½ tsp bicarbonate of soda
(baking soda)
15 ml/1 tbsp milk
Butter, for greasing
Raspberry Jelly Sauce (see page 348)
and pouring cream, to serve

Beat together the margarine, flour, jam and eggs until smooth. Blend together the bicarbonate of soda and milk and stir into the mixture. Turn into a greased 900 ml/1½ pt/3¾ cup pudding basin. Cover with a double thickness of greased greaseproof (waxed) paper or foil, twisting and folding under the rim to secure. Steam for 2 hours. Turn out on to a warmed serving plate and serve with hot Raspberry Jelly Sauce and pouring cream.

Mocha Mould

SERVES 4–6

75 g/3 oz/⅓ cup butter, plus extra for greasing
75 g/3 oz/⅓ cup caster (superfine) sugar)
50 g/2 oz/½ cup plain (semi-sweet) chocolate
1 egg, separated
5 ml/1 tsp instant coffee powder or granules
5 ml/1 tsp water
2.5 ml/½ tsp vanilla essence (extract)
100 g/4 oz/2 cups fresh breadcrumbs
50 g/2 oz/½ cup self-raising (self-rising) flour
60 ml/4 tbsp milk
Coffee Custard (see page 355), to serve

Grease a 1.2 litre/2 pt/5 cup pudding basin or metal mould. Line the base with a circle of greaseproof (waxed) paper. Beat together the remaining butter and the sugar until light and fluffy. Melt the chocolate in a bowl over a pan of hot water or in the microwave. Add to the butter and sugar with the egg yolk and coffee, dissolved in the water, and the vanilla essence. Beat well. Mix together the breadcrumbs and flour and fold half into the mocha mixture with half the milk. Fold in the remaining crumb mixture and milk. Spoon into the prepared basin or mould. Cover with a double thickness of greased greaseproof (waxed) paper or foil, twisting and folding under the rim of the basin or round the edge of the mould to secure. If it doesn't seem very secure on a fluted mould, tie round firmly with a piece of string. Steam for 2 hours. Loosen the edge and turn out on to a warmed serving dish. Spoon a little Coffee Custard over and serve the rest separately.

Cabinet Pudding

SERVES 4–6

Butter, for greasing
A few glacé (candied) cherries, halved
Angelica leaves
6 blanched almonds
50 g/2 oz sponge (lady) fingers, chopped
50 g/2 oz almond macaroons, roughly crushed
300 ml/½ pt/1¼ cups whipping cream
50 g/2 oz/¼ cup caster (superfine) sugar
2 eggs, beaten
2.5 ml/½ tsp vanilla essence (extract)
75 ml/5 tbsp white rum
White Rum Sauce (see page 356), to serve

Thoroughly butter a 900 ml/1½ pt/ 3¾ cup mould. Arrange the cherries, cut sides up, angelica leaves and almonds attractively in the base. Mix together the sponge fingers and macaroons. Whisk the cream with the sugar, eggs, vanilla essence and rum until well blended. Stir in the sponge fingers and macaroons. Leave to soak for 15 minutes. Pour into the mould. Cover with greased foil, twisting and folding under the rim to secure. Steam for 1 hour until set. Leave to stand for 5 minutes. Turn out and serve with White Rum Sauce.

'Little Orange' Pudding

SERVES 6

Butter, for greasing
25 ml/1½ tbsp orange jelly marmalade
  (clear conserve)
300 g/11 oz/1 medium can mandarin
  oranges, drained, reserving the juice
100 g/4 oz/1 cup self-raising (self-
  rising) flour
100 g/4 oz/2 cups fresh soft white
  breadcrumbs
100 g/4 oz/1 cup shredded (chopped)
  vegetable suet
75 g/3 oz/⅓ cup caster (superfine) sugar
150 ml/¼ pt/⅔ cup milk
Classic Custard Sauce (see page 354),
  to serve

Grease a 1.2 litre/2 pt/5 cup pudding basin. Spoon the marmalade into the base. Arrange the 'little oranges' attractively on top. Mix the flour and breadcrumbs in a bowl with the suet and sugar. Mix with enough of the milk to form a soft, dropping consistency. Spoon over the fruit. Cover with a double thickness of greased greaseproof (waxed) paper or foil, twisting and folding under the rim to secure. Steam for 2 hours. Loosen the edge and turn out on to a warmed serving dish. Serve hot with the reserved mandarin juice and Classic Custard Sauce.

Tropical Steamer

SERVES 6

75 g/3 oz/⅓ cup unsalted (sweet) butter,
  plus extra for greasing
50 g/2 oz/¼ cup dark brown sugar
3 ripe bananas
15 ml/1 tbsp dark rum
2 eggs, separated
175 g/6 oz/1½ cups self-raising (self-
  rising) flour, sifted
Dark Rum Sauce (see page 352),
  to serve

Beat together the butter and sugar until light and fluffy. Mash two of the bananas with the rum and beat into the butter mixture with the egg yolks. Fold in the flour with a metal spoon. Whisk the egg whites until stiff, then fold into the mixture with a metal spoon. Thinly slice the remaining banana. Spoon half the mixture into a 1 litre/1¾ pt/4¼ cup greased pudding basin. Top with the banana slices. Spoon over the remaining mixture. Cover with double thickness of greased greaseproof (waxed) paper or foil, with a pleat in the centre to allow for rising. Twist and fold under the rim to secure. Steam for 1½ hours. Loosen the edge and turn out on to a warmed serving plate. Serve with Dark Rum Sauce.

Tuscan Cream

SERVES 4

50 g/2 oz/¼ cup granulated sugar
30 ml/2 tbsp water
600 ml/1 pt/2½ cups milk
3 eggs
25 g/1 oz/2 tbsp castor (superfine)
  sugar
A few drops of almond essence
  (extract)
50 g/2 oz/½ cup toasted chopped
  almonds
15 g/½ oz/1 tbsp unsalted (sweet) butter
Cream, to serve

Put the granulated sugar and water in a heavy-based saucepan. Heat gently, stirring, until the sugar has dissolved. Boil, without stirring, until the sugar caramelises. Remove from the heat, then pour in the milk (being careful as the mixture will splutter). Return to the heat and heat very gently, stirring, until the caramel has melted. Whisk together the eggs and caster sugar. Gradually stir in the caramel milk, the almond essence and the nuts. Thoroughly grease a pudding basin or mould with the butter and pour in the mixture.

Cover with a double thickness of greased greaseproof (waxed) paper or foil, twisting and folding under the rim to secure. Steam for 2 hours. Serve either hot straight from the dish or leave until cold, then chill and turn out. Serve with cream.

Steamed Egg Custard

SERVES 4

2 eggs
15 ml/1 tbsp caster (superfine) sugar
450 ml/¾ pt/2 cups milk
Grated nutmeg

Beat together the eggs and sugar in a basin. Warm the milk and pour over, whisking all the time. Sprinkle with nutmeg. Steam for 1¼ hours until set. Serve warm or cold.

Black Cap Pudding

SERVES 4

Butter, for greasing
15 ml/1 tbsp clear honey
50 g/2 oz/⅓ cup raisins
100 g/4 oz/1 cup plain (all-purpose)
  flour
A pinch of salt
2 eggs
300 ml/½ pt/1¼ cups milk
25 g/1 oz/2 tbsp caster (superfine)
  sugar

Grease a 900 ml/1½ pt/3¾ cup pudding basin. Put the honey in the base, then add the raisins. Sift the flour and salt into a bowl. Beat in the eggs and half the milk until smooth, then stir in the remaining milk and the sugar. Pour over the raisins. Cover with a double thickness of greased greaseproof (waxed) paper or foil and steam for 1½ hours.

Blackcurrant Cap Pudding

SERVES 4

Prepare as for Black Cap Pudding, but substitute 45 ml/3 tbsp blackcurrant jam (conserve) for the honey and raisins.

Little Apricot Puddings

SERVES 4

100 g/4 oz/1 cup self-raising (self-rising) flour
2.5 ml/½ tsp baking powder
100 g/4 oz/½ cup soft tub margarine
100 g/4 oz/½ cup caster (superfine) sugar
2 eggs
225 g/8 oz/1 small can of apricot halves, drained, reserving the juice
75 ml/5 tbsp apricot jam (conserve)
Chantilly Cream (see page 358), to serve

Put the flour, baking powder, margarine, sugar and eggs in a bowl and beat well until smooth. Chop the apricots. Put the juice in a pan with the jam and heat until the jam has melted, stirring all the time. Stir in the fruit. Spoon into four individual soufflé dishes. Spoon in the cake mixture to come half-way up the sides of the dishes. Cover with a double thickness of greased greaseproof (waxed) paper and tie with string. Steam for 35 minutes until risen and firm. Turn out on to individual serving plates and serve with Chantilly Cream.

Steamed Bread Pudding

SERVES 4–6

½ small stale loaf of bread (about 225 g/8 oz)
75 g/3 oz/¾ cup self-raising (self-rising) flour
100 g/4 oz/½ cup light brown sugar
1.5 ml/¼ tsp mixed (apple-pie) spice
75 g/3 oz/¾ cup shredded (chopped) vegetable suet
75 g/3 oz/½ cup dried mixed fruit (fruit cake mix)
1 egg, beaten
Milk
Butter, for greasing
Pouring cream, to serve

Soak the bread in cold water for 30 minutes. Squeeze out the liquid and place the bread in a bowl. Beat well to break up with a fork. Sprinkle the flour, sugar and spice over the surface and beat in. Stir in the suet and fruit. Mix with the beaten egg and a little milk to form a soft, dropping consistency. Turn into a greased 1.2 litre/2 pt/5 cup pudding basin and cover with a double thickness of greased greaseproof (waxed) paper or foil, twisting and folding under the rim to secure. Steam for 2 hours. Turn out and serve with pouring cream.

Perfect Pies and Tarts

Here's an exciting range of crisp, light, melt-in-the-mouth pastries with glorious sweet fillings. Take your pick from these double-crust pies and single-crust tarts, desserts large enough to feed a family or delicate individual servings. Whether served hot or cold, there's a pudding here for every occasion.

Traditional Apple Pie

SERVES 6

For the pastry (paste):
*225 g/8 oz/2 cups plain (all-purpose)
    flour*
A pinch of baking powder
A pinch of salt
*100 g/4 oz/½ cup hard block margarine,
    diced*
Cold water, to mix
For the filling:
10 ml/2 tsp cornflour (cornstarch)
*4 large cooking (tart) apples, peeled and
    sliced*
45 ml/3 tbsp granulated sugar
2 whole cloves (optional)
Milk, to glaze
Caster (superfine) sugar, for sprinkling
Cream or custard, to serve

To make the pastry, sift the flour, baking powder and salt into a bowl. Add the margarine and rub in with the fingertips until the mixture resembles fine breadcrumbs. Mix with cold water to form a firm dough. Knead gently on a lightly floured surface. Cut in half. Roll out one half and line a 23 cm/ 9 in pie plate. Dust with the cornflour.

To fill, top with the apple slices, sprinkle over the sugar and add the cloves, well apart, if using. Brush the edge of the pastry with water. Roll out the remaining pastry. Lay on top and press the edges well together to seal. Trim, knock up the edge and crimp between finger and thumb. Make a hole in the centre to allow steam to escape. Decorate the pie with pastry 'leaves'. Brush with milk and sprinkle with a little caster sugar. Place on a baking (cookie) sheet. Bake in a preheated oven at 200°C/400°F/gas mark 6 for

40 minutes until cooked through. Sprinkle with caster sugar and serve with cream or custard.

Apple and Orange Pie

SERVES 6

Prepare as for Traditional Apple Pie, but substitute 2 oranges, all rind and pith removed and segmented, for 1 of the apples. Omit the cloves. Serve with hot Orange Sauce (see page 350).

Traditional Plum Pie

SERVES 6

Prepare as for Traditional Apple Pie, but substitute 450 g/1 lb plums, halved and stoned (pitted), for the apples and omit the cloves.

Traditional Gooseberry Pie

SERVES 6

Prepare as for Traditional Apple Pie, but substitute 450 g/1 lb gooseberries, topped and tailed, for the apples, and stew for 5 minutes in the sugar until the juice runs. Allow to cool before putting in the pie, adding a little more sugar, if liked. Omit the cloves.

Traditional Blackcurrant Pie

SERVES 6

Prepare as for Traditional Apple Pie, but substitute 450 g/1 lb black-currants for the apples and add an extra 15 ml/1 tbsp sugar. Omit the cloves.

One-crust Pies

SERVES 4–6

Prepare as for any of the traditional pies (left) but use half to two-thirds the amount of pastry (paste). Put the fruit and flavourings in a deep pie dish and stir in the cornflour. Put a pie funnel in the middle.

Roll out the pastry. Cut a strip off the edge of the pastry and place on the dampened rim of the pie dish. Brush with water. Put the pastry 'lid' in position, making a small slit to fit over the pie funnel. Decorate with pastry trimmings. Glaze as for traditional pies and put on a baking (cookie) sheet. Bake as for traditional pies until golden on top and the fruit underneath is bubbling and tender.

Yorkshire Apple Pie

SERVES 6

For the pastry (paste):
225 g/8 oz/2 cups plain (all-purpose) flour
A pinch of salt
50 g/2 oz/¼ cup white vegetable fat (shortening), diced
50 g/2 oz/¼ cup hard block margarine, diced
Cold water, to mix
For the filling:
3 large cooking (tart) apples, sliced
65 g/2½ oz/generous ¼ cup granulated sugar, plus extra for sprinkling
A pinch of ground cloves
75 g/3 oz/¾ cup Wensleydale cheese, crumbled
15 ml/1 tbsp single (light) cream

To make the pastry, sift the flour and salt into a bowl. Add the fats and rub in with the fingertips until the mixture resembles fine breadcrumbs. Mix with enough cold water to form a firm dough. Knead gently on a lightly floured surface. Cut in half. Roll out one half and use to line a pie plate. Prick the base with a fork.

To fill, put a layer of half the apple slices on top. Mix all but 15 ml/1 tbsp of the sugar with the cloves. Sprinkle half over the apples, then sprinkle with half the cheese. Top with the remaining apple slices, then the sugar, then the cheese. Dampen the edges of the pastry with water.

Roll out the remaining pastry and lay over. Press the edges well together to seal. Trim, knock up the edge and flute with the back of a knife. Make a hole in the centre to allow steam to escape. Roll out the trimmings, cut into small leaves and use to decorate the top. Brush with the cream, then sprinkle with sugar. Place on a baking (cookie) sheet and bake in a preheated oven at 220°C/425°F/gas mark 7 for about 30 minutes or until golden brown and cooked through. Serve hot.

Stilton Apple Pie

SERVES 6

Prepare as for Yorkshire Apple Pie, but substitute white or blue Stilton cheese for the Wensleydale.

Cheddar Apple Pie

SERVES 6

225 g/8 oz/2 cups plain (all-purpose)
  flour
A pinch of salt
75 g/3 oz/⅓ cup butter, diced
100 g/4 oz/1 cup Cheddar cheese, grated
1 egg, separated
Cold water, to mix
750 g/1½ lb cooking (tart) apples
15 ml/1 tbsp apple juice or water
60 ml/4 tbsp granulated sugar
Caster (superfine) sugar, for sprinkling

Sift the flour and salt into a bowl. Add the butter and rub in with the fingertips until the mixture resembles breadcrumbs. Stir in the cheese. Add the egg yolk and enough water to form a firm dough. Knead gently on a lightly floured surface. Wrap in clingfilm (plastic wrap) and chill for 30 minutes. Put the apples in a saucepan with the apple juice or water and the granulated sugar. Cover and cook gently for 10 minutes. Leave to cool slightly.

Halve the pastry (paste) and roll out one half. Use to line a 23 cm/9 in pie plate. Roll out the remaining dough to use as a lid. Spoon the apple mixture into the pastry-lined plate and brush the edge with a little of the egg white. Cover with the remaining pastry. Trim, knock up the edge and flute with the back of a knife. Make a hole in the centre to allow steam to escape. Make leaves out of pastry trimmings and use to decorate the pie. Brush with egg white and sprinkle with caster sugar. Bake in a preheated oven at 200°C/400°F/gas mark 6 for 20–25 minutes until golden brown and cooked through. Serve warm.

Minted Apple Pie

SERVES 6–8

275 g/10 oz/2½ cups plain (all-purpose)
  flour
30 ml/2 tbsp icing (confectioners') sugar
175 g/6 oz/¾ cup unsalted (sweet)
  butter, diced
1 egg, separated
Cold water, to mix
900 g/2 lb eating (dessert) apples, sliced
Finely grated rind and juice of 1 lemon
15 ml/1 tbsp dried mint
40 g/1½ oz/3 tbsp caster (superfine)
  sugar
15 ml/1 tbsp cornflour (cornstarch)

Sift the flour and icing sugar into a bowl. Add the butter and rub in with the fingertips. Mix with the egg yolk and enough cold water to form a firm dough. Wrap in clingfilm (plastic wrap) and chill for 30 minutes.

Meanwhile, toss the apple slices in the lemon rind and juice, the mint, 25 g/1 oz/2 tbsp of the caster sugar and the cornflour.

Roll out a good half of the pastry (paste) and use to line a 20 cm/8 in fairly deep pie dish. Fill with the apple mixture. Roll out the remaining pastry. Dampen the edge of the pastry all round the dish and place the remaining pastry in position, pressing gently but firmly round the edge. Trim, knock up and flute with the back of a knife. Use the pastry trimmings to make attractive shapes and use to decorate the top of the pie. Brush with egg white and sprinkle with the remaining caster sugar. Make a hole in the centre to allow steam to escape. Bake in a preheated oven at 200°C/400°F/gas mark 6 for about 35 minutes until crisp, golden and cooked through.

Rosemary Pear Pie

SERVES 6–8

Prepare as for Minted Apple Pie, but substitute dessert pears for the apples, 10 ml/2 tsp crushed rosemary for the mint and add 45 ml/3 tbsp currants to the mixture.

Glazed Pear Pie

SERVES 6–8

225 g/8 oz/2 cups plain (all-purpose) flour
A pinch of salt
100 g/4 oz/½ cup hard block margarine, diced
Cold water, to mix
15 g/½ oz/1 tbsp butter
Demerara sugar
750 g/1½ lb pears, thinly sliced
Finely grated rind and juice of 1 lemon
Caster (superfine) sugar, to taste
Crème fraîche, to serve

Sift the flour and salt into a bowl. Add the margarine and rub in with the fingertips until the mixture resembles fine breadcrumbs. Mix with enough cold water to form a firm dough. Knead gently on a lightly floured surface.
Use the butter to grease a 20 cm/8 in fairly deep pie dish. Sprinkle liberally with demerara sugar. Roll out about two-thirds of the pastry (paste) and use to line the dish. Fill with the pear slices, sprinkling with the lemon rind and juice and caster sugar to taste. Roll out the remaining pastry and use as a lid. Press the edges well together to seal and knock up with the back of a knife. Place on a baking (cookie) sheet. Bake in a preheated oven at 220°C/425°F/gas mark 7 for about 20 minutes until the pastry is browned, then reduce the heat to 180°C/350°F/gas mark 4 and continue cooking for a further 20–30 minutes. Loosen the edge and turn out on to a serving plate so the glazed base is uppermost. Serve warm with crème fraîche.

Tarte Tatin

SERVES 6

175 g/6 oz/1½ cups plain (all-purpose) flour
150 g/5 oz/⅔ cup unsalted (sweet) butter, diced
120 ml/8 tbsp caster (superfine) sugar
1 egg yolk
Cold water, to mix
750 g/1½ lb cooking (tart) apples, peeled, quartered and cored

Sift the flour into a bowl. Add 90 g/3½ oz/scant 1 cup of the butter and rub in with the fingertips. Stir in 15 ml/1 tbsp of the sugar. Mix with the egg yolk and enough cold water to form a firm dough. Wrap in clingfilm (plastic wrap) and chill for 30 minutes.
Meanwhile, butter a deep pie dish with 15 g/½ oz/1 tbsp of the butter. Cover the base with about 75 ml/5 tbsp of the sugar. Top with the apple quarters. Sprinkle with the remaining sugar and dot with the remaining butter.
Roll out the pastry (paste) and use to cover the apples. Trim to fit. Place the dish on a baking (cookie) sheet. Bake in a preheated oven at 190°C/375°F/gas mark 5 for about 30 minutes until cooked through and the sugar has caramelised. Carefully turn out on to a serving plate and serve hot.

Tarte aux Pommes

SERVES 6

45 ml/3 tbsp granulated sugar
300 ml/½ pt/1¼ cups water
30 ml/2 tbsp apricot jam (conserve),
 sieved (strained) if necessary
450 g/1 lb eating (dessert) apples, peeled,
 quartered and cored
100 g/4 oz puff pastry (paste), thawed if
 frozen
Sifted icing (confectioners') sugar, for
 dusting
Whipped cream, to serve

Put the sugar and water in a
saucepan and heat gently, stirring,
until the sugar has dissolved. Boil for
2 minutes, then stir in the jam until
melted. Add the apple quarters, cover,
bring to the boil, reduce the heat and
simmer gently for about 20 minutes
until the apples are tender and
translucent but still hold their shape.
Lift the fruit out of the pan and lay in
the base of a 20–23 cm/8–9 in pie
plate. Brush the rim with water.
 Roll out the pastry and cut a thick
strip to place all round the rim. Brush
with water again. Cut the remaining
pastry into thinner strips and lay in a
lattice pattern over the plate, pressing
gently to seal at the edge. Dust liberally
with icing sugar and bake in a
preheated oven at 220°C/425°F/gas
mark 7 for about 18 minutes until
golden all over. Serve warm with
whipped cream.

Cranapple Pie

SERVES 6

225 g/8 oz/1 cup wholemeal flour
150 g/5 oz/⅔ cup hard block margarine,
 diced
25 g/1 oz/2 tbsp caster (superfine)
 sugar
30 ml/2 tbsp finely chopped almonds
Cold water, to mix
225 g/8 oz cranberries
30 ml/2 tbsp apple juice
4 large cooking (tart) apples, peeled and
 sliced
Granulated sugar, to taste
A little single (light) cream or milk, to
 glaze

Put the flour in a bowl and rub in
almost all of the margarine until the
mixture resembles breadcrumbs. Stir in
the caster sugar and almonds and mix
with enough cold water to form a soft
but not sticky dough. Wrap in clingfilm
(plastic wrap) and chill for 30 minutes.
 Meanwhile, put the cranberries,
apple juice and apple slices in a
saucepan and heat gently until the
cranberries begin to pop. Sweeten to
taste with granulated sugar.
 Roll out about three-quarters of the
pastry (paste) on a lightly floured
surface and use to line a 20 cm/8 in
flan tin (pie pan), lightly greased with
the reserved margarine.
 Roll out the remaining pastry and
cut into an 18 cm/7 in round. Turn the
cooled fruit into the pie and lay the
pastry round in the centre of the top, so
there is an edge of fruit visible all
round. Brush with a little cream or milk
to glaze. Bake in a preheated oven at
200°C/ 400°F/gas mark 6 for about
35 minutes until golden brown and
cooked through. Serve warm.

Chocolate and Pear Pie

SERVES 4

450 g/1 lb puff pastry (paste), thawed if frozen
75 g/3 oz/⅓ cup unsalted (sweet) butter
75 g/3 oz/⅓ cup caster (superfine) sugar, plus extra for sprinkling
1 egg, beaten
150 ml/¼ pt/⅔ cup soured (dairy sour) cream
100 g/4 oz/1 cup self-raising (self-rising) flour
2.5 ml/½ tsp ground ginger
15 ml/1 tbsp cocoa (unsweetened chocolate) powder
25 g/1 oz/¼ cup ground almonds
410 g/14½ oz/1 large can of pear halves, drained, reserving the juice

Cut the pastry into two pieces, one slightly larger than the other. Roll out the smaller piece to a 20 cm/8 in round and the larger to a 23 cm/9 in round. Place the smaller round on a dampened baking (cookie) sheet.

Beat together the butter, sugar and all but 10 ml/2 tsp of the egg. Stir in the cream, flour, ginger, cocoa and almonds. Spread over the pastry on the baking sheet, leaving a small border all round. Top with the pear halves. Brush the border with a little of the reserved egg. Place the larger pastry round over the top and press the edges together to seal. Knock up the edge with the back of a knife. Mark the top with a sharp knife in a criss-cross pattern to decorate, then glaze with the remaining beaten egg. Sprinkle with sugar and bake in a preheated oven at 200°C/400°F/gas mark 6 for about 40 minutes until risen, crisp and golden. Serve warm with the reserved pear juice.

Caramel Pear Pizza Pie

SERVES 6

225 g/8 oz puff pastry (paste), thawed if frozen
15 g/½ oz/1 tbsp butter
200 g/7 oz/scant 1 cup caster (superfine) sugar
3 ripe pears, peeled, cored and sliced
30 ml/2 tbsp cream cheese
Vanilla ice cream (bought or home-made, see page 188), to serve

Roll out the pastry to a 25 cm/10 in round and place on a dampened baking (cookie) sheet. Bake in a preheated oven at 190°C/375°F/gas mark 5 for about 6 minutes until lightly golden. Remove from the oven and leave to cool while making the topping.

Melt the butter in a frying pan (skillet) and add the sugar. Stir until the mixture begins to turn golden, then add the pear slices and toss until they caramelise. Add a little water if they start to stick (be careful as the mixture will splutter). Arrange the pear slices over the pastry and dot with the cheese. Return to the oven for 15 minutes until the pastry is well risen and the pears are a rich golden brown. Serve warm with vanilla ice cream.

Caramel Cinnamon Apple Pizza Pie

SERVES 6

Prepare as for Caramel Pear Pizza Pie, but substitute eating (dessert) apples for the pears and sprinkle with 5 ml/1 tsp ground cinnamon after dotting with the cheese.

Peach and Raspberry Pie

SERVES 6–8

For the pastry (paste):
*225 g/8 oz/2 cups plain (all-purpose)
    flour*
A pinch of salt
5 ml/1 tsp mixed (apple-pie) spice
*100 g/4 oz/½ cup hard block margarine,
    diced*
Cold water, to mix
For the filling:
*4 ripe peaches, skinned, halved, stoned
    (pitted) and sliced*
225 g/8 oz raspberries
45 ml/3 tbsp caster (superfine) sugar
*A little single (light) cream or plain
    yoghurt, to glaze*

To make the pastry, mix the flour, salt and mixed spice in a bowl. Add the margarine and rub in with the fingertips until the mixture resembles fine breadcrumbs. Mix with enough cold water to form a firm dough. Knead gently on a lightly floured surface. Wrap in clingfilm (plastic wrap) and chill for 15 minutes.

To fill, arrange the peaches and raspberries in a 20 cm/8 in pie dish and sprinkle with almost all the caster sugar.

Roll out the pastry to a round a little larger than the pie dish. Cut a strip off all round. Brush the edge of the pie dish with water and lay the strip on the rim. Cover with the pastry round and press the edges well together all round to seal. Knock up the edge and flute with the back of a knife. Make a small hole in the centre to allow steam to escape and cut a few leaves out of any pastry trimmings to decorate. Arrange around the hole and brush all over with cream or yoghurt to glaze. Bake in a preheated oven at 200°C/400°F/gas mark 6 for 30 minutes until golden brown and cooked through. Sprinkle with the remaining caster sugar and serve warm.

Syrup Date Tart

SERVES 8

*175 g/6 oz/1½ cups plain (all-purpose)
    flour*
A pinch of salt
*75 g/3 oz/⅓ cup hard block margarine,
    diced*
Cold water, to mix
100 g/4 oz/2 cups stale cake crumbs
*Finely grated rind and juice of 1 small
    lemon*
75 g/3 oz/½ cup chopped cooking dates
30 ml/2 tbsp golden (light corn) syrup
2 large eggs, beaten

Sift the flour and salt into a bowl. Add the margarine and rub in with the fingertips until the mixture resembles fine breadcrumbs. Mix with enough cold water to form a firm dough. Knead gently on a lightly floured surface. Roll out and use to line a 23 cm/9 in flan tin (pie pan). Trim the edges.

Mix together all the remaining ingredients and pour into the flan case (pie shell). Make a lattice out of pastry (paste) trimmings and lay over the top. Bake in a preheated oven at 180°C/350°F/gas mark 4 for about 40 minutes until golden and the filling is set. Serve warm.

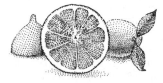

Party Mince Pie

SERVES 5–6

20 ml/4 tsp cornflour (cornstarch)
150 ml/¼ pt/⅔ cup milk
1.5 ml/¼ tsp vanilla essence (extract)
1 egg, separated
25 ml/1½ tbsp caster (superfine) sugar
225 g/8 oz/2 cups plain (all-purpose)
   flour
A pinch of salt
175 g/6 oz/¾ cup butter or margarine,
   softened
1 egg yolk
30 ml/2 tbsp water
225 g/8 oz/⅔ cup mincemeat
Brandy Sauce (see page 356), to serve

Blend the cornflour with a little of the milk in a saucepan. Stir in the remaining milk. Bring to the boil and cook for 1 minute, stirring. Whisk in the vanilla, 1 egg yolk and 15 ml/ 1 tbsp of the sugar. Cook gently for 1 minute, then leave to cool.

Sift the flour, salt and remaining sugar into a bowl. Make a well in the centre. Add the butter or margarine, the remaining egg yolk and water. Work with your hands or a wooden spoon until the mixture forms a soft dough. Wrap in clingfilm (plastic wrap) and chill for 30 minutes.

Cut the pastry (paste) in half. Roll out one half and use to line a 23 cm/ 9 in pie dish. Brush the edge with water. Spoon the cold custard into the dish and top with the mincemeat. Roll out the remaining pastry and use as a lid. Press the edges well together to seal. Trim, knock up the edge and flute with the back of a knife. Cut small stars out of pastry trimmings and arrange on top to decorate. Brush with the lightly beaten egg white to glaze. Bake in a preheated oven at 190°C/375°F/gas mark 5 for 45 minutes or until golden brown and cooked through. Serve warm with Brandy Sauce.

Classic Syrup Tart

SERVES 6

225 g/8 oz/2 cups plain (all-purpose)
   flour
A pinch of salt
100 g/4 oz/½ cup hard block margarine,
   diced
Cold water, to mix
75 g/3 oz/1½ cups white breadcrumbs
90 ml/6 tbsp golden (light corn) syrup
Finely grated rind and juice of 1 small
   lemon
Cream or ice cream, to serve

Sift the flour and salt into a bowl. Add the margarine and rub in with the fingertips until the mixture resembles fine breadcrumbs. Mix with enough cold water to form a firm dough. Knead gently on a lightly floured surface. Roll out and use to line a 23 cm/9 in deep pie plate. Spread the breadcrumbs in the plate. Drizzle the syrup over and sprinkle with the lemon rind and juice. Make a lattice out of pastry (paste) trimmings, if liked, and lay over the tart. Bake in a preheated oven at 220°C/425°F/gas mark 7 for about 30 minutes until golden. Serve warm or cold with cream or ice cream.

Spiced Syrup and Apple Tart

SERVES 6

For the pastry (paste):
225 g/8 oz/2 cups plain (all-purpose) flour
100 g/4 oz/½ cup hard block margarine, diced
25 g/1 oz/2 tbsp caster (superfine) sugar
1 egg, beaten
Cold water, to mix
For the filling:
3 large cooking (tart) apples, finely chopped
100 g/4 oz/⅔ cup sultanas (golden raisins)
175 g/6 oz/3 cups fresh breadcrumbs
1.5 ml/¼ tsp mixed (apple-pie) spice
1.5 ml/¼ tsp ground cinnamon
90 ml/6 tbsp golden (light corn) syrup
Finely grated rind and juice of 1 lime

To make the pastry, put the flour in a bowl. Add the margarine and rub in with the fingertips until the mixture resembles fine breadcrumbs. Stir in the sugar. Add the egg and enough water to form a soft but not sticky dough. Knead gently on a lightly floured surface, then wrap in clingfilm (plastic wrap) and chill for 30 minutes.

Roll out and use to line a 20 cm/ 8 in square shallow baking tin (pan). Trim the edges and reserve the trimmings.

To make the filling, mix together all the ingredients and spoon into the pastry case (pie shell). Roll out the pastry trimmings and cut into thin strips. Use to make a lattice pattern on top of the tart. Brush with a little water, then bake in a preheated oven at 190°C/375°F/gas mark 5 for about 30 minutes or until cooked through and golden brown. Serve warm or cold.

Almond Apple Tart

SERVES 6

450 g/1 lb puff pastry (paste), thawed if frozen
Beaten egg, to glaze
Icing (confectioners') sugar, for dusting
175 g/6 oz white marzipan
2 crisp, green eating (dessert) apples
25 g/1 oz/2 tbsp butter, melted
45 ml/3 tbsp caster (superfine) sugar
Pouring cream, to serve

Roll out the pastry and cut into six 10 cm/4 in squares. Place on a dampened baking sheet and brush with beaten egg. Dust the work surface with icing sugar and roll out the marzipan. Cut into six 7.5 cm/3 in squares and place on top of the pastry squares. Peel, core and slice each apple into 12 pieces. Lay four slices down the centre of each piece of marzipan. Brush with melted butter and sprinkle with caster sugar. Bake in a preheated oven at 220°C/ 425°F/gas mark 7 for 15 minutes until the pastry is golden brown and the apples are caramelised. Serve warm with cream.

American Apple Pie

SERVES 8–10

350 g/12 oz/3 cups plain (all-purpose) flour
A pinch of salt
75 g/3 oz/⅓ cup hard block margarine, diced
75 g/3 oz/⅓ cup white vegetable fat (shortening), diced
Cold water, to mix
1 kg/2¼ lb cooking (tart) apples, thinly sliced
Finely grated rind and juice of ½ lemon
15 ml/1 tbsp cornflour (cornstarch)
175 g/6 oz/¾ cup light brown sugar
5 ml/1 tsp grated nutmeg
2.5 ml/½ tsp mixed (apple pie) spice
30 ml/2 tbsp chopped mixed nuts
25 g/1 oz/2 tbsp unsalted (sweet) butter
A little cream, to glaze
Icing (confectioners') sugar, for dusting
Ice cream, to serve

Sift the flour and salt into a bowl. Add the margarine and white fat and rub in with the fingertips until the mixture resembles fine breadcrumbs. Mix with enough cold water to form a firm dough. Knead gently on a lightly floured surface. Cut in half, roll out one half and to use to line a 25 cm/10 in pie plate.

Mix the apple slices with all the remaining ingredients except the butter. Pile in the centre of the pie. Dot with the butter. Roll out the remaining pastry (paste). Brush the edges of the pie with water and place the pastry over to cover the filling. Press the edges well together to seal, then trim, knock up the edge and flute with the back of a knife. Make a hole in the centre to allow steam to escape. Make leaves out of pastry trimmings and use to decorate the pie. Brush with a little cream to glaze and bake in a preheated oven at 220°C/425°F/gas mark 7 for 10 minutes, then reduce the heat to 190°C/375°F/gas mark 5 for about 35 minutes until golden brown and cooked through. Dust liberally with sifted icing sugar and serve warm with ice cream.

Spiced Carrot and Sultana Pie

SERVES 4

75 g/3 oz/¾ cup plain (all-purpose) flour
75 g/3 oz/¾ cup wholemeal flour
75 g/3 oz/⅓ cup butter, diced
Cold water, to mix
300 ml/½ pt/1¼ cups milk
1 large carrot, grated
50 g/2 oz/1 cup fresh breadcrumbs
50 g/2 oz/¼ cup light brown sugar
30 ml/2 tbsp sultanas (golden raisins)
10 ml/2 tsp mixed (apple-pie) spice
2 eggs, beaten
Fromage frais, to serve

Mix the flours in a bowl. Rub in the butter. Mix with enough cold water to form a firm dough. Knead gently on a lightly floured surface. Roll out the pastry (paste) and use to line a 20 cm/8 in pie dish. Bring the milk just to the boil. Beat in all the remaining ingredients and turn into the pastry-lined dish. Bake in a preheated oven at 190°C/375°F/gas mark 5 for 40 minutes or until set and golden brown. Serve warm with fromage frais.

Apple Turnover Tart

SERVES 6–8

175 g/6 oz/1½ cups wholemeal flour
A pinch of salt
5 ml/1 tsp ground cinnamon
100 g/4 oz/½ cup caster (superfine) sugar
225 g/8 oz/1 cup unsalted (sweet)
  butter
Cold water, to mix
1 kg/2¼ lb cooking (tart) apples, sliced
50 g/2 oz/¼ cup light brown sugar
25 g/1 oz/3 tbsp icing (confectioners')
  sugar
Crème fraîche, to serve

Put the flour, salt and cinnamon in a bowl. Add 25 g/1 oz/2 tbsp of the caster sugar. Dice 100 g/4 oz/½ cup of the butter and rub in with the fingertips until the mixture resembles fine breadcrumbs. Mix with enough cold water to form a firm dough. Wrap in clingfilm (plastic wrap) and chill for 30 minutes.

Melt 75 g/3 oz/⅓ cup of the remaining butter in a pan. Remove from the heat and add the apple slices and remaining caster sugar. Toss thoroughly. Grease a 23 cm/9 in deep round pie dish with the remaining butter. Add the apple mixture in layers with the brown sugar.

Roll out the pastry (paste) to a round and use to cover the pie dish. Trim. Make several slits to allow steam to escape. Bake in a preheated oven at 190°C/375°F/gas mark 5 for about 1 hour or until the apple is tender and the pastry is golden brown. Carefully turn out the tart on to a serving plate. Sprinkle liberally with the icing sugar and flash under a hot grill (broiler) for 3 minutes to caramelise. Serve warm with crème fraîche.

Boxing Day Pie

SERVES 4–5

For the pastry (paste):
100 g/4 oz/1 cup plain (all-purpose) flour
A pinch of salt
50 g/2 oz/¼ cup hard block margarine,
  diced
Cold water, to mix
For the filling:
100 g/4 oz Christmas Pudding (see page
  12)
25 g/1 oz/¼ cup chopped mixed nuts
2 eggs
30 ml/2 tbsp milk
30 ml/2 tbsp brandy
15 ml/1 tbsp dark brown sugar
50 g/2 oz/¼ cup caster (superfine) sugar
Brandy Sauce (see page 356), to serve

To make the pastry, sift the flour and salt into a bowl. Add the margarine and rub in with the fingertips until the mixture resembles fine breadcrumbs. Mix with enough cold water to form a firm dough. Knead gently on a lightly floured surface. Roll out and use to line a 15 cm/6 in flan dish (pie pan).

To make the filling, crumble the Christmas Pudding and mix with the nuts. Separate one of the eggs. Beat the yolk with the whole egg and add to the pudding with the milk, brandy and brown sugar. Mix well. Turn into the pastry case (pie shell). Bake in a preheated oven at 200°C/400°F/gas mark 6 for 20 minutes until the pastry is golden and the filling has set. Whisk the egg white until stiff, then whisk in half the caster sugar until stiff. Fold in the remaining sugar. Pile on top of the pie and return to the oven for 10 minutes until just turning golden brown. Serve hot with Brandy Sauce.

Cherry Pie

SERVES 6

240 g/8½ oz/generous 2 cups plain (all-purpose) flour
125 g/4½ oz/generous ½ cup butter, diced
65 g/2½ oz/generous ¼ cup caster (superfine) sugar
1 egg yolk
Cold water, to mix
750 g/1½ lb cherries, stoned (pitted)
Finely grated rind of 1 orange
A little milk, to glaze
Crème fraîche, to serve

Sift 225 g/8 oz/2 cups of the flour into a bowl. Add 100 g/4 oz/½ cup of the butter and rub in with the fingertips. Stir in 15 g/½ oz/1 tbsp of the sugar. Add the egg yolk and enough water to form a firm dough. Knead gently on a lightly floured surface. Wrap in clingfilm (plastic wrap) and chill for 30 minutes.

Roll out about two-thirds of the pastry (paste) and use to line a 20 cm/8 in pie dish. Put the cherries in a bowl. Mix the remaining sugar and flour with the orange rind and stir in. Spoon into the pastry case (pie shell) and dot with the remaining butter. Roll out the remaining pastry and use as a lid. Press the edges well together to seal. Make a hole in the centre to allow steam to escape. Decorate with leaves made out of the trimmings and brush with a little milk to glaze. Bake in a preheated oven at 220°C/425°F/gas mark 7 for 10 minutes, then reduce the heat to 180°C/350°F/gas mark 4 and continue cooking for 40 minutes. Serve warm or cold with crème fraîche.

Grape Pie

SERVES 6

Prepare as for Cherry Pie, but substitute seedless black or green grapes (or a mixture of the two) for the cherries and the grated rind of 1 lime for the orange.

Edinburgh Tart

SERVES 4–6

50 g/2 oz/¼ cup unsalted (sweet) butter
50 g/2 oz/¼ cup light brown sugar
50 g/2 oz/½ cup chopped mixed (candied) peel
30 ml/2 tbsp sultanas (golden raisins)
15 ml/1 tbsp currants
200 g/7 oz frozen puff pastry (paste), thawed
2 eggs
5 ml/1 tsp whisky (optional)
Atholl Brose Cream (see page 357), to serve

Melt the butter and sugar in a pan. Remove from the heat. Stir in the peel and fruit. Roll out the pastry on a lightly floured surface and use to line a 23 cm/9 in pie plate. Beat the eggs with the whisky, if using, and stir into the fruit mixture. Turn into the pastry-lined plate. Bake in a preheated oven at 220°C/425°F/gas mark 7 for 20 minutes. Reduce the heat to 180°C/350°F/gas mark 4 and continue cooking for a further 15 minutes or until puffy and golden and the filling is set. Serve warm with Atholl Brose Cream.

Pumpkin Pie

SERVES 12

275 g/10 oz/2½ cups plain (all-purpose)
  flour
A pinch of salt
150 g/5 oz/⅔ cup butter, diced
Cold water, to mix
400 g/14 oz/1 large can of pumpkin
  purée
50 g/2 oz/⅓ cup currants
175 g/6 oz/¾ cup light brown sugar
5 ml/1 tsp ground cinnamon
2.5 ml/½ tsp ground ginger
1.5 ml/¼ tsp ground cloves
3 eggs, beaten
300 ml/½ pt/1¼ cups double (heavy)
  cream

Sift the flour and salt into a bowl.
Add the butter and rub in with the
fingertips until the mixture resembles
fine breadcrumbs. Mix with enough
cold water to form a firm dough. Roll
out and use to line two 20 cm/8 in flan
tins (pie pans). Prick the bases with a
fork.
  Blend together the remaining
ingredients, but using only half the
cream. Pour into the flan cases (pie
shells). Bake in a preheated oven at
180°C/350°F/gas mark 4 for about
45 minutes or until the filling is set and
the pastry (paste) is golden brown.
Leave to cool. Whip the remaining
cream and use to decorate the tops of
the pies before serving. Freeze one pie
for up to 3 months, if liked.

Shoo-fly Pie

SERVES 6–8

275 g/10 oz/2½ cups plain (all-purpose)
  flour
A pinch of salt
40 g/1½ oz/3 tbsp white vegetable fat
  (shortening), diced
90 g/3½ oz/scant ½ cup hard block
  margarine, diced
Cold water, to mix
75 g/3 oz/⅓ cup dark brown sugar
5 ml/1 tsp mixed (apple-pie) spice
2.5 ml/½ tsp bicarbonate of soda (baking
  soda)
45 ml/3 tbsp hot water
100 g/4 oz/⅔ cup raisins
Cream, to serve

Sift 175 g/6 oz/1½ cups of the flour
and the salt into a bowl. Add the
white fat and 40 g/1½ oz/3 tbsp of the
margarine and rub in with the fingertips
until the mixture resembles fine
breadcrumbs. Mix with enough cold
water to form a firm dough. Knead
gently on a lightly floured surface. Roll
out and use to line a 20 cm/ 8 in flan
dish (pie pan).
  Sift the remaining flour into a bowl.
Add the remaining margarine and rub
in with the fingertips. Stir in 50 g/
2 oz/¼ cup of the brown sugar and the
mixed spice. Scatter about half this
mixture into the flan case (pie shell).
Blend the bicarbonate of soda with the
water, then mix into the remaining
crumb mixture with the raisins and the
remaining sugar. Spoon into the flan
and level the surface. Bake in a
preheated oven at 180°C/350°F/gas
mark 4 for about 30 minutes until firm
to the touch. Serve warm or cold with
cream.

Damson Rum Pie

SERVES 6

For the pastry (paste):
100 g/4 oz/1 cup wholemeal flour
100 g/4 oz/1 cup self-raising (self-rising)
 flour
100 g/4 oz/½ cup butter, diced
30 ml/2 tbsp dark brown sugar
1 egg, beaten
Cold water, to mix
For the filling:
25 g/1 oz/2 tbsp butter
30 ml/2 tbsp rum
100 g/4 oz/⅔ cup large stoned (pitted)
 (not seedless) raisins, chopped
350 g/12 oz damsons, halved and stoned
50 g/2 oz/¼ cup dark brown sugar
15 ml/1 tbsp milk
Caster (superfine) sugar, for sprinkling
Classic Custard Sauce (see page 354),
 to serve

To make the pastry, mix the flours in a bowl. Add the butter and rub in with the fingertips until the mixture resembles breadcrumbs. Stir in the 30 ml/2 tbsp sugar and mix with the egg and enough cold water to form a soft but not sticky dough. Knead gently on a lightly floured surface, then cut in half. Roll out one half and use to line a pie plate.

To make the filling, mix together the ingredients except the milk and pile on to the pastry-lined plate. Brush the pastry edge with water.

Roll out the remaining pastry, lay over the filled pie and press the edges well together to seal. Trim, then knock up the edge and flute with the back of a knife. Decorate with the pastry trimmings, then brush with the milk and sprinkle with caster sugar. Place the pie on a baking (cookie) sheet and bake in a preheated oven at 200°C/400°F/gas mark 6 for 15 minutes, then reduce the heat to 180°C/350°F/gas mark 4 for a further 20 minutes or until golden brown and cooked through. Serve warm with Classic Custard Sauce.

Lemon Cheese Tart

SERVES 6

175 g/6 oz/1½ cups plain (all-purpose)
 flour
75 g/3 oz/⅓ cup butter, diced
Cold water, to mix
60 ml/4 tbsp lemon curd
100 g/4 oz/½ cup curd (smooth cottage)
 cheese
1 egg, separated

Put the flour in a bowl. Add the butter and rub in with the fingertips until the mixture resembles fine breadcrumbs. Mix with enough cold water to form a firm dough. Knead gently on a lightly floured surface. Roll out and use to line a 20 cm/8 in pie plate.

Beat together the lemon curd and curd cheese with the egg yolk and spoon into the pastry case (pie shell). Roll the pastry (paste) trimmings into strips and use to make a lattice pattern on top. Brush with the egg white to glaze. Bake in a preheated oven at 200°C/400°F/gas mark 6 for 20 minutes or until the pastry is golden and the filling is just set. Serve warm or cold.

Lemon Meringue Pie

SERVES 6

*175 g/6 oz/1½ cups plain (all-purpose)
    flour*
A pinch of salt
90 g/3½ oz/scant ½ cup butter, diced
*25 g/1 oz/3 tbsp icing (confectioners')
    sugar*
3 eggs
Finely grated rind and juice of 2 lemons
30 ml/2 tbsp cornflour (cornstarch)
150 g/5 oz/⅔ cup caster (superfine) sugar

Sift the flour and salt into a bowl. Add 75 g/3 oz/⅓ cup of the butter and rub in with the fingertips until the mixture resembles breadcrumbs. Stir in the icing sugar. Beat one of the eggs and mix in to form a soft but not sticky dough. Knead gently on a lightly floured surface. Wrap in clingfilm (plastic wrap) and chill for 30 minutes.

Roll out and use to line a 20 cm/ 8 in flan tin (pie pan). Fill with crumpled foil and bake in a preheated oven at 200°C/400°F/gas mark 6 for 10 minutes. Remove the foil and bake for a further 5 minutes to dry out.

Make the lemon rind and juice up to 300 ml/½ pt/1¼ cups with water. Blend a little with the cornflour in a saucepan. Stir in the remaining liquid and 25 g/ 1 oz/2 tbsp of the caster sugar. Separate the remaining eggs and whisk the egg yolks into the saucepan. Add the remaining butter. Bring to the boil and cook for 2 minutes, stirring all the time, until thickened. Turn into the cooked flan case (pie shell).

Whisk the egg whites until stiff. Whisk in half the remaining sugar and whisk again until stiff and glossy. Fold in the remaining sugar and pile the meringue on top of the lemon mixture, spreading right to the edges. Reduce the oven temperature to 190°C/375°F/gas mark 5 and cook the pie for about 20 minutes until crisp on top and pale golden brown. Serve warm or cold.

Orange Meringue Pie

SERVES 6

Prepare as for Lemon Meringue Pie, but substitute the finely grated rind and juice of 1 orange for the lemons. Add 10 ml/2 tsp lemon juice and make up the liquid with unsweetened orange juice instead of water.

Pear Meringue Pie

SERVES 6

75 g/3 oz dried pears
300 ml/½ pt/1¼ cups water
5 cm/2 in piece of cinnamon stick
50 g/2 oz/¼ cup granulated sugar
100 g/4 oz/½ cup butter
225 g/8 oz/1 cup caster (superfine) sugar
4 eggs
100 g/4 oz/1cup plain (all-purpose) flour
30 ml/2 tbsp cornflour (cornstarch)
15 ml/1 tbsp lemon juice
Chocolate Custard (see page 355), to
  serve

Soak the pears in the water overnight. Place in a saucepan with the cinnamon stick and granulated sugar. Bring to the boil, reduce the heat and simmer for 20 minutes or until tender. Leave to cool, then discard the cinnamon.

Grease a 20 cm/8 in sponge flan tin (pan). Beat the butter and half the caster sugar until light and fluffy. Beat in 2 of the eggs, one at a time, beating well after each addition. Sift the flour over the surface and fold in with a metal spoon. Turn into the greased tin and smooth the surface. Bake in a preheated oven at 190°C/375°F/gas mark 5 for about 20 minutes until the centre springs back when lightly pressed. Cool slightly, then turn out on to a wire rack to cool completely. Transfer to an ovenproof serving plate.

Lift the pears out of the cold syrup and chop. Blend the cornflour with the lemon juice and stir into the syrup. Bring to the boil and cook for 2 minutes, stirring. Stir in the chopped pears. Separate the remaining eggs and beat the yolks into the pear mixture.

Turn into the sponge flan case (pie shell). Whisk the egg whites until stiff. Whisk in half the remaining sugar and whisk again until stiff and glossy. Fold in the remaining sugar. Pile on top of the flan. Bake in the oven at 190°C/375°F/gas mark 5 for about 10 minutes until lightly coloured. Serve warm with Chocolate Custard.

Pecan Pie

SERVES 4–6

350 g/12 oz puff pastry (paste), thawed
  if frozen
150 g/5 oz/1¼ cups pecan halves
75 g/3 oz/⅓ cup butter
175 g/6 oz/¾ cup light brown sugar
4 eggs
60 ml/4 tbsp golden (light corn) syrup
30 ml/2 tbsp boiling water
5 ml/1 tsp vanilla essence (extract)
Cream or ice cream, to serve

Roll out the pastry and use to line a 20 cm/8 in flan dish (pie pan) on a baking (cookie) sheet. Reserve 25 g/1 oz/¼ cup of the nuts for decoration and roughly chop the remainder.

Beat the butter and sugar until fluffy. Beat in the eggs one at a time, beating well after each addition. Mix the syrup with the boiling water and stir in with the nuts and vanilla essence. Turn into the pastry case (pie shell) and bake in a preheated oven at 200°C/400°F/gas mark 6 for 15 minutes. Remove from the oven and arrange the reserved pecans over. Reduce the heat to 180°C/350°F/gas mark 4 and bake for a further 30 minutes or until deep golden brown and set. Serve warm with cream or ice cream.

Classic Custard Tart

SERVES 6–8

175 g/6 oz/1½ cups plain (all-purpose)
   flour
A pinch of salt
90g/3½ oz/scant ½ cup butter or hard
   block margarine, diced
Cold water, to mix
25 ml/1½ tbsp cornflour (cornstarch)
300 ml/½ pt/1¼ cups milk
2 eggs
15–30 ml/1–2 tbsp caster (superfine)
   sugar
Grated nutmeg, for dusting

Sift the flour and salt into a bowl. Add 75 g/3 oz/⅓ cup of the butter or margarine and rub in with the fingertips until the mixture resembles breadcrumbs. Mix with enough cold water to form a firm dough. Knead gently on a lightly floured surface. Roll out and use to line a 25 cm/10 in pie plate. Place the plate on a baking (cookie) sheet. Decorate the edge by pressing all round with the back of a fork.

Blend the cornflour with a little of the milk in a saucepan. Blend in the remaining milk. Bring to the boil and cook for 2 minutes, stirring. Whisk in the remaining butter or margarine and sweeten to taste with the caster sugar. Cool slightly, then whisk in the eggs. Turn into the prepared dish and dust with nutmeg. Bake in a preheated oven at 190°C/375°F/gas mark 5 for about 25 minutes until golden and just set. Serve hot or cold.

Mississippi Mud Pie

SERVES 8

225 g/8 oz/2 cups plain (all-purpose) flour
25 g/1 oz/¼ cup cornflour (cornstarch)
300 g/11 oz/1⅓ cups unsalted (sweet)
   butter, softened
75 g/3 oz/⅓ cup caster (superfine) sugar
200 g/7 oz/1¾ cups plain (semi-sweet)
   chocolate
15 ml/1 tbsp instant coffee powder or
   granules
15 ml/1 tbsp hot water
3 eggs, beaten
150 ml/¼ pt/⅔ cup single (light) cream
175 g/6 oz/¾ cup dark brown sugar
Pouring cream, to serve

Sift the flour and cornflour into a bowl. Add 200 g/7 oz/scant 1 cup of the butter and the caster sugar and work in with the fingers, gradually drawing in the flour until the mixture forms a ball. (Or put the ingredients in a food processor and blend briefly.) Press into the base and sides of a 23 cm/9 in flan dish (pie pan). Fill with crumpled foil and bake in a preheated oven at 200°C/400°F/gas mark 6 for 10 minutes. Remove the foil and return to the oven for 5 minutes to dry out. Remove from the oven.

Break up the chocolate and place in a saucepan with the remaining butter. Blend the coffee with the water and add. Heat, stirring, until the butter and chocolate have melted. Remove from the heat and beat in the eggs, single cream and brown sugar. Pour into the pastry case (pie shell). Reduce the oven temperature to 190°C/375°F/gas mark 5 and bake for about 40 minutes until set. Leave to cool slightly, then serve warm or cold with pouring cream.

Pear and Orange Pie

SERVES 8

For the filling:
750 g/1½ lb pears, sliced
5 cm/2 in piece of cinnamon stick
50 g/2 oz/¼ cup granulated sugar
300 ml/½ pt/1¼ cups pure orange juice
25 ml/1½ tbsp cornflour (cornstarch)
15 ml/1 tbsp water
For the pastry (paste):
100 g/4 oz/1 cup plain (all-purpose) flour
100 g/4 oz/1 cup wholemeal flour
A pinch of salt
100 g/4 oz/½ cup unsalted (sweet) butter, diced
Cold water, to mix
A little milk or cream, to glaze
Double (heavy) cream, to serve

To make the filling, put the pears in a pan with the cinnamon, sugar and orange juice. Simmer gently for 10 minutes until the fruit is tender but still holds its shape. Blend the cornflour with the water and stir into the saucepan. Bring to the boil and cook for 1 minute, stirring. Leave to cool.

To make the pastry, mix together the flours and salt. Add the butter and rub in with the fingertips. Mix with enough cold water to form a firm dough. Knead gently on a lightly floured surface. Cut in half. Roll out one half and use to line a 23 cm/9 in pie plate. Brush the edge with water. Spoon in the pear mixture.

Roll out the remaining pastry and use as a lid. Press the edges well together to seal. Trim, knock up the edge and flute with the back of a knife. Make leaves out of trimmings and use to decorate the pie. Brush with a little milk or cream to glaze. Bake in a preheated oven at 200°C/400°F/gas mark 6 for about 30 minutes until golden brown. Serve warm with cream.

Peach and Orange Pie

SERVES 8

Prepare as for Pear and Orange Pie, but substitute peaches for the pears. Add the finely grated rind of 1 orange, if liked, to enhance the flavour.

Jam Tart

SERVES 4–8

175 g/6 oz/1½ cups plain (all-purpose) flour
A pinch of salt
75 g/3 oz/⅓ cup hard block margarine, diced
Cold water, to mix
90 ml/6 tbsp jam (conserve)

Sift the flour and salt in a bowl. Add the margarine and rub in with the fingertips until the mixture resembles fine breadcrumbs. Mix with enough cold water to form a firm dough. Knead gently on a lightly floured surface. Roll out and use to line a 20 cm/8 in pie plate. Trim the edge and decorate with the prongs of a fork. Spread the jam in the centre of the pastry. Bake in a preheated oven at 200°C/400°F/gas mark 6 for about 20 minutes until the pastry is golden and the jam is bubbling. Serve warm or cold.

Bakewell Tart

SERVES 6

175 g/6 oz/1½ cups plain (all-purpose) flour
A pinch of salt
40 g/1½ oz/3 tbsp hard block margarine, diced
40 g/1½ oz/3 tbsp white vegetable fat (shortening), diced
Cold water, to mix
60 ml/4 tbsp raspberry jam (conserve)
100 g/4 oz/½ cup butter
100 g/4 oz/½ cup caster (superfine) sugar
2 eggs, beaten
100 g/4 oz/1 cup ground almonds
2.5 ml/½ tsp almond essence (extract)
175 g/6 oz/1 cup icing (confectioners') sugar
30 ml/2 tbsp lemon juice
Halved glacé (candied) cherries, to decorate

Sift the flour and salt into a bowl. Add the margarine and white fat and rub in with the fingertips until the mixture resembles fine breadcrumbs. Mix with enough cold water to form a firm dough. Knead gently on a lightly floured surface. Roll out and use to line a 20 cm/8 in flan dish (pie pan). Prick the base with a fork. Line with crumpled foil and bake in a preheated oven at 200°C/400°F/gas mark 6 for 10 minutes. Remove the foil and cook for a further 5 minutes.

Spread the base with the jam. Beat together the butter and caster sugar until light and fluffy. Beat in the eggs, a little at a time, then fold in the almonds and essence. Spoon into the flan case (pie shell) and bake for 30 minutes

until risen and golden and the mixture feels set. Remove from the oven and leave to cool. Blend the icing sugar with the lemon juice until smooth. Spread over the surface and decorate with halved glacé cherries.

Baked Very Well Tart

SERVES 6

175 g/6 oz/1½ cups plain (all-purpose) flour
A pinch of salt
200 g/7 oz/scant 1 cup hard block margarine, diced
Cold water, to mix
45–60 ml/3–4 tbsp raspberry jam (conserve)
75 g/3 oz/⅓ cup caster (superfine) sugar
2 large eggs
50 g/2 oz/1 cup plain cake crumbs
1.5 ml/¼ tsp vanilla essence (extract)

Sift the flour and salt into a bowl. Add 75 g/3 oz/⅓ cup of the margarine and rub in with the fingertips until the mixture resembles fine breadcrumbs. Mix with enough cold water to form a firm dough. Knead gently on a lightly floured surface, roll out and use to line a 23 cm/9 in pie plate. Decorate the edge with the prongs of a fork.

Spread the jam over the base, avoiding the rim. Beat the remaining margarine in a bowl with the caster sugar. Beat in the eggs, then the cake crumbs and vanilla essence. Spread over the jam. Place the pie plate on a baking (cookie) sheet and bake in a preheated oven at 190°C/375°F/gas mark 5 for about 35 minutes until just set and golden brown. Serve warm.

Festive Bakewell Tart

SERVES 8

225 g/8 oz/2 cups plain (all-purpose)
  flour
225 g/8 oz/1 cup butter, diced
Cold water, to mix
60 ml/4 tbsp mincemeat
150 g/5 oz/⅔ cup caster (superfine) sugar
2 large eggs
A few drops of almond essence (extract)
5 ml/1 tsp baking powder
100 g/4 oz/1 cup ground almonds
30 ml/2 tbsp milk
30 ml/2 tbsp flaked (slivered) almonds

Put 175 g/6 oz/1½ cups of the flour
in a bowl. Add 75 g/3 oz/⅓ cup of
the butter and rub in with the fingertips
until the mixture resembles fine
breadcrumbs. Mix with enough cold
water to form a firm dough. Knead
gently on a lightly floured surface. Roll
out and use to line an 18 × 28 cm/
7 × 11 in shallow baking tin (pan).
Prick with a fork.
  Spread the mincemeat over the
base. Beat the remaining butter with the
sugar until light and fluffy. Beat in the
eggs, one at a time, and add the
almond essence. Sift the remaining flour
with the baking powder over and fold
in with the ground almonds and milk.
Spread over the mincemeat. Sprinkle
with the flaked almonds. Bake in a
preheated oven at 200°C/400°F/gas
mark 6 for about 30 minutes until the
centre springs back when lightly
pressed and the top is golden brown.
Cool slightly, cut into eight rectangles
and serve warm.

Maids of Honour

MAKES 16

For the pastry (paste):
200 g/7 oz/1¾ cups plain (all-purpose)
  flour
A pinch of salt
100 g/4 oz/½ cup butter or hard block
  margarine, diced
Cold water, to mix
For the filling:
175 g/6 oz/¾ cup curd (smooth cottage)
  cheese
40 g/1½ oz/¼ cup currants
50 g/2 oz/¼ cup caster (superfine) sugar,
  plus extra for sprinkling
Finely grated rind of 1 small lemon
15 ml/1 tbsp ground almonds
10 ml/2 tsp brandy or sherry
1 small egg, beaten

To make the pastry, sift the flour and
salt into a bowl. Add 90 g/3½ oz of
the butter or margarine and rub in with
the fingertips until the mixture
resembles fine breadcrumbs. Mix with
enough cold water to form a firm dough.
Knead gently on a lightly floured
surface. Roll out and use to line
16 tartlet tin (patty pan) sections.
  To make the filling, beat together the
curd cheese and the remaining butter or
margarine until well blended. Beat in the
remaining ingredients. Spoon into the
tarts. Cook in a preheated oven at
190°C/375°F/gas mark 5 for about
35 minutes until golden brown. Sprinkle
with a little caster sugar and cool on a
wire rack.

Apricot and Ginger Tart

SERVES 6

100 g/4 oz/1 cup wholemeal flour
A pinch of salt
75 g/6 oz/¾ cup butter, diced
Cold water, to mix
100 g/4 oz/½ cup caster (superfine) sugar
2 large eggs
75 g/3 oz/¾ cup self-raising (self-rising)
   wholemeal flour
25 g/1 oz/¼ cup ground rice
10 ml/2 tsp ground ginger
30 ml/2 tbsp milk
45 ml/3 tbsp apricot jam (conserve)
A few flaked (slivered) almonds, to
   decorate

M ix the wholemeal flour with the
salt in a bowl. Add 50 g/2 oz/
¼ cup of the butter and rub in with the
fingertips until the mixture resembles
fine breadcrumbs. Mix with enough
cold water to form a firm dough. Knead
gently on a lightly floured surface and
use to line a 20 cm/8 in sandwich tin
(pan). Fill with crumpled foil and bake
in a preheated oven at 200°C/400°F/gas
mark 6 for 10 minutes. Remove the foil
and continue cooking for 5 minutes to
dry out. Remove from the oven.

Beat together the remaining butter
and the sugar until light and fluffy. Add
the eggs, one at a time, beating well
after each addition. Mix together the
self-raising wholemeal flour, ginger and
ground rice and sprinkle over the
surface. Fold in with a metal spoon,
adding enough of the milk to form a
soft, dropping consistency. Spread the
jam over the base of the pastry case
(pie shell). Spoon the sponge mixture
over and sprinkle with almonds. Reduce
the oven temperature to 180°C/350°F/
gas mark 4 and cook the tart for about
35 minutes until risen, golden brown
and the centre springs back when
lightly pressed. Leave to cool for
10 minutes, then remove from the tin
and serve warm or cold

Rum Butter Tartlets

MAKES 12

75 g/3 oz/½ cup currants
30 ml/2 tbsp rum
100 g/4 oz/1 cup plain (all-purpose)
   flour
A pinch of salt
75 g/3 oz/⅓ cup butter, diced
Cold water, to mix
15 ml/1 tbsp single (light) cream
100 g/4 oz/½ cup light brown sugar
1 small egg, beaten
Double (heavy) cream, to serve

P ut the currants in small pan with the
rum. Bring to the boil, remove from
the heat and leave to soak for at least
2 hours. Mix the flour and salt in a
bowl. Add 50 g/2 oz/¼ cup of the butter
and rub in with the fingertips. Mix with
enough cold water to form a firm
dough. Knead gently on a lightly
floured surface, roll out and use to line
the 12 sections of a tartlet tin (patty
pan).

Melt the remaining butter in a
saucepan. Add the single cream and
sugar. Stir in the currants and rum and
the egg. Spoon into the tartlets and
bake in a preheated oven at
190°C/375°F/gas mark 5 for about
20 minutes until golden brown and set.
Serve warm with double cream.

Lemon Whisky Tart

SERVES 6

175 g/6 oz/1½ cups plain (all-purpose)
    flour
A pinch of salt
75 g/3 oz/⅓ cup unsalted (sweet) butter,
    diced
Cold water, to mix
75 ml/5 tbsp strawberry jam (conserve)
1 large lemon
100 g/4 oz/½ cup soft tub margarine
100 g/4 oz/½ cup caster (superfine)
    sugar
100 g/4 oz/1 cup self-raising (self-
rising)
    flour
2.5 ml/½ tsp baking powder
2 eggs
225 g/8 oz/1¼ cups icing (confectioners')
    sugar, sifted
15 ml/1 tbsp whisky

Mix the plain flour and salt in a bowl. Add the butter and rub in with the fingertips until the mixture resembles fine breadcrumbs. Mix with enough cold water to form a firm dough. Knead gently on a lightly floured surface. Wrap in clingfilm (plastic wrap) and chill for at least 15 minutes. Roll out and use to line a 23 cm/9 in loose-bottomed flan tin (pie pan). Prick the base with a fork. Spread the jam over the base and chill while preparing the filling.

Finely grate the rind from half the lemon and thinly pare the remainder. Squeeze the juice. Put the margarine, caster sugar, self-raising flour, baking powder and eggs in a bowl with the grated lemon rind. Beat well until smooth. Turn into the flan case (pie shell) and level the surface. Bake in a preheated oven at 190°C/375°F/gas mark 5 for about 30 minutes until cooked through and the centre springs back when lightly pressed.

Meanwhile, cut the thinly pared rind into very thin strips and boil in water for 3 minutes. Drain, rinse with cold water and drain again, then dry on kitchen paper (paper towels). Blend the icing sugar with the lemon juice and whisky until smooth. Remove the tart from the flan tin and place on a serving plate. Spoon the icing over, letting it run down the sides. Scatter the lemon rind over to decorate and serve warm or cold.

Melting Raspberry Pie

SERVES 6

100 g/4 oz/1 cup wholemeal flour
150 g/5 oz/1¼ cups plain (all-purpose)
flour
A pinch of salt
30 ml/2 tbsp icing (confectioners') sugar
100 g/4 oz/½ cup white vegetable fat
(shortening)
90 g/3½ oz/scant ½ cup unsalted (sweet)
butter
75–90 ml/5–6 tbsp water
450 g/1 lb raspberries
45 ml/3 tbsp granulated sugar
Vanilla ice cream (bought or home-made,
see page 188), to serve

Mix together the flours, salt and icing sugar. Beat together the white fat and butter. Gradually work in the flour mixture and water, using an electric beater or wooden spoon. The mixture will be very soft. Draw into a ball and wrap in clingfilm (plastic wrap). Chill for 1 hour.

Cut the dough in half. Roll out one half on a well-floured surface and use to line a 23 cm/9 in pie plate. Mix the raspberries with the granulated sugar and pile into the plate. Brush the edges with water. Roll out the remaining pastry (paste) and use to cover the pie. Trim the edges, then press all round with the prongs of a fork to decorate. Make a small slit in the centre to allow steam to escape. Place on a baking (cookie) sheet. Bake in a preheated oven at 200°C/400°F/gas mark 6 for about 40 minutes until golden brown and cooked through. Serve warm with vanilla ice cream.

Strawberry Custard Tartlets

MAKES 15

175 g/6 oz/1½ cups plain (all-purpose)
flour
5 ml/1 tsp ground cinnamon
75 g/3 oz/⅓ cup butter, diced
15 ml/1 tbsp caster (superfine) sugar
1 egg yolk
Cold water, to mix
½ × 425 g/½ × 15 oz/½ × large can of
custard
15 ml/1 tbsp orange liqueur
15 strawberries
45 ml/3 tbsp redcurrant jelly (clear
conserve)
20 ml/4 tsp water

Sift the flour and cinnamon into a bowl. Add the butter and rub in with the fingertips until the mixture resembles fine breadcrumbs. Stir in the sugar. Mix with the egg yolk and enough cold water to form a firm dough. Knead gently on a lightly floured surface. Wrap in clingfilm (plastic wrap) and chill for 30 minutes.

Roll out and use to line 15 sections of tartlet tins (patty pans). Prick the bases with a fork. Bake in a preheated oven at 200°C/400°F/gas mark 6 for 15 minutes. Transfer to a wire rack to cool. Blend the custard with the orange liqueur and spoon into the cases. Top each with a halved strawberry. Melt the redcurrant jelly in the measured water and brush all over the surface of each tartlet. Chill until ready to serve.

Raspberry Custard Tartlets

MAKES 15

Prepare as for Strawberry Custard Tartlets but top each with 2–3 raspberries instead of the strawberries.

Chester Tart

SERVES 6

225 g/8 oz/2 cups plain (all-purpose) flour
200g/7 oz/scant 1 cup unsalted (sweet) butter, diced
125 g/4½ oz/generous 1 cup caster (superfine) sugar
1 egg yolk
Cold water, to mix
Finely grated rind and juice of 1 lemon
100 g/4 oz/½ cup granulated sugar
4 eggs, separated
60 ml/4 tbsp ground almonds

Sift the flour into a bowl. Add 150 g/5 oz/⅔ cup of the butter and rub in with the fingertips. Stir in 15 ml/1 tbsp of the caster sugar. Mix with the egg yolk and enough cold water to form a firm dough. Knead gently on a lightly floured surface. Wrap with clingfilm (plastic wrap) and chill for 30 minutes. Roll out and use to line a 23 cm/9 in loose-bottomed flan tin (pie pan). Fill with crumpled foil and bake in a preheated oven at 220°C/425°F/gas mark 7 for 10 minutes. Remove the foil and bake for a further 5 minutes.

Meanwhile, melt the remaining butter in a small saucepan. Remove from the heat and whisk in the lemon rind and juice, the granulated sugar and the four egg yolks. Blend in the ground almonds. Return to the heat and cook, stirring, until the mixture thickens but do not allow to boil. Pour into the prepared pastry case (pie shell). Whisk the egg whites until stiff. Whisk in half the remaining sugar and whisk again until glossy and stiff. Fold in the remaining sugar. Pile on top of the tart. Return to the oven for 5 minutes until the meringue is turning colour. Reduce the heat to 160°C/325°F/gas mark 3 and bake for 20–30 minutes until crisp on the outside and a pale biscuit colour. Serve warm or cold.

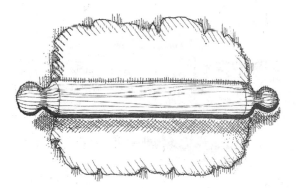

Manchester Tartlets

MAKES 12

For the pastry (paste):
225 g/8 oz/2 cups plain (all-purpose)
  flour
A pinch of salt
100 g/4 oz/¼ cup butter, diced
Cold water, to mix
For the filling:
250 ml/8 fl oz/1 cup milk
20 g/¾ oz/1½ tbsp butter
Grated rind of 1 small lemon
2 large eggs, separated
100 g/4 oz/½ cup caster (superfine) sugar
50 g/2 oz/1 cup fresh breadcrumbs
A little raspberry jam (conserve)

To make the pastry, sift the flour and salt into a bowl. Add the butter and rub in with the fingertips until the mixture resembles fine breadcrumbs. Mix with enough cold water to form a firm dough. Knead gently on a lightly floured surface. Roll out and use to line the 12 sections of a tartlet tin (patty pan). Prick the bases with a fork and fill with crumpled foil. Bake in a preheated oven at 180°C/350°F/gas mark 4 for 15 minutes. Remove the foil after 10 minutes.

To make the filling, put the milk in a saucepan with the butter and lemon rind. Heat until the butter melts. Beat the egg yolks with 25 g/1 oz/2 tbsp of the caster sugar. Whisk in the warm milk mixture, then stir in the breadcrumbs. Leave to stand for 10 minutes. Spoon into the pastry cases (pie shells) and bake for 20 minutes until set. Leave to cool, then carefully lift out of the tins and transfer the tarts to a baking (cookie) sheet. Whisk the egg whites until stiff. Whisk in half the remaining sugar and whisk again until stiff. Fold in the remaining sugar. Spread a little jam over the top of each tart, then top with the meringue mixture. Bake in the oven at 180°C/350°F/gas mark 4 for 5 minutes, then reduce the temperature to 150°C/300°F/gas mark 2 and bake for a further 15 minutes or until the meringue is crisp and a pale biscuit colour.

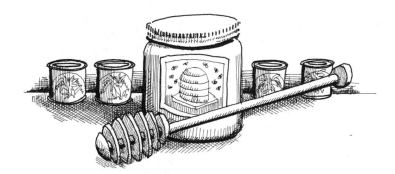

Yorkshire Curd Tartlets

MAKES 10

175 g/6 oz/1½ cups wholemeal flour
A pinch of salt
150 g/5 oz/⅔ cup unsalted (sweet) butter,
  diced
50 g/2 oz/½ cup ground almonds
Cold water, to mix
50 g/2 oz/¼ cup caster (superfine) sugar
1 egg, beaten
225 g/8 oz/1 cup curd (smooth cottage)
  cheese
Finely grated rind of ½ lemon
45 ml/3 tbsp currants
Grated nutmeg, for dusting
Thick cream, to serve

Mix the flour and salt in a bowl. Add 75 g/3 oz/⅓ cup of the butter and rub in with the fingertips until the mixture resembles breadcrumbs. Stir in the almonds. Mix with enough cold water to form a firm dough. Knead gently on a lightly floured surface. Wrap in clingfilm (plastic wrap) and chill for 30 minutes.

Roll out the pastry (paste) and use to line 10 sections of a tartlet tin (patty pan). Beat the remaining butter with the sugar. Beat in the egg, then the cheese, lemon rind and currants. Spoon into the pastry-lined tins and dust with nutmeg. Bake in a preheated oven at 190°C/375°F/gas mark 5 for about 20 minutes until golden and set. Serve warm or cold with thick cream.

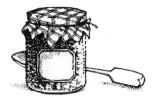

Chocolate Lemon Tartlets

MAKES 9–12

150 g/5 oz/1¼ cups plain (all-purpose)
  flour
A pinch of salt
75 g/3 oz/⅓ cup butter, diced
1 egg yolk
10 ml/2 tsp caster (superfine) sugar
Cold water, to mix
200 g/7 oz/1¾ cups plain (semi-sweet)
  chocolate
150 ml/¼ pt/⅔ cup double (heavy) cream
75 ml/5 tbsp lemon curd

Sift the flour and salt into a bowl. Add the butter and rub in with the fingertips until the mixture resembles breadcrumbs. Add the egg yolk and sugar and enough cold water to form a firm dough. Knead gently on a lightly floured surface. Wrap in clingfilm (plastic wrap) and chill for at least 30 minutes.

Roll out and use to line sections of a tartlet tin (patty pan). Fill each with crumpled foil and bake in a preheated oven at 200°C/400°F/gas mark 6 for 10 minutes. Remove the foil and return to the oven for 5 minutes to dry out. Leave to cool.

Place 100 g/4 oz/1 cup of the chocolate in a bowl over a pan of hot water and stir until melted (or melt in the microwave). Brush all over the insides and round the edges of the pastry cases. Leave to set.

Whip the cream until peaking and fold in the lemon curd. Spoon into the cases (shells). Use a potato peeler to shave curls off the remaining chocolate and use to decorate the tops of the tarts. Chill until ready to serve.

Chocolate Orange Tartlets

MAKES 9–12

Prepare as for Chocolate Lemon Tartlets (see page 57), but substitute orange curd for the lemon.

Classic Mince Pies

MAKES 24

750 g/1½ lb/6 cups plain (all-purpose) flour
A pinch of salt
175 g/6 oz/¾ cup white vegetable fat (shortening), diced
175 g/6 oz/¾ cup hard block margarine, diced
Cold water, to mix
450 g/1 lb/1⅓ cups mincemeat (home-made or bought)
A little milk, to glaze
Caster (superfine) sugar, for sprinkling

Sift the flour and salt into a large bowl. Add the fats and rub in with the fingertips until the mixture resembles fine breadcrumbs. Mix with enough cold water to form a soft but not sticky dough. Knead gently on a lightly floured surface. Wrap in clingfilm (plastic wrap) and chill for 30 minutes.

Roll out just over half the pastry (paste) and cut into 24 rounds, using a 7.5 cm/3 in biscuit (cookie) cutter. Use to line the sections of tartlet tins (patty pans). Roll out the remaining pastry and cut into 24 slightly smaller lids. Fill the pastry cases (pie shells) with mincemeat, then top each with a pastry lid. Brush with a little milk and sprinkle with caster sugar. Bake in a preheated oven at 200°C/400°F/gas mark 6 for about 15 minutes or until golden brown. Transfer to a wire rack to cool. Sprinkle with a little more caster sugar, if liked, and store in an airtight container. They will keep in a cool place for up to two weeks.

Last-minute Mincemeat

MAKES 900 G/2 LB

1 large cooking (tart) apple, quartered
100 g/4 oz/⅔ cup currants
100 g/4 oz/⅔ cup raisins
100 g/4 oz/⅔ cup sultanas (golden raisins)
50 g/2 oz/⅓ cup chopped mixed (candied) peel
100 g/4 oz/1 cup shredded (chopped) vegetable suet
225 g/8 oz/1 cup light brown sugar
2.5 ml/½ tsp mixed (apple-pie) spice
30 ml/2 tbsp brandy or rum

Pass the apple, dried fruit and peel through a coarse mincer (grinder). Stir in the remaining ingredients. Pot, cover and store in the fridge for up to 2 weeks.

Speciality Mince Pies

MAKES 24

Prepare as for Classic Mince Pies but use half the quantity of flour and fats to make enough shortcrust pastry (basic pie crust) to line the tartlet tins (patty pans). Use 375 g/13 oz/1 packet of puff pastry, thawed if frozen, for the lids.

Hot Lemon Tart

SERVES 4–6

225 g/8 oz/2 cups plain (all-purpose) flour
175 g/6 oz/¾ cup unsalted (sweet) butter
125 g/4½ oz/generous ½ cup caster (superfine) sugar
1 egg yolk
Cold water, to mix
3 eggs
Finely grated rind and juice of 2 lemons

Sift the flour into a bowl. Add 100 g/ 4 oz/½ cup of the butter, 15 g/½ oz/ 1 tbsp of the sugar and the egg yolk. Gradually work the flour into the mixture with the fingertips until the mixture forms a ball, adding enough cold water to form a soft but not sticky dough. Knead gently on a lightly floured surface. Wrap in clingfilm (plastic wrap) and chill for 30 minutes.

Roll out and use to line a 20 cm/8 in flan tin (pie pan). Fill with crumpled foil and bake in a preheated oven at 200°C/ 400°F/gas mark 6 for 10 minutes. Remove the foil and return to the oven for a further 5 minutes to dry out.

Whisk the eggs with the remaining sugar until thick and pale. Melt the remaining butter and stir in with the lemon rind and juice. Pour into the pastry case (pie shell) and bake in the oven at 180°C/350°F/gas mark 4 for about 20 minutes until golden brown and just set. Serve hot.

Hot Lime Tart

SERVES 4–6

Prepare as for Hot Lemon Tart but substitute the finely grated rind and juice of 2 limes for the lemons and add 30 ml/2 tbsp lemon juice.

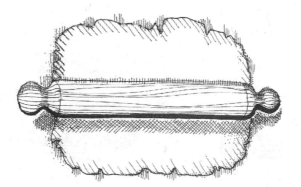

Gorgeous Glazed Apricot Tart

SERVES 8

For the pastry (paste):
150 g/5 oz/1¼ cups plain (all-purpose) flour
50 g/2 oz/⅓ cup icing (confectioners') sugar
150 g/5 oz/⅔ cup butter, softened
Finely grated rind and juice of 1 orange
1 egg yolk
1.5 ml/¼ tsp vanilla essence (extract)
Oil, for greasing
For the filling:
450 g/1 lb/2 cups Ricotta cheese
225 g/8 oz/1 cup caster (superfine) sugar
4 eggs
90 ml/6 tbsp double (heavy) cream
For the topping:
425 g/15 oz/1 large can of apricot halves, drained
30 ml/2 tbsp apricot jam (conserve), sieved (strained), if necessary

To make the pastry, sift the flour and icing sugar into a bowl. Add the butter and half the orange rind and work in with a fork until beginning to form a dough. Add the egg yolk and vanilla essence and mix with the fork, then the hands, until the mixture forms a ball. Wrap in clingfilm (plastic wrap) and chill for 30 minutes.

Roll out half the dough and use to line the base of an oiled 23 cm/9 in springform cake tin (pan). Prick with a fork and bake in a preheated oven at 200°C/400°F/gas mark 6 for 15 minutes. Remove from the oven.

To make the filling, beat the cheese and caster sugar with the remaining orange rind. Add the eggs, one at a time, beating well after each addition. Stir in the cream.

Roll out the remaining dough to a strip and use to line the sides of the cake tin, pressing the strip to the base firmly all round to seal. Pour in the cheese mixture. Bake in the oven at 200°C/400°F/gas mark 6 for 15 minutes, then reduce the heat to 160°C/325°F/gas mark 3 and cook for a further 20 minutes or until set. Arrange the apricot halves, rounded-sides up, on top and return to the oven for 10 minutes. Remove the cake tin. Blend the orange juice and jam in a small saucepan and heat until blended and melted. Brush all over the top of the tart and serve warm or cold.

Flantastic

Some of the most versatile desserts you can make. Whether the bases are made out of sponge, pastry (paste) or crumbs, they can hold a whole variety of glorious fillings from fresh glazed fruit to rich chocolate cream. You can, of course, use ready-made flan cases (pie shells) for any of these recipes, but do try making your own. You won't believe the difference!

Basic Sponge Flan Case

MAKES ONE 20 CM/8 IN FLAN CASE (PIE SHELL)

Butter, for greasing
2 eggs
50 g/2 oz/¼ cup caster (superfine) sugar
50 g/2 oz/½ cup plain (all-purpose) flour

Grease a 20 cm/8 in sponge flan mould. Line the raised centre with greased greaseproof (waxed) paper. Break the eggs into a bowl and add the sugar. Place the bowl over a pan of hot water and whisk with an electric hand whisk until the mixture is thick and pale and leaves a trail when the blades are lifted out. Sift the flour over the surface and fold in gently with a metal spoon. Turn into the prepared mould. Bake in a preheated oven at 190°C/375°F/gas mark 5 for 20 minutes or until risen, golden and the centre springs back when lightly pressed. Allow to cool slightly, trim the edges if the sponge has risen over the edge, then turn out on to a wire rack, remove the paper and leave to cool. Use as required.

Basic Large Sponge Flan Case

MAKES ONE 25 CM/10 IN FLAN CASE (PIE SHELL)

Butter, for greasing
3 eggs
75 g/3 oz/⅓ cup caster (superfine) sugar
75 g/3 oz/¾ cup plain (all-purpose) flour

Prepare as for Basic Sponge Flan Case, but use a 25 cm/10 in sponge flan mould.

Basic Pastry Flan Case

MAKES ONE 20 CM/8 IN FLAN CASE (PIE SHELL)

175 g/6 oz/1½ cups plain (all-purpose)
  flour
A pinch of salt
75 g/3 oz/⅓ cup hard block margarine,
  diced
Cold water, to mix

Sift the flour and salt into a bowl. Add the margarine and rub in with the fingertips until the mixture resembles fine breadcrumbs. Mix with enough cold water to form a firm dough. Knead gently on a lightly floured surface. Wrap the pastry (paste) in clingfilm (plastic wrap) and chill for at least 15 minutes.

Roll out and use to line a 20 cm/ 8 in flan tin (pie pan) or a flan ring set on a baking (cookie) sheet. Prick the base with a fork and fill with crumpled foil. Bake in a preheated oven at 200°C/ 400°F/gas mark 6 for 10 minutes. Remove the foil and bake for a further 5 minutes to dry out. Use as required.

Basic Large Pastry Flan Case

MAKES ONE 25 CM/10 IN FLAN CASE (PIE SHELL)

225 g/8 oz/2 cups plain (all-purpose)
  flour
A pinch of salt
100 g/4 oz/½ cup hard block margarine,
  diced
Cold water, to mix

Prepare as for Basic Pastry Flan Case but use a 25 cm/10 in flan tin (pie pan) or flan ring set on a baking (cookie) sheet.

BASE DIG. BISCI v BUTTER
SLICES BANANAS
BOIL NESTES MILK 1½
POUR OVER BANAN
CREAM ON TOP.

PAMPERS MAXI +
BABY BATH

Sweet Pastry Flan Case

MAKES ONE 20 CM/8 IN FLAN CASE (PIE SHELL)

175 g/6 oz/1½ cups plain (all-purpose)
flour
A pinch of salt
75 g/3 oz/⅓ cup unsalted (sweet) butter,
softened
7.5 ml/1½ tsp caster (superfine) sugar
1 egg yolk
15 ml/1 tbsp water

Sift the flour and salt into a bowl.
Make a well in the centre and add
the butter, sugar and egg yolk.
Gradually knead in the flour until the
mixture forms a ball, adding the water
to form a soft but not sticky dough.
Wrap the pastry (paste) in clingfilm
(plastic wrap) and chill for 30 minutes.
　　Roll out and use to line a 20 cm/8 in
flan ring set on a baking (cookie) sheet.
Prick the base with a fork and fill with
crumpled foil. Bake in a preheated oven
at 200°C/400°F/gas mark 6 for about
10 minutes, then remove the paper and
bake for a further 5 minutes to dry out.
Cool slightly, then remove the flan ring
and transfer the flan case to a serving
plate. Use as required.

Chocolate Flan Case

MAKES ONE 20 CM/8 IN FLAN CASE (PIE SHELL

150 g/5 oz/1¼ cups plain (all-purpose)
flour
45 ml/3 tbsp drinking (sweetened)
chocolate powder
50 g/2 oz/¼ cup hard block margarine,
diced
40 g/1½ oz/3 tbsp white vegetable fat
(shortening), diced
Cold water, to mix

Sift together the flour and drinking
chocolate into a bowl. Add the
margarine and vegetable fat and rub in
with the fingertips until the mixture
resembles breadcrumbs. Mix with
enough cold water to form a firm
dough. Knead gently on a lightly
floured surface. Roll out and use to line
a 20 cm/8 in flan ring set on a baking
(cookie) sheet. Prick the base with a
fork and fill with crumpled foil. Bake in
a preheated oven at 200°C/400°F/gas
mark 6 for 10 minutes. Remove the foil
and return the flan to the oven for
5 minutes to dry out. Use as required.

Almond Pear Flan

SERVES 6–8

1 Basic Large Pastry Flan Case,
  uncooked (see page 62)
75 g/3 oz/⅓ cup unsalted (sweet) butter,
  softened
75 g/3 oz/⅓ cup caster (superfine) sugar
75 g/3 oz/¾ cup ground almonds
25 g/1 oz/¼ cup plain (all-purpose) flour
1 egg, beaten
1 egg yolk
2 ripe pears, peeled and evenly sliced
30 ml/2 tbsp apricot jam (conserve)
15 ml/1 tbsp water

Chill the uncooked flan case (pie shell) while preparing the filling. Beat together the butter and sugar until light and fluffy. Mix in the ground almonds, flour, beaten egg and egg yolk. Turn into the flan case and level with a spatula. Arrange the pear slices attractively over, pressing them down lightly. Bake in a preheated oven at 180°C/350°F/gas mark 4 for 45–50 minutes until the flan is golden and firm to the touch. Heat the jam and water in a saucepan, stirring with a wooden spoon. Sieve (strain) over the flan and brush all over the surface to glaze. Serve warm.

Double Chocolate Flan

SERVES 6

15 ml/1 tbsp powdered gelatine
60 ml/4 tbsp cold water
150 ml/¼ pt/⅔ cup boiling water
2.5 ml/½ tsp instant coffee powder or
  granules
225 g/8 oz/2 cups plain (semi-sweet)
  chocolate
2.5 ml/½ tsp vanilla essence (extract)
2 eggs, separated
50 g/2 oz/¼ cup caster (superfine) sugar
1 Chocolate Flan Case, baked (see page
  63)
150 ml/¼ pt/⅔ cup whipping cream

Sprinkle the gelatine over the cold water in a bowl and leave to soften for 5 minutes. Add the boiling water and stir until completely dissolved. Stir in the coffee. Melt half the chocolate in a bowl over a pan of hot water or in the microwave. Gradually stir in the hot gelatine liquid and vanilla essence. Whisk the egg yolks and sugar until thick and pale and stir into the mixture. Leave until cold and on the point of setting. Whisk the egg whites until stiff and fold into the chocolate mixture. Turn into the flan case (pie shell) and chill until completely set. Melt 75 g/ 3 oz/¾ cup of the remaining chocolate in a bowl as before. Whip the cream until peaking, then whisk in the melted chocolate. Use to swirl all over the top of the flan and grate the remaining chocolate over to decorate.

Chocolate Mint Crisp Flan

SERVES 6

*200 g/7 oz/1 small packet of gingernut
    biscuits (cookies), crushed*
*75 g/3 oz/¾ cup plain (semi-sweet)
    chocolate, melted*
75 g/3 oz/⅓ cup butter, melted
3 egg yolks
*125 g/4½ oz/generous ½ cup caster
    (superfine) sugar*
45 ml/3 tbsp crème de menthe
10 ml/2 tsp powdered gelatine
30 ml/2 tbsp water
A few drops of green food colouring
*250 ml/8 fl oz/1 cup double (heavy)
    cream*
1 egg white
A few mint sprigs
*3 square chocolate after-dinner mints,
    diagonally halved into triangles*

Mix the crushed biscuits with the
melted chocolate and butter. Press
into a 23 cm/9 in flan dish (pie pan).
Chill until firm. Put the egg yolks and
100 g/4 oz/½ cup of the sugar in a bowl
and whisk until thick and pale. Whisk in
the Crème de Menthe until thick.
Sprinkle the gelatine over the water in a
small bowl. Leave to soften for
5 minutes, then stand the bowl in a pan
of hot water and stir until the gelatine
has completely dissolved (or heat briefly
in the microwave). Stir into the egg yolk
mixture with a few drops of green food
colouring. Whip the cream until peaking
and fold about two-thirds into the green
mixture. Turn into the flan case (pie
shell). Chill until set.

Meanwhile, lightly beat the egg
white and brush over the mint sprigs,
then dust with the remaining caster
sugar. Leave on a sheet of greaseproof
(waxed) paper to dry. Just before
serving, decorate the top of the flan with
the remaining whipped cream, the
chocolate triangles and the frosted mint
sprigs.

Apple and Custard Flan

SERVES 6

75 g/3 oz dried apple rings
300 ml/½ pt/1¼ cups water
40 g/1½ oz/3 tbsp granulated sugar
25 g/1 oz/¼ cup plain (all-purpose) flour
1 egg, beaten
300 ml/½ pt/1¼ cups milk
1.5 ml/¼ tsp vanilla essence (extract)
*1 Sweet Pastry Flan Case, baked (see
    page 63)*
*30 ml/2 tbsp apricot jam (conserve),
    sieved (strained), if necessary*

Soak the apple rings in the water
overnight. Place the apple and
soaking water in a saucepan with
15 ml/1 tbsp of the sugar. Bring to the
boil, reduce the heat, cover and simmer
gently for 10 minutes until tender.
Leave to cool.
Blend the flour in a saucepan with
the remaining sugar and the egg. Blend
in the milk. Bring to the boil, reduce the
heat and cook, stirring, for 2 minutes
until thickened and smooth. Cool
slightly, stir in the vanilla essence and
pour into the flan case (pie shell). Drain
the apple rings and arrange on the
custard. Warm the jam in a saucepan
and brush all over the apple to glaze.
Chill until ready to serve.

Coffee Crunch Flan

SERVES 6

*200 g/7 oz/1 small packet of digestive
    biscuits (graham crackers), crushed*
*75 g/3 oz/⅓ cup unsalted (sweet) butter,
    melted*
75 g/5 tbsp caster (superfine) sugar
600 ml/1 pt/2½ cups strong black coffee
15 ml/1 tbsp powdered gelatine
250 ml/8 fl oz/1 cup whipping cream
45 ml/3 tbsp coffee liqueur or brandy
*A few chocolate coffee beans, to
    decorate*

Mix the crushed biscuits with the melted butter and 15 ml/1 tbsp of the sugar. Press into the base and sides of a 20 cm/8 in flan dish (pie pan). Bake in a preheated oven at 180°C/350°F/gas mark 4 for 10 minutes. Remove from the oven and leave to cool.

Meanwhile, put 30 ml/2 tbsp of the coffee in a small bowl. Sweeten the remainder with 30 ml/2 tbsp of the remaining sugar. Sprinkle the gelatine over the coffee in the bowl and leave to soften for 5 minutes. Stand the bowl in a pan of hot water and stir until the gelatine has completely dissolved (or heat briefly in the microwave). Stir into the sweetened coffee and chill until the mixture has the consistency of egg white.

Meanwhile, whip the cream with the remaining sugar and the liqueur or brandy. Fold into the lightly jellied coffee to give a marbled effect. Turn into the flan case (pie shell) and chill until set. Decorate the top with a few chocolate coffee beans in a cluster and serve very cold.

Egg Nog Flan

SERVES 6

*1 Basic Pastry Flan Case, baked (see
    page 62)*
2 eggs
75 g/3 oz/⅓ cup caster (superfine) sugar
25 g/1 oz/¼ cup plain (all-purpose) flour
300 ml/½ pt/1¼ cups milk
5 cm/2 in piece of cinnamon stick
150 ml/¼ pt/⅔ cup double (heavy) cream
15 ml/1 tbsp brandy
Grated nutmeg, for dusting

Transfer the flan case (pie shell) to a serving plate, if necessary. Separate one of the eggs and put the egg yolk with the whole egg and 50 g/2 oz/¼ cup of the sugar in a bowl. Beat well. Whisk in the flour. Heat the milk with the cinnamon stick until almost boiling. Pour over the egg mixture, whisking well. Return to the pan and cook over a gentle heat, stirring, until the mixture boils and thickens. Remove the cinnamon stick. Turn into the cooked pastry case and leave to cool. When cold, chill until set.

Whisk the remaining egg white until stiff. Whisk in the remaining sugar until stiff and glossy. Whip the cream and brandy until softly peaking. Fold the egg white into the cream. Spread over the top of the flan and dust with grated nutmeg.

Butterscotch Beauty

SERVES 6

30 ml/2 tbsp cornflour (cornstarch)
300 ml/½ pt/1¼ cups milk
150 ml/¼ pt/⅔ cup double (heavy) cream
5 ml/1 tsp vanilla essence (extract)
50 g/2 oz/¼ cup butter
100 g/4 oz/½ cup light brown sugar
1 Basic Pastry Flan Case, baked (see page 62)
50 g/2 oz peanut brittle, crushed, to decorate

Blend the cornflour and milk in a saucepan with the cream and vanilla essence. Bring to the boil and cook for 1 minute, stirring, until thickened. Melt the butter and sugar in a saucepan. Stir into the custard. Pour into the flan case and chill until set. Decorate with crushed peanut brittle just before serving.

Kids' Favourite Flan

SERVES 4

1 Basic Sponge Flan Case (see page 62, or use bought)
45 ml/3 tbsp raspberry jam (conserve)
3-4 bananas, sliced
15 ml/1 tbsp lemon juice
250 ml/8 fl oz/1 cup whipping cream, whipped
Grated chocolate, to decorate

Place the baked flan case (pie shell) on a serving plate. Spread the jam over the base. Toss the banana slices with lemon juice to prevent browning and arrange the slices on top of the jam. Cover with whipped cream, sprinkle with grated chocolate and chill until ready to serve.

Banana Grape Flan

SERVES 6

1 Basic Sponge Flan Case (see page 62, or use bought)
25 g/1 oz/¼ cup plain (all-purpose) flour
30 ml/2 tbsp caster (superfine) sugar
1 egg, beaten
170 g/6 oz/1 small can of evaporated milk
2.5 ml/½ tsp vanilla essence (extract)
2 small bananas, sliced
15 ml/1 tbsp lemon juice
100 g/4 oz black grapes, halved and seeded
60 ml/4 tbsp apricot jam (conserve), sieved (strained)

Put the baked flan case (pie shell) on a serving plate. Put the flour and sugar in a saucepan. Blend in the egg until smooth. Make the evaporated milk up to 300 ml/½ pt/1¼ cups with cold water. Gradually blend into the flour mixture. Bring to the boil and cook for 2 minutes, stirring all the time, until thickened and smooth. Stir in the vanilla essence. Pour into the flan case and smooth the surface. Leave until cold.

Toss the banana slices in the lemon juice to prevent browning. Arrange the banana slices and the grapes attractively on top of the custard. Warm the jam, then brush all over the surface of the flan to glaze. Chill until ready to serve.

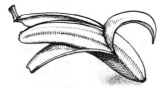

Hedgerow Flan

SERVES 6

10 ml/2 tsp powdered gelatine
90 ml/6 tbsp water
50 g/2 oz/¼ cup granulated sugar
225 g/8 oz ripe blackberries
100 g/4 oz/½ cup medium-fat soft
cheese
150 ml/¼ pt/⅔ cup hazelnut (filbert)
yoghurt
30 ml/2 tbsp finely chopped hazelnuts
1 Basic Sponge Flan Case (see page 62,
or use bought)

Sprinkle the gelatine over 15 ml/
1 tbsp of the water in a small bowl
and leave to soften while cooking the
blackberries. Heat the sugar and the
remaining water in a saucepan until the
sugar has dissolved. Add the blackberries and poach gently for 3 minutes
until tender but still whole. Tilt the pan
so the juice runs to one side. Add the
gelatine to this juice and stir until
dissolved. Turn into a bowl and leave
until just beginning to set.

Meanwhile, beat together the cheese
and yoghurt with the hazelnuts and
spoon into the base of the baked flan
case (pie shell) on a serving plate.
Spoon the blackberry mixture over and
chill until set.

Chocolate Gooseberry Flan

SERVES 6

525 g/1 lb 3 oz/1 large can of
gooseberries
15 ml/1 tbsp powdered gelatine
45 ml/3 tbsp water
15 ml/1 tbsp cornflour (cornstarch)
150 ml/¼ pt/⅔ cup milk
20 ml/4 tsp caster (superfine) sugar
A few drops of green food colouring
300 ml/½ pt/1¼ cups double (heavy)
cream
1 Chocolate Flan Case, baked
(see page 63)

Purée the gooseberries with their juice
in a blender or food processor.
Sprinkle the gelatine over the water in a
small bowl and leave to soften for
5 minutes. Stand the bowl in a pan of
hot water and stir until the gelatine has
completely dissolved. Blend the
cornflour with a little of the milk and
the sugar in a saucepan. Stir in the
remaining milk. Bring to the boil and
cook for 2 minutes, stirring all the time.
Stir in the gooseberry purée, the
gelatine and a few drops of green food
colouring. Leave until cold and on the
point of setting. Whip the cream. Fold
half into the gooseberry mixture and
spoon into the flan case (pie shell). Chill
until set. Decorate with swirls of the
remaining whipped cream before
serving.

Banana Cream Flan

SERVES 6

2 ripe bananas
15 ml/1 tbsp caster (superfine) sugar
15 ml/1 tbsp lemon juice
½ packet of lemon-flavoured jelly (jello)
150 ml/¼ pt/⅔ cup water
150 ml/¼ pt/⅔ cup double (heavy) cream
1 Chocolate Flan Case, baked (see page 63)
Grated chocolate, to decorate

Mash the bananas with the sugar and lemon juice. Dissolve the jelly in the water according to the packet directions. Leave to cool slightly, then stir into the bananas and leave until cold. When the mixture has the consistency of egg white, whip the cream until peaking. Fold half into the banana mixture and turn into the flan case (pie shell). Decorate the top with the remaining whipped cream and grated chocolate. Chill until ready to serve.

Autumn Fruit Crumble Flan

SERVES 4

2 cooking (tart) apples, sliced
100 g/4 oz blackberries
30 ml/2 tbsp apple juice
Caster (superfine) sugar, to taste
10 ml/2 tsp arrowroot
15 ml/1 tbsp cold water
175 g/6 oz/1½ cups wholemeal flour
A pinch of salt
75 g/3 oz/⅓ cup butter or hard block margarine, diced
Cold water, to mix

Put the apples and blackberries in a saucepan with the apple juice. Cover and stew gently until tender. Sweeten to taste with caster sugar. Blend the arrowroot with the water and stir in. Bring to the boil, stirring until thickened. Leave to cool while making the pastry (paste) and crumble.

Mix the flour and salt in a bowl. Add the butter or margarine and rub in with the fingertips until the mixture resembles fine breadcrumbs. Stir in 75 g/3 oz/⅓ cup of caster sugar. Take out 4 heaped tablespoons of the mixture and reserve. Mix the remainder with enough cold water to form a firm dough. Knead gently on a lightly floured surface. Roll out and use to line an 18 cm/7 in flan dish (pie pan). Spoon in the apple and blackberry mixture and sprinkle the reserved crumble mixture over the top. Bake in a preheated oven at 190°C/375°F/gas mark 5 for about 30 minutes until golden brown.

Glazed Orange and Lemon Flan

SERVES 6

1 orange, thinly sliced
1 lemon, thinly sliced
Boiling water
250 g/9 oz/generous 1 cup caster
  (superfine) sugar
75 g/3 oz/¾ cup ground almonds
1 large egg
Finely grated rind of 1 small lemon
1 Sweet Pastry Flan Case, uncooked
  (see page 63)

Put the orange and lemon slices in a
bowl. Cover with boiling water and
leave to stand for 30 minutes.
Meanwhile, mix 50 g/2 oz/¼ cup of the
sugar with the almonds, egg and lemon
rind. Spoon into the flan case (pie shell)
and bake in a preheated oven at
200°C/400°F/gas mark 6 for 25 minutes
until set. Leave to cool.

Meanwhile, simmer the orange and
lemon slices in the soaking water for
5 minutes. Drain, reserving the liquid,
and dry the slices on kitchen paper
(paper towels). Strain 300 ml/½ pt/
1¼ cups of the cooking liquid into a
pan. Add the remaining sugar and heat
gently, stirring, until the sugar has
dissolved. Bring to the boil and boil for
4 minutes. Add the fruit slices and
simmer for a further 3 minutes. Leave
to cool in the syrup.

Lift the slices out of the syrup and
arrange attractively over the flan. Boil
the remaining syrup until reduced by
half, then brush over the top of the
flan. Leave to cool, then chill until
ready to serve.

Lemon Flan

SERVES 4–6

75 g/3 oz/⅓ cup caster (superfine) sugar
2 eggs
Finely grated rind and juice of 1 large
  lemon
25 g/1 oz/2 tbsp unsalted (sweet) butter,
  melted
1 Basic Pastry Flan Case, baked (see
  page 62)
75 ml/5 tbsp double (heavy) cream,
  whipped
30 ml/2 tbsp toasted chopped nuts

Beat together the sugar, eggs, lemon
rind and juice and the melted butter.
Pour into the flan case (pie shell). Bake
in a preheated oven at 180°C/350°F/gas
mark 4 for about 15–20 minutes until
set. Leave to cool, then chill before
decorating with whipped cream and
chopped nuts.

Orange Flan

SERVES 4–6

Prepare as for Lemon Flan, but
substitute the finely grated rind and
juice of 1 orange for the lemon.

Lime Flan

SERVES 4–6

Prepare as for Lemon Flan, but
substitute the finely grated rind and
juice of 2 limes for the lemon and
decorate with pistachio nuts.

Pink Grapefruit Custard Flan

SERVES 6–8

225 g/8 oz/2 cups wholemeal flour
A pinch of salt
30 ml/2 tbsp icing (confectioners')
  sugar
100 g/4 oz/½ cup butter, diced
Cold water, to mix
4 egg yolks
50 g/2 oz/¼ cup caster (superfine) sugar
3 pink grapefruit
25 g/1 oz/¼ cup cornflour (cornstarch)
45 ml/3 tbsp cold water
45 ml/3 tbsp grapefruit marmalade
Thick cream, to serve

Mix the flour, salt and icing sugar in a bowl. Add the butter and rub in with the fingertips. Mix with enough cold water to form a firm dough. Wrap in clingfilm (plastic wrap) and chill for at least 20 minutes.

Knead gently on a lightly floured surface, roll out and use to line a 23 cm/9 in flan dish (pie pan). Prick the base with a fork. Fill with crumpled foil and bake in a preheated oven at 220°C/425°F/gas mark 7 for 10 minutes. Remove the foil and return to the oven for 5 minutes to dry out.

Beat together the egg yolks and sugar in a bowl until thick and pale. Finely grate the rind from one grapefruit and add to the mixture. Squeeze all the juice from that grapefruit and place in a saucepan. Blend the cornflour with the water and stir into the grapefruit juice. Bring to the boil and cook for 2 minutes, stirring. Whisk into the egg yolk mixture and return to the saucepan. Cook, stirring, for 3 minutes until thickened. Turn into the pastry case (pie shell). Cut all the rind and pith from the remaining two grapefruit and segment the fruit. Arrange the segments attractively on top of the flan. Melt the marmalade and brush all over the top to glaze. Leave until cold, then chill and serve with thick cream.

Mallow Mincemeat Flan

SERVES 8

1 Basic Large Pastry Flan Case,
  uncooked (see page 62)
2 large cooking (tart) apples, thinly
  sliced
350 g/12 oz/1 cup mincemeat
75 g/3 oz marshmallows

Put the pastry (paste) lined flan tin (pie pan) on a baking (cookie) sheet. Arrange the apple slices in the base. Spread with the mincemeat. Roll out the pastry trimmings and arrange in a lattice pattern on top. Bake in a preheated oven at 190°C/375°F/gas mark 5 for about 20 minutes.

Snip the marshmallows into halves. Arrange the marshmallows in between the lattice and return to the oven for about 10 minutes until lightly golden and melting. Serve hot.

Apricot Chiffon Flan

SERVES 6

*425 g/15 oz/1 large can of apricot halves,
drained, reserving the juice*
15 ml/1 tbsp powdered gelatine
2 eggs, separated
50 g/2 oz/¼ cup caster (superfine) sugar
300 ml/½ pt/1¼ cups milk
*1 Chocolate Flan Case, baked (see page
63)*
*75 ml/5 tbsp double (heavy) cream,
whipped*

Reserve a few apricots for decoration and finely chop the remainder. Sprinkle the gelatine over 60 ml/4 tbsp of the apricot juice in a small bowl. Leave to soften for 5 minutes, then stand the bowl in a pan of hot water and stir until the gelatine is completely dissolved. Beat the egg yolks and sugar together until thick and pale. Heat the milk, pour over the egg yolk mixture and stir until blended. Return to the pan and cook very gently, stirring, until the mixture thickens. Do not allow to boil or the mixture will curdle. Stir in the dissolved gelatine and chopped apricots. Leave until cold and on the point of setting. Whisk the egg whites until stiff and fold in with a metal spoon. Turn into the flan case (pie shell) and decorate with whipped cream and the reserved apricots. Chill until ready to serve.

Apricot Quark Flan

SERVES 6

15 ml/1 tbsp custard powder
150 ml/¼ pt/⅔ cup milk
*100 g/4 oz/½ cup caster (superfine)
sugar*
*425 g/15 oz/1 large can of apricot halves
in natural juice, drained, reserving
the juice*
175 g/6 oz/¾ cup quark
Finely grated rind of 1 small lemon
150 ml/¼ pt/⅔ cup double (heavy) cream
*1 Sweet Pastry Flan Case, baked (see
page 63)*
*60 ml/4 tbsp apricot jam (conserve),
sieved (strained) if necessary*

Blend the custard powder with a little of the milk and 15 ml/1 tbsp of the sugar in a saucepan. Blend in the remaining milk. Bring to the boil and cook for 2 minutes, stirring until really thick. Remove from the heat. Pour over enough of the apricot juice to cover the surface and leave to cool. Beat the quark with the remaining sugar and the lemon rind. Whip the cream until peaking and fold in. Beat the cold custard to incorporate the juice and fold into the cream mixture. Turn into the flan case (pie shell). Put the apricot jam and 60 ml/4 tbsp of the juice in a saucepan and heat, stirring, until melted. Arrange the apricots, rounded-sides up, all over the top of the flan. Brush with the apricot glaze and chill until ready to serve.

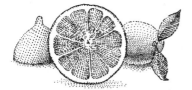

Strawberry Delight Flan

SERVES 6

350 g/12 oz strawberries
25 g/1 oz/2 tbsp caster (superfine)
  sugar
300 ml/½ pt/1¼ cups whipping cream
1 Chocolate Flan Case, baked (see page
  63)
30 ml/2 tbsp redcurrant jelly (clear
  conserve)
15 ml/1 tbsp water

Reserve half the strawberries for decoration and mash the remainder. Sprinkle with the sugar. Whip the cream until peaking and fold in the mashed strawberries. Spoon into the flan case (pie shell). Slice the remaining strawberries and arrange all over the strawberry cream. Melt the redcurrant jelly and water in a saucepan and bring to the boil. Brush all over the strawberries and chill before serving.

Apricot and Ginger Flan

SERVES 4

175 g/6 oz/1½ cups ginger biscuit
  (cookie) crumbs
50 g/2 oz/¼ cup butter, melted
½ × 410 g/½ × 14½ oz/½ × large can of
  apricot pie filling
170 ml/6 fl oz/1 small can of evaporated
  milk, chilled
Halved glacé (candied) cherries and
  angelica leaves, to decorate

Mix the biscuit crumbs with the butter and press into the base and sides of an 18 cm/7 in flan tin (pie pan). Chill until firm. Purée the pie filling. Whisk the evaporated milk until thick and foamy. Gradually whisk in the purée and spoon into the flan case (pie shell). Decorate with halved glacé cherries and angelica leaves and chill until ready to serve.

Banoffee Pie

SERVES 6

350 g/12 oz/1 large can of sweetened
  condensed milk
200 g/7 oz/1 small packet of plain
  biscuits (cookies), crushed
50 g/2 oz/¼ cup butter, melted
2 bananas, sliced
300 ml/½ pt/1¼ cups double (heavy)
  cream
30 ml/2 tbsp caster (superfine) sugar
15 ml/1 tbsp instant coffee powder or
  granules
Drinking (sweetened) chocolate powder
  or grated chocolate, to decorate

Put the unopened can of condensed milk in a saucepan of boiling water and simmer for at least 3 hours, keeping the can submerged all the time. Allow to cool in the water. (It's worth boiling several cans at a time, then storing in the cupboard until ready to use.)

Mix the biscuit crumbs with the butter and press into a 20 cm/8 in flan tin (pie pan). Chill until firm.

Spread the cold caramelised milk on the base. Top with banana slices. Whip together the cream, sugar and coffee and spread or pipe over the bananas. Sprinkle with drinking chocolate powder or grated chocolate and chill until ready to serve.

Chocolate Lemon Flan

SERVES 4–6

*225 g/8 oz/2 cups chocolate digestive
    biscuit (graham cracker) crumbs
100 g/4 oz/½ cup butter, melted
150 ml/¼ pt/⅔ cup double (heavy) cream
Grated rind and juice of 2 lemons
200 g/7 oz/1 small can of sweetened
    condensed milk
Grated chocolate, to decorate*

Mix the biscuit crumbs with the
butter and press into the base and
sides of a 20 cm/8 in flan tin (pie pan).
Chill until firm.
   Whip the cream until softly peaking.
Stir in the lemon rind and juice. Fold in
the condensed milk. Turn into the flan
case (pie shell) and chill for several
hours or overnight. Sprinkle with grated
chocolate before serving.

Ginger Lemon Flan

SERVES 6

Prepare as for Chocolate Lemon Flan
but use gingernut biscuits (cookies)
instead of chocolate digestives (graham
crackers). Decorate the top with finely
chopped crystallised (candied) ginger
instead of chocolate.

Chocolate Mallow Pie

SERVES 6

*200 g/7 oz/1¾ cups chocolate digestive
    biscuit (graham cracker) crumbs
75 g/3 oz/⅓ cup butter, melted
175 g/6 oz/1½ cups plain (semi-sweet)
    chocolate
20 pink and white marshmallows
30 ml/2 tbsp water
1 egg, separated
300 ml/½ pt/1¼ cups double (heavy)
    cream, whipped
8 rose leaves*

Mix the biscuit crumbs with the
butter and press into the base and
sides of an 18 cm/7 in flan tin (pie
pan). Melt 100 g/4 oz/1 cup of the
chocolate with the marshmallows and
water in a saucepan over a gentle heat,
stirring all the time. Cool slightly, then
stir in the egg yolk and leave to cool.
   Whisk the egg white until stiff and
fold into the chocolate mixture with
three-quarters of the cream. Turn into
the flan case (pie shell) and chill until
set.
   Melt the remaining chocolate in a
bowl over a pan of hot water (or in the
microwave). Dip one side of each rose
leaf in the chocolate and place on a
sheet of greaseproof (waxed) paper to
set. Chill. When ready to serve, spread
the remaining cream over the chocolate
pie. Gently peel the leaves off the
chocolate and use the chocolate leaves
to decorate the top.

Tangy Cheese and Rhubarb Flan

SERVES 6

450 g/1 lb rhubarb, cut into short lengths
150 ml/¼ pt/⅔ cup apple juice
100 g/4 oz/½ cup caster (superfine) sugar
30 ml/2 tbsp cornflour (cornstarch)
30 ml/2 tbsp water
1 Basic Pastry Flan Case, baked (see
  page 62)
175 g/6 oz/¾ cup medium-fat soft
  cheese
A few drops of vanilla essence (extract)
1 egg, beaten
A few blanched almonds, to decorate
Vanilla ice cream (see page 188 or use
  bought), to serve

Put the rhubarb in a saucepan with the apple juice and 50 g/2 oz/¼ cup of the sugar. Bring to the boil, reduce the heat and simmer gently for 6 minutes until tender. Purée in a blender or food processor. Blend the cornflour with the water in a saucepan. Stir in the rhubarb purée and bring to the boil, stirring. Cook for 2 minutes until thickened and clear. Turn into the flan case (pie shell) on a baking (cookie) sheet.

Cream together the cheese and vanilla essence. Beat in the egg and the remaining sugar, then spoon over the rhubarb. Decorate the top with blanched almonds and bake in a preheated oven at 180°C/350°F/gas mark 4 for about 40 minutes or until risen, golden and firm to the touch. Leave to cool, then chill. Serve cold with vanilla ice cream.

Raspberry Buttercrisp Flan

SERVES 6

50 g/2 oz/¼ cup butter
50 g/2 oz/⅓ cup icing (confectioners')
  sugar
30 ml/2 tbsp golden (light corn) syrup
100 g/4 oz/2 cups crisp rice cereal
Oil, for greasing
225 g/8 oz raspberries
45 ml/3 tbsp redcurrant jelly (clear
  conserve)
15 ml/1 tbsp water
A little whipped cream, to decorate

Melt the butter in a large saucepan and stir in the sugar and syrup. Remove from the heat and mix in the cereal until completely coated. Oil an 18 cm/7 in flan ring and set on a serving plate. Press the cereal mixture into the base and sides of the flan ring. Leave to cool.

Remove the flan ring. Pile the raspberries into the centre. Melt the redcurrant jelly with the water and lightly brush all over the surface of the fruit to glaze. Chill for at least 30 minutes. Decorate with a little whipped cream just before serving.

Orange Crunch Flan

SERVES 6

200 g/7 oz/1 small packet of digestive
  biscuits (graham crackers), crushed
75 g/3 oz/⅓ cup unsalted (sweet) butter,
  melted
5 ml/1 tsp mixed (apple-pie) spice
15 ml/1 tbsp powdered gelatine
Finely grated rind and juice of 1 large
  orange
10 ml/2 tsp lemon juice
2 eggs, separated
75 g/3 oz/⅓ cup caster (superfine) sugar
300 ml/½ pt/1¼ cups whipping cream
Crystallised (candied) orange slices and
  angelica leaves, to decorate

M ix the crushed biscuits into the
butter and stir in the spice. Press
into the base and sides of a 20 cm/8 in
flan dish (pie pan). Sprinkle the gelatine
over the orange rind and juice and the
lemon juice in a small bowl and leave
to soften for 5 minutes. Stand the bowl
in a pan of hot water and stir until the
gelatine is completely dissolved.

Meanwhile, beat together the egg
yolks and caster sugar until thick and
pale. Stir in the gelatine mixture. Whisk
the egg whites until stiff. In a separate
bowl, whip the cream until peaking.
Fold half the cream, then all the egg
whites into the orange mixture with a
metal spoon. Turn into the flan case
(pie shell) and chill until set. Decorate
with the remaining whipped cream,
crystallised orange slices and angelica
leaves.

Lemon Crunch Flan

SERVES 6

P repare as for Orange Crunch Flan,
but substitute the finely grated rind
and juice of 2 lemons for the orange
and omit the extra 10 ml/2 tsp lemon
juice. Decorate with crystallised
(candied) lemon slices instead of orange
slices.

Lime Crunch Flan

SERVES 6

P repare as for Orange Crunch Flan,
but use chocolate digestive biscuits
(graham crackers) instead of plain and
the finely grated rind and juice of
2 limes instead of the orange. Omit the
lemon juice. Decorate with coarsely
grated chocolate instead of crystallised
(candied) orange slices.

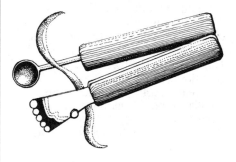

Blackcurrant Whip Flan

SERVES 6

*200 g/7 oz/1 small packet of Marie or
other plain biscuits (cookies),
crushed
75 g/3 oz/⅓ cup unsalted (sweet) butter,
melted
450 g/1 lb blackcurrants, stripped from
the stalks
30 ml/2 tbsp orange juice
3 eggs, separated
100 g/4 oz/½ cup caster (superfine) sugar
15 ml/1 tbsp powdered gelatine
30 ml/2 tbsp water
Orange yoghurt, to serve*

Mix the crushed biscuits with the melted butter and press into a 20 cm/8 in flan dish (pie pan). Chill until firm.

Put the blackcurrants in a pan with the orange juice and stew until the fruit 'pops' and the juice runs. Purée in a blender or food processor, then pass through a sieve (strainer). Put the egg yolks and sugar in a large bowl with the purée. Place the bowl over a pan of hot water and whisk until thick. Sprinkle the gelatine over the water in a small bowl. Leave to soften for 5 minutes, then place the bowl over a pan of hot water and stir until the gelatine has dissolved completely (or heat briefly in the microwave). Stir into the fruit mixture. Whisk the egg whites until stiff and fold into the mixture. Turn into the flan case (pie shell) and chill until set. Serve with orange yoghurt.

Magali

SERVES 4

*100 g/4 oz/1 cup plain (all-purpose) flour
90 g/3½ oz/scant ½ cup butter, diced
10 ml/2 tsp caster (superfine) sugar
Cold water, to mix
150 g/5 oz/1¼ cups plain (semi-sweet)
chocolate
300 ml/½ pt/1¼ cups double (heavy)
cream
15 ml/1 tbsp dark rum or brandy
A few toasted, blanched almonds, to
decorate*

Put the flour in a bowl and rub in 50 g/2 oz/¼ cup of the butter. Stir in the sugar and mix with enough cold water to form a firm dough. Knead gently on a lightly floured surface. Wrap in clingfilm (plastic wrap) and chill for 30 minutes.

Roll out and use to line four individual flan dishes (pie pans). Prick the bases with a fork and fill with crumpled foil. Bake in a preheated oven at 200°C/400°F/gas mark 6 for 8 minutes. Remove the foil and return to the oven for 5 minutes to dry out. Remove from the oven and leave to cool.

Meanwhile, break the chocolate into pieces and place in a saucepan with the remaining butter and 120 ml/4 fl oz/½ cup of the cream. Heat gently, stirring until melted, then beat until thick. Beat in the rum or brandy. If the mixture starts to separate, stir in 5 ml/1 tsp cold water. Spoon into the flan cases (pie shells). Leave to cool, then chill. Whip the remaining cream and use to decorate the flans. Top with the toasted almonds.

Crumbles, Cobblers and Other Family Bakes

Simple to make, delicious to eat and perfect for family meals any day of the week.

Blueberry Almond Crumble

SERVES 4

350 g/12 oz blueberries
175 g/6 oz/¾ cup caster (superfine) sugar
10 ml/2 tsp lemon juice
75 g/3 oz/¾ cup ground almonds
75 g/3 oz/1½ cups plain cake crumbs
2.5 ml/½ tsp ground cinnamon
50 g/2 oz/¼ cup unsalted (sweet) butter, melted
30 ml/2 tbsp flaked (slivered) almonds
Crème fraîche, to serve

Place the blueberries in a shallow, ovenproof dish with 75 g/3 oz/ ⅓ cup of the sugar and the lemon juice. Mix together the remaining sugar, the ground almonds, cake crumbs and cinnamon. Stir in the butter. Sprinkle the mixture over the blueberries and press down lightly. Bake in a preheated oven at 180°C/350°F/gas mark 4 for 20 minutes. Sprinkle the flaked almonds over the top and bake for a further 15–20 minutes until golden brown on top. Serve hot with crème fraîche.

Blackcurrant Hazelnut Crumble

SERVES 4

Prepare as for Blueberry Almond Crumble but substitute blackcurrants for the blueberries and ground hazelnuts (filberts) for the ground almonds. Sprinkle with roughly chopped hazelnuts instead of flaked (slivered) almonds.

Apple Crumble

SERVES 4

750 g/1½ lb cooking (tart) apples
75 g/3 oz/⅓ cup caster (superfine) sugar
1 whole clove (optional)
30 ml/2 tbsp water
100 g/4 oz/1 cup plain (all-purpose) flour
50 g/2 oz/¼ cup butter or hard block margarine, diced

Peel, core and slice the apples and place in an ovenproof dish. Sprinkle with 25 g/1 oz/2 tbsp of the sugar and add the clove, if using, and the water. Put the flour in a bowl and rub in the butter or margarine until the mixture resembles fine breadcrumbs. Stir in the remaining sugar. Sprinkle over the surface of the apples and press down lightly. Bake in a preheated oven at 180°C/350°F/gas mark 4 for 40 minutes until the top is crisp and golden brown and the apples are tender.

Rhubarb Crumble

SERVES 4

Prepare as for Apple Crumble, but substitute rhubarb, cut into small pieces, for the apples. Omit the clove and flavour with the finely grated rind of 1 orange instead, if liked.

Raspberry Oat Bake

SERVES 8

225 g/8 oz/2 cups self-raising (self-rising) flour
2.5 ml/½ tsp salt
175 g/6 oz/¾ cup butter or hard block margarine, diced, plus extra for greasing
175 g/6 oz/1½ cups rolled oats
175 g/6 oz/¾ cup caster (superfine) sugar
300 g/11 oz/1 medium can of raspberries, drained
Easy Custard (see page 354), to serve

Put the flour and salt in a bowl. Rub in the butter or margarine, then stir in the oats and sugar. Grease an 18 × 28 cm/7 × 11 in baking tin (pan) and press half the mixture into the base. Scatter the raspberries over. Cover with the remaining crumble, pressing down firmly. Bake in a preheated oven at 200°C/400°F/gas mark 6 for 30 minutes. Leave to cool for 10 minutes, then cut into pieces and serve warm with custard.

Blackberry and Apple Crumble

SERVES 4

450 g/1 lb cooking (tart) apples
25 g/1 oz/2 tbsp granulated sugar
45 ml/3 tbsp water
175 g/6 oz blackberries
100 g/4 oz/1 cup plain (all-purpose) flour
50 g/2 oz/¼ cup butter or hard block margarine, diced
50 g/2 oz/¼ cup light brown sugar
2.5 ml/½ tsp ground cinnamon

Peel, core and slice the apples and place in a saucepan with the granulated sugar and the water. Bring to the boil and add the blackberries. Cover and cook gently for 5 minutes. Turn into an ovenproof dish.

Meanwhile, put the flour in a bowl and rub in the butter or margarine. Stir in the brown sugar and cinnamon. Spoon over the fruit and press down lightly. Bake in a preheated oven at 190°C/375°F/gas mark 5 for about 20 minutes until lightly golden.

Warming Autumn Crumble

SERVES 4

100 g/4 oz/1 cup wholemeal flour
50 g/2 oz/¼ cup margarine, diced
100 g/4 oz/½ cup light brown sugar
25 g/1 oz/¼ cup flaked (slivered) almonds
225 g/8 oz plums, quartered and stoned (pitted)
450 g/1 lb cooking (tart) apples, sliced
Grated rind and juice of 1 small orange
Classic Custard Sauce (see page 354), to serve

Put the flour in a bowl. Add the margarine and rub in with the fingertips until the mixture resembles breadcrumbs. Stir in half the sugar. Mix the almonds with the plums, apples and orange rind and juice. Stir in the remaining sugar. Turn into a 1.2 litre/2 pt/5 cup ovenproof dish. Sprinkle the crumble over and press down lightly. Bake in a preheated oven at 190°C/375°F/gas mark 5 for about 45 minutes until golden brown and cooked through. Serve hot with Classic Custard Sauce.

Marmalade Crumble Cake

SERVES 6–8

175 g/6 oz/¾ cup butter or hard block
    margarine, diced, plus extra for
    greasing
150 g/5 oz/1¼ cups self-raising (self-
    rising) flour
200 g/7 oz/scant 1 cup caster
    (superfine) sugar
50 g/2 oz/⅓ cup chopped mixed
    (candied) peel
Finely grated rind and juice of 1 orange
2 eggs, lightly beaten
75 g/3 oz/¾ cup plain (all-purpose) flour
30 ml/2 tbsp fine-cut orange
    marmalade, melted
Classic Custard Sauce (see page 354), to
    serve

Grease a 20 cm/8 in deep, round,
loose-bottomed cake tin (pan) and
line with greased greaseproof (waxed)
paper. Put the self-raising flour in a
bowl. Add 150 g/5 oz/⅔ cup of the
butter or margarine and rub in with the
fingertips. Stir in 150 g/5 oz/⅔ cup of
the sugar and the mixed peel. Add the
orange juice and beaten eggs and mix
to a soft, dropping consistency. Turn
into the prepared tin.
    Rub the remaining butter into the
plain flour. Stir in the remaining sugar
and the orange rind. Spread the melted
marmalade over the top of the
uncooked cake, then sprinkle with the
crumble mixture. Bake in a preheated
oven at 180°C/350°F/gas mark 4 for
about 50 minutes until cooked through.
Cool slightly, then carefully remove
from the tin and serve warm with
Classic Custard Sauce.

Raspberry Crumble Cake

SERVES 6–8

Prepare as for Marmalade Crumble
Cake but substitute seedless
raspberry jam (conserve) for the
marmalade.

Tutti Frutti Oatie

SERVES 4

100 g/4 oz/1 cup plain (all-purpose) flour
75 g/3 oz/⅓ cup butter or hard block
    margarine, diced
75 g/3 oz/¾ cup rolled oats
3 cooking (tart) apples, sliced
15 ml/1 tbsp lemon juice
50 g/2 oz/¼ cup sultanas (golden raisins)
50 g/2 oz/½ cup glacé (candied) cherries,
    halved
50 g/2 oz angelica, chopped
75 g/3 oz/⅓ cup light brown sugar
90 ml/6 tbsp pineapple juice
2.5 ml/½ tsp mixed (apple-pie) spice
Pouring cream, to serve

Put the flour in a bowl. Rub in the
butter or margarine and stir in the
oats. Toss the apple slices in the lemon
juice to prevent browning. Layer the
apples in a 1.2 litre/2 pt/5 cup
ovenproof dish with the sultanas,
cherries, angelica and 50 g/2 oz/¼ cup
of the sugar. Mix the remaining sugar
into the crumble mixture. Pour the
pineapple juice over the fruit and
sprinkle with the spice. Scatter the
crumble over and press down lightly.
Bake in a preheated oven at 200°C/
400°F/gas mark 6 for about 30 minutes
until crisp and golden brown. Serve
warm with pouring cream.

Plum Shortcake Crumble

SERVES 6

175 g/6 oz/¾ cup butter, diced, plus extra
  for greasing
250 g/9 oz/2¼ cups plain (all-purpose)
  flour
175 g/6 oz/¾ cup caster (superfine) sugar
450 g/1 lb ripe plums, halved and
  stoned (pitted)
25 g/1 oz/¼ cup chopped almonds
Chantilly Cream (see page 358), to serve

Lightly grease an 18 cm/7 in loose-bottomed cake tin (pan). Sift the flour into a bowl. Add the butter and rub in with the fingertips. Stir in 75 g/3 oz/⅓ cup of the sugar. Spoon about a third of the mixture into a separate bowl and reserve. Knead the remaining mixture until it forms a ball. Press into the base and sides of the tin. Put the halved plums in the tin and sprinkle with the remaining sugar. Scatter the crumble over, then add the almonds. Cook in a preheated oven at 190°C/375°F/gas mark 5 for about 40 minutes until crisp and golden. Leave to cool for 10 minutes, then carefully remove from the tin but leave on the base. Serve warm or cold with Chantilly Cream.

Damson Shortcake Crumble

SERVES 6

Prepare as for Plum Shortcake Crumble, but substitute damsons for the plums and chopped hazelnuts (filberts) for the almonds.

Strawberry Shortcake Crumble

SERVES 6

Prepare as for Plum Shortcake Crumble, but substitute halved strawberries for the plums and sprinkle with 15 ml/1 tbsp lemon juice before adding the sugar and crumble. Sprinkle with walnuts instead of almonds.

Nutty Rhubarb and Apple Crisp

SERVES 6

75 g/3 oz/¾ cup wholemeal flour
50 g/2 oz/½ cup plain (all-purpose) flour
50 g/2 oz/¼ cup butter or hard block
  margarine, diced
50 g/2 oz/½ cup rolled oats
75 g/3 oz/⅓ cup light brown sugar
50 g/2 oz/½ cup walnuts, chopped
3 large cooking (tart) apples, sliced
350 g/12 oz rhubarb, cut into short
  lengths
Granulated sugar, for sprinkling
Whipped cream, to serve

Mix the flours in a bowl. Rub in the butter or margarine until the mixture resembles breadcrumbs. Stir in the oats, brown sugar and nuts. Mix the apples and rhubarb in an ovenproof dish and sprinkle liberally with granulated sugar to taste. Sprinkle over the nut and oat mixture. Press down lightly. Bake in a preheated oven at 180°C/350°F/gas mark 4 for 50 minutes or until golden brown and cooked through. Serve with whipped cream.

Apple Dumplings

SERVES 4

225 g/8 oz/2 cups plain (all-purpose) flour
175 g/6 oz/¾ cup butter, diced
30 ml/2 tbsp caster (superfine) sugar
1 egg, separated
Cold water, to mix
4 large cooking (tart) apples
100 g/4 oz/½ cup light brown sugar
A pinch of ground cloves
Grated rind of 1 lemon
Pouring cream, to serve

Put the flour in a bowl and rub in
100 g/4 oz/½ cup of the butter until
the mixture resembles breadcrumbs. Stir
in the caster sugar. Add the egg yolk
and enough cold water to form a soft
but not sticky dough. Knead gently on
a lightly floured surface. Wrap in
clingfilm (plastic wrap) and chill for
30 minutes.

Meanwhile, peel and core the apples
but leave them whole. Mash the
remaining butter with the brown sugar,
cloves and lemon rind and pack into the
centres of the apples. Cut the pastry
(paste) into four equal pieces. Roll out
each piece to a circle. Place an apple in
the centre of each. Brush the edges with
a little of the lightly beaten egg white.
Gather up over the apples to encase
completely. Place, sealed-sides down, on
a baking (cookie) sheet. Cut leaves out
of pastry trimmings. Brush the
dumplings with egg white to glaze, stick
the leaves in position and brush again.
Bake in a preheated oven at 200°C/
400°F/gas mark 6 for 20 minutes, then
at 180°C/ 350°F/gas mark 4 for about 30
minutes until golden brown and cooked
through. Serve with pouring cream.

Apple and Blackberry Dumplings

SERVES 4

Prepare as for Apple Dumplings, but
fill the centres with blackberries and
the sugar and omit the cloves and
lemon.

Apple Nut Crunch

SERVES 4

100 g/4 oz/1 cup walnuts
750 g/1½ lb eating (dessert) apples,
sliced
Lemon juice
75 g/3 oz/⅓ cup butter
45 ml/3 tbsp clear honey
75 g/3 oz/¾ cup plain (all-purpose) flour
20 ml/4 tsp light brown sugar
120 ml/4 fl oz/½ cup crème fraîche

Reserve 8 walnut halves and
coarsely chop the remainder. Toss
the apple slices in a little lemon juice.
Arrange attractively in a shallow
ovenproof dish. Melt the butter and
honey in a saucepan. Stir in the flour,
sugar and the chopped walnuts. Spoon
over the apples and arrange the
reserved walnut halves on top. Bake for
20 minutes in a preheated oven at
180°C/350°F/gas mark 4 until golden
brown. Serve warm.

Crumble-topped Pear Bake

SERVES 4

2 eggs
75 g/3 oz/⅓ cup caster (superfine) sugar
40 g/1½ oz/⅓ cup plain (all-purpose)
   flour
150 ml/¼ pt/⅔ cup crème fraîche
300 ml/½ pt/1¼ cups milk
900 g/2 lb pears, thickly sliced
50 g/2 oz/¼ cup butter, plus extra for
   greasing
50 g/2 oz/1 cup fresh breadcrumbs
2.5 ml/½ tsp ground cinnamon

Beat the eggs and sugar until thick and pale. Beat in the flour and crème fraîche. Stir in the milk. Lay the pear slices in a buttered shallow ovenproof dish. Pour over the cream mixture. Bake in a preheated oven at 190°C/375°F/gas mark 5 for 30 minutes. Meanwhile, melt the butter in a frying pan (skillet). Add the breadcrumbs and fry (sauté) until crisp and golden, stirring all the time. Stir in the cinnamon. Scatter over the cream mixture and return to the oven for about 10 minutes until set. Serve warm.

Tutti Frutti Roll

SERVES 5–6

A little oil, for greasing
25 g/1 oz/¼ cup glacé (candied) cherries,
   rinsed, dried and roughly chopped
25 g/1 oz/¼ cup chopped almonds
100 g/4 oz/⅔ cup sultanas (golden
   raisins)
75 ml/5 tbsp clear honey
150 g/5 oz/1¼ cups self-raising (self-
   rising) flour
A pinch of salt
50 g/2 oz/½ cup shredded (chopped)
   vegetable suet
1 egg, beaten
60 ml/4 tbsp milk
15 ml/1 tbsp granulated sugar
Crème fraîche, to serve

Oil a baking (cookie) sheet. Mix together the cherries, almonds, sultanas and honey. Sift the flour and salt into a bowl. Stir in the suet. Add all but 15 ml/1 tbsp of the egg and enough of the milk to form a soft but not sticky dough. Knead gently on a lightly floured surface. Roll out to a rectangle about 30 × 20 cm/12 × 8 in. Spread the filling over the surface to within 1 cm/½ in of the edge all round. Brush the edges with a little of the reserved beaten egg. Roll up, starting from a long edge, and press the edges together to seal. Transfer to the baking sheet. Brush with the remaining egg and sprinkle with the sugar. Bake in a preheated oven at 200°C/400°F/gas mark 6 for 20 minutes until crisp and golden. Serve hot, cut into slices, with crème fraîche.

Simple Baked Apples

SERVES 4

4 large even-sized cooking (tart) apples
Light brown sugar
300 ml/½ pt/1¼ cups water
Pouring cream, to serve

Wipe the apples and remove the cores with an apple corer. Make a cut through the skin round the middle of each apple to prevent splitting. Stand the apples in a roasting tin (pan). Pack the centres with brown sugar. Pour the water around and bake in a preheated oven at 200°C/400°F/gas mark 6 for about 30 minutes or until the apples are tender. Serve hot with pouring cream.

Strawberry Baked Apples

SERVES 4

Prepare as for Simple Baked Apples, but fill the centres with strawberry jam (conserve) instead of sugar and sprinkle a little brown sugar over before adding the water. Serve with extra warmed jam, if liked.

Marmalade Baked Apples

SERVES 4

Prepare as for Simple Baked Apples, but fill the centres with marmalade instead of sugar and sprinkle with a little brown sugar before adding the water. Serve with Orange Sauce (see page 350).

Fruit and Nut Baked Apples

SERVES 4

Prepare as for Simple Baked Apples, but fill the centres with a mixture of chopped nuts and sultanas (golden raisins) instead of sugar and drizzle a little golden (light corn) syrup over each one before adding the water. Serve with extra warmed golden syrup, if liked.

Mincemeat Apples

SERVES 4

Prepare as for Simple Baked Apples, but fill the centres with mincemeat instead of sugar, sprinkle with a little granulated sugar and ground cinnamon and top each with half a glacé (candied) cherry before adding the water.

Frinklies

SERVES 4

50 g/2 oz/¼ cup soft margarine
50 g/2 oz/¼ cup caster (superfine) sugar
2 eggs
50 g/2 oz/½ cup plain (all-purpose) flour
150 ml/¼ pt/⅔ cup milk
Warmed jam (conserve) or clear honey
Sifted icing (confectioners') sugar, for dusting

Beat together the margarine, sugar, eggs and flour until smooth, then stir in the milk (don't worry if it curdles). Grease the 12 sections of a bun tin (muffin pan). Spoon in the mixture and bake in a preheated oven at 200°C/400°F/gas mark 6 for 15–20 minutes until set and golden. They will sink when they come out of the oven – but they're supposed to! Arrange three on each of four serving plates. Spoon a little warmed jam or clear honey over and dust with icing sugar before serving.

Fantastic Flapjacks

MAKES 9

75 g/3 oz/⅓ cup butter or margarine, plus extra for greasing
25 g/1 oz/2 tbsp light brown sugar
30 ml/2 tbsp golden (light corn) syrup
175 g/6 oz/1½ cups oat crunch cereal
50 g/2 oz/½ cup plain (all-purpose) flour
A pinch of salt
Custard or ice cream, to serve

Put the butter or margarine, sugar and syrup in a saucepan and heat until melted. Stir in the cereal, flour and salt until well blended. Turn into a greased 18 cm/7 in square baking tin (pan) and press out evenly. Bake in a preheated oven at 190°C/375°F/gas mark 5 for about 12 minutes until golden brown. Leave to cool slightly, then cut into nine squares. Leave to cool completely in the tin, then serve with custard or ice cream. Store any remainder in an airtight tin to serve as a snack.

Popover Morsels

MAKES 9

50 g/2 oz/½ cup plain (all-purpose) flour
A pinch of salt
1 egg
150 ml/¼ pt/⅔ cup milk and water mixed
50 g/2 oz/⅓ cup dried mixed fruit (fruit cake mix)
A little oil
Lemon Honey Sauce (see page 346), to serve

Sift the flour and salt into a bowl. Add the egg and half the milk and water and beat until smooth. Stir in the remaining liquid and the fruit. Put about 2.5 ml/½ tsp oil in the base of nine sections of a tartlet tin (patty pan). Place in a preheated oven at 220°C/425°F/gas mark 7 until sizzling. Spoon the batter mixture into the tins. Bake in the oven for about 15 minutes until risen, crisp and golden. Serve piping hot with Lemon Honey Sauce.

Raspberry Oaties

MAKES 15

225 g/8 oz/2 cups self-raising (self-
rising) flour
A pinch of salt
175 g/6 oz/¾ cup hard block margarine,
diced
175 g/6 oz/1½ cups rolled oats
175 g/6 oz/¾ cup light brown sugar
A few drops of vanilla essence (extract)
425 g/15 oz/1 large can of raspberries,
drained, reserving the juice
10 ml/2 tsp cornflour (cornstarch)
10 ml/2 tsp lemon juice
Fromage frais, to serve

Put the flour in a bowl with the salt. Add the margarine and rub in with the fingertips until the mixture resembles breadcrumbs. Stir in the oats, sugar and vanilla essence. Press half the mixture into the base of a lightly greased 18 × 28 cm/7 × 11 in shallow baking tin (pan). Spread the raspberries over. Cover with the remaining oat mixture and press down well. Bake in a preheated oven at 200°C/400°F/gas mark 6 for 30 minutes. Allow to cool for 5 minutes, then cut into 15 squares. Pile on to a serving dish.

Blend the cornflour with a little of the reserved juice in a saucepan. Add the remaining raspberry juice and the lemon juice. Bring to the boil and cook for 2 minutes, stirring until thickened and clear. Serve the raspberry squares warm, with the raspberry sauce and fromage frais.

Pineapple Upside-down Pudding

SERVES 6

15 g/½ oz/1 tbsp butter
30 ml/2 tbsp light brown sugar
225 g/8 oz/1 small can of pineapple
slices, drained, reserving the juice
Glacé (candied) cherries, halved
Angelica leaves
100 g/4 oz/½ cup soft tub margarine
100 g/4 oz/1 cup self-raising (self-
rising) flour
100 g/4 oz/½ cup caster (superfine)
sugar
5 ml/1 tsp baking powder
2 eggs

Grease a 20 cm/8 in sandwich tin (pan) liberally with the butter, especially in the base. Cover the base with the brown sugar. Arrange the pineapple slices on top and place a halved glacé cherry, cut-side up, in the centre of each ring. Place angelica leaves in the gaps.

Put the remaining ingredients in a bowl and beat well until smooth, adding 15 ml/1 tbsp of the reserved pineapple juice. Spread over the pineapple. Bake in a preheated oven at 190°C/375°F/gas mark 5 for 20 minutes or until risen, golden and the centre springs back when lightly pressed. Leave to cool slightly, then loosen the edge all round and turn the pudding out on to a warmed serving plate. Serve with the reserved juice.

Chocolate Pear Upside-down Pudding

SERVES 6

Prepare as for Pineapple Upside-down Pudding but substitute pear halves for the pineapple, walnut halves for the cherries and 30 ml/2 tbsp cocoa (unsweetened chocolate) powder for the same amount of flour.

Chocolate Orange Upside-down Pudding

SERVES 6

Prepare as for Chocolate Pear Upside-down Pudding, but substitute 300 g/ 11 oz/1 medium can of drained mandarin oranges and 30 ml/2 tbsp flaked (slivered) almonds for the pears and walnuts.

Queen of Puddings

SERVES 4

50 g/2 oz/1 cup fresh breadcrumbs
2 eggs, separated
100 g/4 oz/½ cup caster (superfine) sugar
300 ml/½ pt/1¼ cups milk
Finely grated rind of 1 lemon
Strawberry, raspberry or apricot jam
(conserve)

Put the breadcrumbs in an ovenproof dish. Whisk together the egg yolks and half the sugar. Warm the milk and whisk into the eggs and sugar. Pour over the breadcrumbs and stir in the lemon rind. Leave to soak for 15 minutes. Bake in a preheated oven at 180°C/350°F/gas mark 4 for about

35 minutes until set. Whisk the egg whites until stiff and fold in the remaining sugar. Spread a little jam over the surface of the pudding, then pile on the meringue mixture. Return to the oven for about 20 minutes until the meringue is crisp and lightly golden. Serve warm.

Hazelnut Queen of Puddings

SERVES 4–6

Prepare as for Queen of Puddings, but omit the lemon rind and use 2.5 ml/ ½ tsp vanilla essence (extract) instead. Use raspberry jam (conserve) and fold 50 g/2 oz/½ cup ground hazelnuts (filberts) into the meringue mixture and decorate the top with a few whole hazelnuts before baking.

Almond Queen of Puddings

SERVES 4–6

Prepare as for Queen of Puddings, but use 2.5 ml/½ tsp almond essence (extract) instead of lemon rind. Use apricot jam (conserve) and fold 50 g/2 oz/½ cup ground almonds into the meringue mixture. Top with a few flaked almonds before baking.

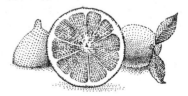

West Country Apple Cake

SERVES 8–10

3 large cooking (tart) apples, sliced
3 eggs
250 g/9 oz/generous 1 cup caster
   (superfine) sugar
100 g/4 oz/½ cup margarine
150 ml/¼ pt/⅔ cup cider
200 g/7 oz/1¾ cups plain (all-purpose)
   flour
15 ml/1 tbsp baking powder
1.5 ml/¼ tsp ground cloves
Hot Lemon Sauce (see page 346), to
   serve

Put the apple slices in cold water to prevent browning. Whisk together the eggs and 225 g/8 oz/1 cup of the sugar until thick and pale and the whisk leaves a trail when lifted out of the mixture. Melt the margarine in a saucepan with the cider. Bring to the boil and stir into the eggs and sugar. Sift the flour and baking powder over the surface and fold in with a metal spoon. Pour into a greased and floured roasting tin (pan). Lay the apple slices attractively over.

Mix the remaining sugar with the ground cloves and sprinkle over. Bake in a preheated oven at 200°C/400°F/gas mark 6 for about 40 minutes until golden and the centre springs back when lightly pressed. Cut the cake into squares and transfer to warmed serving plates. Serve with Hot Lemon Sauce.

Apple and Raisin Meringue

SERVES 6

450 g/1 lb cooking (tart) apples, sliced
30 ml/2 tbsp water
Caster (superfine) sugar, to taste
50 g/2 oz/⅓ cup raisins
5 ml/1 tsp ground cinnamon
40 g/1½ oz/3 tbsp cornflour
   (cornstarch)
450 ml/¾ pt/2 cups milk
2 eggs, separated
Glacé (candied) cherries and angelica
   leaves, to decorate

Put the apple slices in a saucepan with the water. Cover and cook gently until pulpy, stirring occasionally. Sweeten to taste with the caster sugar and stir in the raisins and cinnamon. Turn into a 1.2 litre/2 pt/5 cup ovenproof dish. Blend the cornflour with a little of the milk and 40 g/1½ oz/3 tbsp caster sugar in a saucepan. Whisk in the egg yolks and stir in the remaining milk. Bring to the boil and cook for 2 minutes, stirring all the time, until thickened and smooth. Pour over the apple mixture.

Whisk the egg whites until stiff and whisk in 50 g/2 oz/¼ cup caster sugar. Fold in a further 50 g/2 oz/¼ cup caster sugar. Pile on top of the custard and decorate with cherries and angelica leaves. Bake in a preheated oven at 160°C/325°F/gas mark 3 for 10–15 minutes until the meringue is a pale biscuit colour.

Apple Charlotte Meringue

SERVES 5–6

100 g/4 oz/½ cup caster (superfine) sugar
75 g/3 oz/⅓ cup butter or margarine,
softened
6 thick slices of white or wholemeal
bread, crusts removed
550 g/1¼ lb cooking (tart) apples, sliced
15 ml/1 tbsp water
A small piece of cinnamon stick
Granulated sugar, to taste
2 eggs, separated

Beat together 15 ml/1 tbsp of the sugar and the butter or margarine and spread over the bread slices. Cut each slice into three strips. Arrange around the sides and in the base of an 18 cm/7 in soufflé dish, buttered-sides out. Bake in a preheated oven at 180°C/350°F/gas mark 4 for 20 minutes.

Meanwhile, put the apple slices in a saucepan with the water and cinnamon stick. Cook gently, stirring occasionally, until pulpy and sweeten to taste with granulated sugar. Remove the cinnamon stick. Beat the egg yolks into the apple. Turn the mixture into the soufflé dish. Whisk the egg whites until stiff.

Whisk in half the remaining sugar and whisk until stiff and glossy. Fold in the remaining sugar. Pile on top of the apple mixture and return to the oven for about 8–10 minutes until the meringue is just turning colour. Serve hot.

Apple and Blackberry Charlotte Meringue

SERVES 5–6

Prepare as for Apple Charlotte Meringue, but use 450 g/1 lb apples and 100 g/4 oz blackberries instead of all apples.

Apple Charlotte

SERVES 4–5

450 g/1 lb cooking (tart) apples
75 g/3 oz/⅓ cup demerara or light
brown sugar
5 slices of bread
75 g/3 oz/⅓ cup butter or margarine,
melted

Peel, core and slice the apples and mix with 50 g/2 oz/¼ cup of the sugar. Cut four of the slices of bread into triangles and dip in the melted butter. Use to line a 1 litre/1¾ pt/4¼ cup ovenproof dish. Fill with the apple slices and sugar. Dice the remaining bread and toss in the remaining butter. Scatter over the top and sprinkle with the remaining sugar. Cook in a preheated oven at 180°C/350°F/gas mark 4 for about 40 minutes until golden brown and cooked through.

Apple and Ginger Charlotte

SERVES 4–5

Prepare as for Apple Charlotte, but mix 15 ml/1 tbsp grated fresh root ginger with the apples and sugar before filling the dish.

91

Apple Nut and Raisin Charlotte

SERVES 4–5

Prepare as for Apple Charlotte (see page 91), but flavour with a pinch of ground cinnamon and stir in 50 g/ 2 oz/1 small packet of mixed nuts and raisins, chopped, into the apple when adding the sugar.

Citrus Charlotte

SERVES 4–5

Prepare as for Apple Charlotte (see page 91), but add the finely grated rind of 1 orange and 1 lemon to the apple, with the segmented orange flesh and the juice from the lemon. Use wholemeal bread and light brown sugar for a change, too.

Apple Amber

SERVES 4–6

900 g/2 lb cooking (tart) apples, sliced
100 g/4 oz/½ cup granulated sugar
Finely grated rind and juice of 1 lemon
50 g/2 oz/¼ cup butter
3 eggs, separated
45 ml/3 tbsp caster (superfine) sugar,
*   plus extra for sprinkling*
Cream, to serve

Put the apple slices in a saucepan with the granulated sugar, lemon rind and juice and the butter. Cook gently, stirring occasionally, until pulpy. Beat well until fairly smooth. Beat in the egg yolks and pour into an ovenproof dish.
   Whisk the egg whites until stiff. Whisk in half the sugar until stiff and glossy. Fold in the remaining sugar. Pile on top of the pudding, sprinkle with caster sugar and bake in a preheated oven at 150°C/300°F/gas mark 2 for about 35 minutes or until the meringue is a pale biscuit colour.

Apricot Amber

SERVES 4–6

Prepare as for Apple Amber, but substitute fresh apricots, quartered and stoned (pitted), for the apples.

Danish Apple Cake

SERVES 6

200 g/7 oz/scant 1 cup unsalted (sweet)
butter
900 g/2 lb cooking (tart) apples, sliced
2 whole cloves
Finely grated rind and juice of ½ lemon
Caster (superfine) sugar
1 small stale loaf, crusts removed
Whole blanched almonds, toasted, to
decorate
Crème fraîche, to serve

Melt 25 g/1 oz/2 tbsp of the butter in a saucepan. Add the apple slices, cloves, lemon rind and juice and cook gently until pulpy, stirring occasionally. Sweeten to taste with caster sugar. Leave to cool.

Make the loaf into crumbs. Melt a quarter of the remaining butter in a frying pan (skillet) and add enough crumbs to absorb the fat. Fry (sauté) until crisp and golden. Remove from the pan and drain on kitchen paper (paper towels). Repeat until all the crumbs are fried.

Remove the cloves from the apple mixture. Layer the fruit and crumbs in a glass serving dish, finishing with a layer of crumbs. Press down lightly. Sprinkle with a little caster sugar and decorate with a few toasted almonds. Chill for at least 2 hours before serving.

Apricot Pudding

SERVES 6

225 g/8 oz/1 cup butter or margarine,
softened, plus extra for greasing
225 g/8 oz/1 cup light brown sugar
3 eggs, beaten
2.5 ml/½ tsp almond essence (extract)
100 g/4 oz/1 cup ground almonds
225 g/8 oz/2 cups self-raising (self-
rising) flour
2.5 ml/½ tsp baking powder
100 g/4 oz/⅔ cup ready-to-eat dried
apricots, chopped
30 ml/2 tbsp flaked (slivered) almonds
15 ml/1 tbsp demerara sugar
Classic Custard Sauce (see page 354), to
serve

Beat together the butter and sugar until light and fluffy. Beat in half the egg and the almond essence, then the ground almonds, then the remaining egg. Sift the flour and baking powder over the surface and scatter the apricots over. Fold in with a metal spoon. Turn into a greased and lined 18 cm/7 in square cake tin (pan). Sprinkle with the demerara sugar and the flaked almonds. Bake in a preheated oven at 150°C/300°F/gas mark 2 for about 2 hours or until the centre springs back when lightly pressed and the cake is shrinking from the sides of the tin. Turn out, remove the paper and serve warm with Classic Custard Sauce.

Norwegian Pear Cake

SERVES 10

2 eggs
250 g/9 oz/generous 1 cup caster
    (superfine) sugar
95 g/3¾ oz/scant ½ cup butter, plus
    extra for greasing
150 ml/¼ pt/⅔ cup milk
190 g/6½ oz/generous 1½ cups plain (all-
    purpose) flour
15 ml/1 tbsp baking powder
6 pears, sliced
Classic Custard Sauce (see page 354), to
    serve

Beat the eggs and 225 g/8 oz/1 cup
of the sugar together until thick and
pale. Melt the butter in the milk and
bring to the boil. Pour into the eggs and
sugar. Sift the flour and baking powder
over the surface and fold in with a
metal spoon. Turn into a buttered
roasting tin (pan). Arrange the pear
slices over and sprinkle with the
remaining sugar. Bake in a preheated
oven at 200°C/400°F/gas mark 6 for
about 25 minutes or until risen and
cooked through. Serve warm, cut into
squares, with Classic Custard Sauce.

Pear and Cinnamon Clafoutie

SERVES 4–5

Prepare as for Plum Clafoutie (right),
but substitute peeled, cored and
thickly sliced pears for the plums.
Sprinkle with 5 ml/1 tsp ground
cinnamon instead of the flaked
(slivered) almonds before baking.

Plum Clafoutie

SERVES 4–5

350 g/12 oz ripe plums, halved and
    stoned (pitted)
75 g/3 oz/⅓ cup granulated sugar
250 ml/8 fl oz/1 cup water
50 g/2 oz/¼ cup butter, melted
100 g/4 oz/1 cup plain (all-purpose) flour
2 eggs
300 ml/½ pt/1¼ cups milk
30 ml/2 tbsp flaked (slivered) almonds
    (optional)
Icing (confectioners') sugar, for dusting

Put the plums in a saucepan with the
sugar and water. Heat gently until
the sugar melts, then simmer gently for
8 minutes. Brush a 1 litre/1¾ pt/4¼ cup
ovenproof dish with a little of the
melted butter. Lift the plums out of the
syrup with a draining spoon and lay,
cut-sides down, in the dish. Pour the
syrup into a serving jug.
    Put the flour in a bowl. Make a well
in the centre and add the eggs and half
the milk. Beat well until smooth, then
stir in the remaining milk and melted
butter. Pour over the plums and scatter
with flaked almonds, if using. Bake in a
preheated oven at 200°C/400°F/gas
mark 6 for about 30 minutes until risen
and golden. Dust with a little icing
sugar and serve warm with the reserved
plum syrup.

Cherry Clafoutie

SERVES 4–5

Prepare as for Plum Clafoutie, but
substitute halved and stoned (pitted)
black cherries for the plums.

Peach Clafoutie

SERVES 4–5

Prepare as for Plum Clafoutie, but substitute 3–4 ripe peaches, skinned, halved and stoned (pitted), for the plums.

Chocolate Nut Puddings

SERVES 4

40 g/1½ oz/⅓ cup self-raising (self-rising) flour
40 g/1½ oz/¾ cup fresh breadcrumbs
100 g/4 oz/1 cup chopped mixed nuts
50 g/2 oz/¼ cup butter or margarine
50 g/2 oz/¼ cup light brown sugar
15 ml/1 tbsp golden (light corn) syrup
15 ml/1 tbsp cocoa (unsweetened chocolate) powder
5 ml/1 tsp vanilla essence (extract)
2 eggs, separated
15 ml/1 tbsp hot water
A little icing sugar and 4 walnut halves, to decorate
Chocolate Custard (see page 355), to serve

Mix together the flour and breadcrumbs. Stir in the nuts. Melt together the butter, sugar, syrup, cocoa and vanilla essence. Stir into the flour and breadcrumbs. Beat in the egg yolks and water. Whisk the egg whites until stiff, then fold into the mixture with a metal spoon. Spoon into four individual soufflé dishes. Cover with foil and bake in a preheated oven at 180°C/350°F/gas mark 4 for about 30 minutes until lightly set. Loosen the edges and turn out on to warmed serving plates. Dust each with icing sugar, top with a walnut half and serve with Chocolate Custard.

Baked Chocolate Pudding

SERVES 8

Oil, for greasing
100 g/4 oz/1 cup self-raising (self-rising) flour
5 ml/1 tsp baking powder
30 ml/2 tbsp cocoa (unsweetened chocolate) powder
2.5 ml/½ tsp ground cinnamon
100 g/4 oz/½ cup soft tub margarine
100 g/4 oz/½ cup light brown sugar
2 eggs
30 ml/2 tbsp hot water
Drinking (sweetened) chocolate powder, for dusting
Dark Rum Sauce (see page 356), to serve

Oil an 18 cm/7 in deep round cake tin (pan) and line the base with greased, greaseproof (waxed) paper. Sift together the flour, baking powder, cocoa and cinnamon. Beat together the margarine and sugar until fluffy. Beat in the eggs one at a time. Fold in the sifted mixture and add the hot water to form a soft, dropping consistency. Spoon into the tin and level the surface. Bake in a preheated oven at 160°C/325°F/gas mark 3 for about 25–30 minutes until firm to the touch. Turn out of the cake tin, remove the paper, dust with drinking chocolate powder and serve with Dark Rum Sauce.

Baked Apple and Cranberry Pudding

SERVES 6

A little butter, for greasing
150 g/5 oz/1¼ cups plain (all-purpose) flour
A pinch of salt
100 g/4 oz/½ cup caster (superfine) sugar
4 large eggs
375 ml/13 fl oz/1½ cups single (light) cream
350 g/12 oz cranberries
2 eating (dessert) apples, sliced
Icing (confectioners') sugar, for dusting

Butter an 18 cm/7 in flan dish (pie pan). Sift the flour and salt into a bowl and stir in the sugar. Beat together the eggs and cream and gradually beat into the flour to form a smooth batter. Put the cranberries in the flan dish and lay the apple slices over. Pour on the batter. Bake in a preheated oven at 200°C/400°F/gas mark 6 for 45 minutes. Turn out on to a warmed serving dish, if liked, and dust with icing sugar before serving.

Lemon Sauce Pudding

SERVES 4

50 g/2 oz/¼ cup unsalted (sweet) butter, softened, plus extra for greasing
75 g/3 oz/⅓ cup caster (superfine) sugar
2 eggs, separated
15 ml/1 tbsp plain (all-purpose) flour
Finely grated rind and juice of 2 small lemons
200 ml/7 fl oz/scant 1 cup milk
Lightly whipped cream, to serve

Beat together the butter and sugar until light and fluffy. Beat in the egg yolks, flour, lemon rind and juice together. Stir in the milk. Whisk the egg whites until stiff, then fold in with a metal spoon. Turn into a lightly greased ovenproof dish and bake in a preheated oven at 180°C/350°F/gas mark 4 for 45 minutes or until risen and golden brown. The mixture will separate into a golden sponge with a buttery lemon sauce underneath. Serve with lightly whipped cream.

Yummy Chocolate Pudding

SERVES 4–6

45 ml/3 tbsp cocoa (unsweetened chocolate) powder
90 g/3½ oz/scant 1 cup self-raising (self-rising) flour
5 ml/1 tsp baking powder
100 g/4 oz/½ cup butter or margarine, softened, plus extra for greasing
100 g/4 oz/½ cup light brown sugar
2 eggs
45 ml/3 tbsp dark chocolate spread
45 ml/3 tbsp hot water
Cream, to serve

Sift 30 ml/2 tbsp of the cocoa, the flour and baking powder into a bowl. Add the butter or margarine, sugar and eggs and beat thoroughly until well blended. Butter a 1.2 litre/2 pt/5 cup ovenproof dish. Blend the chocolate spread with the hot water and remaining cocoa powder and pour into the dish. Spoon the chocolate sponge cake mixture over the top. Bake in a preheated oven at 190°C/375°F/gas mark 5 for about 30 minutes or until risen and the cake springs back when lightly pressed. Serve hot with cream.

Built-in Chocolate Sauce Pudding

SERVES 6–8

175 g/6 oz/1½ cups self-raising (self-rising) flour
50 g/2 oz/½ cup cocoa (unsweetened chocolate) powder
200 g/7 oz/scant 1 cup light brown sugar
150 ml/¼ pt/⅔ cup milk
10 ml/2 tsp vanilla essence (extract)
50 g/2 oz/¼ cup unsalted (sweet) butter, melted, plus extra for greasing
300 ml/½ pt/1¼ cups very hot water
Crème fraîche, to serve

Sift the flour and half the cocoa powder into a bowl. Add 150 g/5 oz/⅔ cup of the sugar, the milk, vanilla essence and melted butter and mix well. Turn into a buttered 1.5 litre/2½ pt/6 cup ovenproof dish. Blend the remaining cocoa powder with the remaining sugar and sprinkle over. Pour over the very hot water and bake in a preheated oven at 190°C/375°F/gas mark 5 for about 40 minutes or until firm to the touch and the mixture has formed a sauce underneath. Serve with crème fraîche.

Basic Bread Pudding

MAKES 20 PIECES

Butter, for greasing
750 g/1½ lb stale bread, sliced
350 g/12 oz/2 cups dried mixed fruit
  (fruit cake mix)
175 g/6 oz/¾ cup dark brown sugar
15 ml/1 tbsp mixed (apple-pie) spice
50 g/2 oz/¼ cup caster (superfine) sugar
Cream or custard, to serve

Butter a large roasting tin (pan). Put the bread in a large bowl. Cover with cold water and leave to soak for 1 hour. Squeeze out all excess water. Return to the bowl and beat until smooth. Add the remaining ingredients except the caster sugar and mix well. Spread in the prepared tin. Bake in a preheated oven at 190°C/375°F/gas mark 5 for about 1¾ hours until brown and crisp on top. Sprinkle with the caster sugar, leave to cool slightly, then cut into squares. Serve warm or cold with cream or custard. Store any remainder in an airtight container.

Special Bread Pudding

SERVES 6–8

8 slices of day-old bread
100 g/4 oz/⅔ cup dried mixed fruit
  (fruit cake mix)
30 ml/2 tbsp apricot jam (conserve)
10 ml/2 tsp mixed (apple-pie) spice
50 g/2 oz/¼ cup butter or margarine,
  melted, plus extra for greasing
75 g/3 oz/⅓ cup light brown sugar
Caster (superfine) sugar, for sprinkling
Ice cream, to serve

Break up the bread and place in a bowl. Soak in water for 15 minutes, then squeeze dry with the hands. Return to the bowl and beat with a fork until smooth. Stir in the remaining ingredients. Turn into a greased 1.75 litre/3 pt/7½ cup baking tin (pan). Bake in a preheated oven at 190°C/375°F/gas mark 5 for about 1½ hours or until golden and firm. Sprinkle with caster sugar and serve warm with ice cream.

Enriched Bread Pudding

SERVES 6–8

100 g/4 oz wholemeal bread, cubed
150 ml/¼ pt/⅔ cup milk
3 eggs, lightly beaten
50 g/2 oz/¼ cup dark brown sugar
5 ml/1 tsp ground cinnamon
5 ml/1 tsp grated nutmeg
5 ml/1 tsp ground mace
175 g/6 oz/1 cup dried mixed fruit (fruit
  cake mix)
20 g/¾ oz/1½ tbsp butter, melted
Caster (superfine) sugar, for sprinkling
Cream or custard, to serve

Put the bread in a bowl. Add the milk and leave to soak for 30 minutes. Beat well with a fork. Mix in the eggs, sugar, spices and fruit. Brush a 1.5 litre/2½ pt/6 cup ovenproof dish with some of the butter. Turn the mixture into the dish and level the surface. Drizzle with the remaining butter. Bake in a preheated oven at 180°C/350°F/gas mark 4 for about 1 hour or until golden brown and set. Allow to cool slightly, sprinkle with caster sugar and serve cut into squares with cream or custard.

Rhubarb Fingers

MAKES 18

6 sticks of young rhubarb
175 g/6 oz/1½ cups plain (all-purpose)
*   flour*
A pinch of salt
75 g/3 oz/⅓ cup hard block margarine,
*   diced*
25 g/1 oz/2 tbsp caster (superfine)
*   sugar*
1 egg, separated
Cold water, to mix
Icing (confectioners') sugar, for dusting
Classic Custard Sauce (see page 354), to
*   serve*

Trim the rhubarb and cut into 30 cm/12 in lengths. Sift the flour and salt into a bowl. Add the margarine and rub in with the fingertips until the mixture resembles fine breadcrumbs. Stir in the sugar. Mix with the egg yolk and enough cold water to form a firm dough. Knead gently on a lightly floured surface. Roll out to a rectangle 46 × 33 cm/18 × 13 in. Cut into six equal strips, 33 cm/13 in long. Place a stick of rhubarb on each strip. Brush the edges of the pastry (paste) with a little egg white and fold over to cover the rhubarb completely, pressing the edges firmly together to seal. Repeat with the remaining rhubarb. Knock up the edges with the back of a knife and transfer to a baking (cookie) sheet. Brush with more egg white and bake in a preheated oven at 190°C/375°F/gas mark 5 for 25 minutes until golden and cooked through. Cut each stick into 7.5 cm/3 in pieces. Dust with sifted icing sugar and serve warm or cold with Classic Custard Sauce.

Rhubarb and Custard Meringue Bake

SERVES 4–6

450 g/1 lb rhubarb, chopped
4 trifle sponges, sliced
50 g/2 oz/¼ cup granulated sugar
Finely grated rind and juice of 2
*   clementines or satsumas*
2 eggs, separated
300 ml/½ pt/1¼ cups single (light) cream
100 g/4 oz/½ cup caster (superfine)
*   sugar*

Layer the rhubarb in an ovenproof dish with the sponge slices and granulated sugar. Whisk the fruit rind and juice with the egg yolks and cream and pour over. Bake in a preheated oven at 190°C/375°F/gas mark 5 for about 40 minutes until the custard is set and the fruit is tender.

Whisk the egg whites until stiff. Whisk in half the sugar until stiff and glossy. Fold in the remaining sugar. Pile on top of the pudding and bake for a further 10 minutes or until the meringue is just turning colour. Serve warm.

Eve's Pudding

SERVES 6

A little butter, for greasing
750 g/1½ lb cooking (tart) apples, sliced
5 ml/1 tsp ground cinnamon
15 ml/1 tbsp water
75 g/3 oz/⅓ cup light brown sugar
50 g/2 oz/¼ cup soft tub margarine
50 g/2 oz/¼ cup caster (superfine) sugar,
    plus extra for sprinkling
1 egg, beaten
100 g/4 oz/1 cup self-raising (self-
    rising) flour
30 ml/2 tbsp milk
Pouring cream, to serve

Butter a 1.2 litre/2 pt/5 cup ovenproof dish. Mix together the apple slices and cinnamon and place in the dish. Add the water and cover with the brown sugar. Beat together the margarine and caster sugar until light and fluffy. Beat in the egg. Sift the flour over the surface and fold in with a metal spoon. Add enough of the milk to form a soft, dropping consistency. Spread over the apple mixture. Bake in a preheated oven at 180°C/350°F/gas mark 4 for 45 minutes until firm, well risen and the apples are cooked through. Sprinkle with a little extra caster sugar and serve with pouring cream.

Rhubarb Eve's Pudding

SERVES 6

Prepare as for Eve's Pudding, but substitute rhubarb for apples and ground ginger for cinnamon. Omit the water.

Spiced Apple Pudding

SERVES 8

150 g/5 oz/⅔ cup unsalted (sweet)
    butter, plus extra for greasing
225 g/8 oz/1 cup caster (superfine)
    sugar
2 eggs, beaten
225 g/8 oz/2 cups self-raising (self-
    rising) flour
5 ml/1 tsp mixed (apple-pie) spice
30 ml/2 tbsp chopped walnuts
450 g/1 lb cooking (tart) apples, sliced
Cream, to serve

Beat together the butter and sugar until light and fluffy. Add the eggs, a little at a time, beating well after each addition. Sift the flour and spice over the surface and scatter the walnuts over. Fold in with a metal spoon. Turn into a buttered 20 cm/8 in deep loose-bottomed cake tin (pan). Cover with the apple slices. Bake in a preheated oven at 160°C/325°F/gas mark 3 for 1½ hours or until risen and golden and a skewer inserted in the centre comes out clean. Carefully remove from the tin and serve warm with cream.

Sweet Pizza Base

SERVES 4–6

225 g/8 oz/2 cups self-raising (self-rising) flour
A pinch of salt
50 g/2 oz/¼ cup butter or hard block margarine, diced
5 ml/1 tsp caster (superfine) sugar
1 egg, beaten
30 ml/2 tbsp milk

Sift the flour and salt into a bowl. Add the fat and rub in with the fingertips. Stir in the sugar. Mix in the egg and enough of the milk to form a soft but not sticky dough. Knead gently on a lightly floured surface. Roll out and use to line a 23 cm/9 in pizza plate or place the round on a greased baking (cookie) sheet. Cover with your chosen filling (see below) and topping (see page 102) and bake in a preheated oven at 200°C/400°F/gas mark 6 for about 30 minutes until cooked through. Serve hot or cold.

Vanilla Custard Pizza Filling

ENOUGH FOR ONE 23 CM/9 IN PIZZA

15 g/½ oz/2 tbsp plain (all-purpose) flour
25 g/1 oz/2 tbsp granulated sugar
1 egg, beaten
150 ml/¼ pt/⅔ cup milk
1.5 ml/¼ tsp vanilla essence (extract)

Blend the flour and sugar in a saucepan. Whisk in the egg and a little of the milk. Stir in the remaining milk. Bring to the boil and cook for 2 minutes, stirring all the time. Add the vanilla essence, cover with a circle of wetted greaseproof (waxed) paper and leave to cool. Spread over the pizza base and add your chosen topping.

Chocolate Custard Pizza Filling

ENOUGH FOR ONE 23 CM/9 IN PIZZA

Prepare as for Vanilla Custard Pizza Filling, but beat 45 ml/3 tbsp chocolate spread and an extra 15 ml/1 tbsp milk into the custard before cooling.

Almond Custard Pizza Filling

ENOUGH FOR ONE 23 CM/9 IN PIZZA

Make as for Vanilla Custard Pizza Filling, but substitute almond essence (extract) to taste for the vanilla essence.

Sweet Cheese Pizza Filling

ENOUGH FOR ONE 23 CM/9 IN PIZZA

100 g/4 oz/½ cup cream cheese
15 ml/1 tbsp caster (superfine) sugar
Finely grated rind of 1 lemon
15 ml/1 tbsp single (light) cream

Beat together all the ingredients to form a smooth paste. Spread over the pizza base and add your chosen topping.

Lemon Pie Pizza Filling

ENOUGH FOR ONE 23 CM/9 IN PIZZA BASE

1 packet of lemon meringue pie filling
250 ml/8 fl oz/1 cup water
1 egg yolk
30 ml/2 tbsp fromage frais

Blend the pie filling with the water in a saucepan. Bring to the boil and cook for 2 minutes, stirring. Whisk in the egg yolk and fromage frais. Leave to cool. Spread over the pizza base and add your chosen topping.

Sweet Pizza Toppings

You can use any of the fillings with any fruit topping of your choice. Here are a few novel ideas to get you started.

- **Cherry Nut:** use Sweet Cheese or Almond Custard Pizza Filling, topped with 400 g/14 oz/1 large can of red cherry pie filling and 30 ml/2 tbsp flaked (slivered) almonds. Bake as instructed.

- **Black Forest:** use Chocolate Custard Pizza Filling, topped with 400 g/ 14 oz/1 large can of black cherry pie filling. Bake as instructed. Sprinkle with 45 ml/3 tbsp grated chocolate before serving.

- **Strudel Topping:** use Sweet Cheese Pizza Filling, topped with 2 eating (dessert) apples, thinly sliced and tossed in 30 ml/2 tbsp granulated sugar and 10 ml/2 tsp ground cinnamon. Brush with 45 ml/3 tbsp apricot jam (conserve), warmed with 15 ml/1 tbsp lemon juice. Bake as instructed.

- **Just a Trifle:** use Vanilla Custard Pizza Filling, topped with 400 g/ 14 oz/1 large can of strawberry pie filling and drizzled with 15 ml/1 tbsp sweet sherry. Bake as instructed. Serve cold, topped with whipped cream.

- **Caribbean Banana:** use Lemon Pie Pizza Filling, topped with thickly sliced bananas. Sprinkle thickly with dark brown sugar and moisten with 30 ml/2 tbsp dark rum. Bake as instructed. Serve hot or cold with ice cream.

Baked Banana Bonanza

SERVES 4

750 g/1¾ lb ripe bananas
45 ml/3 tbsp lemon jelly marmalade
*   (clear conserve)*
150 ml/¼ pt/⅔ cup grapefruit juice
25 g/1 oz/2 tbsp light brown sugar
15 ml/1 tbsp chopped glacé (candied)
*   cherries*
10 ml/2 tsp chopped angelica
Brandy Snaps (see page 124), to serve

Peel the bananas and slice thickly. Place in an ovenproof dish. Melt the marmalade with the grapefruit juice and pour over. Sprinkle with the sugar. Cover with foil and bake in a preheated oven at 180°C/350°F/gas mark 4 for about 30 minutes until cooked through, basting occasionally with the sauce. Scatter the cherries and angelica over and serve hot with Brandy Snaps.

Posh Pastries

Choux, puff and filo pastries (pastes) can create a selection
of truly mouth-watering desserts. Choux pastry is really easy to
make at home but, for the best results, I suggest you buy fresh or
frozen puff and filo pastry as they are very time-consuming and
fairly tricky to make.

Custard Slice

SERVES 8

*375 g/13 oz/1 packet of puff pastry
(paste), thawed if frozen*
2 egg yolks
25 g/1 oz/2 tbsp caster (superfine) sugar
15 g/½ oz/2 tbsp plain (all-purpose) flour
150 ml/¼ pt/⅔ cup milk
1.5 ml/¼ tsp vanilla essence (extract)
*60 ml/4 tbsp strawberry or raspberry
jam (conserve)*
*175 g/6 oz/1 cup icing (confectioners')
sugar, sifted*
15 ml/1 tbsp water
*Glacé (candied) cherries and angelica
leaves, to decorate*

Roll out the pastry thinly to a 33 cm/
13 in square on a lightly floured
surface. Cut into three 11 cm/4¼ in
wide strips. Place on a dampened
baking (cookie) sheet. Bake in a
preheated oven at 220°C/425°F/gas
mark 7 for about 10 minutes until
risen, crisp and golden. Transfer to a
wire rack to cool.

Blend the egg yolks with the sugar
and flour in a bowl. Bring the milk
almost to the boil, then pour into the
bowl, stirring all the time. Return to the
saucepan, bring to the boil over a gentle
heat and cook for 2 minutes, stirring all
the time, until thickened and smooth.
Stir in the vanilla essence, cover with a
circle of wetted greaseproof (waxed)
paper and leave to cool.

Place one sheet of pastry on a
serving plate. Spread with a little jam,
then half the custard. Spread a second
layer of pastry with jam and place on
top. Cover with the remaining custard.
Top with the remaining sheet of pastry.

Blend the icing sugar with enough
water to form a smooth paste. Spread
over the top. Decorate with halved glacé
cherries and angelica leaves and chill
until ready to serve.

Cream Horns

MAKES 10

*225 g/8 oz puff pastry (paste), thawed
if frozen*
A little milk
Caster (superfine) sugar, for sprinkling
Raspberry jam (conserve)
*150 ml/¼ pt/⅔ cup double (heavy) or
whipping cream, whipped*
A few raspberries, to serve (optional)

Roll out the pastry thinly and trim to
a rectangle 25 × 30 cm/10 × 12 in.
Cut into 10 strips, 2.5 cm/1 in wide and
30 cm/12 in long. Wrap a strip of
pastry round a cream horn tin (pan),
slightly overlapping along the edge and
place on a baking (cookie) sheet with
the end underneath. Repeat with the
remainder. Chill for 30 minutes.

Brush with milk and sprinkle with
caster sugar. Bake in a preheated oven
at 220°C/425°F/gas mark 7 for about
20 minutes until crisp and golden.
Allow to cool slightly, then carefully
remove the tins. Cool on a wire rack.
Put 10 ml/2 tsp jam in the base of each
and fill with piped or spooned whipped
cream. Place on serving plates and add
a few fresh raspberries to the side of
each horn, if liked.

Lemon Mille Feuille

SERVES 8

*375 g/13 oz/1 packet of puff pastry
  (paste), thawed if frozen*
*225 g/8 oz/²⁄₃ cup apricot jam
  (conserve)*
60 ml/4 tbsp water
300 ml/½ pt/1¼ cups double (heavy) cream
300 ml/½ pt/1¼ cups lemon curd
Lemon juice (optional)
*Crystallised (candied) lemon slices and
  angelica leaves, to decorate*

Roll out the pastry thinly and cut two 23 cm/9 in rounds. Using a small tea plate, cut out the centre to leave two rings. Place on dampened baking (cookie) sheets and bake in a preheated oven at 220°C/425°F/gas mark 7 for about 10 minutes until risen, crisp and golden. Meanwhile, re-knead the inner circles, roll out and cut into a 23 cm/ 9 in round. Cut some stars, half moons or other shapes out of the trimmings and place beside the pastry round on a dampened baking sheet. Bake for about 15 minutes until crisp and golden. Transfer all the pastry pieces to wire racks to cool.

When cold, warm the apricot jam and water in a saucepan. Place the complete round on a serving plate and brush with a little jam. Top with one ring and brush again. Top with the remaining ring. Brush with more jam and arrange the pastry shapes round the top. Brush again with any remaining glaze. Whip the cream until peaking and reserve about a third for decoration.

Fold the lemon curd into the remainder and spike with lemon juice, if liked. Spoon into the pastry ring. Decorate with the remaining whipped cream, crystallised lemon slices and angelica leaves and chill until ready to serve.

Strawberry Mille Feuille

SERVES 8

Prepare as for Lemon Mille Feuille, but for the filling fold 350 g/12 oz crushed strawberries into 200 ml/ 7 fl oz/scant 1 cup double (heavy) cream, whipped. Sweeten to taste and spike with lemon juice, if liked. Decorate the top with about 100 ml/ 3½ fl oz/scant ½ cup double (heavy) cream, whipped, and a few whole strawberries.

Cream Slices

MAKES 8

225 g/8 oz puff pastry (paste), thawed,
*   if frozen*
300 ml/½ pt/1¼ cups double (heavy)
*   cream*
90 ml/6 tbsp strawberry jam (conserve)
225 g/8 oz/1⅓ cups icing (confectioners')
*   sugar*
30 ml/2 tbsp water
4 glacé (candied) cherries, halved
16 angelica leaves

Roll out the pastry to a 40 × 10 cm/
16 × 4 in rectangle. Cut into eight
10 × 5 cm/4 × 2 in pieces. Place on a
dampened baking (cookie) sheet. Bake
in a preheated oven at 230°C/450°F/gas
mark 8 for 10 minutes or until risen,
golden and puffy. Transfer to a wire
rack to cool.

When cold, slit horizontally into
halves. Whip the cream until stiff.
Sandwich the slices back together with
the jam and whipped cream. Place on
the wire rack. Blend the icing sugar
with the water until smooth. Spread
over the tops and decorate each with
half a glacé cherry and two angelica
leaves.

Baklavas

MAKES 10

225 g/8 oz/1 cup unsalted (sweet)
*   butter, melted*
225 g/8 oz filo pastry (paste)
275 g/10 oz/2½ cups walnuts, chopped
75 g/3 oz/⅓ cup caster (superfine) sugar
10 ml/2 tsp ground cinnamon
5 ml/1 tsp grated nutmeg
For the syrup:
225 g/8 oz/1 cup granulated sugar
Finely grated rind and juice of 1 small
*   lemon*
A little rose water (optional), to serve

Brush a 28 × 18 cm/11 × 7 in
shallow baking tin (pan) with a
little of the melted butter. Line with a
sheet of filo pastry. Brush with butter
and repeat until you have four layers of
buttered pastry. Mix together the nuts,
caster sugar and spices and spread over
the pastry. Top with the remaining
layers of pastry, again brushing with
butter in between each layer and then
on top. Score the top layer in a criss-
cross pattern, with lines about 2.5 cm/
1 in apart. Bake in a preheated oven at
180°C/350°F/gas mark 4 for 40 minutes
or until golden brown and cooked
through.

Meanwhile, put the syrup
ingredients in a saucepan and heat
gently, stirring, until the sugar has
dissolved. Boil rapidly for 4 minutes.
When the pastry is cooked, mark the
top into 10 squares and spoon the hot
syrup over. Leave to cool, then chill
until the next day. Cut into squares and
sprinkle with a few drops of rosewater
before serving, if liked.

Kateifi

SERVES 9–12

550 g/1¼ lb/2½ cups granulated sugar
250 ml/8 fl oz/1 cup water
10 ml/2 tsp lemon juice
225 g/8 oz/2 cups walnuts, finely chopped
30 ml/2 tbsp ground cinnamon
275 g/10 oz/1¼ cups unsalted (sweet) butter
12 shredded wheat cereal biscuits

Mix 450 g/1 lb/2 cups of the sugar in a pan with the water. Heat very gently, stirring, until the sugar has dissolved, then boil until the syrup is thick but not coloured. Stir in the lemon juice. Place the base of the pan in cold water to prevent further cooking and leave to cool.

Mix the nuts with the remaining sugar and the cinnamon. Melt the butter. Dip each cereal biscuit in the butter to soak well, then press half the biscuits in a buttered 23–25 cm/9–10 in baking tin (pan). Spread the nut mixture over, then press the remaining buttered biscuits firmly over the top. Drizzle over any remaining butter. Bake in a preheated oven at 190°C/375°F/gas mark 5 for about 30 minutes until turning golden brown round the edges. Remove from the oven and pour the cold syrup over to cover completely. Leave to cool, then cut into pieces.

Greek Puffs

MAKES 12

75 g/3 oz/⅓ cup unsalted (sweet) butter
45 ml/3 tbsp clear honey
40 g/1½ oz/⅓ cup chopped mixed nuts
3 shredded wheat cereal biscuits, crushed
215 g/7½ oz puff pastry (paste), thawed if frozen
15 ml/1 tbsp caster (superfine) sugar
2.5 ml/½ tsp ground cinnamon
Greek-style Yoghurt (see page 359), to serve

Put the butter and honey in a saucepan and heat until the butter has melted. Remove from the heat and stir in the nuts and crushed cereal. Cut the pastry in half. Roll out one half and use to line the base of an 18 × 28 cm/ 7 × 11 in Swiss roll tin (jelly roll pan). Roll out the other half to a rectangle the same size. Brush the pastry in the tin with water. Spoon in the honey filling and spread evenly. Brush the second piece of pastry with water and lay on top, brushed-side down. Press down fairly firmly. Brush the top with water. Mix together the sugar and cinnamon and sprinkle over. Bake in a preheated oven at 220°C/425°F/gas mark 7 for 25 minutes until risen and golden brown. Leave to cool in the tin for 10 minutes, then cut into squares and serve warm with Greek-style Yoghurt.

Jam Turnovers

SERVES 4–6

*225 g/8 oz puff pastry (paste), thawed
if frozen
Any flavour jam (conserve)
Milk, to glaze
Caster (superfine) sugar, for sprinkling
Cream or Easy Custard (see page 354)*

Roll out the pastry and cut into four or six squares. Put a good spoonful of jam in the centre of each square. Brush the edges with milk. Fold over to form a triangle, then press the edges well together to seal. Knock up the edges and flute with the back of a knife. Transfer to a dampened baking (cookie) sheet. Brush with milk and sprinkle with caster sugar. Bake in a preheated oven at 230°C/450°F/gas mark 8 for about 15 minutes until well risen, puffy and golden. Serve warm with cream or custard.

Apple Turnovers

SERVES 4–6

Prepare as for Jam Turnovers, but fill the pastry (paste) with sliced cooking (tart) apples, sweetened to taste with granulated sugar mixed with a tiny pinch of ground cloves or cinnamon.

Pear Turnovers

SERVES 4–6

Prepare as for Jam Turnovers, but fill the pastry (paste) with sliced pears and flavour with a pinch of ground ginger.

Apple and Sultana Plait

SERVES 8

*450 g/1 lb cooking (tart) apples, diced
15 ml/1 tbsp lemon juice
75 g/3 oz/⅓ cup light brown sugar
2.5 ml/½ tsp ground cinnamon
100 g/4 oz/⅔ cup sultanas (golden
raisins)
375 g/13 oz/1 packet of puff pastry
(paste), thawed if frozen
A little cream, to glaze
100 g/4 oz/⅔ cup icing (confectioners')
sugar
15 ml/1 tbsp water*

Toss the diced apple in the lemon juice and mix in the brown sugar, cinnamon and sultanas. Roll out the pastry to a 40 × 35 cm/16 × 14 in rectangle. Make a series of 11 cm/4½ in long diagonal cuts along both long sides of the pastry, about 2.5 cm/1 in apart. Spoon the filling down the centre. Fold in the top and bottom edges, then fold the strips over the filling, alternating from each side, to form a plait.

Carefully transfer to a dampened baking (cookie) sheet. Brush with a little cream and bake in a preheated oven at 200°C/400°F/gas mark 6 for about 20 minutes until golden, risen and cooked through. Allow to cool slightly, then transfer to a wire rack to finish cooling. Mix the icing sugar with the water and drizzle over the top. Leave until set, then serve sliced.

Minted Currant Puffs

SERVES 8

*225 g/8 oz/2 cups plain (all-purpose)
  flour*
A pinch of salt
*175 g/6 oz/¾ cup white vegetable fat
  (shortening), diced*
Cold water, to mix
30 ml/2 tbsp chopped mint
45 ml/3 tbsp granulated sugar
100 g/4 oz/⅔ cup currants
A little milk, to glaze
Caster (superfine) sugar, for sprinkling
Whipped or clotted cream, to serve

Make the rough puff pastry: sift the
flour and salt into a bowl. Add the
vegetable fat and leave in cubes. Mix
with enough cold water to form a soft,
lumpy dough. Draw the mixture into a
ball, then roll out on a floured surface to
a rectangle about 1 cm/½ in thick. Fold
the top third down and the bottom third
up over it. Press the edges with the
rolling pin to seal and give the dough a
quarter turn. Roll and fold twice more,
giving a quarter turn after each folding.
Wrap in clingfilm (plastic wrap) and
chill for 30 minutes.

Meanwhile, mix the mint with the
granulated sugar and currants. Roll out
the chilled dough thinly and cut into
16 rounds using a 10 cm/4 in cutter or
a small saucer as a guide. Re-knead
and roll any trimmings, if necessary, to
make the final rounds. Divide the filling
between the centres of the rounds.
Dampen the edges and draw up over
the filling, sealing the edges well
together. Turn over and roll lightly with
a rolling pin to flatten so that you can
see the currants through the pastry.
Transfer to baking (cookie) sheets.

Brush with a little milk and sprinkle
with caster sugar. Bake in a preheated
oven at 200°C/400°F/gas mark 6 for
about 15 minutes until puffy and
golden. Serve warm with whipped or
clotted cream.

Strawberry Shortcake

SERVES 6

*175 g/6 oz/1½ cups self-raising (self-
  rising) flour*
5 ml/1 tsp baking powder
30 ml/2 tbsp icing (confectioners') sugar
75 g/3 oz/⅓ cup butter, diced
120 ml/4 fl oz/½ cup milk
350 g/12 oz strawberries, hulled
30 ml/2 tbsp caster (superfine) sugar
*300 ml/½ pt/1¼ cups double (heavy)
  cream*
A few drops of vanilla essence (extract)

Sift the flour, baking powder and icing
sugar into a bowl. Add the butter
and rub in with the fingertips until the
mixture resembles fine breadcrumbs.
Stir in the milk to form a soft, slightly
sticky dough. Knead gently on a lightly
floured surface. Shape into a round and
press gently into a greased 18 cm/7 in
round cake tin (pan). Bake in a
preheated oven at 230°C/450°F/gas
mark 8 for about 15 minutes until well
risen and golden brown. Turn out on to
a wire rack to cool.

Split horizontally. Slice half the
strawberries and sprinkle with half the
sugar. Whip the cream with a few drops
of vanilla essence and the remaining
sugar until softly peaking. Sandwich the
shortcake halves together with half the
cream and the sliced strawberries.
Spread the remaining cream on top and
decorate with the whole strawberries.

Traditional Cheesecake Squares

MAKES 9

For the pastry (paste):
175 g/6 oz/1½ cups plain (all-purpose)
   flour
A pinch of salt
5 ml/1 tsp ground cinnamon
75 g/3 oz/⅓ cup butter, diced
15 ml/1 tbsp icing (confectioners') sugar
Cold water, to mix
For the filling:
75 g/3 oz/⅓ cup butter, softened
50 g/2 oz/¼ cup caster (superfine) sugar
Grated rind of 1 lemon
175 g/6 oz/¾ cup medium-fat soft cheese
30 ml/2 tbsp soured (dairy sour) cream
   or plain yoghurt
2 eggs, beaten
100 g/4 oz/⅔ cup sultanas (golden raisins)
A little sifted icing sugar, for dusting

To make the pastry, sift the flour, salt and cinnamon into a bowl. Add the butter and rub in with the fingertips until the mixture resembles fine bread-crumbs. Stir in the icing sugar. Mix with enough cold water to form a firm dough. Knead gently on a lightly floured surface and use to line an 18 cm/7 in square shallow baking tin (pan).

To make the filling, beat the softened butter with the sugar, lemon rind, cheese and soured cream until smooth. Gradually beat in the eggs and sultanas. Spoon into the pastry-lined tin and level the surface.

Roll out the pastry trimmings and cut into thin strips. Arrange in a lattice pattern over the filling. Bake in a preheated oven at 180°C/350°F/gas mark 4 for 35 minutes or until golden and set. Leave to cool for 10 minutes, then cut into squares and transfer to a wire rack to cool completely. Dust with icing sugar before serving.

Easy Apple Strudels

SERVES 4

1 cooking (tart) apple, chopped
40 g/1½ oz/3 tbsp granulated sugar
30 ml/2 tbsp sultanas (golden raisins)
2.5 ml/½ tsp ground cinnamon
4 sheets of filo pastry (paste)
20 g/¾ oz/1½ tbsp butter, melted

Mix the apple with the sugar, sultanas and cinnamon. Brush the pastry sheets with a little of the butter. Fold into halves and brush again. Divide the filling equally between the pastry rectangles, placing it towards the middle of one edge. Fold in the sides, then roll up. Transfer to a lightly greased baking (cookie) sheet and brush with any remaining butter. Bake in a preheated oven at 190°C/375°F/gas mark 5 for 10–15 minutes until golden and cooked through.

Easy Pear and Ginger Strudels

SERVES 4

Prepare as for Easy Apple Strudels, but substitute 2 ripe pears, chopped, and 2 pieces of stem ginger in syrup, chopped, for the apple and sultanas. Serve with a little warmed syrup from the ginger jar spooned over.

Almond Slices

MAKES 14

225 g/8 oz/2 cups plain (all-purpose) flour
A pinch of salt
100 g/4 oz/½ cup hard block margarine,
*   diced*
1 egg, separated
Cold water, to mix
45 ml/3 tbsp apricot jam (conserve)
100 g/4 oz/½ cup caster (superfine) sugar
100 g/4 oz/½ cup icing (confectioners')
*   sugar*
175 g/6 oz/1½ cups ground almonds
1 egg
2.5 ml/½ tsp almond essence (extract)
40 g/1½ oz/⅓ cup flaked (slivered)
*   almonds*
Ice cream, to serve

Sift the flour and salt into a bowl. Add the margarine and rub in with the fingertips. Mix with the egg yolk and enough cold water to form a firm dough. Knead gently on a lightly floured surface. Roll out and use to line an 18 × 28 cm/7 × 11 in shallow baking tin (pan). Spread the jam in the base. Mix together the caster and icing sugars with the ground almonds. Stir in the whole egg, the remaining egg white and the almond essence. Spread into the tin and decorate with the flaked almonds. Bake in a preheated oven at 200°C/400°F/gas mark 6 for about 25 minutes until golden brown and set. Leave to cool slightly, then slice. Serve warm or cold with ice cream. (These are also good served cold for tea.)

Hazelnut Slices

MAKES 14

Prepare as for Almond Slices, but substitute ground hazelnuts (filberts) instead of almonds, vanilla essence (extract) for almond, raspberry jam (conserve) for apricot and decorate with whole blanched hazelnuts instead of flaked (slivered) almonds.

Chocolate Walnut Slices

MAKES 14

Prepare as for Almond Slices, but substitute ground walnuts for ground almonds, vanilla essence (extract) for almond, and chocolate spread for jam (conserve), and decorate with walnut halves instead of flaked (slivered) almonds.

Glazed Apple Shortbread Layer

SERVES 6

225 g/8 oz/2 cups plain (all-purpose)
  flour
225 g/8 oz/1 cup unsalted (sweet)
  butter, diced, plus extra for greasing
100 g/4 oz/1 cup ground almonds
100 g/4 oz/½ cup caster (superfine)
  sugar
225 g/8 oz/1 cup granulated sugar
120 ml/4 fl oz/½ cup water
Grated rind and juice of 2 lemons
4 large cooking (tart) apples, chopped
50 g/2 oz/½ cup flaked (slivered) almonds
75 g/3 oz/½ cup icing (confectioners')
  sugar
Hot water, if necessary

Put the flour in a bowl. Add the butter and rub in with the fingertips until the mixture resembles coarse crumbs. Stir in the ground almonds and caster sugar. Mix to form a firm dough. Knead gently on a lightly floured surface. Wrap in clingfilm (plastic wrap) and chill for 30 minutes.

Cut into quarters and roll out each piece to a 23 cm/9 in round. Place on lightly greased baking (cookie) sheets and bake in a preheated oven at 190°C/375°F/gas mark 5 for 15 minutes until a pale biscuit brown. Cool on wire racks.

Meanwhile, put the granulated sugar and water in a pan. Heat gently, stirring, until the sugar dissolves. Boil rapidly for 2 minutes, then add the rind and juice of one of the lemons, the chopped apple and the flaked almonds. Cook until thick. Leave to cool.

When cold, place the first layer of shortbread on a serving plate. Spread a third of the apple mixture on top, then repeat the layers, finishing with a layer of shortbread. Sift the icing sugar into a bowl. Add the rind and juice of the remaining lemon and mix to a smooth paste. If necessary, add hot water, a little at a time, to form a glossy, pouring consistency. Drizzle over the shortbread and chill overnight before serving.

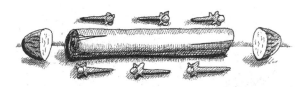

Eccles Cakes

SERVES 4

100 g/4 oz puff pastry (paste), thawed if
   frozen
25 g/1 oz/2 tbsp unsalted (sweet) butter,
   softened
25 g/1 oz/2 tbsp light brown sugar
25 g/1 oz/2 tbsp chopped mixed
   (candied) peel
Finely grated rind of ½ lemon
50 g/2 oz/⅓ cup currants
1 egg white, lightly beaten
A little caster (superfine) sugar, for
   sprinkling
Clotted Cream (see page 359 or use
bought), to serve

Roll out the pastry very thinly and
cut into eight rounds using a 9 cm/
3½ in plain cutter. Beat together the
butter and brown sugar and work in the
peel, lemon rind and currants. Divide
the mixture between the pastry rounds.
Draw the edges over the filling to form
a parcel. Turn over and roll gently with
a rolling pin until the currants show
through the pastry, taking care not to
break the surface. Transfer to a
dampened baking (cookie) sheet,
sealed sides down. Make two or three
slashes in the top of each to decorate.
Leave to stand for 15 minutes. Brush
with the egg white, then sprinkle with
caster sugar. Bake in a preheated oven
at 230°C/450°F/gas mark 8 for 12–15
minutes until puffy and golden. Serve
warm with Clotted Cream.

Lovers' Dessert

SERVES 6

175 g/6 oz/1½ cups plain (all-purpose)
   flour
100 g/4 oz/½ cup unsalted (sweet)
   butter, diced, plus extra for greasing
50 g/2 oz/¼ cup caster (superfine) sugar
Grated rind and juice of 1 orange
100 g/4 oz strawberries
150 ml/¼ pt/⅔ cup double (heavy) cream
Icing (confectioners') sugar, for dusting

Make a heart-shaped template out of
card or greaseproof (waxed) paper,
about 10 cm/4 in long. Sift the flour
into a bowl. Add the butter and rub in
with the fingertips until the mixture
resembles coarse breadcrumbs. Stir in
the sugar and orange rind and knead to
form a firm dough. Roll out on a lightly
floured surface and cut out 12 heart
shapes, using the template as a guide.
Re-roll the trimmings to make the last
ones. Place on two greased baking
(cookie) sheets. Cut a heart-shaped
hole, about 5 cm/2 in long, out of six of
the hearts, using a sharp pointed knife.
Bake in a preheated oven at 160°C/
325°F/gas mark 3 for about 20 minutes
until a pale golden brown. Leave to
cool, then transfer to a wire rack until
completely cold.
   Slice two or three of the strawberries
and mash the remainder. Whip the
cream and orange juice until stiff and
lightly fold in the mashed strawberries.
Place the uncut hearts on six serving
plates. Top with the strawberry cream,
then the cut heart shapes. Dust with
sifted icing sugar and decorate with the
sliced strawberries.

Jalousie

SERVES 6–8

225 g/8 oz puff pastry (paste), thawed if frozen
Raspberry jam (conserve)
Milk, to glaze
Icing (confectioners') sugar, for dusting
Whipped cream, to serve

Cut the pastry in half and roll out one half on a lightly floured surface to a rectangle about 20 × 25 cm/8 × 10 in. Transfer to a dampened baking (cookie) sheet. Roll out the other half to the same size. Dust with a little flour and fold in half lengthways. Make a series of cuts along the folded edge to within 2.5 cm/1 in of the open edge (like the paper lanterns you made as a child). Spread the uncut rectangle generously with jam to within 2.5 cm/1 in of the edges. Brush the edges with water, then carefully unfold the cut rectangle and lay over the top. Press the edges well together to seal, then knock up and flute with the back of a knife. Bake in a preheated oven at 220°C/425°F/gas mark 7 for 15 minutes or until golden and puffy. Dust with a little sifted icing sugar and serve warm with whipped cream.

Mincemeat Jalousie

SERVES 6–8

Prepare as for Jalousie, but substitute mincemeat for the jam (conserve), topping it with the finely grated rind of 1 small lemon. Brush with milk and sprinkle with demerara sugar before baking. Serve with Brandy Sauce (see page 356).

Pear and Chocolate Rolls

SERVES 6

410 g/14½ oz/1 large can of pears, drained, reserving the juice
50 g/2 oz/½ cup chocolate chips
6 sheets of filo pastry (paste)
Melted butter, for brushing
15 ml/1 tbsp cocoa (unsweetened chocolate) powder
15 ml/1 tbsp cornflour (cornstarch)
Granulated sugar, to taste

Chop the pears and mix with the chocolate chips. Brush a pastry sheet with a little butter and fold in half. Brush lightly again. Place a sixth of the pear mixture along the centre of one long edge. Fold in the sides, then roll up. Place on a lightly buttered baking (cookie) sheet. Repeat with the remaining pastry and pear mixture. Brush the rolls with a little melted butter and bake in a preheated oven at 200°C/400°F/gas mark 6 for about 15 minutes until crisp and golden.

Meanwhile, make the reserved pear juice up to 300 ml/½ pt/1¼ cups with water. Blend a little with the cocoa and cornflour in a saucepan. Add the remaining liquid. Bring to the boil and cook for 2 minutes, stirring all the time, until thickened. Sweeten to taste with granulated sugar. Serve the rolls hot with the chocolate sauce spooned over.

Strawberry Cream Buns

MAKES 10

For the choux pastry (paste):
*150 g/5 oz/1¼ cups plain (all-purpose)
   flour
A pinch of salt
300 ml/½ pt/1¼ cups water
50 g/2 oz/¼ cup butter
2 eggs, beaten*
For the filling and topping:
*225 g/8 oz strawberries
25 g/1 oz/2 tbsp caster (superfine)
   sugar
5 ml/1 tsp lemon juice
150 ml/¼ pt/⅔ cup double (heavy) cream
A little icing (confectioners') sugar, for
   dusting*

To make the pastry, sift the flour and salt on to a sheet of greaseproof (waxed) paper. Heat the water and butter in a saucepan until the butter melts. Bring to the boil. Remove from the heat and add the flour all in one go. Beat with a wooden spoon until the mixture is smooth and leaves the sides of the pan clean. Remove from the heat and allow to cool slightly. Beat in the eggs a little at a time, beating well after each addition, until smooth and glossy but still holding its shape. Put 15 ml/ 1 tbsp of the mixture, well apart, on greased baking (cookie) sheets. Bake in a preheated oven at 220°C/425°F/gas mark 7 for 10 minutes. Reduce the heat to 180°C/ 350°F/gas mark 4 and continue cooking for a further 20 minutes until puffy and a rich golden brown. Transfer to a wire rack and make a slit in the side of each bun to allow the steam to escape.

To make the filling, reserve a few strawberries with stalks on for decoration and chop the remainder. Mix with the caster sugar and lemon juice. Whip the cream until stiff and fold in the strawberry mixture. Use to fill the choux buns. Pile on a serving plate, dust with a little sifted icing sugar and decorate with the reserved strawberries.

Peach Cream Buns

MAKES 10

Prepare as for Strawberry Cream Buns, but substitute 3 skinned, chopped peaches for the strawberries.

Raspberry Cream Buns

MAKES 10

Prepare as for Strawberry Cream Buns, but substitute lightly crushed raspberries for the strawberries.

Melba Buns

MAKES 10

Prepare the buns as for Strawberry Cream Buns, but fill with Chantilly Cream (see page 358), and sliced white peaches, and drizzle with Brandied Loganberry Sauce (see page 349) just before serving.

Christmas Peach Parcels

MAKES ABOUT 8

8 sheets of filo pastry (paste)
75 g/3 oz/⅓ cup butter, melted
410 g/14½ oz/1 large can of peach
* halves, drained, reserving the juice*
450 g/1 lb/1 medium jar of mincemeat

For each parcel, brush a pastry sheet with a little butter. Fold in half widthways and brush again. Place a peach half in the centre and add a tablespoonful of mincemeat to the cavity. Draw the pastry up over the fruit to form a parcel. Transfer to a buttered baking (cookie) sheet. Brush with a little more butter. Repeat with the remaining peach halves. Bake in a preheated oven at 200°C/400°F/gas mark 6 for about 15 minutes until golden brown. Serve hot or cold with a little of the reserved juice poured over.

Christmas Pear Parcels

MAKES ABOUT 8

Prepare as for Christmas Peach Parcels, but substitute drained canned pear halves for the peaches.

Minted Christmas Crackers

MAKES 8

1 large cooking (tart) apple, chopped
100 g/4 oz/⅔ cup sultanas (golden
* raisins)*
30 ml/2 tbsp ground almonds
5 ml/1 tsp dried mint
15 ml/1 tbsp granulated sugar
225 g/8 oz puff pastry (paste), thawed
* if frozen*
Milk, to glaze
Caster (superfine) sugar, for sprinkling
45 ml/3 tbsp icing (confectioners')
* sugar*
Lemon juice
Silver cake balls, to decorate

Mix the apple with the sultanas, almonds, mint and granulated sugar. Roll out the pastry to a rectangle about 40 × 30 cm/16 × 12 in and cut into eight equal rectangles. Divide the apple mixture between the centre of each rectangle. Brush the long edges with milk. Roll up over the filling and place sealed-sides down on a dampened baking (cookie) sheet. Pinch the pastry firmly each side of the filling to form cracker shapes. Brush with milk and sprinkle with caster sugar. Bake in a preheated oven at 220°C/425°F/gas mark 7 for about 10 minutes until crisp and golden. Mix the icing sugar with a little lemon juice until the consistency of thick cream. Drizzle over the crackers, stud with silver balls and serve hot. (Or leave until cold and add the icing (frosting) and decoration when ready to serve.)

Chocolate Eclairs

MAKES ABOUT 9

For the choux pastry (paste):
65 g/2½ oz/generous ½ cup plain (all-purpose) flour
A pinch of salt
150 ml/¼ pt/⅔ cup water
25 g/1 oz/2 tbsp butter
1 egg, beaten
For the filling and topping:
150 ml/¼ pt/⅔ cup double (heavy) cream
10 ml/2 tsp caster (superfine) sugar
15 ml/1 tbsp cocoa (unsweetened chocolate) powder
100 g/4 oz/⅔ cup icing (confectioners') sugar
20 ml/4 tsp cold water

To make the pastry, sift the flour and salt on to a sheet of greaseproof (waxed) paper. Heat the water and butter in a saucepan until the butter melts. Bring to the boil. Remove from the heat and add the flour all in one go. Beat with a wooden spoon until the mixture is smooth and leaves the sides of the pan clean. Remove from the heat and allow to cool slightly. Beat in the egg a little at a time, beating well after each addition, until smooth and glossy but still holding its shape. Spoon into a piping bag fitted with a large plain tube (tip) and pipe lengths of choux, about 7.5 cm/3 in long, well apart on a greased baking (cookie) sheet. Cook in a preheated oven at 220°C/425°F/gas mark 7 for 15 minutes, then reduce the heat to 180°C/350°F/gas mark 4 and continue cooking for a further 10 minutes until puffy, crisp and golden. Transfer to a wire rack and make a slit in the side of each to allow steam to escape. Leave to cool.

To make the filling, whip the cream and sugar until peaking and use to fill the éclairs. Sift together the icing sugar and cocoa and mix with enough of the water to form a smooth paste. Spread over each éclair and leave until set.

Coffee Eclairs

MAKES ABOUT 9

Prepare as for Chocolate Eclairs, but for the icing use 10 ml/2 tsp instant coffee powder or granules instead of the cocoa (unsweetened chocolate) powder, dissolved in 15 ml/1 tbsp water, then blended into the sifted icing sugar.

Chocolate Profiteroles

SERVES 4

Make as for Chocolate Eclairs, but spoon or pipe the mixture into small balls on the baking (cookie) sheet. Bake in a preheated oven at 200°C/400°F/gas mark 6 for about 15–18 minutes until puffy, crisp and golden. Cool on a wire rack, fill with sweetened cream as for Chocolate Eclairs, but pile up and top with Simple Chocolate Sauce (see page 351) instead of the icing (frosting).

Belgian Profiteroles

SERVES 4

Prepare as for Chocolate Profiteroles, but top with Belgian Chocolate Sauce (see page 351) instead of Simple Chocolate Sauce.

Raspberry Profiteroles

SERVES 4

Prepare as for Chocolate Profiteroles (see page 117), but drizzle over hot All-year Raspberry Sauce (see page 348) instead of Simple Chocolate Sauce.

Apricot Profiteroles

SERVES 4–6

Prepare as for Chocolate Profiteroles (see page 117), but drizzle over Fresh Apricot Sauce (see page 348), instead of Simple Chocolate Sauce.

Gaelic Coffee Profiteroles

SERVES 4

Prepare as for Chocolate Profiteroles (see page 117), but fill either with sweetened cream or Coffee Cream (see page 358) and drizzle over Gaelic Coffee Sauce (see page 353).

Krümeltorte

SERVES 6–8

1 kg/2¼ lb cooking (tart) apples, thickly sliced
15 ml/1 tbsp water
175 g/6 oz/¾ cup caster (superfine) sugar, plus extra for sprinkling
10 ml/2 tsp vanilla essence (extract)
275 g/10 oz/2½ cups plain (all-purpose) flour
150 g/5 oz/⅔ cup unsalted (sweet) butter, diced
1 egg, beaten
Chantilly Cream (see page 358), to serve

Put the apple slices in a saucepan with the water, 100 g/4 oz/½ cup of the sugar and half the vanilla essence. Cook gently for 4 minutes until almost cooked. Leave to cool.

Put the flour in a bowl. Add the butter and rub in with the fingertips. Mix in the remaining sugar and vanilla essence. Mix with the egg and, if necessary, a little water, to form a firm dough. Knead gently on a lightly floured surface. Roll out half the pastry and use to line the base of a 20 cm/8 in springform tin (pan). Pile the apple mixture on the pastry (paste), leaving a border of pastry all round. Flatten the top of the fruit. Crumble the remaining pastry in the fingers and sprinkle round the apples and over the top. Bake in a preheated oven at 220°C/425°F/gas mark 7 for 30 minutes until golden brown. Carefully remove the sides of the tin, sprinkle with a little extra caster sugar and serve hot with Chantilly Cream.

Genuine Cherry Strudel

SERVES 8

For the strudel dough:
300 g/11 oz/2¾ cups plain (all-purpose) flour
2.5 ml/½ tsp salt
1 egg, beaten
30 ml/2 tbsp sunflower oil
120 ml/4 fl oz/½ cup lukewarm water
50 g/2 oz/¼ cup butter, melted
For the filling:
50 g/2 oz/1 cup cake crumbs
50 g/2 oz/½ cup ground almonds
900 g/2 lb cherries, stoned (pitted)
5 ml/1 tsp ground cinnamon
175 g/6 oz/¾ cup caster (superfine) sugar
Icing (confectioners') sugar, sifted

To make the dough, sift the flour and salt into a bowl. Add the egg and oil and mix with enough lukewarm water to form a ball. Turn out on to a floured board and knead until smooth and elastic. Wrap loosely in clingfilm (plastic wrap) and leave in the bowl for 1 hour to rest. Place the dough on a large floured cloth (such as a tablecloth or sheet) and roll out to a rectangle about 5 mm/¼ in thick. Then, using the knuckles, gently stretch the dough from the centre underneath until it is very large and wafer thin (don't worry if you make the odd hole). (If possible, work on a table that you can move all round, but you can use the cloth to turn to dough round to work the other side.) Trim the edges to a rectangle about 60 × 40 cm/24 × 16 in and brush all over with melted butter.

To make the filling, mix the crumbs and almonds together and scatter over the surface. Mix the cherries with the cinnamon and caster sugar and spread over to within 5 cm/2 in of the edges. Fold the edges in over the filling, then use the cloth to help roll up the strudel from one of the long sides. Transfer to a buttered baking (cookie) sheet, curving the strudel into a horseshoe shape. Brush with any remaining butter. Bake in a preheated oven at 200°C/400°F/gas mark 6 for about 40 minutes until golden and cooked through. Dust with the icing sugar and serve warm, or leave until cold and carefully transfer to a large serving plate.

Apfelstrudel

SERVES 8

Prepare as for Genuine Cherry Strudel, but substitute 900 g/2 lb cooking (tart) apples, chopped, and 100 g/4 oz/⅔ cup sultanas (golden raisins) for the cherries and add the finely grated rind of ½ lemon mixed with the fruit.

Mocha Eclairs

MAKES 8

For the choux pastry (paste):
65 g/2½ oz/⅔ cup plain (all-purpose) flour
A pinch of salt
50 g/2 oz/¼ cup hard block margarine
150 ml/¼ pt/⅔ cup water
2 eggs, beaten
For the filling and topping:
50 g/2 oz/½ cup plain (semi-sweet) chocolate
200 g/7 oz/scant 1 cup fromage frais
5 ml/1 tsp instant coffee powder or granules
15 ml/1 tbsp water
100 g/4 oz/⅔ cup icing (confectioners') sugar

To make the pastry, sift the flour and salt on to a sheet of greaseproof (waxed) paper. Heat the margarine and water in a small saucepan until the fat melts. Bring to the boil. Remove from the heat and add the flour all in one go.

Beat with a wooden spoon until the mixture is smooth and leaves the sides of the pan clean. Remove from the heat and allow to cool slightly. Beat in the eggs a little at a time, beating well after each addition, until smooth and glossy but still holding its shape. Spoon into a piping bag fitted with a large plain tube (tip). Pipe strips of the mixture about 13 cm/5 in long, well apart to allow for rising, on to a greased baking (cookie) sheet. Bake in a preheated oven at 200°C/400°F/gas mark 6 for about 30 minutes until puffy, crisp and golden. Transfer to a wire rack and make a slit in the side of each to allow steam to escape. Leave to cool.

To make the filling, melt the chocolate in a bowl either over a pan of hot water or briefly in a microwave. Cool slightly, then beat in the fromage frais. Blend the coffee with the water and stir in the sifted icing sugar. Fill the éclairs with the chocolate cheese and place on a serving plate. Spread the icing (frosting) over the tops. Chill until ready to serve and eat within 3 hours.

Rum Baba

SERVES 6

*225 g/8 oz/2 cups plain (all-purpose)
  flour*
2.5 ml/½ tsp salt
10 ml/2 tsp easy-blend dried yeast
4 eggs, beaten
150 ml/¼ pt/⅔ cup milk, hand-hot
*100 g/4 oz/½ cup butter, melted, plus
  extra for greasing*
45 ml/3 tbsp currants
225 g/8 oz/1 cup granulated sugar
300 ml/½ pt/1¼ cups water
10 ml/2 tsp lemon juice
60 ml/4 tbsp dark rum
*Whipped cream and glacé (candied)
  cherries, to decorate*

Sift the flour and salt into a bowl. Stir
in the yeast. Make a well in the
centre and add the eggs, milk and
butter. Gradually work in the flour, then
beat to form a smooth batter. Butter a
large ring tin (pan) and sprinkle in the
currants. Add the batter, cover and
leave in a warm place until the batter
has risen to the top of the tin.

Cook in a preheated oven at
200°C/400°F/gas mark 6 for about
40 minutes until golden brown. Leave
in the tin.

Put the sugar in a saucepan with
the water. Heat gently until the sugar
has dissolved. Bring to the boil and boil
for 5 minutes until syrupy. Stir in the
lemon juice and rum. Prick the warm
baba all over with a skewer. Spoon the
syrup over until thoroughly soaked.
Leave to cool. Turn out on to a serving
plate. Fill the centre with whipped
cream and decorate with glacé cherries
before serving.

Individual Rum Babas

SERVES 6–8

Prepare as for Rum Baba, but turn
the mixture into six to eight
individual Yorkshire pudding tins (pans)
or flan tins (pie pans). Cook in a
preheated oven at 220°C/425°F/gas
mark 7 for 15–20 minutes, then
continue as for Rum Baba.

Fresh Peach Dumplings

SERVES 4

*225 g/8 oz/2 cups plain (all-purpose)
  flour*
*100 g/4 oz/½ cup unsalted (sweet)
  butter, diced*
30 ml/2 tbsp caster (superfine) sugar
1 egg, beaten
15 ml/1 tbsp light brown sugar
5 ml/1 tsp ground cinnamon
15 ml/1 tbsp ground almonds
*4 peaches, skinned, halved and stoned
  (pitted)*
Melted butter, for brushing
*Classic Custard Sauce (see page 354), to
  serve*

Put the flour in a bowl. Add the
butter and rub in with the fingertips.
Stir in half the caster sugar. Mix with
enough egg to form a firm dough.
Knead gently on a lightly floured
surface. Wrap in clingfilm (plastic wrap)
and chill for 30 minutes.

Mix together the brown sugar,
cinnamon and almonds. Spoon into the
cavities of the peaches. Roll out the
pastry (paste) and cut into quarters.
Re-form the peach halves in pairs and
place on the centres of the rounds.
Brush the edges of the pastry with
water and gather up over the fruit to
cover completely. Place on a baking
(cookie) sheet, sealed-sides down.
Brush with a little melted butter and
sprinkle with the remaining caster
sugar. Bake in a preheated oven at
200°C/400°F/gas mark 6 for about
30 minutes until a rich golden brown.
Serve warm with Classic Custard Sauce.

Crisp Creations

Thin, lacy Brandy Snap Baskets filled with whipped Chantilly Cream and fresh strawberries, melting Cigarettes Russes with a sensuous chocolate mousse, crisp but light Meringue Nests oozing with luscious fillings, or melting Shortbread Triangles to add glorious texture to a velvety syllabub. These and many more evocative delights can be found right here.

Palmiers

MAKES 24

75 g/3 oz/⅓ cup caster (superfine) sugar
225 g/8 oz puff pastry (paste), thawed
* if frozen*
25 g/1 oz/2 tbsp butter, melted

Sprinkle the work surface with a little sugar. Roll out the pastry thinly to about 25 × 30 cm/10 × 12 in. Brush with a little melted butter and sprinkle liberally with sugar. Fold the long sides in so they nearly meet in the middle, then flip one folded side over the other. Wrap in clingfilm (plastic wrap) and chill for at least 30 minutes.

Using a sharp knife, cut into 24 slices and place on a wetted baking (cookie) sheet. Bake in a preheated oven at 220°C/425°F/gas mark 7 for 10 minutes. Turn each palmier over and bake for a further 3–4 minutes until crisp and golden brown all over. Sprinkle immediately with more sugar and transfer to a wire rack to cool. Store in an airtight tin.

Arlettes

MAKES 16

225 g/8 oz puff pastry (paste) in a
* block, thawed if frozen*
Icing (confectioners') sugar, for dusting

Cut the pastry block into 1 cm/½ in slices. Roll out each slice as thinly as possible on a board dusted with sifted icing sugar. Cut each thin rectangle in half. Dust the pastry thickly with icing sugar, then transfer as many as possible to two dampened baking (cookie) sheets. Bake near the bottom of the oven at 180°C/350°F/gas mark 4 for 6 minutes, then remove from the oven and dust

again with more icing sugar. Return to the top of the oven at 220°C/425°F/gas mark 7 for a further 3 minutes or until shiny and brown. Cool on a wire rack. Repeat with the remaining pastry pieces. Store in an airtight container.

Brandy Snaps

MAKES 16

50 g/2 oz/¼ cup butter
50 g/2 oz/¼ cup caster (superfine) sugar
30 ml/2 tbsp golden (light corn) syrup
50 g/2 oz/½ cup plain (all-purpose) flour
2.5 ml/½ tsp ground ginger
5 ml/1 tsp brandy
Finely grated rind of ½ lemon (optional)
Whipped cream (optional), to serve

Line two baking (cookie) sheets with non-stick baking parchment. Melt the butter, sugar and syrup on a saucepan over a gentle heat. Sift in the flour and ginger and add the brandy and lemon rind, if using. Mix thoroughly until well blended. Drop 5 ml/1 tsp amounts of the mixture 10 cm/4 in apart on the baking sheets and bake in a preheated oven at 180°C/350°F/gas mark 4 for 7–10 minutes until golden brown and bubbly.

Meanwhile, grease the handle of a wooden spoon. Remove the first sheet of biscuits from the oven and quickly lift off the baking sheet with a fish slice. Mould loosely around the wooden spoon handle, one at a time, then cool on a wire rack. If the biscuits harden before you get a chance to mould them, return to the oven for a few minutes to soften. Store in an airtight container for up to 1 week. Serve with a little whipped cream piped or spooned into each end of the brandy snaps, if liked.

Brandy Snap Baskets

MAKES 8

1 quantity of Brandy Snap mixture
Fresh fruit, to serve

Prepare as for brandy snaps, but put 10 ml/2 tsp amounts of the mixture well apart on the lined baking (cookie) sheets. Mould over a greased orange or small individual bowl instead of the spoon handle. Serve filled with fresh fruit.

Lemon Baskets

SERVES 8

2 lemons
175 g/6 oz/¾ cup granulated sugar
45 ml/3 tbsp water
2 egg whites
250 ml/8 fl oz/1 cup double (heavy) cream, whipped
8 Brandy Snap Baskets

Thinly pare the rind from 1 lemon. Cut the rind into very thin strips and boil in water for 3 minutes. Drain, rinse with cold water and drain again. Reserve for decoration. Finely grate the rind of the second lemon. Squeeze the juice from both lemons. Put the sugar, water, lemon rind and juice in a saucepan. Heat gently, stirring, until the sugar has dissolved. Bring to the boil and boil until thick and syrupy but not coloured. Whisk the egg whites until stiff. Gradually whisk into the hot syrup, whisking all the time, until the mixture is cold. Fold in the cream. Chill until stiffened. Spoon into the Brandy Snap Baskets and decorate with the reserved lemon strips.

Chocolate Sundae Baskets

SERVES 8

8 Brandy Snap Baskets
8 large scoops of Dark Chocolate Ice Cream (see page 189, or use bought)
150 ml/¼ pt/⅔ cup whipping cream, whipped
1 quantity Simple Chocolate Sauce (see page 351), cold
2 chocolate flake bars, crumbled

Put the Brandy Snap Baskets on individual serving plates. Add a large scoop of ice cream to each. Pile on the whipped cream and drizzle with Simple Chocolate Sauce. Sprinkle with the crumbled flake and serve.

Strawberry Baskets

SERVE 8

8 Brandy Snap Baskets
2 quantities Chantilly Cream (see page 358)
175 g/6 oz small strawberries, halved
2 quantities Smooth Strawberry Sauce (see page 349)
A little icing (confectioners') sugar, for dusting

Put the baskets on individual serving plates. Spoon in the Chantilly Cream. Top with strawberries. Spoon the sauce around the base of each basket and dust the tops with a little sifted icing sugar.

Brandy Hazelnut Cones

MAKES 10

4 eggs, separated
75 g/3 oz/⅓ cup caster (superfine) sugar
1 egg yolk
40 g/1½ oz/⅓ cup plain (all-purpose) flour
40 g/1½ oz/⅓ cup cornflour (cornstarch)
A pinch of salt
40 g/1½ oz/3 tbsp unsalted (sweet)
*   butter, melted*
150 ml/¼ pt/⅔ cup double (heavy) cream
150 ml/¼ pt/⅔ cup hazelnut (filbert)
*   yoghurt*
15 ml/1 tbsp brandy
1 kiwi fruit, cut into 5 slices
Toasted chopped hazelnuts, to decorate

Line two baking (cookie) sheets with non-stick baking parchment. Whisk the egg whites until stiff and fold in half the caster sugar. Whisk the five egg yolks with the remaining sugar until thick and pale. Sift the flours and salt over the surface and fold in with the butter. Fold in the egg whites. Put five spoonfuls of the mixture well apart on each baking sheet and spread each one out slightly, still keeping it fairly round. Bake in a preheated oven at 220°C/ 425°F/gas mark 7 for about 10 minutes or until lightly golden and turning brown at the edges. Lift off with a fish slice and quickly shape each into a cone, preferably round cream horn tins (pans). Leave to cool, covered in a clean tea towel (dish cloth).

Whip together the cream, yoghurt and brandy until stiff. Spoon into the cold cones. Halve the kiwi fruit slices. Decorate each cone with a half slice of kiwi fruit and a few toasted chopped hazelnuts.

Strawberry Cones

MAKES 10

Prepare as for Brandy Hazelnut Cones, but substitute strawberry yoghurt and orange liqueur for the hazelnut (filbert) yoghurt and brandy. Decorate each with a whole or halved strawberry instead of kiwi fruit and omit the nuts.

Apricot Cones

MAKES 10

Prepare as for Brandy Hazelnut Cones, but substitute apricot yoghurt and amaretto for the hazelnut (filbert) yoghurt and brandy. Decorate with chopped ready-to-eat dried apricots and a few toasted flaked (slivered) almonds instead of the kiwi fruit and hazelnuts.

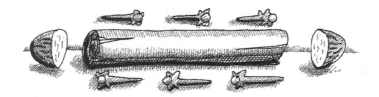

Shortbread Triangles

MAKES 8

75 g/3 oz/¾ cup plain (all-purpose) flour
25 g/1 oz/¼ cup rice flour or cornflour (cornstarch)
A pinch of salt
65 g/2½ oz/scant ⅓ cup caster (superfine) sugar
100 g/4 oz/½ cup butter, diced

Sift the flours and salt into a bowl. Add 50 g/2 oz/¼ cup of the sugar and the butter and rub in with the fingertips until the mixture resembles fine breadcrumbs. Press into an 18 cm/7 in sandwich tin (pan). Prick all over with a fork and mark into eight equal triangles. Chill for 1 hour.

Bake in a preheated oven at 150°C/300°F/gas mark 2 for about 1 hour until a very pale golden brown. Sprinkle with the remaining caster sugar. Leave to cool in the tin, then transfer to a wire rack and break or cut into triangles before serving.

Viennese Fingers

MAKES 12

150 g/5 oz/⅔ cup butter
75 g/3 oz/½ cup icing (confectioners') sugar, sifted
150 g/5 oz/1¼ cups plain (all-purpose) flour, sifted
100 g/4 oz/1 cup plain (semi-sweet) chocolate
A few drops of vanilla essence (extract)

Grease two baking (cookie) sheets. Beat 100 g/4 oz/½ cup of the butter with 25 g/1 oz/3 tbsp of the icing sugar, then work in the flour. Place in a piping bag with a large star tube (tip)

and pipe twelve 5 cm/2 in long strips on to each baking sheet. Bake in a preheated oven at 190°C/375°F/gas mark 5 for 10–15 minutes until a pale golden brown. Transfer to a wire rack to cool.

Melt the chocolate in a bowl over a pan of hot water or in the microwave. Beat together the remaining butter and icing sugar with a few drops of vanilla essence. Sandwich the biscuits together in pairs with the butter icing, then dip one end of each in melted chocolate. When hardened, dip the other ends in the chocolate. When set, store in an airtight container for up to 1 week.

Cigarettes Russes

MAKES ABOUT 16

100 g/4 oz/½ cup caster (superfine) sugar
2 egg whites, lightly beaten
50 g/2 oz/¼ cup unsalted (sweet) butter, melted
50 g/2 oz/½ cup plain (all-purpose) flour, sifted
4 drops of vanilla essence (extract)

Whisk the sugar into the egg whites until smooth. Stir in the butter and flour and add the vanilla essence. Grease and flour a baking (cookie) sheet. Spread spoonfuls into small oblongs well apart on the sheet. Bake in a preheated oven at 200°C/400°F/gas mark 6 for 5–6 minutes until lightly golden. Remove from the oven, remove one at a time from the baking sheet and place upside-down on the work surface. Quickly roll tightly round a wooden spoon handle, holding firmly with the hand until it sets. Cool on a wire rack. Repeat with the remaining mixture. Store in an airtight container.

Amaretti Biscuits

MAKES ABOUT 24

90 g/3½ oz/scant 1 cup ground almonds
175 g/6 oz/¾ cup caster (superfine)
  sugar
2.5 ml/½ tsp vanilla essence (extract)
2 egg whites
30 ml/2 tbsp amaretto
Flaked (slivered) almonds
Icing (confectioners') sugar, for dusting

Beat the almonds with the sugar, vanilla essence and one of the egg whites until smooth. Beat in the liqueur. Whisk the second egg white until stiff and fold into the mixture with a metal spoon. Divide the mixture into walnut-sized pieces and roll into balls. Place on a baking (cookie) sheet lined with baking parchment and press a flaked almond on top of each ball. Bake in a preheated oven at 180°C/350°F/gas mark 4 for about 25 minutes or until golden brown. Leave the biscuits (cookies) on the baking sheet for 5 minutes then dust with sifted icing sugar and transfer to a wire rack to cool. Store in an airtight container.

Almond Macaroons

MAKES 12

2 egg whites
150 g/5 oz/⅔ cup caster (superfine)
  sugar
A few drops of almond essence
  (extract)
150 g/5 oz/1¼ cups ground almonds
Rice paper
12 whole blanched almonds, to
  decorate

Lightly whisk the egg whites. Add the sugar, almond essence and almonds. Mix to a paste. Roll into 12 balls and place well apart on a baking (cookie) sheet lined with rice paper. Top each ball with an almond. Bake in a preheated oven at 190°C/375°F/gas mark 5 for about 20 minutes until pale biscuit coloured. Leave to cool for 10 minutes, then cut or tear the rice paper round each macaroon and transfer to a wire rack to cool completely. Store in an airtight container.

Hazelnut Macaroons

MAKES 12

Prepare as for Almond Macaroons but substitute vanilla essence (extract) for almond and ground hazelnuts (filberts) for ground almonds. Decorate with whole hazelnuts instead of almonds.

Coconut Macaroons

MAKES 12

Prepare as for Almond Macaroons, but substitute vanilla essence (extract) for almond and desiccated (shredded) coconut for ground almonds. Decorate with halved glacé (candied) cherries instead of whole nuts.

Chocolate Macaroons

MAKES 12

Prepare as for Almond Macaroons, but substitute 25 g/1 oz/¼ cup cocoa (unsweetened chocolate) powder for the same amount of ground almonds.

Lemon Fingers

MAKES 24

50 g/2 oz/¼ cup butter, softened
50 g/2 oz/¼ cup caster (superfine) sugar
1 small egg, beaten
100 g/4 oz/1 cup plain (all-purpose) flour
2.5 ml/½ tsp baking powder
A pinch of salt
Finely grated rind of 1 small lemon

Beat together the butter and sugar until light and fluffy. Beat in the egg. Sift the flour, baking powder and salt over the surface, sprinkle over the lemon rind and fold in with a metal spoon. Shape the dough into a soft ball, wrap in clingfilm (plastic wrap) and chill for 30 minutes.

Roll out thinly on a lightly floured surface and cut into fingers. Transfer to buttered baking (cookie) sheets and bake in a preheated oven at 180°C/350°F/gas mark 4 for about 15 minutes or until a very pale biscuit colour. Do not allow to brown much. Allow to cool slightly, then transfer to a wire rack to cool completely. Store in an airtight tin.

Langues de Chat

MAKES 24

100 g/4 oz/½ cup butter, softened, plus extra for greasing
100 g/4 oz/½ cup caster (superfine) sugar
A few drops of vanilla essence (extract)
3 egg whites
100 g/4 oz/1 cup plain (all-purpose) flour
25 g/1 oz/¼ cup cornflour (cornstarch)

Beat together the butter and sugar until light and fluffy. Beat in a few drops of vanilla essence. Whisk the egg whites until stiff and fold in with a metal spoon. Sift the flours over the surface and lightly fold in with a metal spoon. Use to fill a piping bag fitted with a large plain tube (tip). Pipe small finger lengths a little apart on buttered baking (cookie) sheets. Bake in a preheated oven at 180°C/350°F/gas mark 4 for about 20 minutes or until brown round the edges. Do not overcook – they should still be pale on top. Allow to cool slightly, then transfer to a wire rack until completely cold. Store in an airtight container.

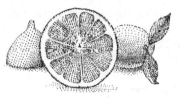

Almond Tuiles

MAKES ABOUT 20

75 g/3 oz/⅓ cup unsalted (sweet) butter
75 g/3 oz/⅓ cup caster (superfine) sugar
50 g/2 oz/½ cup plain (all-purpose)
flour, sifted
75 g/3 oz/¾ cup blanched almonds, cut
into thin strips

Beat together the butter and sugar until light and fluffy. Work in the flour and almonds. Put 5 ml/1 tsp mounds of the mixture well apart on a baking (cookie) sheet, lined with non-stick baking parchment and flatten with a wet palette knife. Bake in a preheated oven at 200°C/400°F/gas mark 6 for about 7 minutes until lightly golden. Remove from the oven. Lift off the baking sheet with a palette knife and curl round a rolling pin until firm. Cool on a wire rack. Store in an airtight container.

Anzacs

MAKES 24

100 g/4 oz/½ cup granulated sugar
50 g/2 oz/½ cup plain (all-purpose) flour
50 g/2 oz/½ cup wholemeal flour
40 g/1½ oz/⅓ cup chopped hazelnuts
(filberts)
40 g/1½ oz/⅓ cup desiccated (shredded)
coconut
50 g/2 oz/¼ cup butter or margarine,
plus extra for greasing
15 ml/1 tbsp golden (light corn) syrup
2.5 ml/½ tsp bicarbonate of soda
(baking soda)
15 ml/1 tbsp milk

Mix together the sugar, flours, hazelnuts and coconut in a bowl. Heat the butter or margarine and syrup in a saucepan, stirring, until the fat melts. Blend the bicarbonate of soda with the milk. Add the liquids to the flour mixture and mix thoroughly. Shape into 24 small balls and place well apart on greased baking (cookie) sheets. Bake in a preheated oven at 180°C/350°F/gas mark 4 for about 20 minutes until spread out and golden. Transfer to wire racks to cool and harden. Store in an airtight container.

Almond Petits Fours

MAKES ABOUT 30

2 egg whites
100 g/4 oz/1 cup ground almonds
50 g/2 oz/¼ cup caster (superfine) sugar
1.5 ml/¼ tsp almond essence (extract)
Rice paper
Glacé (candied) cherries, angelica leaves
and whole blanched almonds, to
decorate

Whisk the egg whites until stiff. Fold in the almonds, sugar and almond essence. Spoon into a piping bag fitted with a large star tube (tip) and pipe small rosettes and 's' shapes on to rice paper on baking (cookie) sheets. Decorate some with halved glacé cherries, some with angelica leaves and some with blanched almonds. Bake in a preheated oven at 180°C/350°F/gas mark 4 for 20 minutes until golden brown. Leave until cold, then cut the rice paper round each petit four. Store in an airtight tin.

Ginger Snaps

MAKES ABOUT 30

100 g/4 oz/1 cup self-raising (self-rising)
* flour*
5 ml/1 tsp ground ginger
5 ml/1 tsp ground mace
50 g/2 oz/¼ cup unsalted (sweet) butter,
* diced, plus extra for greasing*
40 g/1½ oz/3 tbsp caster (superfine)
* sugar*
15 ml/1 tbsp black treacle (molasses)
Milk, to mix

Sift the flour, ginger and mace into a
bowl. Rub in the butter and stir in
the sugar. Warm the treacle with 15 ml/
1 tbsp milk and stir in, adding enough
extra milk to form a stiff dough. Knead
gently on a lightly floured surface. Roll
out thinly and cut into 30 rounds, using
a 5 cm/2 in cutter. Transfer to greased
baking (cookie) sheets and bake in a
preheated oven at 180°C/350°F/gas
mark 4 for about 10 minutes until
golden brown. Leave to cool for 5
minutes, then transfer to a wire rack to
cool completely. Store in an airtight tin.

White Meringue Nests

MAKES 8 NESTS

You can use bought meringue nests for
quick individual desserts but the real
things are in a completely different class
– sophisticated and sumptuous.

3 egg whites
175 g/6 oz/¾ cup caster (superfine)
* sugar*
A few drops of vanilla essence (extract)

Lay a sheet of baking parchment on a
dampened baking (cookie) sheet.
Whisk the egg whites until stiff. Add
15 ml/1 tbsp of the sugar and the
vanilla and whisk again until stiff and
glossy. Gradually whisk in half the
remaining sugar, then fold in the
remainder with a metal spoon. Spoon
eight round heaps of the mixture a little
apart on the baking sheet and hollow
out slightly in the centres to form nests.
Rough up the mixture slightly round
the tops. Bake in a preheated oven at
110°C/225°F/gas mark ¼ for 2–3 hours
or until crisp but still white. Remove
from the oven and leave to cool.
Carefully lift off the paper and store in
an airtight container.

Brown Meringue Nests

MAKES 8

3 egg whites
A pinch of cream of tartar
175 g/6 oz/¾ cup soft dark brown sugar

Whisk the egg whites with the
cream of tartar until stiff. Whisk
in the sugar 15 ml/1 tbsp at a time,
whisking well between each addition,
until stiff and glossy. Use to fill a piping
bag fitted with a large star tube (tip)
and pipe eight nests well apart on
baking parchment on a baking (cookie)
sheet. Alternatively, spoon the mixture
into mounds and hollow out to form
nests. Bake in a preheated oven at
120°C/250°F/gas mark ½ for about 1
hour or until crisp and dry. Turn off the
oven and leave there until cold. Store in
an airtight container until ready to use.

Bite-sized Meringues

MAKES ABOUT 24

Prepare the meringue mixture as for White or Brown Meringue Nests (see page 131). Put small spoonfuls on baking parchment on two baking (cookie) sheets. Bake as for the nests until crisp and dry. Cool, then store in an airtight container.

Fresh Strawberry Nests

MAKES 8

8 White or Brown Meringue Nests (see page 131)
250 ml/8 fl oz/1 cup double (heavy) or whipping cream
30 ml/2 tbsp orange liqueur or orange juice
175–225 g/6–8 oz strawberries, sliced

Place the meringue nests on serving plates. Whip the cream with the orange liqueur until stiff. Spoon into the meringues and top with sliced strawberries. Serve straight away.

Fresh Raspberry Nests

SERVES 8

Prepare as for Fresh Strawberry Nests, but substitute amaretto for orange liqueur and whole raspberries for the strawberries.

Fresh Peach Nests

SERVES 8

Prepare as for Fresh Strawberry Nests, but substitute peach liqueur or brandy for the orange liqueur and four sliced peaches for the strawberries.

Ginger Cream Nests

SERVES 4

150 ml/¼ pt/⅔ cup double (heavy) cream
2 pieces of stem ginger in syrup, finely chopped
4 Brown Meringue Nests (see page 131)

Whip the cream until stiff. Fold in half the ginger. Spoon into the nests and sprinkle with the remaining ginger.

Florentines

MAKES ABOUT 30

100 g/4 oz/½ cup caster (superfine) sugar
90 g/3¾ oz/scant ½ cup unsalted (sweet) butter
100 g/4 oz/1 cup chopped mixed nuts
25 g/1 oz/¼ cup chopped mixed (candied) peel
10 glacé (candied) cherries, chopped
30 ml/2 tbsp sultanas (golden raisins), chopped
15 ml/1 tbsp double (heavy) cream, whipped
175 g/6 oz/1½ cups plain (semi-sweet) chocolate, or half plain and half white chocolate

Put the sugar and butter in a saucepan and heat gently, stirring, until melted, then boil for 1 minute. Remove from the heat. Stir in the nuts, peel, cherries and sultanas. Fold in the whipped cream. Allow to cool slightly. Put small mounds of the mixture, well apart, on baking parchment on baking (cookie) sheets, four or five on each. Bake in a preheated oven at 190°C/375°F/gas mark 5 for about 10 minutes or until golden and bubbling. Remove from the oven, leave to cool briefly, then lift from the baking sheet and cool on a wire rack.

When all the Florentines are cooked, melt the chocolate in a bowl over hot water (or the two chocolates separately). Spread the base of each with chocolate and ripple the surface with the prongs of a fork. Place with the chocolate-coated bases facing up on wire racks to set. Store in an airtight container.

Raspberry Nut Meringue

SERVES 8

3 eggs, separated
250 g/9 oz/generous 1 cup caster (superfine) sugar
Oil, for greasing
45 ml/3 tbsp finely chopped hazelnuts (filberts)
Finely grated rind and juice of 1 lime
250 ml/8 fl oz/1 cup double (heavy) cream
225 g/8 oz raspberries

Whisk the egg whites until stiff. Whisk in 75 g/3 oz/⅓ cup of the sugar and whisk again until stiff and glossy. Fold in a further 75 g/3 oz/⅓ cup of the sugar. Spoon the meringue mixture into an oiled, fairly large, shallow ovenproof serving dish. Spread out so it covers the base fairly thinly and the sides more thickly. Sprinkle with the hazelnuts. Bake in a preheated oven at 110°C/225°F/gas mark ¼ for several hours until crisp.

Put the egg yolks in a bowl with the remaining sugar and the lime rind and juice. Whisk over a pan of hot water until thick and pale. Whip the cream until peaking. Fold about two-thirds into the custard. Pour into the meringue and chill for at least 6 hours, preferably overnight. Pile the raspberries on top and decorate with the remaining whipped cream.

Nectarine Meringue

SERVES 8

Prepare as for Raspberry Meringue, but substitute 3 sliced nectarines for the raspberries and the finely grated rind and juice of 1 lemon for the lime.

Strawberry Meringue

SERVES 8

Prepare as for Raspberry Meringue (see page 133), but substitute sliced strawberries for the raspberries and the finely grated rind and juice of 1 small orange for the lime.

Frosty Mountain

SERVES 8–10

4 egg whites
225 g/8 oz/1 cup caster (superfine) sugar
600 ml/1 pt/2½ cups whipping cream
2 × 300 g/2 × 11 oz/2 medium cans of lychees, drained
410 g/14½ oz/1 large can of pear halves, drained

Line two baking (cookie) sheets with baking parchment and draw an 18 cm/7 in round on each using a plate as a guide. Whisk the egg whites until stiff. Add half the sugar and whisk again until stiff and glossy. Fold in the remaining sugar. Divide the mixture between the two rounds and spread out evenly. Bake in a preheated oven at 110°C/225°F/gas mark ¼ for 2 hours until crisp but still white. Remove from the oven and leave to cool.

Whip the cream until peaking. Take out about 60 ml/4 tbsp for decoration. Chop the fruit, reserving a few whole lychees and one pear half for decoration. Mix the chopped fruit with the cream and use to sandwich the meringue rounds together on a serving plate. Decorate the top with the reserved whipped cream, a few whole lychees and thick slices of pear.

Strawberry Italian Meringue Basket

SERVES 6

3 large egg whites
175 g/6 oz/1 cup icing (confectioners') sugar
1 quantity Chantilly Cream (see page 358)
350 g/12 oz strawberries, halved
Mint sprigs, to decorate

Line two baking (cookie) sheets with baking parchment, draw a 23 cm/9 in circle on each. Lightly whisk the egg whites. Sift a little of the icing sugar over the surface and whisk in. Repeat until all the sugar has been added, whisking all the time. Place the bowl over a pan of hot water and continue whisking for about 5 minutes until the meringue is thick, stiff and glossy. Put about a third of the meringue in a piping bag fitted with a large star tube (tip). Pipe a ring round the edge of one of the circles. Fill the bag with the remaining meringue and pipe a ring round the outside of the second circle, then continue piping to fill in this circle (this will be the base). Bake the ring on the shelf below the disc in a preheated oven at 140°C/275°F/gas mark 1 for 1½ hours, then turn off the oven and leave the meringue there to cool completely.

When ready to serve, place the meringue disc on a serving plate. Spread a little of the Chantilly Cream round the edge and stick the ring on top. Fill the centre with the remaining Chantilly Cream and top with the halved strawberries. Decorate with a few mint sprigs and serve.

Raspberry Italian Meringue Basket

SERVES 6

Prepare as for Strawberry Italian Meringue Basket, but substitute raspberries for the strawberries.

Apricot Italian Meringue Basket

SERVES 6

Prepare as for Strawberry Italian Meringue Basket, but substitute 550 g/1¼ lb/1 very large can of apricot halves, drained, for the strawberries. Decorate with a few toasted flaked (slivered) almonds instead of mint sprigs.

Pear Italian Meringue Basket

SERVES 6

Prepare as for Strawberry Italian Meringue Basket, but substitute 550 g/1¼ lb/1 very large can of pear quarters, drained, for the strawberries and drizzle with cold Simple Chocolate Sauce (see page 351) to decorate. Omit the mint sprigs.

Kiwi Pavlova

SERVES 8

4 egg whites
225 g/8 oz/1 cup caster (superfine) sugar
15 ml/1 tbsp cornflour (cornstarch)
1.5 ml/¼ tsp vanilla essence (extract)
10 ml/2 tsp vinegar
Whipped cream
3–4 kiwi fruit, sliced

Whisk the egg whites until stiff. Gradually whisk in the sugar, then the cornflour, vanilla and vinegar. Spoon in a large circle on baking parchment on a baking (cookie) sheet, making a slight hollow in the centre. Bake in a preheated oven at 150°C/300°F/gas mark 2 for 1½ hours until a pale biscuit colour, crisp on the outside and slightly fluffy in the middle. Leave to cool. Transfer to a serving plate, fill the centre with whipped cream and top with the kiwi fruit.

Strawberry Pavlova

SERVES 8

Prepare as for Kiwi Pavlova, but substitute 175 g/6 oz small strawberries, halved, for the kiwi fruit.

Mandarin and Raspberry Pavlova

SERVES 8

Prepare as for Kiwi Pavlova, but substitute 100 g/4 oz raspberries and 300 g/11 oz/1 medium can of mandarins, drained, for the kiwi fruit.

Apricot Custard Pavlova

SERVES 6

2 eggs, separated
5 ml/1 tsp cornflour (cornstarch)
5 ml/1 tsp vinegar
5 ml/1 tsp almond essence (extract)
175 g/6 oz/¾ cup caster (superfine)
*   sugar*
25 g/1 oz/¼ cup plain (all-purpose) flour
150 ml/¼ pt/⅔ cup milk
430 g/15½ oz/1 large can of apricot
*   halves, drained, reserving the juice*
150 ml/¼ pt/⅔ cup whipping cream,
*   whipped*
15 ml/1 tbsp amaretto
Toasted flaked (slivered) almonds, to
*   decorate*

Line a baking (cookie) sheet with non-stick baking parchment and mark a 20 cm/8 in circle on it. Whisk the egg whites until stiff. Mix together the cornflour, vinegar and almond essence and whisk into the egg whites with 150 g/5 oz/⅔ cup of the caster sugar. Continue whisking until stiff and glossy. Spoon on to the round on the baking sheet, hollowing out the mixture slightly in the centre to form a nest. Bake in a preheated oven at 150°C/300°F/gas mark 2 for 5 minutes, then reduce the heat to 140°C/275°F/gas mark 1 and continue cooking for 1 hour. Turn off the oven and leave in there to cool completely.

When cold, carefully remove from the paper and transfer to a serving plate. Meanwhile, blend the flour and remaining sugar with a little of the milk in a saucepan. Stir in the remaining milk and apricot juice. Bring to the boil and cook for 2 minutes, stirring all the time. Whisk in the egg yolks and cook gently for 1 minute. Remove from the heat and whisk in the amaretto. Cover with a circle of wet greaseproof (waxed) paper and leave until cold.

Fold in the whipped cream. Spoon into the cold Pavlova. Arrange the apricot halves attractively over the top and scatter with a few toasted, flaked almonds.

Meringue Shells Chantilly

MAKES 9 FILLED MERINGUES

3 egg whites
175 g/6 oz/¾ cup caster (superfine) sugar
300 ml/½ pt/1¼ cups double (heavy) cream
20 ml/4 tsp icing (confectioners') sugar
A few drops of vanilla essence

Line two baking (cookie) sheets with non-stick baking parchment. Put the egg whites in a large bowl (preferably stainless steel). Whisk until so stiff that the bowl can be held upside down without the egg whites slipping out. Add half the caster sugar and whisk again until stiff and glossy. Lightly fold in the remainder with a metal spoon. Take out 15 ml/1 tbsp quantities of the mixture and gently work the top of the mixture against the side of the bowl to smooth the surface. Use a second spoon to scoop the meringue gently out of the first spoon on to the baking sheet. Repeat until you have 18 shells (nine on each sheet). Dry out in the oven at 110°C/225°F/gas mark ¼ for about 2 hours or until they are crisp and turning a very pale biscuit colour. Lightly press the flat base of each meringue to create a small hollow, then replace on the baking sheets, hollowed-sides up. Return to the oven for a further 20–30 minutes until completely dry. Transfer to a wire rack to cool.

Whip the cream with the icing sugar and vanilla essence until peaking. Use a teaspoon to fill the hollows in the meringues with the sweetened cream, then sandwich them together in pairs. Serve within two hours of filling. The unfilled meringues can be stored in an airtight container for up to 10 days.

Chocolate Meringue Shells

MAKES 9 FILLED MERINGUES

Prepare as for Meringue Shells Chantilly, but fill with 1 quantity of Chocolate Cream (see page 357) instead of the sweetened cream.

Coffee Meringue Shells

MAKES 9 FILLED MERINGUES

Prepare as for Meringue Shells Chantilly, but fill with 1 quantity of Coffee Cream (see page 358) instead of the sweetened cream.

Brandied Meringue Shells

MAKES 9 FILLED MERINGUES

Prepare as for Meringue Shells Chantilly, but fill with 1 quantity of Brandy Cream (see page 358) instead of the sweetened cream. Place on a wire rack and drizzle the meringues with a little melted plain (semi-sweet) chocolate to decorate, if liked. Leave to set and chill before serving.

Tia Maria Meringue Shells

MAKES 9 FILLED MERINGUES

Prepare as for Meringue Shells Chantilly, but fill with 1 quantity of Tia Maria Cream (see page 359) instead of the sweetened cream. Serve with slices of fresh pear on one side.

Burnt Almond Meringue Shells

MAKES 9 FILLED MERINGUES

Prepare as for Meringue Shells Chantilly (see page 137), but fill with 1 quantity of Burnt Almond Cream (see page 357) instead of the sweetened cream. Serve with fresh cherries on the side.

Crème de Menthe Meringue Shells

MAKES 9 FILLED MERINGUES

Prepare as for Meringue Shells Chantilly (see page 137), but fill with 1 quantity of Crème de Menthe Cream (see page 358) instead of the sweetened cream. Stud the cream, where visible,with quartered thin chocolate mints.

Framboise Meringue Shells

MAKES 9 FILLED MERINGUES

Prepare as for Meringue Shells Chantilly (see page 137), but fill with 1 quantity of Framboise Cream (see page 359) instead of the sweetened cream. Serve a pile of fresh raspberries on the side.

Chocolate Orange Pavlova

SERVES 8

3 egg whites
225 g/8 oz/1 cup caster (superfine) sugar
15 ml/1 tbsp cornflour (cornstarch)
30 ml/2 tbsp cocoa (unsweetened chocolate) powder
5 ml/1 tsp vinegar
150 ml/¼ pt/⅔ cup double (heavy) cream
45 ml/3 tbsp chocolate spread
3–4 oranges, segmented

Whisk the egg whites until stiff. Gradually mix in the sugar, whisking well after each addition, until stiff and glossy. Sift the cornflour and cocoa over the surface, add the vinegar and fold in gently with a metal spoon. Spread into a 23 cm/9 in circle on a piece of baking parchment on a baking (cookie) sheet, hollow out the centre slightly. Bake in a preheated oven at 140°C/275°F/gas mark 1 for about 2 hours until crisp. Leave to cool.

Carefully slide off the paper and transfer to a serving plate. Whip the cream until peaking and fold in the chocolate spread. Spread over the pavlova and decorate with the orange segments. Serve within 2 hours.

Chocolate Raspberry Pavlova

SERVES 8

Prepare as for Chocolate Orange Pavlova, but use 175 g/6 oz raspberries instead of the oranges for decoration and serve with Fresh Raspberry Sauce (see page 348).

Sweet Set Menus

Jellies, set creams and custards are amongst some of the most popular desserts. They can be made hours or even days in advance, which makes them particularly useful when entertaining. I have called for ordinary powdered gelatine in the recipes but do use a vegetarian equivalent if you prefer. Make sure you follow the directions on the packet for how to dissolve it as the procedure can vary from product to product.

Fresh Blackcurrant Jelly

SERVES 6

850 g/1¾ lb blackcurrants
45 ml/3 tbsp water
Juice of ½ lemon
100 g/4 oz/½ cup caster (superfine)
*   sugar, plus extra for frosting*
20 g/¾ oz/1½ tbsp powdered gelatine
Fromage frais, to serve

Strip 750 g/1½ lb of the blackcurrants from their stalks and place in a saucepan with the measured water. Simmer until the fruit pops and is becoming pulpy. Purée in a blender or food processor, then pass through a sieve (strainer). Return to the saucepan. Make the lemon juice up to 600 ml/ 1 pt/2½ cups with water. Add to the pan with the sugar. Heat gently, stirring until the sugar has dissolved. Tilt the pan and sprinkle on the gelatine. Stir until the gelatine has completely dissolved. Allow to cool slightly. Turn into a glass serving dish. Leave until cold, then chill until set. Meanwhile, dip the reserved blackcurrant sprigs in cold water, then dust liberally with caster sugar. Leave to dry. Lay the frosted blackcurrant sprigs on top of the set jelly before serving with fromage frais.

Fresh Redcurrant Jelly

SERVES 6

Prepare as for Fresh Blackcurrant Jelly but substitute redcurrants for the blackcurrants. Use the juice of half an orange instead of lemon, if liked.

Port and Claret Jelly

SERVES 6

100 g/4 oz/½ cup granulated sugar
15 ml/1 tbsp redcurrant jelly (clear
*   conserve)*
5 cm/2 in piece of cinnamon stick
1 whole clove
250 ml/8 fl oz/1 cup water
250 ml/8 fl oz/1 cup claret
15 ml/1 tbsp powdered gelatine
150 ml/¼ pt/⅔ cup ruby port
15 ml/1 tbsp brandy
Cigarettes Russes (see page 127), to
*   serve*

Put the sugar, redcurrant jelly, cinnamon stick, clove and water in a saucepan and heat gently, stirring, until the sugar has dissolved completely. Pour a little of the claret into a small bowl. Sprinkle the gelatine over and leave to soften for 5 minutes. Stand the bowl over a pan of hot water and heat, stirring until the gelatine has completely dissolved (or dissolve briefly in the microwave). Stir in the remaining claret, then stir into the flavoured water with the port and brandy. Leave until cold, then strain into six wine goblets and chill until set. Serve with Cigarettes Russes.

Raspberry and Apple Jelly

SERVES 4

10 ml/2 tsp powdered gelatine
30 ml/2 tbsp lemon juice
1 packet of raspberry-flavoured jelly
(jello)
750 ml/1¼ pts/3 cups medium-sweet
cider
1 eating (dessert) apple
100 g/4 oz raspberries

Put the gelatine in a small bowl with the lemon juice and leave to soften for 5 minutes. Stand the bowl in a pan of hot water until dissolved (or dissolve briefly in the microwave). Meanwhile, break up the jelly and dissolve in 300 ml/½ pt/1¼ cups of the cider in a saucepan or in the microwave. Peel the apple and cut into very thin matchsticks. Add to the dissolved jelly. Stir in the dissolved gelatine and the remaining cider. Divide the raspberries between four glass serving dishes. Pour the jelly and apple mixture over. Leave until completely cold, then chill until set.

Cloudy Apple Jelly

SERVES 4

450 g/1 lb cooking (tart) apples, sliced
Apple juice
Caster (superfine) sugar, to taste
15 ml/1 tbsp powdered gelatine

Put the apple slices in a saucepan with 30 ml/2 tbsp apple juice. Cover and cook very gently until pulpy. Sweeten to taste with caster sugar. Meanwhile, sprinkle the gelatine over 30 ml/2 tbsp apple juice in a small bowl. Leave to soften for 5 minutes, then stir into the stewed apple until completely dissolved. Purée in a blender or food processor. Turn into a measuring jug. Make up to 600 ml/1 pt/2½ cups with apple juice. Turn into a wetted 600 ml/1 pt/2½ cup jelly (jello) mould and chill until set. Dip the mould briefly in hot water, then turn out on to a serving plate.

Claret and Cranberry Jelly

SERVES 4

75 g/3 oz/⅓ cup caster (superfine) sugar
30 ml/2 tbsp lemon juice
30 ml/2 tbsp brandy
150 ml/¼ pt/⅔ cup cranberry juice
15 ml/1 tbsp powdered gelatine
300 ml/½ pt/1¼ cups claret
Whipped cream, to serve

Put the sugar, lemon juice, brandy and cranberry juice in a saucepan. Sprinkle over the gelatine and leave to soften for 5 minutes. Heat gently until the gelatine has dissolved completely. Do not allow to boil. Stir in the claret. Pour into a jelly mould. Allow to cool, then chill until set. Turn out on to a serving plate and serve with whipped cream.

Fresh Orange Jelly

SERVES 4

Finely grated rind and juice of 1 orange
15 ml/1 tbsp powdered gelatine
Pure orange juice

Put the orange rind and juice in a measuring jug and sprinkle the gelatine over. Leave to soften for 5 minutes. Stand the jug in a pan of hot water and stir until the gelatine has dissolved (or dissolve briefly in the microwave). Make up to 600 ml/1 pt/2½ cups with orange juice. Turn into a 600 ml/1 pt/2½ cup jelly (jello) mould and chill until set. Dip the mould briefly in hot water, then turn out on to a serving plate and serve cold.

Fresh Lemon Jelly

SERVES 4

Prepare as for Fresh Orange Jelly, but use the finely grated rind and juice of 2 lemons and make up with pure pineapple juice instead of orange juice.

Season's Greetings Jelly

SERVES 10

225 g/8 oz/1 packet of dried fruit salad
50 g/2 oz/½ cup glacé (candied) cherries
300 ml/½ pt/1¼ cups water
15 ml/1 tbsp brandy
2 packets of black cherry-flavoured jelly (jello) tablets
50 g/2 oz/½ cup plain (semi-sweet) chocolate
A few holly leaves
150 ml/¼ pt/⅔ cup double (heavy) cream, whipped

Soak the fruit salad and cherries in the water and brandy for at least 3 hours or overnight. Drain off any liquid into a measuring jug. Chop the fruit, discarding any stones (pits). Make up the liquid to 1 litre/1¾ pts/4¼ cups with water. Dissolve the jelly tablets in a little of the measured liquid in a saucepan (or dissolve in a bowl in the microwave). Remove from the heat and stir in the remaining liquid. Chill until the consistency of egg white. Stir in the chopped fruit and turn into a wetted 1.25 litre/2¼ pt/5½ cup pudding basin. Chill until set.

Meanwhile, melt the chocolate in a small bowl over a pan of hot water or in the microwave. Dip the holly leaves in the chocolate to coat on one side. Leave to dry on a sheet of greaseproof (waxed) paper. Chill until firm, then gently peel off the holly to leave chocolate leaves. When ready to serve, dip the basin briefly in a bowl of hot water, then turn the jelly out on to a serving plate. Pipe or spoon the whipped cream on top and decorate with the chocolate holly leaves.

Lemon Custard Jelly

SERVES 4

Thinly pared rind and juice of 2 lemons
75 g/3 oz/⅓ cup granulated sugar
500 ml/17 fl oz/2¼ cups water
15 ml/1 tbsp powdered gelatine
3 eggs
Almond Tuiles (see page 130), to serve

Put the lemon rind in a saucepan with the sugar and all but 45 ml/ 3 tbsp of the water. Heat gently, stirring, until the sugar has dissolved. Bring to the boil, remove from the heat and leave to stand for 15 minutes. Meanwhile, sprinkle the gelatine over the remaining water in a small bowl. Leave to soften for 5 minutes, then stand the bowl in a pan of hot water and stir until the gelatine has completely dissolved (or dissolve in the microwave). Remove the lemon rind from the syrup. Whisk the eggs until blended. Whisk in the syrup. Stand the bowl over a pan of hot water and cook, stirring, until the mixture looks thickened and creamy. Stir in the dissolved gelatine and the lemon juice. Pour into a wetted 600 ml/1 pt/2½ cup jelly (jello) mould. Chill until set. Dip the mould briefly in hot water, then turn out on to a serving plate and serve with Almond Tuiles.

Pear Pleasure

SERVES 6

300 ml/½ pt/1¼ cups water
60 ml/4 tbsp clear honey
2 limes
4 pears, peeled, quartered and cores
*   removed*
1 packet of lime-flavoured jelly (jello)
Maraschino cherries, drained
*   thoroughly and halved*
300 ml/½ pt/1¼ cups apple juice
Crème fraîche, to serve

Put the water and honey in a saucepan. Finely grate the rind and squeeze the juice from one of the limes and add to the pan. Add the pear quarters and simmer gently until the pears look almost transparent and are just tender. Leave until cold. Strain off the liquid and, if necessary, make up to 300 ml/½ pt/1¼ cups with water. Return the liquid to the saucepan. Add half the jelly and heat until dissolved. Pour this mixture into a round glass serving dish and chill until set. Arrange the pears in a starburst pattern over the top and decorate in between with halved maraschino cherries. Meanwhile, dissolve the remaining jelly in the apple juice. Leave until cold but not set. Pour gently over the pears and cherries and chill until set. Serve with crème fraîche.

Chocolate Crème Caramel

SERVES 4–5

100 g/4 oz/½ cup granulated sugar
60 ml/4 tbsp water
2 large eggs
15 ml/1 tbsp caster (superfine) sugar
375 ml/13 fl oz/1½ cups milk
75 g/3 oz/¾ cup plain (semi-sweet)
* chocolate, broken into pieces*
A few drops of vanilla essence (extract)

Put the granulated sugar in a heavy-based pan with half the water. Heat gently, stirring, until the sugar has dissolved completely. Do not allow to boil. When dissolved, bring to the boil and boil until the mixture turns a rich golden brown. Do not stir. Remove from the heat and immediately add the remaining water (be careful as it will splutter). Return to the heat and heat gently, stirring, until the caramel has dissolved. Pour into four individual soufflé dishes. Place the dishes in a roasting tin (pan) containing 2.5 cm/ 1 in boiling water. Beat together the eggs and caster sugar until thick and pale. Put the milk in a saucepan with the chocolate and vanilla. Heat gently, stirring until the chocolate has melted, then bring to the boil. Pour over the eggs and sugar and mix well. Strain over the caramel. Bake in a preheated oven at 140°C/275°F/gas mark 1 for about 45 minutes or until set. Leave until cold, then chill overnight. Turn out on to serving plates before serving.

Chocolate Amaretti Creams

SERVES 4

4 Amaretti Biscuits (see page 128, or
* use bought), crushed*
250 g/9 oz/2¼ cups plain (semi-sweet)
* chocolate*
30 ml/2 tbsp glycerine
30 ml/2 tbsp amaretto
150 ml/¼ pt/⅔ cup double (heavy) cream
Single (light) cream, to serve

Line the bases of four ramekins (custard cups) with greaseproof (waxed) paper and divide the crushed biscuits between the dishes. Gently melt the chocolate with the glycerine and amaretto in a bowl over a pan of hot water or in the microwave. Whip the double cream until softly peaking. Stir 30 ml/2 tbsp of it into the chocolate mixture, then add the remainder, folding in with a metal spoon until well blended. Turn into the ramekins and level the surfaces. Chill until set. Run a round-bladed knife round the edge of each, cover with a serving plate and invert on to the plate. Remove the paper and serve with single cream.

Vanilla Creams

SERVES 4

15 ml/1 tbsp powdered gelatine
30 ml/2 tbsp water
300 ml/½ pt/1¼ cups milk
100 g/4 oz/½ cup caster (superfine)
*   sugar*
2 egg yolks
7.5 ml/1½ tsp cornflour (cornstarch)
2.5 ml/½ tsp vanilla essence (extract)
150 ml/¼ pt/⅔ cup double (heavy) cream
Oil, for greasing
Fresh Raspberry Sauce (see page 348),
*   to serve*
Mint sprigs, to decorate

Sprinkle the gelatine over the water in
a small bowl. Leave to stand for
5 minutes to soften. Reserve 15 ml/
1 tbsp of the milk and heat the
remainder in a saucepan with the sugar.
Heat gently, stirring until the sugar
dissolves, then bring almost to the boil.
Blend the remaining milk with the egg
yolks, cornflour and vanilla essence.
Whisk in a little of the hot milk. Return
to the saucepan and cook over a gentle
heat, whisking all the time, for
2–3 minutes until thick and smooth.
Stir in the gelatine until completely
dissolved. Leave to cool.

Whip the cream until softly peaking
and fold into the cold but not set
custard. Turn into four lightly oiled
individual moulds and chill until set.
When ready to serve, loosen the edges
with a round-bladed knife and turn out
on to serving plates. Pour a pool of
Fresh Raspberry Sauce around and
serve decorated with mint sprigs.

Crème Caramel

SERVES 6

175 g/6 oz/¾ cup granulated sugar
60 ml/4 tbsp cold water
6 egg yolks
15 ml/1 tbsp caster (superfine) sugar
750 ml/1¼ pts/3 cups single (light) cream
5 ml/1 tsp vanilla essence (extract)

Put the granulated sugar in a pan
with the water. Heat gently, stirring,
until the syrup is clear and all the sugar
has dissolved. Bring to the boil and boil
without stirring until the mixture is a
rich caramel colour. Pour into six
ramekins (custard cups). Beat the egg
yolks with the caster sugar in a bowl
over a pan of hot water until thick and
pale. Whisk in the cream and vanilla
essence. Cook gently, stirring, until the
custard thickens. Strain over the
caramel, allow to cool, then chill until
set. Either turn out on to serving plates
or eat as they are.

Quark Dessert

SERVES 4

1 packet of any fruit-flavoured jelly
*   (jello)*
450 ml/¾ pt/2 cups water
100 g/4 oz/½ cup quark

Make up the jelly using the water
and chill until the consistency of
egg white. Whisk in the quark and chill
until set.

Austrian Rice Mould

SERVES 6

65 g/2½ oz/generous ¼ cup short-grain
*   rice*
600 ml/1 pt/2½ cups milk
40 g/1½ oz/3 tbsp granulated sugar
10 ml/2 tsp powdered gelatine
45 ml/3 tbsp water
1 eating (dessert) apple, finely diced
15 ml/1 tbsp lemon juice
250 g/9 oz strawberries
150 ml/¼ pt/⅔ cup crème fraîche
15 ml/1 tbsp icing (confectioners')
*   sugar*

Put the rice in a saucepan with the milk. Bring to the boil, reduce the heat and simmer gently for 20 minutes or until tender. Stir in the granulated sugar. Meanwhile, put the gelatine in a small bowl and stir in the cold water. Leave to soften for 5 minutes. Stir into the hot rice and continue to stir until completely dissolved. Leave to cool.

Toss the diced apple in lemon juice to prevent browning. Quarter half the strawberries. Mix with the apple into the crème fraîche, then fold into the cold but not set rice. Turn into a 900 ml/1½ pt/3¾ cup jelly (jello) mould and chill until set. Meanwhile, purée the remaining strawberries in a blender or food processor with the icing sugar. Dip the jelly mould briefly into hot water, then turn the rice dessert out on to a serving plate. Spoon the strawberry sauce around and serve.

Jellied Fruit Layer

SERVES 6

1 packet of lemon-flavoured jelly (jello)
450 ml/¾ pt/2 cups water
15 ml/1 tbsp lemon juice
225 g/8 oz/1 cup medium-fat soft
*   cheese*
75 g/3 oz/⅓ cup unsalted (sweet) butter,
*   softened*
50 g/2 oz/⅓ cup icing (confectioners')
*   sugar*
50 g/2 oz maraschino cherries, plus
*   extra for decoration*
25 g/1 oz/¼ cup chopped pistachio nuts
30 ml/2 tbsp milk
8 trifle sponges, diced

Break up the jelly and place in a saucepan with 150 ml/¼ pt/⅔ cup of the water and heat gently, stirring, until dissolved. Stir in the remaining water and the lemon juice (or place in a bowl and dissolve in the microwave). Beat together the cheese, butter and icing sugar until soft and fluffy. Quarter the cherries and stir into the mixture with the pistachios and milk.

Put a layer of sponge in the base of a 900 ml/1½ pt/3¾ cup jelly (jello) mould. Pour enough jelly over to soak completely. Top with half the cheese mixture. Cover with more sponge, then top up to the sponge with jelly. Add the remaining cheese mixture, then the remaining sponge. Pour the remaining jelly over. Cover and chill until set. Dip the mould briefly in hot water, then turn out on to a serving dish and decorate with a few maraschino cherries.

Apricot Fruit Topper

SERVES 4

1 packet of lemon-flavoured jelly (jello)
Boiling water
410 g/14½ oz/1 large can of apricots,
drained, reserving the juice
Finely grated rind of 1 lemon
150 ml/¼ pt/⅔ cup apricot yoghurt
150 g/5 oz green and black grapes, in
tiny bunches
100 g/4 oz cherries, in pairs or threes
1 egg white
Caster (superfine) sugar, for frosting

Break up the jelly and place in a measuring jug. Make up to 150 ml/ ¼ pt/⅔ cup with boiling water. Stir until completely dissolved. Make up to 300 ml/½ pt/1¼ cups with the apricot juice. Purée the apricots in a blender or food processor and stir into the jelly with the lemon rind and yoghurt. Mix well, then turn into a 600 ml/1 pt/ 2½ cup wetted jelly (jello) mould. Chill until set.

Meanwhile, brush all the clusters of fruit with egg white and sprinkle liberally with caster sugar. Place on a sheet of greaseproof (waxed) paper to set. Turn the jelly out on to a serving dish and arrange clusters of fruit on top and round the edge. Serve cold.

Apricot Crisp

SERVES 6

100 g/4 oz/⅔ cup dried apricots
450 ml/¾ pt/2 cups water
15 ml/1 tbsp granulated sugar
1 packet of orange-flavoured jelly (jello)
15 ml/1 tbsp lemon juice
25 g/1 oz/2 tbsp butter
15 ml/1 tbsp golden (light corn) syrup
50 g/2 oz/1 cup bran flakes
150 ml/¼ pt/⅔ cup crème fraîche

Put the apricots in a pan with the water and leave to soak overnight. Stir in the sugar. Bring to the boil, reduce the heat and simmer gently for 10 minutes until the fruit is tender. Remove the fruit with a draining spoon and leave to cool.

Dissolve the jelly in the juice in the saucepan. Stir in the lemon juice. Purée the apricots in a blender or food processor with some of the dissolved jelly. Stir in the remainder and pour into six glasses. Chill until set.

Melt the butter and syrup in a saucepan and stir in the bran flakes. Spread the crème fraîche over the set apricot mixture. Top with the buttery bran flake mixture and chill again until firm.

Jelly Berry Loaf

SERVES 8

15 ml/1 tbsp powdered gelatine
600 ml/1 pt/2½ cups pure orange juice
15 ml/1 tbsp caster (superfine) sugar
2 bananas
Lemon juice
8 strawberries, sliced
100 g/4 oz blueberries
100 g/4 oz raspberries

Sprinkle the gelatine over a little of the orange juice and the sugar in a small bowl. Leave to soften for 5 minutes. Stand the bowl in a pan of hot water and stir until the gelatine has dissolved completely. Stir into the remaining orange juice. Chill until on the point of setting.

Meanwhile, slice the bananas and toss in lemon juice to prevent browning. Pour a little of the orange mixture in the base of a 1.2 litre/2 pt/5 cup loaf tin (pan) or terrine. Arrange a layer of banana slices on top. Pour on more of the nearly set jelly (jello) and add a layer of sliced strawberries. Repeat with the blueberries, then the raspberries. Continue layering, finishing with a layer of the rest of the jelly. Chill until set. Dip the base of the tin briefly in hot water, then turn out on to a serving plate. Serve sliced.

Apple Chartreuse

SERVES 6

300 ml/½ pt/1¼ cups water
45 ml/3 tbsp granulated sugar
Thinly pared rind and juice of 1 lemon
4 cooking (tart) apples, thickly sliced
15 ml/1 tbsp powdered gelatine
Apple juice
Chantilly Cream (see page 358), to
serve

Put the water, sugar, lemon rind and juice in a saucepan. Heat gently, stirring, until the sugar has dissolved. Add the apple slices bring to the boil, reduce the heat and poach gently until the apples are translucent but still hold their shape. Lift out with a draining spoon and transfer to a 900 ml/1½ pt/ 3¾ cup mould. Stir the gelatine into the hot syrup and stir until completely dissolved. Strain into a measuring jug. Make up to 600 ml/1 pt/2½ cups with apple juice. Leave until cold, then chill until the consistency of egg white. Pour into the mould. Chill until set. Dip the base of the mould briefly in hot water, then turn out on to a serving plate and serve with Chantilly Cream.

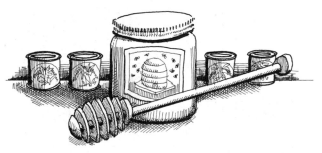

Cherries Jubilee

SERVES 6

1 packet of cherry-flavoured jelly (jello)
Boiling water
450 ml/¾ pt/2 cups American ginger ale
450 g/1 lb ripe cherries, stoned (pitted)
75 ml/5 tbsp double (heavy) cream,
  whipped
Crystallised (candied) ginger pieces, to
  decorate

Break up the jelly and place in a measuring jug. Make up to 150 ml/ ¼ pt/⅔ cup with boiling water. Stir until completely dissolved. Make up to 600 ml/1 pt/2½ cups with the ginger ale, stirring until well blended. Leave until cold, then chill until the consistency of egg white. Put the cherries in a 1 litre/1¾ pt/4¼ cup jelly (jello) mould. Pour the cherry jelly over. Chill until set. Dip the mould briefly in hot water and turn the jelly out on to a serving plate. Decorate round the base with swirls of whipped cream and top with pieces of crystallised ginger.

Milk Jelly

SERVES 4

1 packet of fruit flavoured jelly (jello)
150 ml/¼ pt/⅔ cup boiling water
450 ml/¾ pt/2 cups milk

Dissolve the jelly in the water and whisk in the milk. Turn into a wetted 600 ml/1 pt/2½ pt jelly (jello) mould or glass dish and chill until set. If set in a mould, dip briefly in hot water and turn the jelly out on to a serving plate.

Lemon Milk Jelly

SERVES 4

1 lemon
20 ml/4 tsp powdered gelatine
30 ml/2 tbsp water
600 ml/1 pt/2½ cups milk
50 g/2 oz/¼ cup caster (superfine) sugar
Yellow food colouring (optional)
Angelica leaves, to decorate

Finely grate the rind from the lemon. Cut off all the white pith, then cut the fruit into slices, then into quarters. Sprinkle the gelatine over the lemon rind and water in a small bowl. Leave to soften for 5 minutes. Stand the bowl in a pan of hot water and stir until the gelatine has dissolved completely. Warm the milk in a saucepan. Stir in the sugar until dissolved. Mix a little of the milk into the gelatine, then pour back into the remaining milk and stir well. Colour lightly with food colouring, if liked. Pour into a wetted 750 ml/ 1¼ pt/3 cup jelly (jello) mould and leave to cool. Chill until set. Turn the jelly out on to a serving plate, decorate with the quartered lemon slices and angelica leaves.

Orange Milk Jelly

SERVES 4

Prepare as for Lemon Milk Jelly, but substitute the finely grated rind of ½ orange for the lemon, use orange instead of yellow colouring, if liked, and decorate with quartered orange slices.

Lime Milk Jelly

SERVES 4

Prepare as for Lemon Milk Jelly (see page 149), but substitute the finely grated rind of 1 lime for the lemon, use a little green food colouring instead of yellow, if liked, and decorate with quartered lime slices.

Coffee Milk Jelly

SERVES 4

Prepare as for Lemon Milk Jelly (see page 149), but omit the lemon. Flavour the milk with 15 ml/1 tbsp instant coffee powder or granules, dissolved in the milk with the sugar. Decorate with whipped cream and chopped walnuts, if liked.

Honey and Lemon Milk Jelly

SERVES 4

Prepare as for Lemon Milk Jelly (see page 149), but substitute 30 ml/ 2 tbsp clear honey for the sugar.

Chocolate Milk Jelly

SERVES 4

Prepare as for Lemon Milk Jelly (see page 149), but omit the lemon. Flavour the milk with 75 g/3 oz/¾ cup grated or chopped plain (semi-sweet) chocolate when warming, stirring all the time, until melted and well blended. Decorate with whipped cream and grated chocolate, if liked.

Honey Milk Jelly

SERVES 4

Prepare as for Lemon Milk Jelly (see page 149), but omit the lemon. Substitute 30 ml/2 tbsp clear honey for the sugar and add a few drops of vanilla essence (extract). Decorate with whipped cream and roughly crushed chocolate honeycomb bar.

Avocado Smoothies

SERVES 6

1 packet of lemon-flavoured jelly (jello)
150 ml/¼ pt/⅔ cup water
300 ml/½ pt/1¼ cups apple juice
1 ripe avocado
5 ml/1 tsp lemon juice
60 ml/4 tbsp crème fraîche
4 small mint sprigs

Dissolve the jelly in the water according to the packet directions. Stir in the apple juice. Scoop out all the flesh from the avocado into a blender or food processor, discarding the stone (pit). Add the lemon juice and blend until smooth. Blend in the dissolved jelly mixture. Turn into four individual serving dishes and chill until set. Top each with a spoonful of crème fraîche and decorate with a mint sprig before serving.

Quark Orange Jelly

SERVES 4

1 packet of orange-flavoured jelly (jello)
Boiling water
Finely grated rind and juice of 1 orange
100 g/4 oz/½ cup quark
2 oranges, rinded, sliced and quartered

Break up the jelly and place in a measuring jug. Make up to 150 ml/ ¼ pt/⅔ cup with boiling water. Stir until completely dissolved. Add the orange rind and juice and make up to 450 ml/ ¾ pt/2 cups with cold water. Chill until the consistency of egg white. Stir in the quark and turn into glasses. Chill until set. Decorate all over the top with quartered orange slices.

Junket

SERVES 4

600 ml/1 pt/2½ cups full-cream milk
15 ml/1 tbsp caster (superfine) sugar
30 ml/2 tbsp brandy (optional)
5 ml/1 tsp essence of rennet (or
*   according to manufacturer's*
*   instructions, if different)*
Grated nutmeg
Clotted Cream (see page 359), to serve
*   (optional)*

Warm the milk with the sugar and brandy, if using, to blood heat (when it feels neither hot nor cold). Pour into a serving dish and stir in the rennet. Leave undisturbed until set. Dust with grated nutmeg and chill, if time. Serve with Clotted Cream, if liked.

Coffee Junket

SERVES 4

Prepare as for Junket, but flavour the milk with 15 ml/1 tbsp instant coffee powder or granules when adding the sugar. Omit the brandy, if preferred.

Chocolate Junket

SERVES 4

Prepare as for Junket, but omit the sugar and add 45 ml/3 tbsp drinking (sweetened) chocolate powder to the milk when warming. Make sure it is completely dissolved before adding the rennet. Omit the brandy, if preferred.

Orange Junket

SERVES 4

Prepare as for Junket, but omit the brandy and add the finely grated rind of ½ orange to the milk when warming. Colour with orange food colouring, if liked, and decorate with crystallised (candied) orange slices or slices of fresh orange.

Lemon Junket

SERVES 4

Prepare as for Junket, but omit the brandy and flavour the milk with the finely grated rind of 1 small lemon. Decorate with crystallised (candied) lemon slices or slices of the fresh lemon, if liked.

Strawberry Junket

SERVES 3–4

600 ml/1 pt/2½ cups milk
30 ml/2 tbsp strawberry milkshake
　syrup
10 ml/2 tsp caster (superfine) sugar
A few drops of pink food colouring
5 ml/1 tsp essence of rennet (or
　according to manufacturer's
　instructions, if different)
100 g/4 oz fresh or thawed frozen
　strawberries, sliced
Whipped cream, to decorate

Warm the milk with the syrup, sugar and food colouring too blood heat. Stir in the rennet. Pour into three or four glass serving dishes and leave at room temperature until set, then chill. Top each with a spoonful of strawberries and a dollop of whipped cream before serving.

Banana Junket

SERVES 3–4

Prepare as for Strawberry Junket, but substitute banana milkshake syrup for strawberry. Decorate the top with sliced bananas tossed in lemon juice instead of the strawberries.

French Blancmange

SERVES 6

600 ml/1 pt/2½ cups milk
100 g/4 oz/½ cup granulated sugar
2.5 ml/½ tsp almond essence (extract)
5 cm/2 in piece of cinnamon stick
25 ml/1½ tbsp powdered gelatine
45 ml/3 tbsp water
150 ml/¼ pt/⅔ cup double (heavy) cream
30 ml/2 tbsp Cognac
Apricot Jam Sauce (see page 347)
　(optional), to serve

Put the milk, sugar, almond essence and cinnamon stick in a saucepan and heat gently, stirring, until the sugar has dissolved. Leave to stand for 5 minutes. Meanwhile, sprinkle the gelatine over the water in a small bowl and leave to soften for 5 minutes. Stand the bowl in a pan of hot water and stir until the gelatine has dissolved. Stir into the milk. Remove the cinnamon stick. Blend in the cream and Cognac. Pour into a wetted 1 litre/1¾ pt/4¼ cup jelly (jello) mould and chill until set. Dip the mould briefly in hot water, then turn the jelly out on to a serving plate. Pour the Apricot Jam Sauce around the base, if using.

English Vanilla Blancmange

SERVES 4

45 ml/3 tbsp cornflour (cornstarch)
40 g/1½ oz/3 tbsp granulated sugar
600 ml/1 pt/2½ cups milk
Vanilla essence (extract), to taste
15 g/½ oz/1 tbsp unsalted (sweet) butter
Cream (optional), to serve

Blend the cornflour and sugar with a little of the milk until smooth. Bring the remaining milk just to the boil and pour over the cornflour mixture, stirring. Return to the pan, bring to the boil and cook for 2 minutes, stirring all the time, until thickened and smooth. Flavour with vanilla to taste and stir in the butter. Turn into a wetted 600 ml/ 1 pt/2½ cup jelly (jello) mould and leave until cold. Chill until set. Turn out on to a serving plate and serve cold with cream, if liked.

Vanilla Cream Blancmange

SERVES 4

Prepare as for English Vanilla Blancmange, but substitute 300 ml/ ½ pt/1¼ cups single (light) cream for half the milk.

Honey and Ginger Blancmange

SERVES 4

Prepare as for English Vanilla Blancmange, but substitute 30 ml/ 2 tbsp clear honey for the sugar and 2.5 ml/½ tsp ground ginger for the vanilla.

Syrup Blancmange

SERVES 4

Prepare as for English Vanilla Blancmange, but substitute 30 ml/ 2 tbsp golden (light corn) syrup for the sugar. Add a piece of cinnamon stick to the milk when warming and discard before setting.

Lemon Blancmange

SERVES 4

Prepare as for English Vanilla Blancmange, but substitute the finely grated rind of 1 lemon to the milk for the vanilla essence and add a few drops of yellow food colouring, if liked.

Orange Blancmange

SERVES 4

Prepare as for English Vanilla Blancmange, but substitute the finely grated rind of 1 orange for the vanilla and add a few drops of orange food colouring, if liked.

Chocolate Blancmange

SERVES 4

Prepare as for English Vanilla Blancmange, but add 75 g/3 oz/ ¾ cup grated chocolate to the milk when heating, stirring until completely melted, and continue as before.

Coffee Blancmange

SERVES 4

Prepare as for English Vanilla Blancmange (see page 153), but add 15 ml/1 tbsp instant coffee powder or granules to the milk when heating.

Strawberry Blancmange

SERVES 4

300 g/11 oz/1 medium can of strawberries in syrup
Cold milk
45 ml/3 tbsp cornflour (cornstarch)
Caster (superfine) sugar, to taste
Pink food colouring (optional)
15 g/½ oz/1 tbsp unsalted (sweet) butter
Smooth Strawberry Sauce (see page 349) (optional), to serve

Purée the can of strawberries and make up to 600 ml/1 pt/2½ cups with milk. Blend the cornflour with a little of the mixture in a saucepan, then stir in the remainder. Bring to the boil and cook for 2 minutes, stirring all the time, until thickened and smooth. Sweeten to taste, add a few drops of pink food colouring, if liked, and stir in the butter. Turn into a wetted 600 ml/1 pt/2½ cup wetted jelly (jello) mould. Leave until cold, then chill until set. Turn out on to a serving plate and serve with Smooth Strawberry Sauce, if liked.

Peach Jelly Cream

SERVES 4

6 ripe peaches, skinned, halved and stoned (pitted)
1 packet of lemon-flavoured jelly (jello)
Boiling water
300 ml/½ pt/1¼ cups single (light) cream

Purée four of the peaches in a blender or food processor. Slice the remainder and reserve for decoration. Break up the jelly and place in a measuring jug. Make up to 150 ml/¼ pt/⅔ cup with boiling water and stir until dissolved. Leave to cool, then stir in the peach purée and cream. Turn into a 600 ml/1 pt/2½ cup wetted jelly (jello) mould and chill until set. Dip the mould briefly in hot water, turn the jelly out on to a serving plate and decorate with the peach slices.

Apricot Jelly Cream

SERVES 4

Prepare as for Peach Jelly Cream, but substitute 450 g/1 lb ripe apricots for the peaches. Purée three-quarters of them and quarter the remainder for decoration.

Fluffy Frivolities

Mousses and hot and cold soufflés always make a spectacular finale to a special meal. They are not half as difficult to make as you may think – the skill lies in the lightness of hand when folding in the whisked egg whites or whipped cream to give a truly fluffy texture. Other gorgeous whips include syllabubs and Zabaglione   a warm froth of sweet wine and eggs that slips down like nectar.

Crème Marron

SERVES 6

2 egg whites
300 ml/½ pt/1¼ cups double (heavy)
   cream
60 ml/4 tbsp unsweetened chestnut purée
   (paste)
15 ml/1 tbsp brandy
50 g/2 oz marrons glacés, finely chopped
Caster (superfine) sugar
Cigarettes Russes (see page 127), to
   serve

Whisk the egg whites until stiff.
Whip the cream until peaking.
Fold the egg whites into the cream.
Beat the chestnut purée with the brandy
and half the marrons glacés. Reserve
45 ml/3 tbsp of the cream mixture for
decoration and fold the chestnut
mixture into the remainder. Sweeten to
taste with caster sugar. Spoon into six
glasses. Top with the reserved cream
and sprinkle with the remaining
marrons. Serve with Cigarettes Russes.

Foolproof Chocolate Mousse

SERVES 6

4 eggs, separated
200 g/7 oz/1¾ cups plain (semi-sweet)
   chocolate
75 ml/5 tbsp strong hot coffee
2.5 ml/½ tsp vanilla essence (extract)
A little whipped cream and grated
   chocolate, to decorate

Whisk the egg whites until stiff.
Break up the chocolate and place
in a food processor or blender. Run the
machine until the chocolate is
completely crushed. Add the hot coffee
and continue running the machine until
the mixture is smooth. Add the egg
yolks and vanilla essence and blend for
a further 1 minute. Pour the chocolate
mixture slowly over the whites and fold
in lightly but thoroughly. Spoon into six
individual dishes or a large serving dish
and chill until set. Top with a little
whipped cream and a sprinkling of
grated chocolate.

Meringue Fruit Crush

SERVES 4

300 ml/½ pt/1¼ cups double (heavy)
   cream
225 g/8 oz soft summer fruits
   (strawberries, raspberries,
   loganberries etc.)
100 g/4 oz meringues, lightly crushed
40 g/1½ oz/⅓ cup chopped toasted
   hazelnuts (filberts)
Grated chocolate, to decorate

Whip the cream until softly peaking.
Lightly crush the fruit. Layer the
fruit, meringue and nuts in four glasses.
Top with a layer of cream. Sprinkle with
grated chocolate and chill before
serving.

Lemon Honeycomb Mould

SERVES 6

15 ml/1 tbsp powdered gelatine
60 ml/4 tbsp water
2 eggs, separated
75 g/3 oz/⅓ cup caster (superfine) sugar
Finely grated rind and juice of 2 lemons
300 ml/½ pt/1¼ cups milk
Oil, for greasing
Crystallised (candied) lemon slices and angelica leaves, to decorate

Sprinkle the gelatine over the water in a small bowl and leave to soften for 5 minutes. Whisk together the egg yolks, sugar and lemon rind. Bring the milk to the boil and pour over the egg yolk mixture, whisking all the time. Return to the saucepan and cook, stirring, over a gentle heat until the custard thickens and coats the back of a spoon. Do not allow to boil. Remove from the heat and stir in the gelatine until completely dissolved. Strain in the lemon juice. Whisk the egg whites until stiff and fold into the mixture with a metal spoon. Pour into a lightly oiled 900 ml/1½ pt/3¾ cup fluted mould. Chill until set. Turn out on to a serving plate and decorate with crystallised lemon slices and angelica leaves before serving.

Vanilla Honeycomb Mould

SERVES 4–6

Prepare as for Lemon Honeycomb Mould, but substitute 5 ml/1 tsp vanilla essence (extract) for the lemon rind and juice.

Coffee Honeycomb Mould

SERVES 6

3 eggs, separated
125 g/4½ oz/generous ½ cup caster (superfine) sugar
450 ml/¾ pt/2 cups milk
15 ml/1 tbsp powdered gelatine
150 ml/¼ pt/⅔ cup water
20 ml/4 tsp instant coffee powder or granules
Chantilly Cream (see page 358), to serve

Whisk together the egg yolks and sugar in a bowl until thick and pale. Warm the milk until almost boiling and pour over the mixture. When well blended, return to the saucepan and cook, stirring, over a very gentle heat, until thickened. Do not allow to boil or the mixture will curdle. Meanwhile, sprinkle the gelatine over 60 ml/4 tbsp of the water in a small bowl. Leave to soften for 5 minutes. Stand the bowl in a pan of hot water and stir until the gelatine has dissolved completely (or dissolve in the microwave). Blend the coffee with the remaining water and stir into the custard with the dissolved gelatine. Whisk the egg whites until stiff and fold into the mixture with a metal spoon. Turn into a 1.2 litre/2 pt/5 cup wetted jelly (jello) mould and chill until set. Dip the mould briefly in hot water, then turn out on to a serving dish. The mixture should have separated into a clear jelly top and a fluffy base. Serve with Chantilly Cream.

Almond Melting Meringue

SERVES 6

Oil, for greasing
50 g/2 oz/½ cup sugared almond sweets
4 egg whites
100 g/4 oz/½ cup caster (superfine)
  sugar
1 quantity All-year Raspberry Sauce
  (see page 348), cooled

Oil a 15 cm/6 in soufflé dish or cake tin (pan). Reserve three almonds for decoration and crush the remainder. Whisk the egg whites until stiff. Lightly fold in the sugar with a metal spoon. Put 60–75 ml/4–5 tbsp of the meringue mixture in the tin. Sprinkle about 30 ml/2 tbsp of the crushed almonds over. Repeat the layers and finish with a layer of the meringue mixture. Tap the container sharply on the work surface to settle the mixture. Place in a roasting tin (pan) containing 2.5 cm/ 1 in boiling water. Bake in a preheated oven at 190°C/375°F/gas mark 5 for 30 minutes until risen and set. Leave to cool in the tin, then turn out on to a serving plate. Spoon a little of the raspberry sauce over and decorate with the reserved almonds. Serve the remaining sauce separately.

Café Crème

SERVES 6

15 ml/1 tbsp powdered gelatine
150 ml/¼ pt/⅔ cup strong black coffee
150 ml/¼ pt/⅔ cup milk
150 ml/¼ pt/⅔ cup single (light) cream
50 g/2 oz/⅓ cup semolina (cream of
  wheat)
75 g/3 oz/⅓ cup light brown sugar
2 eggs, separated
150 ml/¼ pt/⅔ cup double (heavy)
  cream, whipped
A little instant coffee powder, to
  decorate

Sprinkle the gelatine over the coffee in a small bowl and leave to soften for 5 minutes. Stand the bowl in a pan of hot water and stir until the gelatine has dissolved completely. Leave to cool. Put the milk and single cream in a saucepan and stir in the semolina. Stir until blended. Bring to the boil and cook for 3 minutes, stirring all the time, until thickened. Beat in the sugar and egg yolks, then stir in the gelatine mixture. Leave until cold and just beginning to set. Whisk the egg whites until stiff. Fold into the coffee mixture. Turn into a glass serving dish and chill until set. Cover with whipped cream and dust with instant coffee powder just before serving.

Crème au Citron

SERVES 6

Prepare as for Café Crème, but substitute the finely grated rind and juice of 1 lemon for the coffee, made up to 150 ml/¼ pt/⅔ cup with apple juice.

Crème à l'Orange

SERVES 6

Prepare as for Café Crème, but substitute the finely grated rind and juice of 1 orange for the coffee, made up to 150 ml/¼ pt/⅔ cup with pure orange juice. Decorate with crystallised (candied) orange slices and angelica leaves instead of the coffee powder.

Mocha Rum Mousse

SERVES 8

175 g/6 oz/1½ cups plain (semi-sweet) chocolate
7.5 ml/1½ tsp instant coffee powder or granules
15 ml/1 tbsp hot water
4 large eggs, separated
5 ml/1 tsp vanilla essence (extract)
300 ml/½ pt/1¼ cups double (heavy) cream
45 ml/3 tbsp rum
Grated chocolate, to decorate

Break up the chocolate and melt in a bowl over a pan of hot water, (or melt in the microwave). Dissolve the coffee in the water. Whisk into the egg yolks, then beat into the chocolate with the vanilla. Whisk the egg whites until stiff, then the cream and rum until peaking. Fold the cream, then the egg whites into the chocolate mixture. Turn into a glass serving dish. Chill for several hours until set. Decorate with a little grated chocolate before serving.

Lemon Curd Mousse

SERVES 6

7.5 ml/1½ tsp powdered gelatine
30 ml/2 tbsp water
3 eggs, separated
100 g/4 oz/½ cup caster (superfine) sugar
Grated rind and juice of 2 small lemons
65 g/2½ oz/generous ¼ cup butter
Mint sprigs, to decorate

Sprinkle the gelatine over the water in a small bowl. Leave to soften for 5 minutes, then stand the bowl in a pan of gently simmering water until dissolved (or heat briefly in the microwave). Whisk the egg yolks with 25 g/1 oz/2 tbsp of the sugar until thick and pale. Put the lemon rind, juice and butter in a saucepan and heat until the butter melts. Bring to the boil. Add the gelatine and turn into a blender or food processor with the yolks mixture. Run the machine for 1½–2 minutes. Whisk the egg whites until stiff. Whisk in the remaining sugar, then fold in the hot lemon mixture. Turn into six individual glass serving dishes, leave until cold, then chill until set. Decorate each with a small sprig of mint before serving.

Orange Curd Mousse

SERVES 6

Prepare as for Lemon Curd Mousse, but substitute the grated rind and juice of 1 large orange for the lemons.

Lime Curd Mousse

SERVES 6

Prepare as for Lemon Curd Mousse (see page 159), but substitute the grated rind and juice of 2 limes for the lemons.

Chocolate Coffee Cups

SERVES 6

150 g/5 oz/1¼ cups plain (semi-sweet) chocolate
20 ml/4 tsp instant coffee powder or granules
30 ml/2 tbsp hot water
4 egg whites
100 g/4 oz/½ cup caster (superfine) sugar
Chocolate mint sticks, to decorate

Break up the chocolate and melt in a bowl over a pan of hot water (or melt in the microwave). Dissolve the coffee in the water and stir into the chocolate. Whisk the egg whites until stiff. Whisk in half the sugar until stiff and glossy. Fold in the remainder. Fold into the chocolate mixture. Spoon into six coffee cups and chill until set. Serve on the saucers with two chocolate mint sticks on the side of each cup of mousse.

White Chocolate Mousse

SERVES 6

250 g/9 oz/2¼ cups white chocolate
25 g/1 oz/2 tbsp unsalted (sweet) butter
5 eggs, separated
25 g/1 oz/¼ cup plain (semi-sweet) chocolate, coarsely grated

Break up 225 g/8 oz/2 cups of the white chocolate and place in a bowl with the butter. Place over a pan of hot water or in the microwave to melt. Beat in the egg yolks. Whisk the egg whites until stiff and fold into the chocolate mixture. Turn into six ramekins (custard cups) and chill until set. Coarsely grate the remaining white chocolate and use to decorate the mousses with the grated plain chocolate.

Whisky MacDream

SERVES 6

30 ml/2 tbsp whisky
15 ml/1 tbsp ginger wine
30 ml/2 tbsp ginger marmalade
Finely grated rind and juice of ½ lemon
30 ml/2 tbsp caster (superfine) sugar
300 ml/½ pt/1¼ cups double (heavy) cream
2 egg whites
Shortbread Triangles (see page 127), to serve

Warm the whisky, ginger wine, marmalade, lemon rind and juice and the sugar in a pan until the marmalade and sugar have melted. Leave to cool. Whip the cream until softly peaking, then whisk in the cooled whisky mixture until thick. Whisk the egg whites until stiff and fold into the cream mixture with a metal spoon. Turn into six serving dishes and chill for 1 hour. Serve with Shortbread Triangles.

Honey Apple Snow

SERVES 6

12 mint leaves
2 eggs, separated
60 ml/4 tbsp caster (superfine) sugar
300 ml/½ pt/1¼ cups milk
900 g/2 lb cooking (tart) apples, sliced
Finely grated rind and juice of 1 small
  lemon
45 ml/3 tbsp clear honey
15 ml/1 tbsp powdered gelatine
45 ml/3 tbsp water
150 ml/¼ pt/⅔ cup whipping cream,
  whipped

Brush the mint leaves with a little of the lightly beaten egg white, then dust with some of the caster sugar to coat completely. Leave to dry on a sheet of greaseproof (waxed) paper. Put the egg yolks in a bowl with the remaining caster sugar. Whisk until thick and pale. Warm the milk in a saucepan. Pour into the eggs and sugar and mix until smooth. Return to the saucepan and cook gently, stirring, until the custard thickens. Do not boil. Remove from the heat and leave to cool.

Put the apple slices in a separate pan with the lemon rind and juice. Cook gently, stirring occasionally, until pulpy. Sweeten to taste with the honey and leave to cool. Sprinkle the gelatine over the water in a small bowl. Leave to soften for 5 minutes. Stand the bowl in a pan of hot water and stir until completely dissolved (or dissolve briefly in a microwave). Purée the apple and custard in a blender or food processor with the gelatine. Leave until on the point of setting. Whisk the egg whites until stiff and fold into the mixture with a metal spoon. Turn into a glass serving dish and chill until set. Cover with whipped cream and decorate with the frosted mint leaves before serving.

Boozy Chocolate Mousse

SERVES 6

200 g/7 oz/1¾ cups plain (semi-sweet)
  chocolate
3 eggs, separated
15–30 ml/1–2 tbsp brandy
150 ml/¼ pt/⅔ cup double (heavy) cream
Coarsely grated chocolate, to decorate

Melt the chocolate over a pan of hot water (or in the microwave). Beat in the egg yolks and brandy. Whisk the egg whites until stiff, then the cream in a separate bowl until peaking. Fold the cream, then egg whites into the chocolate mixture. Turn into a glass serving dish and chill until firm. Sprinkle with coarsely grated chocolate before serving.

Chocolate Orange Mousse

SERVES 8

1 orange
225 g/8 oz/2 cups plain (semi-sweet)
chocolate
600 ml/1 pt/2½ cups milk
15 ml/1 tbsp powdered gelatine
3 eggs, separated
40 g/1½ oz/3 tbsp caster (superfine)
sugar
300 ml/½ pt/1¼ cups double (heavy)
cream
30 ml/2 tbsp orange liqueur

Pare off a strip of orange rind, cut into very thin strips and boil in water for 3 minutes. Drain, rinse with cold water and drain again. Reserve for decoration. Finely grate the remaining rind and squeeze the juice. Using a potato peeler, pare off a few chocolate curls and reserve for decoration, then break up the remainder and place in a bowl over a pan of hot water to melt, or melt in the microwave. Stir in the milk and grated orange rind until well blended. Sprinkle the gelatine over the orange juice in a small bowl and leave to soften for 5 minutes, then stand the bowl in a pan of hot water and stir until the gelatine has dissolved completely (or heat briefly in the microwave). Whisk the egg yolks and sugar together until thick and pale. Whisk in the chocolate milk and gelatine. Leave until on the point of setting. Whisk the egg whites until stiff and whip the cream until softly peaking. Fold all but 60 ml/ 4 tbsp of the cream into the mixture with the orange liqueur, then fold in the egg whites. Turn into a serving dish and chill until set, preferably overnight, to allow the flavours to develop. Decorate with the reserved whipped cream, the chocolate curls and thin strips of orange rind.

North Angel Mousse

SERVES 6

10 ml/2 tsp powdered gelatine
15 ml/1 tbsp water
2 eggs, separated
100 g/4 oz/⅔ cup icing (confectioners')
sugar
15 ml/1 tbsp brandy
15 ml/1 tbsp dark rum
250 ml/8 fl oz/1 cup double (heavy)
cream
Shortbread Triangles (see page 127), to
serve

Sprinkle the gelatine over the water in a small bowl and leave to soften for 5 minutes. Stand the bowl in a pan of hot water and stir until the gelatine has dissolved completely (or heat briefly in the microwave). Whisk together the egg yolks and icing sugar until thick and pale. Whisk in the brandy and rum. Whisk the egg whites until stiff, then whip the cream until peaking. Fold the cream, then the egg whites into the brandy and rum mixture. Divide between six wine goblets and chill until set. Serve with Shortbread Triangles.

Rhubarb and Ginger Mousse

SERVES 6

*450 g/1 lb rhubarb, cut into short
    lengths*
100 g/4 oz/½ cup granulated sugar
150 ml/¼ pt/⅔ cup water
15 ml/1 tbsp powdered gelatine
3 eggs, separated
2.5 ml/½ tsp ground ginger
*30 ml/2 tbsp ginger syrup from a jar of
    stem ginger*
300 ml/½ pt/1¼ cups whipping cream
2 pieces of stem ginger, chopped

Put the rhubarb in a pan with the sugar and water. Bring to the boil, reduce the heat, part-cover and simmer until the fruit is pulpy. Stir in the gelatine and stir until completely dissolved. Allow to cool slightly, then purée in a blender or food processor. Turn into a bowl. Whisk together the egg yolks, ground ginger and ginger syrup, then stir into the purée. Whip the cream until peaking. Fold half into the rhubarb mixture. Whisk the egg whites until stiff and fold in with a metal spoon. Turn into a glass serving dish and chill until set. Decorate with the remaining whipped cream and the chopped ginger.

Peach Mousse

SERVES 6

10 ml/2 tsp powdered gelatine
30 ml/2 tbsp water
*3 large ripe peaches, skinned, stoned
    (pitted) and chopped*
50 g/2 oz/¼ cup caster (superfine) sugar
15 ml/1 tbsp lemon juice
15 ml/1 tbsp peach or orange liqueur
*300 ml/½ pt/1½ cups double (heavy)
    cream*
*A few drops of orange food colouring
    (optional)*
Angelica leaves, to decorate

Sprinkle the gelatine over the water in a small bowl and leave to soften for 5 minutes. Stand the bowl in a pan of hot water and stir until the gelatine has dissolved completely (or dissolve in the microwave). Purée the peaches with the sugar, lemon juice and liqueur in a blender or food processor. Blend in the dissolved gelatine. Whip the cream until peaking. Lightly fold into the peach mixture with a metal spoon, adding a few drops of orange food colouring, if liked. Turn into a glass dish and chill until set. Decorate with angelica leaves before serving.

Mango Mousse

SERVES 4

2 limes
1 large ripe mango
150 ml/¼ pt/⅔ cup water
15 ml/1 tbsp powdered gelatine
30 ml/2 tbsp clear honey
300 ml/½ pt/1¼ cups whipping cream,
   plus extra to decorate

Finely grate the rind and squeeze the juice from one of the limes. Thinly slice the other lime and reserve for decoration. Peel the mango, cut all the flesh off the stone (pit) and place in a saucepan. Add the water and lime rind and juice. Bring to the boil, reduce the heat and simmer gently for about 5 minutes or until tender. Sprinkle the gelatine over and stir until completely dissolved. Purée in a blender or food processor, then stir in the honey. Leave until cold and the consistency of egg white. Whip the cream until peaking and fold into the mixture with a metal spoon. Spoon into a serving dish and chill until set. Decorate with a little whipped cream and lime twists before serving.

Nectarine Mousse

SERVES 4

Prepare as for Mango Mousse, but substitute 2–3 ripe nectarines for the mango.

Prickly Pear Mousse

SERVES 4

Prepare as for Mango Mousse, but substitute 3 prickly pears, halved and the flesh scooped out, for the mango.

Pawpaw Mousse

SERVES 4

Prepare as for Mango Mousse, but substitute a large pawpaw, halved, seeded and peeled, for the mango.

Chocolate and Orange Pots

SERVES 4

150 g/5 oz/1¼ cups plain (semi-sweet)
   chocolate
Grated rind and juice of 1 small orange
2 eggs, separated
15 ml/1 tbsp caster (superfine) sugar
Whipped cream, to decorate

Break up the chocolate and melt in a bowl over a pan of hot water (or melt in the microwave). Stir in the orange rind and juice. Place the egg yolks and sugar in one bowl and the egg whites in another. Whisk the egg whites until stiff, then the egg yolks and sugar until thick and pale. Stir the chocolate mixture into the egg yolk mixture. Fold in the egg whites with a metal spoon. Turn into four individual pots and chill until set. Decorate with whipped cream before serving.

Chocolate Roulade

SERVES 6

*175 g/6 oz/1½ cups plain (semi-sweet)
  chocolate
4 eggs, separated
150 g/5 oz/⅔ cup caster (superfine)
  sugar, plus extra for sprinkling
15 ml/1 tbsp hot water
150 ml/¼ pt/⅔ cup double (heavy) or
  whipping cream, whipped
Icing (confectioners') sugar, for dusting*

Line an 18 × 28 cm/7 × 11 in Swiss roll tin (jelly roll pan) with non-stick baking parchment so the paper stands about 2.5 cm/1 in above the tin all round. Melt the chocolate in a bowl over a pan of hot water or in the microwave. Whisk together the yolks and caster sugar until thick and pale. Stir in the melted chocolate and the hot water. Whisk the egg whites until stiff and fold into the chocolate mixture with a metal spoon. Turn into the prepared tin and spread out evenly. Bake towards the top of a preheated oven at 180°C/350°F/gas mark 4 for about 15–18 minutes until firm to the touch.

Put a clean tea towel (dish cloth) on the work surface and cover with a sheet of baking parchment. Sprinkle with caster sugar. Turn the chocolate roulade out on to the paper and carefully loosen the cooking paper but leave in place. Cover with another clean tea towel and leave until cold. Remove the cooking paper. Trim the edges, if liked, then spread with the whipped cream. Carefully roll up from one short edge, using the paper underneath to help. Wrap in the paper and chill until ready to serve. Unwrap on to a serving plate, dust with sifted icing sugar and serve cut into slices.

Coffee and Walnut Roulade

SERVES 8

*Oil, for greasing
4 eggs, separated
100 g/4 oz/½ cup caster (superfine)
  sugar, plus extra for sprinkling
100 g/4 oz/2 cups plain cake crumbs
A few drops of vanilla essence (extract)
45 ml/3 tbsp ground walnuts
15 ml/1 tbsp instant coffee powder or
  granules
15 ml/1 tbsp coffee liqueur or water
250 ml/8 fl oz/1 cup double (heavy) cream
Icing (confectioners') sugar, for dusting*

Grease and line a Swiss roll tin (jelly roll pan) with greased greaseproof (waxed) paper. Beat together the egg yolks and sugar until thick and pale. Beat in the cake crumbs, vanilla and ground walnuts. Whisk the egg whites until stiff and fold into the mixture with a metal spoon. Turn into the prepared tin and smooth the surface. Bake in a preheated oven at 200°C/400°F/gas mark 6 for about 15 minutes until firm. Remove from the oven and turn out on to a sheet of greaseproof paper, sprinkled with caster sugar, on a tea towel (dish cloth). Cover with another tea towel and leave until cold.

Dissolve the coffee in the liqueur or water. Whip the cream until peaking and whisk in the dissolved coffee. Remove the covering cloth and cooking paper and trim the edges of the roulade, if liked. Spread with the cream and roll up from one short edge, using the paper underneath to help. Transfer to a serving plate. Dust with sifted icing sugar and chill until ready to serve.

Chocolate Snow Cake

SERVES 6–8

Oil, for greasing
175 g/6 oz/1½ cups plain (semi-sweet)
  chocolate
3 eggs, separated
2 egg whites
175 g/6 oz/¾ cup caster (superfine)
  sugar
45 ml/3 tbsp warm water
300 ml/½ pt/1¼ cups crème fraîche
A little grated chocolate, to decorate

Oil two 20 cm/8 in sandwich tins
(pans) and line the bases with oiled
greaseproof (waxed) paper. Break up
the chocolate and melt in a bowl over a
pan of hot water or in the microwave.
Put the egg yolks and caster sugar in a
bowl over a pan of hot water and whisk
until thick and pale. Stir the warm
water into the melted chocolate, then
beat into the sugar mixture. Whisk the
egg whites until stiff and fold in with a
metal spoon. Turn into the prepared tins
and level the surfaces. Bake in a
preheated oven at 180°C/350°F/gas
mark 4 for about 15 minutes. The cakes
may sink slightly in the centre, but
don't worry! Remove from the oven
and cover the tins with greaseproof
paper and a damp tea towel (dish
cloth). Leave until cold. Turn out of the
tins and remove the paper. Sandwich
the cakes together with a little of the
crème fraîche and pile the remainder on
top. Decorate with a little grated
chocolate and chill until ready to serve.

Plum and Ginger Whip

SERVES 6

450 g/1 lb ripe red plums, halved and
  stoned (pitted)
60 ml/4 tbsp water
45 ml/3 tbsp granulated sugar
2 eggs, separated
2 pieces of stem ginger in syrup, finely
  chopped
15 ml/1 tbsp kirsch
15 ml/1 tbsp powdered gelatine
30 ml/2 tbsp water
300 ml/½ pt/1¼ cups double (heavy)
  cream
6 fresh mint leaves, to decorate

Put the plums in a saucepan with the
water and sugar. Heat gently until
the juices start to run, then cover and
cook gently for 10 minutes until pulpy.
Cool slightly, then stir in the egg yolks.
Purée in a blender or food processor.
Stir in the ginger and kirsch. Sprinkle
the gelatine over the water in a small
bowl and leave to soften for 5 minutes.
Stand the bowl in a pan of gently
simmering water and stir until
completely dissolved (or dissolve in the
microwave). Stir the dissolved gelatine
into the plum purée. Whisk the egg
whites until stiff, then whip the cream
until softly peaking. Using a metal
spoon, fold half the cream into the plum
purée, then fold in the egg whites. Turn
into six dessert glasses and chill until
set. Decorate with the remaining
whipped cream and the mint leaves.

Banana Chocolate Orange Mousse Bombe

SERVES 6

*1 large chocolate Swiss (jelly) roll,
  thinly sliced*
Finely grated rind and juice of 1 orange
20 ml/4 tsp powdered gelatine
*225 g/8 oz/2 cups plain (semi-sweet)
  chocolate*
*400 g/14 oz/1 large can of evaporated
  milk, chilled*
2 large bananas
5 ml/1 tsp lemon juice
Grated chocolate, to decorate

Line a 1.2 litre/2 pt/5 cup pudding basin with the Swiss roll slices. Put the orange rind and juice in a bowl. Sprinkle the gelatine over and leave to soften for 5 minutes. Stand the bowl in a pan of hot water and stir until dissolved (or dissolve in the microwave). Break up the chocolate and melt in a bowl over a pan of hot water or in the microwave. Stir in the gelatine. Whip the evaporated milk until foamy. Mash the banana thoroughly with the lemon juice. Fold the milk and banana into the chocolate. Turn into the prepared basin and chill until set. Turn out on to a serving plate and decorate with a little grated chocolate.

Irish Rock

SERVES 6

*100 g/4 oz/²⁄₃ cup icing (confectioners')
  sugar*
*100 g/4 oz/½ cup unsalted (sweet)
  butter, softened*
*300 ml/½ pt/1¼ cups double (heavy)
  cream, lightly whipped*
*225 g/8 oz/2 cups ground hazelnuts
  (filberts)*
15 ml/1 tbsp Irish whiskey
A few drops of rose water
2 egg whites
*Rose petals and a few rose or angelica
  leaves, to decorate*
Palmiers (see page 124), to serve

Beat together the sugar and butter until light and fluffy. Gently fold in the cream, then the nuts, whiskey and rose water. Whisk the egg whites until stiff and fold into the mixture with a metal spoon. When thoroughly blended turn into a shallow dish and chill until firm. Break into rough pieces with a fork and pile into open champagne cups or shallow sundae dishes. Scatter with a few rose petals and stud with leaves. Serve with Palmiers.

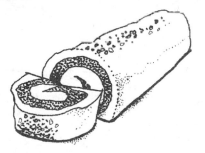

Vanilla Bavarois

SERVES 8

25 ml/1½ tbsp powdered gelatine
75 ml/5 tbsp water
6 egg yolks
75 g/3 oz/⅓ cup caster (superfine) sugar
600 ml/1 pt/2½ cups milk
5 ml/1 tsp vanilla essence (extract)
300 ml/½ pt/1¼ cups double (heavy)
 cream
15 ml/1 tbsp redcurrant jelly (clear
 conserve)

Sprinkle the gelatine over the water in a small bowl and leave to soften for 5 minutes. Stand the bowl in a pan of hot water and stir until the gelatine has dissolved completely. Whisk together the egg yolks and sugar until thick and pale. Warm the milk and stir into the eggs and sugar. Add the vanilla. Stand the bowl over a pan of hot water and stir until the custard thickens and coats the back of a spoon. Do not allow to boil. Test by lifting the spoon out of the mixture and drawing a finger across the back of the spoon: if it leaves a clear line in the custard it is ready. Remove the bowl from the pan and stir in the gelatine. Leave until cool and on the point of setting.

Whip the cream until softly peaking. Reserve 60 ml/4 tbsp for decoration and fold in the remainder with a metal spoon. Turn into a serving dish and chill until set. Spread the reserved cream over and pipe lines of redcurrant jelly over the surface. Use a skewer or cocktail stick (toothpick) to draw across the lines one way, then the other, to form a feathered pattern.

Cranberry Nirvana

SERVES 6

450 g/1 lb fresh cranberries
60 ml/4 tbsp water
Granulated sugar, to taste
2 egg whites
100 g/4 oz/½ cup caster (superfine)
 sugar
2.5 ml/½ tsp vanilla essence (extract)
Single (light) cream, to serve

Put the cranberries in a pan with the water. Heat gently until the fruit begins to pop. Stir in granulated sugar to taste. Turn into an ovenproof serving dish. Whisk the egg whites until stiff. Whisk in half the caster sugar and the vanilla essence. Fold in the remaining caster sugar and pile on top of the cranberries. Bake in a preheated oven at 140°C/275°F/gas mark 1 for 1 hour until crisp and pale. Serve warm with single cream.

Coffee Marbled Bavarois

SERVES 6–8

*30 ml/2 tbsp instant coffee powder or
  granules*
15 ml/1 tbsp hot water
600 ml/1 pt/2½ cups milk
2 eggs, separated
2 egg yolks
15 ml/1 tbsp powdered gelatine
45 ml/3 tbsp cold water
2.5 ml/½ tsp vanilla essence (extract)
*300 ml/½ pt/1¼ cups double (heavy)
  cream, whipped*
Oil, for greasing
Chopped walnuts, to decorate

Dissolve the coffee in the hot water.
Put the milk in a saucepan and
bring to the boil. Remove from the heat.
Whisk together all four egg yolks and
the sugar until thick and pale, then stir
in the hot milk. Return to the saucepan
and heat gently, stirring with a wooden
spoon, until thickened and the mixture
coats the back of a spoon. Do not allow
to boil. Test by lifting the spoon out of
the mixture and drawing a finger across
the back of the spoon: if it leaves a clear
line in the custard it is ready. Sprinkle
the gelatine over the cold water in a
small bowl. Leave to soften for
5 minutes, then stand the bowl in a pan
of hot water and stir until the gelatine
dissolves (or dissolve in the
microwave). Stir the gelatine into the
custard. Pour half the mixture into a
separate bowl. Add the coffee to one
half and stand the bowl in cold water to
speed up setting. Leave until the
mixture has the consistency of egg

white, stirring occasionally. Stir the
vanilla essence into the other half and
cool in the same way.

When on the point of setting, fold
half the whipped cream into the vanilla
mixture. Whisk the egg whites until stiff
and fold into the coffee mixture. Turn
the vanilla mixture into a lightly oiled
900 ml/1½ pt/3¾ cup ring mould. Top
with the coffee mixture and swirl the
mixtures together lightly to give a
marbled effect. Chill until set. Turn out
on to a serving plate, fill the centre with
the remaining whipped cream and
sprinkle with chopped nuts.

Norwegian Cream

SERVES 6

6 eggs, separated
100 g/4 oz/½ cup caster (superfine) sugar
15 ml/1 tbsp powdered gelatine
20 ml/4 tsp orange juice
Jam (conserve)
Whipped cream
*Grated chocolate or crumbled chocolate
  flake bar, to decorate*

Whisk the egg whites until stiff.
Add the sugar and whisk again
until peaking. Whisk the yolks in a
separate bowl and fold into the
meringue mixture. Dissolve the gelatine
in the orange juice in a bowl over a pan
of hot water or in the microwave. Fold
into the egg mixture. Turn into a soufflé
dish and chill until set. When set,
spread the top with jam, then whipped
cream, and cover with grated chocolate
or crumbled flake bar.

Lychee Bavarois

SERVES 6

1 packet of lemon-flavoured jelly (jello)
15 ml/1 tbsp lemon juice
Boiling water
425 g/15 oz/1 large can of lychees,
    drained, reserving the syrup
150 ml/¼ pt/⅔ cup milk
30 ml/2 tbsp custard powder
30 ml/2 tbsp caster (superfine) sugar
150 ml/¼ pt/⅔ cup double (heavy) cream

Break up the jelly and place in a
measuring jug. Add the lemon juice
and make up to 150 ml/¼ pt/⅔ cup with
boiling water. Stir until dissolved. Add
the lychee syrup and make up to
450 ml/¾ pt/2 cups with water, if
necessary. Quarter the lychees. Put
them in the base of a 900 ml/1½ pt/
3¾ cup jelly (jello) mould and pour over
about half the jelly to cover. Chill until
set.
    Meanwhile, blend a little of the milk
with the custard powder and sugar in a
saucepan. Add the remaining milk.
Bring to the boil and cook for
2 minutes, stirring, to form a thick
custard. Stir in the remaining jelly.
Leave until cool and on the point of
setting. Whip the cream until softly
peaking and fold in. Spoon over the
lychees and chill until set. When ready
to serve, dip the mould briefly in hot
water and turn out on to a serving
plate. Serve very cold.

Coffee Russe

SERVES 4–6

10 sponge (lady) fingers, halved
    widthways
20 ml/4 tsp instant coffee powder or
    granules
15 ml/1 tbsp powdered gelatine
45 ml/3 tbsp cold water
2 eggs, separated
50 g/2 oz/¼ cup caster (superfine) sugar
250 ml/8 fl oz/1 cup double (heavy)
    cream
Chocolate coffee beans, to decorate

Line the base of a 15 cm/6 in round,
deep loose-bottomed cake tin (pan)
with baking parchment. Arrange the
sponge fingers, cut ends down, round
the edge of the tin. Blend together the
coffee, gelatine and water in a small
bowl and leave to soften for 5 minutes.
Stand the bowl in a pan of hot water
and stir until the gelatine has dissolved
completely (or dissolve in the
microwave). Whisk together the egg
yolks and caster sugar until thick and
pale. Stir in the gelatine mixture. Whisk
the egg whites until stiff, then whip the
cream until peaking. Fold about two-
thirds of the cream, then all the egg
white into the coffee mixture. Turn into
the sponge-lined tin and smooth the
surface. Chill until set. Just before
serving, remove the tin and slide the
Russe out on to a serving plate.
Decorate the top with the remaining
whipped cream and some chocolate
coffee beans.

Orange Russe

SERVES 6

Finely grated rind and juice of 1 orange
1 packet of orange-flavoured jelly (jello)
75 g/3 oz/1 small packet of sponge (lady)
* fingers, halved widthways*
25 ml/1½ tbsp custard powder
300 ml/½ pt/1¼ cups milk
25 ml/1½ tbsp granulated sugar
1 egg, separated
150 ml/¼ pt/⅔ cup double (heavy) cream

Line the base of an 18 cm/7 in round, loose-bottomed cake tin (pan) with greaseproof (waxed) paper. Put the orange rind and juice in a measuring jug and make up to 300 ml/½ pt/1¼ cups with water. Break up the jelly and add to the liquid. Heat in the microwave or put in a saucepan and stir until dissolved. Allow to cool.

Dip the sides of the sponge fingers in the jelly and use to line the prepared tin. Blend the custard powder and sugar with a little of the milk in a saucepan. Blend in the remaining milk. Bring to the boil and boil for 2 minutes, stirring until thickened. Remove from the heat and beat in the egg yolk. Cover with a circle of wetted greaseproof paper and leave to cool. Whisk the egg white, then whip the cream until peaking. Whisk the cream into the custard with 150 ml/¼ pt/⅔ cup of the cold but not set jelly. Fold in the egg white. Turn into the prepared tin. Chill until set. Chill the remaining jelly separately until set. Just before serving, turn the Russe out on to a serving plate. Remove the greaseproof paper. Chop the set jelly and arrange all round the edge of the Russe to decorate.

Charlotte Malakoff

SERVES 8

24 sponge (lady) fingers
100 g/4 oz/½ cup unsalted (sweet)
* butter, softened*
100 g/4 oz/1 cup ground hazelnuts
* (filberts)*
100 g/4 oz/⅔ cup icing (confectioners')
* sugar*
450 ml/¾ pt/2 cups double (heavy)
* cream*
30 ml/2 tbsp dark rum
Toasted whole hazelnuts, to decorate

Line a 15 cm/6 in deep round cake tin (pan) with greaseproof (waxed) paper. Line the sides of the tin with sponge fingers, sugared sides out. Put the butter, ground hazelnuts and icing sugar in a bowl and beat until light and fluffy. Whip the cream until peaking. Fold about two-thirds into the nut mixture with the rum. Turn half the mixture into the prepared tin. Crush the remaining sponge fingers and scatter over. Top with the remaining nut mixture. Chill for several hours or overnight. Trim the sponge fingers level with the mixture. Turn out on to a serving plate. Pipe the remaining whipped cream round the top edge and decorate with a few whole toasted hazelnuts.

Charlotte Russe

SERVES 6

1 packet of lemon-flavoured jelly (jello)
Glacé (candied) cherries and angelica
* leaves, to decorate*
12–14 sponge (lady) fingers
150 ml/¼ pt/⅔ cup milk
150 ml/¼ pt/⅔ cup single (light) cream
3 egg yolks
20 ml/4 tsp caster (superfine) sugar
25 ml/1½ tbsp powdered gelatine
30 ml/2 tbsp water
A few drops of vanilla essence (extract)
300 ml/½ pt/1¼ cups whipping cream

Make up the jelly according to the packet directions. When cold but not set, pour a little into the base of a 900 ml/1½ pt/3¾ cup charlotte mould or cake tin (pan) (not a loose-bottomed one). Leave to set. Arrange pieces of cherry and angelica leaves attractively on the jelly and gently pour a little more jelly over, just to cover. Chill again until set.

Line the tin with the sponge fingers, trimming to fit. Bring the milk and single cream just to the boil. Whisk together the egg yolks and sugar until thick and pale. Pour on the milk, whisking all the time. Return the mixture to the pan and cook very gently, stirring, until the mixture thickens and coats the back of a spoon. Do not allow to boil. To test, lift the spoon out of the mixture and draw a finger across the back of the spoon: if it leaves a clear line the custard is ready. Sprinkle the gelatine over the water in a small bowl. Leave to soften for 5 minutes, then stand the bowl in a pan of hot water and stir until the gelatine has dissolved completely (or dissolve in the microwave). Stir into the custard and flavour to taste with vanilla. Leave until cold and on the point of setting.

Whip the cream until peaking and fold into the mixture with a metal spoon. Turn into the prepared tin. Cover with foil and chill until set. Trim the tips of the sponge fingers level with the top of the filling. Dip the base of the tin briefly in hot water, then turn out on to a serving plate. Chop the remaining jelly and arrange around the base to decorate.

Sparkling Sabayon

SERVES 4–6

4 egg yolks
45 ml/3 tbsp caster (superfine) sugar
Juice of ½ lemon
300 ml/½ pt/1¼ cups sweet sparkling
* wine at room temperature*
30 ml/2 tbsp brandy
4–6 ratafias

Whisk the egg yolks, sugar, lemon juice and half the wine in a bowl over a pan of hot water until frothy. Gradually whisk in the remaining wine, whisking all the time, and continue to whisk until really thick and the mixture has doubled in volume. Whisk in the brandy. Place a ratafia in the base of each of four to six wine goblets. Spoon the sabayon over and serve hot.

Strawberry Russe

SERVES 6

350 g/12 oz strawberries
1 packet of strawberry-flavoured jelly
* (jello)*
Angelica leaves, to decorate
12–14 sponge (lady) fingers
3 egg yolks
20 ml/4 tsp caster (superfine) sugar
150 ml/¼ pt/⅔ cup single (light) cream
25 ml/1½ tbsp powdered gelatine
30 ml/2 tbsp water
A few drops of vanilla essence (extract)
300 ml/½ pt/1¼ cups whipping cream

Purée 225 g/8 oz of the strawberries in a blender or food processor and slice the remainder. Make up the jelly according to the packet directions. When cold but not set, pour a little into the base of a 900 ml/1½ pt/3¾ cup charlotte mould or cake tin (pan) (not a loose-bottomed one). Leave to set. Arrange the strawberry slices and angelica leaves attractively on the jelly and gently pour a little more jelly over, just to cover. Chill again until set.

Line the tin with the sponge fingers, trimming to fit. Whisk together the egg yolks and sugar until thick and pale, then stir in the strawberry purée. Bring the single cream just to the boil and pour over the strawberry mixture, whisking all the time. Return the mixture to the pan and cook very gently, stirring, until the mixture thickens and coats the back of a spoon. Do not allow to boil. To test, lift the spoon out of the mixture and draw a finger across the back of the spoon: if it leaves a clear line, the custard is ready. Sprinkle the gelatine over the water in a small bowl. Leave to soften for 5 minutes, then stand the bowl in a pan of hot water and stir until the gelatine has dissolved completely (or dissolve briefly in the microwave). Stir into the custard and flavour to taste with vanilla. Leave until cold and on the point of setting.

Whip the cream until peaking and fold into the mixture with a metal spoon. Turn into the prepared tin. Cover with foil and chill until set. Trim the tips of the sponge fingers level with the top of the filling. Dip the base of the tin briefly in hot water, then turn out on to a serving plate. Chop the remaining jelly and arrange around the base to decorate.

Zabaglione

SERVES 4

2 eggs
25 g/1 oz/2 tbsp caster (superfine)
* sugar*
45 ml/3 tbsp Marsala or sweet sherry
Sponge (lady) fingers, to serve

Put the eggs, sugar and Marsala or sherry in a large bowl over a pan of gently simmering water. Whisk until thick, creamy and voluminous. (An electric whisk is quickest, a balloon whisk will give you greater volume.) Pour into four glasses and serve straight away with sponge fingers.

Traditional Syllabub

SERVES 6

2 small lemons
150 ml/¼ pt/⅔ cup fruity white wine
50 ml/3½ tbsp brandy
450 ml/¾ pt/2 cups double (heavy)
cream
150 g/5 oz/⅔ cup caster (superfine)
sugar

Thinly pare the rind of 1 lemon. Cut into wafer thin strips and boil in water for 2 minutes. Drain, rinse with cold water and drain again. Finely grate the rind of the second lemon and squeeze the juice from both. Mix the wine and brandy with the lemon juice. Whip the cream and sugar until peaking. Gradually whisk in the liquid until thick and softly peaking. Spoon into six glasses and sprinkle with the reserved lemon rind. Chill for at least 2 hours.

Cider Syllabub

SERVES 4

150 ml/¼ pt/⅔ cup double (heavy) cream
Finely grated rind and juice of ½ lemon
50 g/2 oz/¼ cup caster (superfine) sugar
120 ml/4 fl oz/½ cup medium-sweet
cider
Shortbread Triangles (see page 127), to
serve

Whip the cream with the lemon rind and juice and the sugar. Stir in the cider. Spoon into four glasses and chill for at least 2 hours. Serve with Shortbread Triangles.

Fluffy Lemon Syllabub

SERVES 4

1 small lemon
2 large egg whites
300 ml/½ pt/1¼ cups double (heavy)
cream
75 g/3 oz/⅓ cup caster (superfine) sugar
300 ml/½ pt/1¼ cups Chardonnay or
other fragrant white wine

Thinly pare the rind from the lemon and cut into thin strips. Boil in a little water for 2 minutes. Drain, rinse with cold water and drain again. Reserve for decoration. Squeeze the juice from the lemon. Whisk the egg whites until stiff, then whip the cream until softly peaking (there is no need to wash the blades in between). Fold the cream, sugar, wine and lemon juice into the egg whites. Quickly spoon into four glasses and chill for at least 2 hours. The mixture will separate to give a foamy top and a lemony wine liquid underneath. Decorate with the thinly pared lemon rind before serving.

Fluffy Orange Syllabub

SERVES 4

Prepare as for Fluffy Lemon Syllabub, but use the finely grated rind and juice of 1 orange instead of the lemon.

Rum Punch Syllabub

SERVES 6

120 ml/4 fl oz/½ cup rum
Finely grated rind and juice of 1 orange
Finely grated rind and juice of 1 lemon
A good pinch of freshly grated nutmeg
75 g/3 oz/⅓ cup caster (superfine) sugar
450 ml/¾ pt/2 cups double (heavy) cream

Mix together the rum, fruit rind and juice, nutmeg and sugar and stir until the sugar has dissolved. Whip the cream until peaking. Gradually whisk in the liquid. Spoon into six glasses and chill for at least 2 hours.

Strawberry Syllabub

SERVES 6

350 g/12 oz strawberries
100 g/4 oz/½ cup caster (superfine) sugar
15 ml/1 tbsp lemon juice
150 ml/¼ pt/⅔ cup dry white wine
300 ml/½ pt/1¼ cups double (heavy) cream

Purée the fruit in a blender or food processor. Place the remaining ingredients in a bowl and whisk until softly peaking. Gently fold in the strawberry purée with a metal spoon. Spoon into six wine goblets and chill before serving.

Raspberry Syllabub

SERVES 6

Prepare as for Strawberry Syllabub, but substitute raspberries for the strawberries and pass through a sieve (strainer) after puréeing to remove the pips.

Nectar Syllabub

SERVES 6

Prepare as for Strawberry Syllabub, but substitute 150 ml/¼ pt/⅔ cup bottled fruit nectar for the the puréed strawberries and halve the quantity of sugar.

Passion Fruit Soft Cheese Syllabub

SERVES 4

2 passion fruit
225 g/8 oz/1 cup medium-fat soft cheese
25 g/1 oz/3 tbsp icing (confectioners') sugar
50 ml/3½ tbsp milk
Finely grated rind and juice of ½ lime
2 egg whites

Halve the passion fruit and scoop out the flesh and seeds into a sieve (strainer) over a bowl. Rub through with a wooden spoon. Discard the seeds. Beat in the cheese, sugar, milk, lime rind and juice. Whisk the egg whites until stiff and fold into the mixture with a metal spoon. Turn into four glasses and chill for at least 2 hours. The mixture will separate.

Whisky Lemon Syllabub

SERVES 4

30 ml/2 tbsp caster (superfine) sugar
Finely grated rind and juice of 1 lemon
30 ml/2 tbsp whisky
300 ml/½ pt/1¼ cups single (light) cream
300 ml/½ pt/1¼ cups double (heavy)
  cream
Shortbread Triangles (see page 127), to
  serve

Heat the sugar, lemon rind and juice and whisky in a saucepan until the sugar has dissolved. Leave to cool. Whip the creams together until softly peaking. Whisk in the whisky mixture. Pour into four glasses and chill for at least 2 hours before serving with Shortbread Triangles.

Flummery

SERVES 4

15 ml/1 tbsp powdered gelatine
45 ml/3 tbsp water
3 eggs, separated
100 g/4 oz/½ cup caster (superfine)
  sugar
150 ml/¼ pt/⅔ cup soured (dairy sour)
  cream
1 large lemon
Mint sprigs, to decorate

Sprinkle the gelatine over the water in a small bowl and leave to soften for 5 minutes. Stand the bowl in a pan of hot water and stir until the gelatine has dissolved completely. Whisk together the egg yolks and sugar until thick and pale. Whisk in the dissolved gelatine. Stir in the soured cream. Cut four slices from the lemon and reserve for

decoration. Finely grate the rind and squeeze the juice from the remainder. Stir into the cream mixture. Leave until on the point of setting. Whisk the egg whites until stiff and fold in with a metal spoon. Turn into four glasses and chill until set. Decorate each with a lemon twist and a mint sprig.

Coffee Feather Soufflé

SERVES 6

4 eggs, separated
100 g/4 oz/½ cup light brown sugar
30 ml/2 tbsp instant coffee powder or
  granules
150 ml/¼ pt/⅔ cup hot water
15 ml/1 tbsp powdered gelatine
300 ml/½ pt/1¼ cups double (heavy)
  cream
Walnut halves, to decorate

Tie a collar of double thickness greaseproof (waxed) paper round an 15 cm/6 in soufflé dish so it comes about 5 cm/2 in above the rim. Put the egg yolks and sugar in a bowl and whisk until thick and pale. Dissolve the coffee in the water. Sprinkle the gelatine over and stand the bowl in a pan of hot water. Stir until the gelatine has dissolved (or melt in the microwave). Whisk into the yolks and sugar. Leave to cool, then chill until on the point of setting. Whisk the egg whites until stiff, then whip the cream until softly peaking. Fold half the cream into the coffee mixture, then fold in the egg whites. Turn into the prepared dish and chill until set. Carefully remove the collar. Decorate the top with the remaining cream and a few walnut halves.

Tropical Flummery

SERVES 4

100 g/4 oz/½ cup granulated sugar
150 ml/¼ pt/⅔ cup water
Thinly pared rind and juice of 1 lemon
A small piece of cinnamon stick
1 star anise (optional)
3 guavas
120 ml/4 fl oz/½ cup milk
10 ml/2 tsp powdered gelatine
225 g/8 oz/1 cup fromage frais
60 ml/4 tbsp crème fraîche
Poppy seeds, for sprinkling

Put the sugar, water, lemon rind and juice and the spices in a saucepan. Heat gently until the sugar dissolves, then bring to the boil. Peel and quarter the guavas and remove the seeds. Poach in the syrup for 1 minute. Remove from the heat and leave to cool.

Put the milk in a small saucepan. Sprinkle the gelatine over and leave to soften for 5 minutes. Heat gently until dissolved but do not let the milk boil. Leave to cool. Beat the cool gelatine milk into the fromage frais. Discard the spices and lemon rind from the guava syrup. Reserve two pieces of guava for decoration. Purée the remainder with the syrup in a blender or food processor. Fold into the fromage frais mixture. Spoon into four glasses and chill until set. Chop the reserved guava pieces. Put 15 ml/1 tbsp of the crème fraîche on top of each flummery, top with the chopped guava and sprinkle with a few poppy seeds.

Orange Posset

SERVES 6

Finely grated rind and juice of 1 large orange
600 ml/1 pt/2½ cups double (heavy) cream
150 ml/¼ pt/⅔ cup sweet white wine
5 ml/1 tsp lemon juice
Icing (confectioners') sugar, sifted
3 egg whites
Crystallised (candied) orange slices, to decorate

Whisk together the orange rind and cream until stiff. Whisk in the wine and orange and lemon juices and sweeten to taste with icing sugar. Whisk the egg whites until stiff and fold in with a metal spoon. Turn into a glass serving dish and chill. Whisk again to blend before serving and decorate with crystallised (candied) orange slices.

Lemon Posset

SERVES 6

Prepare as for Orange Posset, but substitute the finely grated rind and juice of 2 lemons for the orange and omit the extra lemon juice. Decorate with crystallised lemon slices.

Lime Posset

SERVES 6

Prepare as for Orange Posset, but substitute the finely grated rind and juice of 2 limes for the orange and omit the lemon juice. Decorate with crystallised (candied) lime slices instead of orange.

Grapefruit Posset

SERVES 6

Prepare as for Orange Posset (see page 177), but substitute the finely grated rind and juice of 1 grapefruit for the orange and omit the lemon juice. Decorate with toasted flaked (slivered) almonds instead of crystallised (candied) orange slices.

Strawberry Mallows

SERVES 4

100 g/4 oz marshmallows
12 even-sized perfectly shaped
strawberries, unhulled
50 g/2 oz/¹⁄₂ cup desiccated (shredded)
coconut, toasted
50 g/2 oz any-sized strawberries
Caster (superfine) sugar, to taste
2.5 ml/¹⁄₂ tsp lemon juice
150 ml/¹⁄₄ pt/²⁄₃ cup double (heavy) cream

Put the marshmallows in a bowl and stand the bowl over a pan of hot water. Stir until melted. Push a cocktail stick into each of the 12 strawberries. Dip in the melted marshmallow to coat completely, then coat with toasted coconut. Stick the cocktail sticks in a potato and leave to set.

Meanwhile, mash the 50g/2 oz strawberries until pulpy and sweeten to taste with the sugar. Spike with the lemon juice. Whip the cream until stiff. Fold in the strawberry pulp. Pile on to four serving plates and arrange three coconut strawberries attractively on each plate.

Cool Chocolate Velvet Soufflé

SERVES 4–6

10 ml/2 tsp powdered gelatine
15 ml/1 tbsp water
4 eggs, separated
50 g/2 oz/¹⁄₄ cup caster (superfine) sugar
100 g/4 oz/1 cup plain (semi-sweet)
chocolate
15 ml/1 tbsp coffee liqueur or strong
coffee
300 ml/¹⁄₂ pt/1¹⁄₄ cups double (heavy)
cream
Chopped pistachio nuts, to decorate

Tie a collar of doulbe thickness greaseproof (waxed) paper round a 15 cm/6 in soufflé dish so it stands about 5 cm/2 in above the dish. Sprinkle the gelatine over the water in a small bowl and leave to soften for 5 minutes. Stand the bowl in a pan of hot water and stir until the gelatine has dissolved (or dissolve briefly in the microwave). Put the egg yolks and sugar in a bowl and whisk until thick and pale. Melt the chocolate in a bowl over a pan of hot water or in the microwave. Stir in the liqueur or coffee. Whisk the egg whites until stiff, then whip the cream until peaking. Stir the chocolate into the egg yolk mixture, then stir in the gelatine. Fold in half the cream, then all the egg whites. Turn into the prepared soufflé dish and chill until set. Carefully remove the collar. Decorate the top with the reserved cream and sprinkle with pistachio nuts.

Strawberry Soufflé

SERVES 6

15 ml/1 tbsp powdered gelatine
30 ml/2 tbsp water
450 g/1 lb ripe strawberries
3 eggs, separated
75 g/3 oz/⅓ cup caster (superfine) sugar
15 ml/1 tbsp lemon juice
30 ml/2 tbsp water
150 ml/¼ pt/⅔ cup double (heavy) cream
30–45 ml/2–3 tbsp toasted chopped nuts

Tie a collar of double-thickness greaseproof (waxed) paper firmly round a 15 cm/6 in soufflé dish to stand about 5 cm/2 in above the rim. Sprinkle the gelatine over the cold water and leave to soften for 5 minutes. Stand the bowl in a pan of hot water and stir until the gelatine has completely dissolved (or dissolve briefly in the microwave). Reserve about six even-sized strawberries for decoration. Purée the remainder in a blender or food processor. Put the egg yolks and sugar in one bowl with the lemon juice and water and the egg whites in another bowl. Stand the egg yolk bowl over a pan of hot water and whisk until thick and pale. Stir in the gelatine. Whisk the egg whites until stiff and whip the cream until peaking. Fold the strawberry purée into the egg yolk mixture. Reserve half the cream for decoration and fold the remainder into the strawberry mixture with a metal spoon. Fold in the egg whites. Turn into the prepared soufflé dish. Level the surface and chill until set. Carefully remove the greaseproof collar and decorate the sides of the soufflé with the chopped nuts. Pipe the reserved cream on the top and decorate with the reserved strawberries.

Hot Boozy Orange Soufflé

SERVES 4–6

Butter, for greasing
50 g/2 oz/¼ cup caster (superfine) sugar, plus extra for sprinkling
4 eggs, separated
Finely grated rind and juice of 2 oranges
25 g/1 oz/¼ cup plain (all-purpose) flour
200 ml/7 fl oz/scant 1 cup milk
60 ml/4 tbsp Cointreau or brandy
Sifted icing (confectioners') sugar, for dusting
Pouring cream, to serve

Grease a 1.2 litre/2 pt/5 cup soufflé dish with butter and sprinkle with caster sugar. Shake out any excess. Whisk together the sugar and egg yolks with the orange rind until thick and pale. Whisk together the flour and orange juice and stir into the egg yolk mixture. Bring the milk just to the boil. Pour the milk over, whisking all the time. Return to the saucepan and cook gently, stirring, until thick and smooth. Cool slightly, then whisk in the Cointreau or brandy. Whisk the egg whites until stiff. Beat 30 ml/2 tbsp into the orange mixture to slacken it slightly, then fold in the remainder with a metal spoon. Turn into the prepared dish and bake in a preheated oven at 220°C/425°F/gas mark 7 for about 15 minutes until puffy, golden and just set. Dust quickly with icing sugar and serve straight away with pouring cream.

Prune Soufflé

SERVES 6

225 g/8 oz prunes
300 ml/½ pt/1¼ cups cold tea
Thinly pared rind and juice of 1 lemon
3 eggs, separated
75 g/3 oz/⅓ cup caster (superfine) sugar
15 ml/1 tbsp powdered gelatine
45 ml/3 tbsp water
150 ml/¼ pt/⅔ cup double (heavy) cream
1 White or Brown Meringue Nest (see
* page 131, or use bought), crushed, to*
* decorate*
Crème fraîche or Greek-style Yoghurt
* (see page 359, or use bought), to*
* serve*

Put the prunes in a bowl. Cover with cold tea and leave to soak overnight. Tie a collar of double thickness greaseproof (waxed) paper round a 15 cm/6 in soufflé dish so it stands at least 5 cm/2 in above the rim. Put the prunes and tea in a saucepan with the lemon rind. Bring to the boil, reduce the heat and stew for 10 minutes until tender. Discard the lemon rind and remove the stones (pits) from the fruit. Purée the prunes with their juice in a blender or food processor. Add the lemon juice. Whisk the egg yolks and sugar until thick and pale. Sprinkle the gelatine over the water in a small bowl. Leave to soften for 5 minutes, then stand the bowl in a pan of hot water and stir until dissolved(or dissolve briefly in the microwave). Whisk the egg whites until stiff, then whip the cream until peaking. Stir the gelatine and purée into the egg yolk mixture. Fold in the cream, then the egg whites. Turn into the prepared dish and chill until set. Carefully remove the collar. Put a rim of crushed meringue round the top edge of the soufflé to decorate and serve with crème fraîche or Greek-style Yoghurt.

Hot Chocolate Soufflés

SERVES 4

4 eggs, separated
40 g/1½ oz/3 tbsp caster (superfine)
* sugar*
30 ml/2 tbsp plain (all-purpose) flour
15 ml/1 tbsp cocoa (unsweetened
* chocolate) powder*
200 ml/7 fl oz/scant 1 cup milk
A few drops of vanilla essence (extract)
Icing (confectioners') sugar, for dusting
Whipped cream, to serve

Put the egg yolks in a bowl with the caster sugar and whisk until thick and pale. Blend the flour and cocoa with a little of the milk in a saucepan. Stir in the remaining milk and the vanilla. Bring to the boil and cook for 2 minutes, stirring all the time, until thickened and smooth. Allow to cool slightly, then whisk into the egg yolk mixture. Whisk the egg whites until stiff and fold into the mixture with a metal spoon. Turn into four greased individual soufflé dishes. Bake in a preheated oven at 180°C/350°F/gas mark 4 for about 25 minutes until risen and just set. Remove from the oven, dust quickly with a little sifted icing sugar and serve straight away with whipped cream.

Chocolate Brandy Soufflés

SERVES 4

Prepare as for Hot Chocolate Soufflés, but add 15 ml/1 tbsp brandy to the mixture before folding in the egg whites.

Hot Lemon Soufflé

SERVES 4

50 g/2 oz/¼ cup butter, plus extra for greasing
100 g/4 oz/½ cup caster (superfine) sugar, plus extra for sprinkling
Finely grated rind and juice of 2 lemons
4 eggs, separated
Icing (confectioners') sugar, for dusting
Cream or Brandied Loganberry Sauce (see page 349), to serve

Grease a 1 litre/1¾ pt/4¼ cup soufflé dish, sprinkle with a little caster sugar, then shake out any excess. Put the butter, 50 g/2 oz/¼ cup of the sugar and the lemon juice in a saucepan and heat, stirring, until the butter and sugar have melted. Remove from the heat and, using an electric beater, beat in the egg yolks and lemon rind. Continue beating until thick and pale. Whisk the egg whites until stiff and whisk in half the remaining sugar until stiff and glossy. Fold in the remainder. Fold the meringue mixture into the lemon mixture with a metal spoon. Spoon into the prepared dish and bake in a preheated oven at 220°C/425°F/gas mark 7 for about 10–15 minutes until risen and golden. Dust quickly with sifted icing sugar and serve straight away with cream or Brandied Loganberry Sauce.

Ginger Soufflé

SERVES 4

Butter, for greasing
75 g/3 oz/⅓ cup caster (superfine) sugar, plus extra for sprinkling
4 eggs, separated
25 g/1 oz/¼ cup plain (all-purpose) flour
2.5 ml/½ tsp ground ginger
250 ml/8 fl oz/1 cup milk
2 pieces of stem ginger in syrup, finely chopped
15 ml/1 tbsp ginger syrup
Whipped cream, to serve

Grease a 1 litre/1¾ pt/4¼ cup soufflé dish and sprinkle with caster sugar. Shake out any excess. Put half the sugar in a bowl with the egg yolks, flour and ground ginger and whisk together well. Bring the milk just to the boil and pour into the egg mixture, whisking until smooth. Return to the saucepan. Slowly bring to the boil and cook for 2 minutes, stirring all the time, until thick and smooth. Cool slightly, then stir in the chopped ginger and ginger syrup. Whisk the egg whites until stiff. Whisk in half the remaining sugar and whisk again until stiff and glossy. Fold in the remaining sugar. Beat 30 ml/2 tbsp of the egg mixture into the ginger mixture to slacken it slightly, then fold in the remainder with a metal spoon. Turn into the prepared dish and bake in a preheated oven at 220°C/425°F/gas mark 7 for about 12 minutes until risen, golden and just set. Sprinkle with a little caster sugar and serve straight away with whipped cream.

Hot Raspberry and Lemon Soufflés

MAKES 8

65 g/2½ oz/generous ¼ cup unsalted (sweet) butter
75 g/3 oz/⅓ cup caster (superfine) sugar
100 g/4 oz raspberries
30 ml/2 tbsp kirsch
40 g/1½ oz/⅓ cup plain (all-purpose) flour
Finely grated rind and juice of 2 lemons
3 eggs, separated
150 ml/¼ pt/⅔ cup milk
Icing (confectioners') sugar, for dusting
Cream, to serve

Butter eight ramekin dishes (custard cups) with a little of the butter and sprinkle with 25 g/1 oz/2 tbsp of the caster sugar. Divide the raspberries between the dishes and sprinkle with kirsch. Melt the remaining butter in a saucepan, add the flour and cook, stirring, for 1 minute. Remove from the heat and gradually blend in the lemon juice and milk. Return to the heat, bring to the boil and cook, stirring, for 2 minutes. Remove from the heat and beat in the egg yolks, remaining sugar and lemon rind. Whisk the egg whites until stiff. Stir 30 ml/2 tbsp into the thick mixture to slacken it slightly, then fold in the remainder with a metal spoon. Spoon into the ramekin dishes and place a little apart on a baking (cookie) sheet. Bake in a preheated oven at 190°C/375°F/gas mark 5 for about 12 minutes until risen, golden and just set. Quickly dust with sifted icing sugar and serve straight away with cream.

Hot Strawberry and Orange Soufflés

MAKES 8

Prepare as for Hot Raspberry and Lemon Soufflés, but substitute sliced strawberries for the raspberries, orange liqueur for the kirsch and 1 large orange for the lemons.

Hot Loganberry and Lime Soufflés

MAKES 8

Prepare as for Hot Raspberry and Lemon Soufflés, but substitute halved loganberries for the raspberries, brandy for the kirsch and 2 limes for the lemons.

Hot Pear and Orange Soufflés

SERVES 4

1 large orange
1 pear, diced
20 g/¾ oz/1½ tbsp butter, plus extra for greasing
20 g/¾ oz/3 tbsp plain (all-purpose) flour
150 ml/¼ pt/⅔ cup milk
25 g/1 oz/2 tbsp caster (superfine) sugar
2 eggs, separated
Icing (confectioners') sugar, for dusting
Orange Sauce (see page 350), to serve

Finely grate the rind from the orange. Cut off all the white pith and slice, then roughly chop the flesh. Mix with the pear and spoon into four buttered individual soufflé dishes. Melt the butter in a saucepan. Remove from the heat and blend in the flour and milk. Return to the heat and bring to the boil, stirring, until very thick and bubbling. Remove from the heat and beat in the sugar, egg yolks and the orange rind. Whisk the egg whites until stiff. Beat 15 ml/1 tbsp into the mixture to slacken, then fold in the remainder with a metal spoon. Spoon on top of the fruit. Place the dishes on a baking (cookie) sheet and bake in a preheated oven at 200°C/400°F/gas mark 6 for about 15 minutes or until risen and golden. Dust with sifted icing sugar and serve straight away with hot Orange Sauce.

Chocolate Strawberry Cups

SERVES 4

150 g/5 oz/1¼ cups plain (semi-sweet) chocolate
8 rose leaves
2 trifle sponges, crumbled
30 ml/2 tbsp kirsch
120 ml/4 fl oz/½ cup double (heavy) cream
30 ml/2 tbsp strawberry jam (conserve)
5 ml/1 tsp lemon juice
4 small strawberries (optional)

Break up the chocolate and place in a bowl over a pan of hot water. Stir until melted. Dip the rose leaves on one side only in the chocolate and leave to dry, chocolate-side up, on a sheet of greaseproof (waxed) paper. Brush the remaining chocolate liberally over the insides of four paper cake cases (cupcake papers) until thickly coated. Chill until set.

When firm, gently peel away the paper to leave chocolate cases. Mix the crumbled sponges with the kirsch and spoon into the cases. Whip the cream until peaking, then whisk in the jam and lemon juice. Spoon into the cases and chill until set. Gently peel away the rose leaves from the chocolate and use the chocolate leaves to decorate the cups with a fresh strawberry on each, if liked.

Chocolate Apricot Cups

SERVES 4

Prepare as for Chocolate Strawberry Cups, but substitute apricot jam (conserve) for strawberry and decorate each with a whole toasted almond with the chocolate leaves, if liked.

Rhubarb and Orange Mallow

SERVES 4

1 orange
750 g/1½ lb forced rhubarb, cut into
  short lengths
300 ml/½ pt/1¼ cups water
75 g/3 oz/⅓ cup caster (superfine) sugar
2 eggs, separated
100 g/4 oz marshmallows
10 ml/2 tsp powdered gelatine

Thinly pare the rind from half the orange, cut into thin strips and boil in water for 3 minutes. Drain, rinse with cold water and drain again. Finely grate the remaining rind and squeeze the juice from the orange.

Put the rhubarb in a pan with the water and sugar. Bring to the boil, reduce the heat and simmer gently for about 6 minutes or until the rhubarb is tender. Drain, reserving the juice. Turn the rhubarb into a glass serving dish. Put the egg yolks, marshmallows, grated rind and 30 ml/2 tbsp of the orange juice in a saucepan and whisk over a low heat until the marshmallows have melted. Remove from the heat and stir in
150 ml/¼ pt/⅔ cup of the rhubarb juice.

Put the remaining rhubarb juice in a small bowl. Sprinkle the gelatine over and leave to soften for 5 minutes. Stand the bowl in a pan of hot water and stir until the gelatine has completely dissolved. Stir into the mallow mixture. Whisk the egg whites until stiff and fold into the mallow mixture with a metal spoon. Spoon over the rhubarb and chill until set. Sprinkle the orange strips over and serve very cold.

Rhubarb Fluff

SERVES 4

170 g/6 oz/1 small can of evaporated
  milk
450 g/1 lb rhubarb, cut into short
  lengths
175 g/6 oz/¾ cup light brown sugar
150 ml/¼ pt/⅔ cup pure orange juice
Viennese Fingers (see page 127), to
  serve

Boil the can of evaporated milk in a saucepan of water for 15 minutes. Drain, leave to cool, then chill for at least 2 hours. Meanwhile, put the rhubarb, sugar and orange juice in a saucepan. Bring to the boil, stirring, then cover and simmer gently until really tender. Leave until cold. Empty the chilled can of milk into a bowl. Whisk until thick and peaking. Beat the rhubarb until pulpy and fold into the whipped milk. Turn into four glass serving dishes and serve straight away with Viennese Fingers.

Avocado Whip

SERVES 6

1 lime
2 small ripe avocados
60 ml/4 tbsp caster (superfine) sugar
2 large egg whites
250 ml/8 fl oz/1 cup whipping cream,
 lightly whipped
Shortbread Triangles (see page 127), to
 serve

Thinly pare the rind off the lime and cut into thin strips. Boil in water for 2 minutes. Drain, rinse with cold water and drain again. Squeeze the lime juice. Peel the avocados, remove the stones (pits), then mash the flesh with the lime juice. Sweeten to taste with some or all of the sugar. Whisk the egg whites until stiff, then whip the cream until softly peaking. Reserve about a quarter of the cream and fold the remainder into the avocado mixture. Lightly fold in the egg whites. Spoon into six glass serving dishes and top each with a spoonful of the remaining whipped cream. Chill for up to 1 hour. Decorate with the shredded lime rind and serve with Shortbread Triangles.

Fluffy Apricot Dessert

SERVES 6

4 eggs, separated
40 g/1½ oz/3 tbsp caster (superfine)
 sugar
5 ml/1 tsp cornflour (cornstarch)
150 ml/¼ pt/⅔ cup single (light) cream
410 g/14½ oz/1 large can of apricot
 halves, drained, reserving the juice
90 ml/6 tbsp double (heavy) cream
Toasted flaked (slivered) almonds, to
 decorate

Put the egg yolks in a bowl with the sugar and cornflour and whisk until smooth. Heat the cream until almost boiling. Pour over the egg mixture and whisk until well blended. Place the bowl over a pan of hot water and whisk until thickened and the mixture coats the back of a spoon. To test, lift the spoon out of the mixture and draw a finger through the mixture on the spoon: if it leaves a clear line, the custard is ready. Leave until cold.

Purée the apricots in a blender or food processor. Stir into the cold custard. Whisk the egg whites until stiff and fold into the mixture with a metal spoon. Turn into six glass serving dishes and chill for at least 1 hour. Whisk the cream with 15 ml/1 tbsp of the apricot juice until peaking. Spoon on top of the desserts and decorate with toasted flaked almonds.

Queen Mab's Pudding

SERVES 6

3 eggs
50 g/2 oz/¼ cup caster (superfine) sugar
300 ml/½ pt/1¼ cups milk
300 ml/½ pt/1¼ cups single (light) cream
2.5 ml/½ tsp vanilla essence (extract)
15 ml/1 tbsp powdered gelatine
45 ml/3 tbsp water
75 g/3 oz/¾ cup glacé (crystallised)
  cherries
50 g/2 oz/½ cup chopped mixed
  (candied) peel
30 ml/2 tbsp chopped angelica
300 ml/½ pt/1¼ cups double (heavy)
  cream

Whisk together the eggs and caster sugar in a bowl. Warm the milk, single cream and vanilla together until almost boiling. Pour over the eggs and sugar, whisking all the time. Return to the saucepan and heat gently, stirring, until the custard thickens and coats the back of a spoon. Do not allow to boil or the custard will curdle. To test, lift the spoon out of the mixture and draw a finger through the mixture on the spoon: if it leaves a clear line, the custard is ready. Allow to cool slightly. Meanwhile, sprinkle the gelatine over the water and leave to soften for 5 minutes. Stand the bowl in a pan of hot water and stir until the gelatine has dissolved completely (or dissolve in the microwave). Stir into the custard.

Halve 25 g/1 oz/¼ cup of the cherries and chop the remainder. Stir the chopped cherries into the custard with the peel and chopped angelica. Leave until cold and on the point of setting. Whip the cream until peaking. Fold half into the custard and turn into a 900 ml/1½ pt/3¾ cup wetted mould. Chill until set. Dip the base of the mould briefly in hot water, then turn out on to a serving plate. Decorate with the remaining whipped cream and the halved glacé cherries.

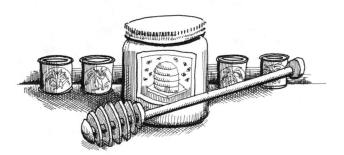

Frozen Assets

Ice creams, sorbets and other frozen delights await you here. From the simplest vanilla ice cream to an exotic chocolate bombe, you will find all the frozen desserts you could wish to try.

Real Vanilla Ice Cream

MAKES 1 LITRE/1¾ PTS/4¼ CUPS

450 ml/¾ pt/2 cups single (light) cream
2 eggs
2 egg yolks
100 g/4 oz/½ cup caster (superfine) sugar
5 ml/1 tsp vanilla essence (extract)
300 ml/½ pt/1¼ cups double (heavy)
 cream

Warm the single cream in a saucepan but do not let it boil. Whisk the eggs, egg yolks and all but 15 ml/1 tbsp of the sugar together until thick and pale. Whisk in the warm cream and the vanilla. Place the bowl over a pan of gently simmering water and continue whisking until the mixture thickens and will coat the back of a spoon. To test, lift the spoon out of the mixture and draw a finger through the mixture on the spoon: if it leaves a clear line, the custard is ready. Stand the bowl in cold water to cool quickly. Sprinkle the surface with the reserved caster sugar to prevent a skin forming and leave until cold.

Whip the double cream until softly peaking, then whisk into the cold custard. Turn into a rigid container, cover and freeze for 1 hour. Whisk thoroughly with a fork to break up the ice crystals. Repeat the freezing and whisking twice more, then freeze until firm.

Light Vanilla Ice Cream

MAKES 1 LITRE/1¾ PTS/4¼ CUPS

Prepare as for Real Vanilla Ice Cream, but substitute semi-skimmed milk for the single (light) cream.

Economy Vanilla Ice Cream

MAKES 1 LITRE/1¾ PTS/4¼ CUPS

600 ml/1 pt/2½ cups milk
30 ml/2 tbsp custard powder
100 g/4 oz/½ cup caster (superfine) sugar
5 ml/1 tsp vanilla essence (extract)
1 sachet of Dream Topping mix

Set aside 150 ml/¼ pt/⅔ cup of the milk to make up the Dream Topping. Blend the custard powder with a little of the remaining milk and the sugar in a saucepan. Add the remaining milk, bring to the boil and cook for 2 minutes, stirring all the time, until thick and smooth. Stir in the vanilla essence. Cover with a circle of wetted greaseproof (waxed) paper to prevent a skin forming and leave until cold.

Make up the Dream Topping with the reserved milk as directed on the packet. Fold into the custard. Turn into a freezerproof container and freeze for 1½ hours. Whisk with a fork to break up the ice crystals, then freeze until firm.

Fresh Strawberry Ice Cream

MAKES 1.2 LITRES/2 PTS/5 CUPS

Prepare as for any of the vanilla ice creams, but blend in 225 g/8 oz strawberries puréed with 5 ml/1 tsp lemon juice before whisking in the whipped cream or Dream Topping.

Fresh Raspberry Ice Cream

MAKES 1.2 LITRES/2 PTS/5 CUPS

Prepare as for any of the vanilla ice creams, but blend in 225 g/8 oz raspberries, puréed then passed through a sieve (strainer) to remove the seeds, before whisking in the whipped cream or Dream Topping.

Raspberry Ripple Ice Cream

MAKES 1.2 LITRES/2 PTS/5 CUPS

Prepare as for any of the vanilla ice creams, but after the final whisking fold in 1 quantity of All-year Raspberry Sauce (see page 348) until it forms a rippled effect, then freeze until firm.

Chocolate Chip Ice Cream

MAKES 1.2 LITRES/2 PTS/5 CUPS

Prepare as for any of the vanilla ice creams, but add 100 g/4 oz/1 cup chocolate chips at the last whisking, then freeze until firm.

Dark Chocolate Ice Cream

MAKES 1.2 LITRES/2 PTS/5 CUPS

Prepare as for any of the vanilla ice creams, but melt 200 g/7 oz/ 1¾ cups plain (semi-sweet) chocolate in the single (light) cream before adding to the egg mixture.

Chocolate and Coconut Ice Cream

MAKES 1 LITRE/1¾ PTS/4¼ CUPS

Prepare as for any of the vanilla ice creams, but whisk 45 ml/3 tbsp cocoa (unsweetened chocolate) powder and 30 ml/2 tbsp grated creamed coconut into the warmed cream before making the custard.

Chocolate Mint Chip Ice Cream

MAKES 1.2 LITRES/2 PTS/5 CUPS

Prepare as for any of the vanilla ice creams, but substitute peppermint essence for vanilla and whisk in a few drops of green food colouring and 8–10 finely chopped chocolate mints at the final whisking, then freeze until firm.

Coffee Ice Cream

MAKES 1 LITRE/1¾ PTS/4¼ CUPS

Prepare as for any of the vanilla ice creams, but whisk in 15 ml/1 tbsp instant coffee powder or granules dissolved in 10 ml/2 tsp water before folding in the whipped cream or Dream Topping.

Toasted Sesame Ice Cream

MAKES 1 LITRE/1¾ PTS/4¼ CUPS

Prepare as for any of the vanilla ice creams, but whisk in 30 ml/2 tbsp toasted sesame seeds at the final whisking, then freeze until firm.

Orange Ice Cream

MAKES 1 LITRE/1¾ PTS/4¼ CUPS

Prepare as for any of the vanilla ice creams (see page 188), but omit the vanilla essence and add the finely grated rind and juice of 1 orange to the mixture at the final whisking, then freeze until firm.

Lemon Ice Cream

MAKES 1 LITRE/1¾ PTS/4¼ CUPS

Prepare as for any of the vanilla ice creams (see page 188), but omit the vanilla essence (extract) and whisk in the finely grated rind and juice of 1 large or 2 small lemons at the final whisking, then freeze until firm.

Lime Ice Cream

MAKES 1 LITRE/1¾ PTS/4¼ CUPS

Prepare as for any of the vanilla ice creams (see page 188), but omit the vanilla essence (extract) and whisk in the finely grated rind and juice of 2 limes at the final whisking, then freeze until firm.

Grapefruit Ice Cream

MAKES 1 LITRE/1¾ PT/4¼ CUPS

Prepare as for any of the vanilla ice creams (see page 188), but omit the vanilla essence (extract) and whisk in the finely grated rind and juice of 1 small grapefruit at the final whisking, then freeze until firm.

Almond Macaroon Ice Cream

MAKES 1 LITRE/1¾ PT/4¼ CUPS

Prepare as for any of the vanilla ice creams (see page 188), but substitute almond essence (extract) for the vanilla and fold in 100 g/4 oz/1 cup crushed almond macaroons at the final whisking, then freeze until firm.

Mincemeat Ice Cream

MAKES 1.2 LITRES/2 PTS/5 CUPS

Prepare as for any of the vanilla ice creams (see page 188), but stir in 225 g/8 oz/⅔ cup mincemeat and 15 ml/1 tbsp brandy after the final whisking, then freeze until firm.

Melon Ice Cream

MAKES .2 LITRES/2 PTS/5 CUPS

Prepare as for any of the vanilla ice creams (see page 188), but fold in the finely chopped flesh of 1 small ripe melon after the final whisking, then freeze until firm.

Passion Fruit Ice Cream

MAKES 1 LITRE/1¾ PTS/4¼ CUPS

Prepare as for any of the vanilla ice creams (see page 188), but scoop out the flesh and seeds of 3 passion fruit and pass through a sieve (strainer). Whisk in the juice at the final whisking, then freeze until firm.

Honey and Ginger Ice Cream
MAKES 1 LITRE/1¾ PTS/4¼ CUPS

Prepare as for any of the vanilla ice creams (see page 188), but substitute clear honey for the sugar and add 2 pieces of finely chopped stem ginger in syrup at the final whisking, then freeze until firm.

Pistachio Ice Cream
MAKES 1 LITRE/1¾ PTS/4¼ CUPS

Prepare as for any of the vanilla ice creams (see page 188), but add 50 g/2 oz/½ cup finely chopped or ground pistachio nuts to the mixture after the final whisking and colour with a few drops of green food colouring, if liked. Freeze until firm.

Almond Ice Cream
MAKES 1 LITRE/1¾ PTS/4¼ CUPS

Prepare as for any of the vanilla ice creams (see page 188), but substitute almond essence (extract) for the vanilla and whisk in 50 g/2 oz/½ cup finely chopped or ground almonds after the final whisking, then freeze until firm.

Peanut Brittle Ice Cream
MAKES 1.2 LITRES/2 PTS/5 CUPS

Prepare as for any of the vanilla ice creams (see page 188), but add 100 g/4 oz/1 cup finely crushed peanut brittle after the final whisking, then freeze until firm.

Maraschino Cherry Ice Cream
MAKES 1.2 LITRES/2 PTS/5 CUPS

Prepare as for any of the vanilla ice creams (see page 188), but add 200 g/7 oz/1 small jar of maraschino cherries, chopped, and 30 ml/2 tbsp of the syrup to the mixture after the final whisking, then freeze until firm.

Banana Ice Cream
SERVES 4–6

400 g/14 oz/1 large can of evaporated milk, chilled
3 ripe bananas
15 ml/1 tbsp lemon juice
Caster (superfine) sugar

Whisk the evaporated milk until thick and fluffy. Mash the bananas thoroughly with the lemon juice. Sweeten to taste with caster sugar, then fold into the whipped milk. Turn into a freezerproof container and freeze for about 1 hour or until firm around the edges. Whisk with a fork to break up the ice crystals. Freeze until firm. Remove from the freezer 10 minutes before serving.

Banana and Coconut Ice Cream
SERVES 4–6

Prepare as for Banana Ice Cream, but whisk in 45 ml/3 tbsp toasted desiccated (shredded) coconut after whisking to break up the ice crystals.

Blackcurrant Ice Cream

SERVES 8

450 g/1 lb blackcurrants, stripped from
their stalks
150 ml/¼ pt/⅔ cup water
75 g/3 oz/⅓ cup caster (superfine) sugar
3 eggs, separated
300 ml/½ pt/1¼ cups single (light) cream
300 ml/½ pt/1¼ cups double (heavy)
cream

Put the blackcurrants in a pan with the water and sugar. Heat gently, stirring, until the sugar dissolves, then bring to the boil and boil for 5 minutes. Purée in a blender or food processor, then pass through a sieve (strainer). Beat the egg yolks, then gradually whisk in the purée. Cool slightly, then stir in the single cream. Turn into a freezerproof container and freeze for 1–1½ hours until half-frozen. Whisk thoroughly with a fork to break up the ice crystals. Whisk the egg whites until stiff, then whip the double cream until peaking. Fold the cream, then the egg whites, into the mixture and freeze until firm.

Redcurrant Ice Cream

SERVES 8

Prepare as for Blackcurrant Ice Cream, but substitute redcurrants for the blackcurrants.

Raspberry Meringue Bombe

SERVES 8

1 quantity any vanilla ice cream (see
page 188), before freezing
225 g/8 oz raspberries
4 White Meringue Nests (see page 131,
or use bought), crushed

Spoon half the ice cream mixture into a freezerproof container and freeze for 1 hour. Purée the raspberries, then pass through a sieve (strainer) to remove the seeds. Stir into the other half of the ice cream. Pour into a freezerproof container and freeze for 1 hour.

Place a 1 litre/1¾ pt/ 4¼ cup pudding basin in the freezer. Whisk both ice creams with a fork to break up the ice crystals and freeze again for 1 hour. Whisk thoroughly again. Fold the crushed meringue into the vanilla mixture. Press into the base and up the sides of the chilled basin to form a shell of vanilla ice cream. Pack the raspberry mixture into the centre. Cover and freeze again until firm. Transfer to the fridge 30 minutes before serving. Dip the basin briefly in hot water, then turn out on to a serving plate. Serve straight away.

Caramel Ice Cream

SERVES 4

10 ml/2 tsp arrowroot
100 g/4 oz/½ cup light brown sugar
150 ml/¼ pt/⅔ cup water
25 g/1 oz/2 tbsp butter
10 ml/2 tsp lemon juice
400 g/14 oz/1 large can of evaporated
   milk, chilled
2.5 ml/½ tsp vanilla essence (extract)

Blend the arrowroot with 15 ml/
1 tbsp water in a small bowl. Put
the sugar and water in a saucepan with
the butter and lemon juice. Heat gently,
stirring, until the sugar and butter have
melted. Add the blended arrowroot and
cook, stirring, until thickened. Leave to
cool. Whisk the evaporated milk until
thick and fold into the caramel sauce
with the vanilla essence. Turn into a
freezerproof container and freeze for
1½ hours. Whisk with a fork to break
up the ice crystals, then freeze again for
1 hour. Whisk again, then freeze until
firm.

Brown Bread Ice Cream

SERVES 4

300 ml/½ pt/1¼ cups double (heavy)
   cream
75 g/3 oz/⅓ cup caster (superfine) sugar
5 ml/1 tsp vanilla essence (extract)
50 g/2 oz/¼ cup butter
50 g/2 oz/1 cup fresh wholemeal
   breadcrumbs
50 g/2 oz/¼ cup light brown sugar

Whip the cream with all but 15 ml/
1 tbsp of the caster sugar and the
vanilla essence until stiff. Turn into a
freezerproof container and freeze for
1 hour until firm around the edges.
Meanwhile, melt the butter in a frying
pan (skillet). Stir in the breadcrumbs
and brown sugar. Cook, stirring, over a
moderate heat until golden and crisp.
Stir in the remaining caster sugar and
cook for 1 minute. Turn out on to a
plate to cool. Whisk the half-frozen
cream to break up the ice crystals.
Whisk in the breadcrumbs. Return to
the freezer and freeze until firm.

Brown Bread and Mango Ice Cream

SERVES 4-6

Prepare as for Brown Bread Ice
Cream, but omit the vanilla and add
1 ripe mango, peeled, stoned (pitted)
and mashed to the whipped cream
before starting to freeze.

Lemon Mint Ice Cream

SERVES 6

4 eggs, separated
100 g/4 oz/½ cup caster (superfine)
* sugar*
300 ml/½ pt/1¼ cups double (heavy)
* cream*
Finely grated rind and juice of 2 large
* lemons*
4 mint sprigs, finely chopped
A mint sprig, to decorate

Whisk the egg whites until stiff. Whisk in the sugar a little at a time, whisking well after each addition. In a separate bowl, whip the cream until peaking with the lemon rind and juice. Lightly beat the egg yolks and fold into the meringue mixture. Add this to the cream mixture and fold in with the chopped mint until just mixed but totally blended. Turn into a 1.5 litre/ 2½ pt/6 cup pudding basin. Cover and freeze until firm. Remove from the freezer 20 minutes before serving. Stand the basin briefly in hot water, then turn out on to a serving plate. Decorate with a mint sprig and serve.

Crème Brulée Glacé au Fruits

SERVES 6

2 bananas
10 ml/2 tsp lemon juice
2 oranges
300 ml/½ pt/1¼ cups double (heavy)
* cream*
150 ml/¼ pt/⅔ cup single (light) cream
15 ml/1 tbsp caster (superfine) sugar
100 g/4 oz seedless black grapes, halved
1 kiwi fruit, halved and sliced
100 g/4 oz/½ cup light brown sugar

Slice the bananas and toss in the lemon juice. Cut off and discard all the rind and pith from the oranges and separate into segments. Halve the segments. Whip together the creams and caster sugar. Put the bananas in a large shallow flameproof and freezerproof dish. Top with a quarter of the cream. Cover with the orange pieces and top with more cream. Cover with the grapes and kiwi fruit, then all the remaining cream. Cover the cream completely with the brown sugar and freeze until firm. When ready to serve, place under a preheated grill (broiler) until the sugar caramelises, then serve immediately.

Orange Cheese Sherbet

SERVES 6

225 g/8 oz/1 cup cottage cheese
5 ml/1 tsp finely grated orange rind
30 ml/2 tbsp orange juice
60 ml/4 tbsp clear honey
150 ml/¼ pt/⅔ cup plain yoghurt
A pinch of ground ginger
1 egg white
Thinly pared orange rind, to decorate

Purée all the ingredients except the egg white in a blender or food processor, or pass the cheese through a sieve (strainer) and beat in the remaining ingredients. Turn into a metal or plastic container, cover with foil and freeze for 2 hours. Whisk thoroughly with a fork to break up the ice crystals. Whisk the egg white until stiff and fold into the mixture with a metal spoon. Re-cover and freeze for 1½ hours. Whisk again with a fork, then freeze until firm. To serve, spoon into wine goblets and sprinkle with thinly pared orange rind.

Lemon Cheese Sherbet

SERVES 6

Prepare as for Orange Cheese Sherbet, but substitute lemon rind and juice for orange and ground cinnamon for ginger.

Grapefruit Cheese Sherbet

SERVES 6

Prepare as for Orange Cheese Sherbet, but substitute grapefruit rind and juice for orange.

Mandarin Cheese Sherbet

SERVES 6

Prepare as for Orange Cheese Sherbet, but substitute mandarin rind and juice for orange and mixed (apple-pie) spice for the ground ginger. Scatter with mandarin orange segments instead of decorating with thinly pared orange rind.

Lime Cheese Sherbet

SERVES 6

Prepare as for Orange Cheese Sherbet, but substitute lime rind and juice for orange and ground cinnamon for ginger.

Honey Lemon Parfait

SERVES 4–6

Finely grated rind and juice of ½ lemon
150 ml/¼ pt/⅔ cup water
30 ml/2 tbsp clear honey
2 egg whites
150 ml/¼ pt/⅔ cup double (heavy) cream
Cigarettes Russes (see page 127), to
serve

Put the lemon rind, juice, water and honey in a saucepan. Bring to the boil and boil until thick and syrupy. Remove from the heat. Whisk the egg whites until stiff. Gradually whisk in the syrup and continue whisking until the mixture is cold. Whip the cream and fold into the mixture. Turn into a freezerproof container and freeze until half frozen. Whisk thoroughly with a fork to break up the ice crystals, then freeze again until firm. Serve in dishes with Cigarettes Russes.

Vanilla Yoghurt Ice Cream

SERVES 6–8

4 eggs, separated
175 g/6 oz/¾ cup caster (superfine) sugar
300 ml/½ pt/1¼ cups thick vanilla yoghurt
300 ml/½ pt/1¼ cups crème fraîche
2.5 ml/½ tsp vanilla essence (extract)

Whisk together the egg yolks and sugar until thick and pale. Fold in the yoghurt, crème fraîche and vanilla essence. Turn into a freezerproof container and freeze for 2 hours. Turn the mixture into a large bowl. Whisk well with a fork to break up the ice crystals. Whisk the egg whites until stiff and fold into the yoghurt mixture. Return to the freezer container and freeze until firm.

Peach and Hazelnut Yoghurt Ice Cream

SERVES 6–8

Prepare as for Vanilla Yoghurt Ice Cream, but substitute 1 small carton of peach yoghurt and 1 small carton of hazelnut (filbert) yoghurt for the vanilla yoghurt.

Caribbean Ice

SERVES 8–10

30 ml/2 tbsp cornflour (cornstarch)
900 ml/1½ pts/3 cups milk
100 g/4 oz/½ cup granulated sugar
100 g/4 oz creamed coconut, crumbled
225 g/8 oz/1 cup curd (smooth cottage) cheese
Jewelled Pineapple Sauce (see page 350), to serve

Blend the cornflour with a little of the milk and the sugar in a bowl. Put the remaining milk in a saucepan with the crumbled coconut and heat, stirring, until the coconut melts. Pour over the cornflour mixture and stir well. Return to the saucepan, bring to the boil and cook, stirring, for 2 minutes until thickened and smooth. Cover with a circle of wetted greaseproof (waxed) paper and leave to cool. When cold, beat in the curd cheese. Turn into a freezerproof container and freeze until firm around the edges. Whisk well with a fork to break up the ice crystals. Return to the freezer and freeze until firm. Remove from the freezer about 15 minutes before serving with Jewelled Pineapple Sauce.

Tutti Frutti Ice

SERVES 6

220 g/7¾ oz/1 small can of sliced
peaches, drained, reserving the juice
2 egg whites
60 ml/4 tbsp icing (confectioners') sugar
300 ml/½ pt/1¼ cups double (heavy)
cream
50 g/2 oz/⅓ cup raisins
50 g/2 oz/⅓ cup sultanas (golden raisins)
25 g/1 oz/¼ cup chopped mixed (candied)
peel
25 g/1 oz/¼ cup glacé (candied) cherries,
chopped
25 g/1 oz/¼ cup pistachio nuts, chopped

Purée about three-quarters of the peaches with 15 ml/1 tbsp of the syrup in a blender or food processor. Chop the remaining peaches. Whisk the egg whites until stiff. Whisk in the icing sugar. Whip the cream until peaking, then fold in the egg whites. Spoon half the mixture into a separate bowl. Fold the peach purée into one half. Turn into a 900 ml/1½ pt/3¾ cup pudding basin. Press a 600 ml/1 pt/2½ cup basin into the mixture so that it is squeezed up between the two basins to within 1 cm/½ in of the top. Freeze until firm.

Mix the chopped peaches with the remaining ingredients into the rest of the cream mixture. When the cream between the basins is frozen, half-fill the inner basin with hot water and leave for a few seconds before carefully lifting it out. Fill the centre of the ice cream with the mixed fruit mixture and level the surface. Cover with foil and freeze until firm. When ready to serve, dip the basin briefly in hot water, then turn out on to a serving plate.

Lemon Sorbet

SERVES 8

600 ml/1 pt/2½ cups water
225 g/8 oz/1 cup granulated sugar
Thinly pared rind and juice of 2 large
lemons
Bottled lemon juice
2 egg whites

Put the water and sugar in a saucepan. Heat gently, stirring, until the sugar has dissolved. Bring to the boil and simmer gently for 10 minutes until thick but not coloured. Add the lemon rind and leave until cold. Make the freshly squeezed lemon juice up to 450 ml/¾ pt/2 cups with bottled lemon juice. Stir into the syrup. Strain into a freezerproof container and freeze for about 1½ hours until frozen round the edges. Whisk with a fork to break up the ice crystals. Whisk the egg whites until stiff and fold in with a metal spoon. Return to the freezer and freeze until firm.

Orange Sorbet

SERVES 8

Prepare as for Lemon Sorbet, but substitute the thinly pared rind and juice of 2 oranges for the lemons and spike to taste with lemon juice, if liked

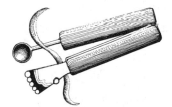

American Orange Sorbet

SERVES 8

60 ml/4 tbsp lemon juice
10 ml/2 tsp liquid sweetener
Finely grated rind and juice of 2 oranges
250 ml/8 fl oz/1 cup frozen concentrated
  orange juice, thawed
2 egg whites

Mix together the lemon juice and sweetener and make up to 600 ml/ 1 pt/2½ cups with water. Add the orange rind and juices and mix well. Pour into a freezerproof container and freeze for 2 hours until just firm. Whisk with a fork to break up the ice crystals. Whisk the egg whites until stiff and fold into the mixture with a metal spoon. Freeze until firm. Transfer to the fridge about 20 minutes before serving to soften slightly.

Grapefruit and Gin Sorbet

SERVES 6

175 g/6 oz/¾ cup granulated sugar
300 ml/½ pt/1¼ cups water
2 grapefruit, all pith and rind removed
  and segmented
75 ml/5 tbsp gin
1 egg white
Langues de Chat (see page 129), to
  serve

Put the sugar and water in a saucepan and heat gently until the sugar has dissolved. Bring to the boil and simmer for 5 minutes, without stirring. Leave to cool. Purée the grapefruit flesh in a blender or food processor with the gin. Stir into the cold syrup and freeze for 1½ hours until firm around the edges. Whisk thoroughly with a fork to break up the ice crystals. Whisk the egg white until stiff and fold in with a metal spoon. Return to the freezer and freeze until firm. Remove from the freezer about 15 minutes before serving with Langues de Chat.

Strawberry Sorbet

SERVES 6

100 g/4 oz/½ cup caster (superfine)
  sugar
300 ml/½ pt/1¼ cups water
225 g/8 oz ripe strawberries
Juice of 1 small lemon
1 egg white

Put the sugar and water in a saucepan. Heat gently until the sugar has dissolved completely. Leave to cool. Purée the strawberries in a blender or food processor. Pass through a sieve (strainer) if liked, to remove the pips. Stir into the syrup with the lemon juice. Turn into a freezerproof container and freeze until firm around the edges. Whisk with a fork to break up the ice crystals. Whisk the egg white until stiff and fold into the sorbet. Return to the freezer until firm. Remove from the freezer 10 minutes before serving to soften slightly.

Honey Sorbet

SERVES 6

15 ml/1 tbsp powdered gelatine
60 ml/4 tbsp apple juice
200 ml/7 fl oz/scant 1 cup water
60 ml/4 tbsp clear honey
250 ml/8 fl oz/1 cup crème fraîche
3 egg whites
40 g/1½ oz/3 tbsp caster (superfine)
*   sugar*

Sprinkle the gelatine over the apple juice in a small bowl and leave to soften for 5 minutes. Stand the bowl in a pan of hot water and stir until the gelatine has dissolved completely (or dissolve in the microwave). Blend the water and honey in a bowl. Stir in the dissolved gelatine and the crème fraîche. Freeze for 1½ hours. Remove from the freezer and whisk with a fork to break up the ice crystals. Whisk the egg whites until stiff. Whisk in the sugar until stiff and glossy. Fold into the half-frozen mixture with a metal spoon. Return to the freezer and freeze until firm.

Raspberry Leaf Sorbet

SERVES 4

175 g/6 oz/¾ cup granulated sugar
600 ml/1 pt/2½ cups water
Finely grated rind and juice of 2 large
*   lemons*
4 good handfuls of young raspberry
*   leaves*
1 small egg white

Dissolve the sugar in the water over a gentle heat, stirring, then bring to the boil and boil for 2 minutes without stirring. Stir in the lemon rind and juice. Add the raspberry leaves and leave to infuse until the mixture is cold. Whisk the egg white until stiff. Strain the mixture into the egg white and stir well. Pour into a freezerproof container and freeze until the mixture is half-frozen. Whisk with a fork to break up the ice crystals and freeze again until firm. Remove from the freezer 10 minutes before serving.

Elderflower Sorbet

SERVES 4

Prepare as for Raspberry Leaf Sorbet, but substitute freshly picked, just-flowering elderflowers for the raspberry leaves.

Blackcurrant Leaf Sorbet

SERVES 4

Prepare as for Raspberry Leaf Sorbet, but substitute blackcurrant leaves for the raspberry leaves.

Vine Leaf Sorbet

SERVES 4

Prepare as for Raspberry Leaf Sorbet, but substitute young vine leaves for the raspberry leaves.

Fresh Mint Sorbet

SERVES 4

Prepare as for Raspberry Leaf Sorbet, but substitute freshly picked mint sprigs for the raspberry leaves.

Lemon Water Ice

SERVES 4–6

3 lemons
300 ml/½ pt/1¼ cups water
5 ml/1 tsp powdered gelatine
100 g/4 oz/⅔ cup icing (confectioners')
  sugar
1 egg white

Thinly pare the rind from the lemons and simmer in the water for 5 minutes. Remove the rind. Sprinkle the gelatine over the water and stir until completely dissolved. Stir in the sugar until dissolved. Squeeze the juice from the lemons and stir in. Turn into a freezerproof container and freeze until half-frozen. Whisk with a fork to break up the ice crystals. Whisk the egg white until stiff and fold into the mixture with a metal spoon. Freeze until firm.

Orange Water Ice

SERVES 4–6

Prepare as for Lemon Water Ice, but substitute the rind and juice of 2 large oranges, made up to 150 ml/¼ pt/⅔ cup with pure orange juice, if necessary, for the lemons.

Apricot Water Ice

SERVES 4–6

450 g/1 lb apricots, halved and stoned
  (pitted)
300 ml/½ pt/1¼ cups water
Finely grated rind and juice of 1 lemon
5 ml/1 tsp powdered gelatine
75 g/3 oz/⅓ cup icing (confectioners')
  sugar
1 egg white

Put the apricots in a saucepan with the water, lemon rind and juice. Bring to the boil, reduce the heat, cover and simmer gently until the apricots are tender. Stir in the gelatine until dissolved. Purée in a blender or food processor with the sugar. Turn into a freezerproof container and leave until cold. Freeze until half-frozen. Whisk with a fork to break up the ice crystals. Whisk the egg white until stiff and fold into the mixture with a metal spoon. Freeze until firm.

Greengage Water Ice

SERVES 4

Prepare as for Apricot Water Ice, but substitute ripe greengages for the apricots.

Blackcurrant Sorbet

SERVES 6

325 ml/11 fl oz/1½ cups water
225 g/8 oz blackcurrants, stripped from
  their stalks
100 g/4 oz/½ cup caster (superfine)
  sugar
5 ml/1 tsp lemon juice
2 egg whites

Put 30 ml/2 tbsp of the water in a saucepan with the blackcurrants and stew gently for 10 minutes. Meanwhile, in a separate saucepan, gently heat the remaining water and the sugar, stirring until the sugar has dissolved, then bring to the boil and boil for 5 minutes. Purée the blackcurrants and sugar syrup in a blender or food processor. Add the lemon juice. Pass through a sieve (strainer) to remove the seeds. Turn into a freezerproof container, leave until cold, then freeze until firm around the edges. Whisk thoroughly with a fork to break up the ice crystals. Whisk the egg whites until stiff and fold in with a metal spoon. Return to the freezer and freeze until firm.

Coffee Granita

SERVES 4

600 ml/1 pt/2½ cups boiling water
40 ml/2½ tbsp instant coffee powder or
  granules
75 g/3 oz/⅓ cup caster (superfine) sugar
Amaretti Biscuits (see page 128), to
  serve

Mix together the water, coffee and sugar until completely dissolved. Leave until cold. Pour into a freezer-proof container and freeze for about 45–60 minutes or until firm around the edges. Whisk with a fork to break up the ice crystals. Repeat this process two or three times more until frozen and granular – about 3 hours in all. Spoon into glasses and serve with Amaretti Biscuits.

Lemon Granita

SERVES 4

100 g/4 oz/½ cup granulated sugar
300 ml/½ pt/1¼ cups water
Finely grated rind and juice of 2 lemons
Bottled lemon juice

Put the sugar and water in a saucepan and heat gently, stirring, until the sugar has dissolved. Bring to the boil and boil without stirring for 5 minutes. Leave to cool. Make the lemon rind and juice up to 250 ml/ 8 fl oz/1 cup with bottled lemon juice. Stir into the syrup. Turn into a freezerproof container and freeze until half-frozen. Whisk with a fork to break up the ice crystals. Freeze again until firm. Turn out of the container and crush coarsely. Serve immediately in rough chunks.

Orange Granita

SERVES 4

Prepare as for Lemon Granita (see page 201), but substitute the finely grated rind and juice of 2 oranges, made up to 250 ml/8 fl oz/1 cup with pure orange juice, for the lemons.

Victoria Ice

SERVES 6

450 g/1 lb ripe Victoria plums, quartered and stoned (pitted)
45 ml/3 tbsp icing (confectioners') sugar
120 ml/4 fl oz/½ cup water
30 ml/2 tbsp kirsch or schnapps
175 g/6 oz/¾ cup caster (superfine) sugar
2 large egg whites
A pinch of salt
300 ml/½ pt/1¼ cups double (heavy) cream
Almond Tuiles (see page 130), to serve

Put the plums in a pan with the icing sugar, 30 ml/2 tbsp of the water and the kirsch or schnapps. Cover and stew gently until the plums are soft. Purée in a blender or food processor. Dissolve the caster sugar in the remaining water. Bring to the boil and boil for 2 minutes. Whisk the egg whites with the salt until stiff. Add the boiling sugar syrup in a thin stream, whisking all the time. Gradually whisk in the plum purée. Whip the cream until peaking and fold into the mixture with a metal spoon. Turn into a metal or plastic container and freeze until firm. Remove from the freezer 5 minutes before serving with Almond Tuiles.

Fireside Ice Cream

SERVES 6

4 egg yolks
225 g/8 oz/⅔ cup thick honey
A pinch of ground cloves
600 ml/1 pt/2½ cups double (heavy) cream
150 ml/¼ pt/⅔ cup whisky

Whisk the egg yolks with the honey and cloves until thick and doubled in volume. Whip together the cream and whisky until peaking, then lightly whisk or fold into the honey mixture. Turn into a freezerproof container and freeze until firm.

Peach Melba

SERVES 4

100 g/4 oz raspberries
30 ml/2 tbsp redcurrant jelly (clear conserve)
15 ml/1 tbsp icing (confectioners') sugar
2 peaches, skinned, halved and stoned (pitted)
8 scoops of any vanilla ice cream (see page 188, or use bought)
150 ml/¼ pt/⅔ cup double (heavy) cream, whipped
45 ml/3 tbsp chopped pistachio nuts

Pass the raspberries through a sieve (strainer) to purée and remove the seeds. Place in a saucepan with the redcurrant jelly and icing sugar. Heat gently until the jelly and sugar have dissolved. Leave to cool. Place each peach half on an individual serving dish. Top each with a scoop of ice cream and pipe or pile the whipped cream over. Drizzle with the raspberry sauce and sprinkle with the pistachio nuts.

Banana Splits

SERVES 4

4 bananas
8 scoops of any vanilla ice cream (see
page 188, or use bought)
Whipped cream (optional), to decorate
1 quantity Simple Chocolate Sauce (see
page 351)
Toasted chopped nuts, for sprinkling
2 glacé (candied) cherries, halved

Halve the bananas lengthways and place two halves in each of four shallow serving dishes (preferably oval ones), to resemble two sides of a boat. Add two scoops of ice cream to the centre of each. Top with a little whipped cream, if using. Drizzle with hot Simple Chocolate Sauce, sprinkle with chopped nuts, top with half a glacé cherry and serve immediately.

Colourful Fruit Sundaes

SERVES 4

295 g/10½ oz/1 small can of raspberries,
drained, reserving the juice
2 nectarines, chopped, discarding the
stones (pits)
2 kiwi fruit, peeled, halved and sliced
500 ml/17 fl oz/2¼ cups of any vanilla
ice cream (see page 188, or use
bought)
50 g/2 oz fresh raspberries

Purée the canned raspberries in a blender or food processor. Pass through a sieve (strainer) to remove the seeds, then stir in enough of the juice to give a pouring consistency. Put half the chopped nectarines in the base of four sundae glasses. Top with half the kiwi

fruit. Top each with a scoop of the ice cream, then drizzle with half the raspberry sauce. Repeat the layers. Top with the fresh raspberries and serve straight away.

Lemon Coolers

SERVES 6–8

6–8 lemons (depending on size)
200 ml/7 fl oz/scant 1 cup water
300 g/11 oz/scant 1½ cups granulated
sugar
5 ml/1 tsp cornflour (cornstarch)
4 large egg yolks
375 ml/13 fl oz/1½ cups Greek-style
Yoghurt (see page 359, or use
bought)
Mint sprigs, to decorate

Cut the tops off the lemons and reserve. Scoop out the flesh into a saucepan, leaving the skins intact. Add the water and sugar to the saucepan. Heat gently until the sugar dissolves, pressing the fruit firmly on the sides of the pan to extract the juice. Bring to the boil and cook for 4 minutes. Strain. Put the cornflour and egg yolks in a bowl and whisk thoroughly until thick and pale. Gradually whisk in the lemon syrup and continue whisking until the mixture is thick and foamy. Leave to cool, then fold in the yoghurt. Turn into a freezer container and freeze for 2 hours. Whisk well, then spoon into the lemon shells, replace the tops and wrap individually in foil. Freeze for at least 3 hours until firm. Transfer to the fridge 20 minutes before eating. Unwrap and place in wine goblets. Decorate each with a mint sprig.

Raspberry Knickerbocker Glory

SERVES 4

1 packet of raspberry-flavoured jelly (jello)
4 trifle sponges
30 ml/2 tbsp sweet sherry or orange juice
225 g/8 oz raspberries
15 ml/1 tbsp caster (superfine) sugar
4 scoops of Raspberry Ripple Ice Cream (see page 189, or use bought)
150 ml/¼ pt/⅔ cup double (heavy) cream, whipped
Chopped nuts and coloured sprinkles, to decorate

M ake up the jelly according to the packet directions. Chill until set. Crumble the trifle sponges in a bowl and mix in the sherry or orange juice. When soaked, divide between four tall sundae glasses. Divide the raspberries between the glasses. Sprinkle with the sugar. Chop up the jelly and spoon over the raspberries. Top each with a scoop of ice cream. Smother in whipped cream and decorate with chopped nuts and coloured sprinkles.

Strawberry Knickerbocker Glory

SERVES 4

P repare as for Raspberry Knickerbocker Glory, but substitute strawberry jelly (jello) for the raspberry, sliced strawberries for the raspberries and either all strawberry or half strawberry and half vanilla or chocolate ice cream for the raspberry ripple.

St Clement's Knickerbocker Glory

SERVES 4

1 packet of lemon-flavoured jelly (jello)
300 g/11 oz/1 medium can of mandarin oranges, drained, reserving the juice
1 sachet of Dream Topping mix
150 ml/¼ pt/⅔ cup milk
150 ml/¼ pt/⅔ cup fromage frais
Finely grated rind and juice of 1 lemon or orange
Caster (superfine) sugar (optional)
8 scoops of any vanilla ice cream (see page 188, or use bought)
Crystallised (candied) orange and lemon slices, to decorate

M ake up the jelly according to the packet directions, using the mandarin orange juice for the some of the water. Chill until set, then roughly chop. Make up the Dream Topping with the milk according to the packet directions. Blend the fromage frais with the orange or lemon rind and juice. Sweeten to taste, if liked, with sugar. Spoon half the jelly into four knickerbocker glory glasses or other tall glasses. Top with the mandarin oranges. Spoon the fromage frais over. Top with the remaining jelly. Add 2 scoops of ice cream to each. Pile the Dream Topping over and decorate with orange and lemon slices.

Chestnut Sundae

SERVES 4

*8 scoops of any vanilla ice cream (see
page 188, or use bought)*
*170 g/6 oz/1 small can of sweetened
chestnut purée (paste)*
*60 ml/4 tbsp double (heavy) cream,
whipped*
4 maraschino cherries

Put the ice cream in four sundae
glasses. Pipe or spoon the chestnut
purée over. Top each with 15 ml/1 tbsp
whipped cream, then with a maraschino
cherry.

Frozen Strawberry Mousse

SERVES 4

*350 g/12 oz strawberries, plus extra to
decorate*
Finely grated rind and juice of ½ lemon
Caster (superfine) sugar
2 egg whites
150 ml/¼ pt/⅔ cup double (heavy) cream

Purée the strawberries in a blender or
food processor. Add the lemon rind
and juice and sweeten to taste with
caster sugar. Whisk the egg whites until
stiff, then the cream until peaking. Fold
the cream, then the egg whites into the
purée. Turn into a freezerproof container
and freeze until firm. Remove from the
freezer 15 minutes before serving. Serve
scooped into glass dishes with a few
strawberries scattered over.

Frozen Raspberry Mousse

SERVES 4

Prepare as for Frozen Strawberry
Mousse, but substitute raspberries,
sieved (strained) after puréeing to
remove the pips, for the strawberries.

Frozen Peach Mousse

SERVES 4

Prepare as for Frozen Strawberry
Mousse, but substitute 4 ripe
peaches, skinned, quartered and stoned
(pitted), for the strawberries. Use an
extra peach, unskinned and sliced, to
decorate.

Melon Belle Hélène

SERVES 4

2 small cantaloupe melons
*4 scoops of any vanilla ice cream (see
page 188, or use bought)*
*1 quantity Belgian Chocolate Sauce (see
page 351), to serve*

Halve the melons and scoop out the
seeds. Put a scoop of ice cream in
the centre of each and spoon the
Belgian Chocolate Sauce over.

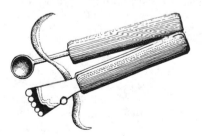

Frozen Coffee Crunch Soufflés

SERVES 4

175 g/6 oz/¾ cup caster (superfine) sugar
90 ml/6 tbsp cold water
2 egg whites
7.5 ml/1½ tsp instant coffee powder or granules
7.5 ml/1½ tsp boiling water
15 ml/1 tbsp amaretto
375 ml/13 fl oz/1½ cups double (heavy) cream
8 Amaretti Biscuits (see page 128, or use bought), crushed
Icing (confectioners') sugar, for dusting
4 toasted almonds

Tie greaseproof (waxed) paper around four ramekins (custard cups) so it stands 5 cm/2 in above the rims. Heat the sugar and cold water gently in a saucepan until the sugar dissolves, then bring to the boil and boil for 3 minutes. Meanwhile, whisk the egg whites until stiff. Pour the syrup on the egg whites, whisking all the time until cool and glossy. Dissolve the coffee in the boiling water and stir in the liqueur. Whisk into the meringue mixture. Whip the cream until peaking and fold into the egg mixture. Pour into the ramekins until they are half-full, then sprinkle with a layer of about two-thirds of the crushed Amaretti Biscuits. Top with the remaining soufflé mixture (it should stand about 2.5 cm/1 in above the rim of each dish). Freeze for at least 2 hours until firm. Carefully remove the paper collars and coat the edges in the remaining crushed biscuits. Dust the tops with sifted icing sugar and top

each with a toasted almond. Leave in the fridge for 15–20 minutes to soften slightly before serving.

Melon Glacé Melba

SERVES 4

2 small ogen melons
4 scoops of any vanilla ice cream (see page 188, or use bought)
Fresh Raspberry Sauce (see page 348), to serve

Halve the melons and scoop out the seeds. Add a scoop of ice cream to the centre of each and spoon the Fresh Raspberry Sauce over.

Melon Glacé

SERVES 4

2 small ogen, cantaloupe, galia or charentais melons
4 scoops of any vanilla ice cream (see page 188, or use bought)
30 ml/2 tbsp ginger wine

Halve the melons, scoop out the seeds and place the melon halves in four serving dishes. Add a scoop of ice cream to each cavity and spoon the ginger wine over. Serve straight away.

Iced Coffee Meringue Ring

SERVES 6

---

3 eggs, separated
225 g/8 oz/1 cup caster (superfine) sugar
30 ml/2 tbsp instant coffee powder or
  granules
170 g/6 oz/1 small can of evaporated milk
300 ml/½ pt/1¼ cups whipping cream
60 ml/4 tbsp coffee liqueur
Extra whipped cream and a little instant
  coffee powder, to decorate

Whisk the egg whites until stiff. Reserve 45 ml/3 tbsp of the sugar. Whisk half the remaining sugar into the egg whites and whisk again. Fold in the remaining half. Place small spoonfuls on a baking (cookie) sheet lined with baking parchment. Bake in a preheated oven at 150°C/300°F/gas mark 2 for about 1 hour or until pale biscuit-coloured and crisp. Remove from the oven and leave to cool on a wire rack.

Meanwhile, put the egg yolks in a bowl with the remaining 45 ml/3 tbsp of the sugar. Whisk until thick and pale. Put the coffee in a measuring jug. Add the evaporated milk and make up to 300 ml/½ pt/1¼ cups with water. Heat gently in a saucepan until hot but not boiling. Whisk into the egg yolk mixture. Return to the pan and cook, stirring, until the custard thickens and coats the back of a wooden spoon. Do not allow to boil. To test, lift the spoon out of the mixture and draw a finger across the back of the spoon: there should be a clear line left. Leave to cool, stirring occasionally.

Whip together the cream and liqueur until peaking and fold into the coffee custard with a metal spoon. Turn into a freezerproof container and freeze for 2 hours or until partly frozen. Whisk thoroughly with a fork to break up the ice crystals. Roughly crush the meringues and fold into the mixture. Spoon into a 1.5 litre/2½ pt/6 cup ring mould. Freeze until firm. When ready to serve, dip the base of the mould briefly in hot water, then turn out on to a serving plate. Fill the centre with whipped cream, dust with coffee powder and serve straight away.

Iced Christmas Pud

SERVES 8

---

4 eggs, separated
100 g/4 oz/½ cup caster (superfine) sugar
225 g/8 oz bought Christmas pudding or
  rich fruit cake, broken into small
  pieces
300 ml/½ pt/1¼ cups double (heavy)
  cream, whipped
45 ml/3 tbsp brandy or rum
A small holly sprig, to decorate

Whisk together the egg yolks and sugar until thick and pale. Fold in the crumbled pudding, then the cream and the brandy or rum. Whisk the egg whites until stiff and fold in with a metal spoon. Turn into a 1.5 litre/2½ pt/ 6 cup pudding basin (or two small basins), cover and freeze until firm. When ready to serve, loosen the edge with a round-bladed knife. Dip the basin briefly in hot water, turn out on to a serving plate and decorate with a small holly sprig. Serve straight away.

Raspberry Baked Alaska

SERVES 8

Oil, for greasing
175 g/6 oz/¾ cup caster (superfine) sugar
50 g/2 oz/½ cup self-raising (self-rising)
  flour
2.5 ml/½ tsp baking powder
50 g/2 oz/¼ cup soft tub margarine
1 egg
15 ml/1 tbsp kirsch or raspberry liqueur
4 egg whites
500 ml/17 fl oz/2¼ cups Raspberry
  Ripple Ice Cream (see page 189, or
  use bought)
350 g/12 oz raspberries
Whole blanched almonds, to decorate

Grease an 18 cm/7 in sandwich tin (pan) and line the base with greased greaseproof (waxed) paper. Put 50 g/2 oz/¼ cup of the sugar in a bowl with the flour, baking powder, margarine and whole egg. Beat well until smooth with a wooden spoon or hand beater. Turn into the prepared tin and level the surface. Bake in a preheated oven at 190°C/375°F/gas mark 5 for 15–20 minutes until risen, golden and the centre springs back when lightly pressed. Turn out on to a wire rack, remove the paper and leave to cool.

When ready to serve, place on an ovenproof serving dish and sprinkle with the kirsch or raspberry liqueur. Whisk the egg whites until stiff. Whisk in half the remaining sugar until stiff and glossy. Fold in the remainder with a metal spoon. Pile the ice cream up on the centre of the sponge round. Cover all over with the raspberries. Smother completely in the meringue mixture and decorate with a few blanched almonds. Bake in a preheated oven at 230°C/450°F/gas mark 8 for about 5 minutes until the peaks of the meringue are just turning colour. Serve straight away.

Christmas Bombe

SERVES 6

100 g/4 oz/⅔ cup dried mixed fruit (fruit
  cake mix)
50 g/2 oz/½ cup glacé (candied) cherries,
  chopped
30 ml/2 tbsp brandy
2.5 ml/½ tsp mixed (apple-pie) spice
500 ml/17 fl oz/2¼ cups any vanilla ice
  cream (see page 188, or use bought),
  slightly softened
90 ml/6 tbsp double (heavy) cream,
  lightly whipped
50 g/2 oz/½ cup toasted, chopped mixed
  nuts
A holly sprig, to decorate

Put the dried fruit and cherries in a bowl and mix in the brandy and spice. Cover with clingfilm (plastic wrap) and leave to soak for 3 hours or overnight. Mash the ice cream briefly and fold in the cream, soaked fruit and nuts. Turn into a 1 litre/1¾ pt/4¼ cup pudding basin. Cover and freeze until firm. When ready to serve, loosen the edge, stand the basin briefly in hot water, then turn out, decorate with a holly sprig and serve.

Coffee Maple Pecan Alaska

SERVES 6

100 g/4 oz/1 cup plain (all-purpose) flour
A pinch of salt
50 g/2 oz/¼ cup butter, diced
90 g/3½ oz/scant ½ cup caster (superfine) sugar
40 g/1½ oz/⅓ cup pecan nuts
1 egg yolk
15 ml/1 tbsp water
3 egg whites
500 g/17 fl oz/2¼ cups Coffee Ice Cream (see page 189, or use bought)
Maple syrup, to serve

Sift the flour and salt into a bowl. Add the butter and rub in with the fingertips until the mixture resembles breadcrumbs. Stir in 15 ml/1 tbsp of the sugar. Chop 25 g/1 oz/¼ cup of the pecans and stir into the mixture. Add the egg yolk and water and mix to form a firm dough. Knead gently on a lightly floured surface. Place on a greased baking (cookie) sheet and roll out to a rectangle about 15 × 10 cm/6 × 4 in. Bake in a preheated oven at 180°C/350°F/gas mark 4 for about 30 minutes until pale golden brown. Allow to cool slightly, then transfer to a wire rack until completely cold.

Place on an ovenproof serving plate. Whisk the egg whites until stiff. Whisk in half the remaining sugar until stiff and glossy. Fold in the remaining sugar. Put the ice cream on the shortcake base, either in a block or in scoops. Cover completely with the meringue mixture and decorate with the remaining pecans. Bake immediately in a hot oven at 230°C/450°F/gas mark 8 for about 3–5 minutes until just turning colour. Serve immediately with maple syrup.

Baked Alaska

SERVES 4–6

1 Basic Sponge Flan Case (pie shell) (see page 62, or use bought)
3 egg whites
175 g/6 oz/¾ cup caster (superfine) sugar
2.5 ml/½ tsp vanilla essence (extract)
8 scoops of any vanilla ice cream (see page 188, or use bought)

Put the sponge case (pie shell) on an ovenproof plate. Whisk the egg whites until stiff. Whisk in half the sugar and the vanilla essence and continue whisking until stiff and glossy. Fold in the remaining sugar. Pile the scoops of ice cream in the flan case. Cover completely with the meringue mixture. Bake in a preheated oven at 230°C/450°F/gas mark 8 for 2 minutes until the meringue is just turning golden. Serve straight away before the ice cream melts.

Golden Baked Alaska

SERVES 6

18 cm/7 in Basic Sponge Flan Case
  (see page 62, or use bought)
2 peaches, stoned (pitted) and chopped
30 ml/2 tbsp peach or orange liqueur or
  orange juice
3 eggs, separated
15 ml/1 tbsp caster (superfine) sugar,
  plus extra for sprinkling
500 ml/17 fl oz/2¼ cups any vanilla ice
  cream (see page 188, or use bought)

Put the flan case (pie shell) on an ovenproof serving plate. Top with the chopped fruit and drizzle with the liqueur or orange juice. Whisk the egg whites until stiff, then the egg yolks and sugar until thick and pale. Fold the egg whites into the egg yolk mixture. Pile scoops of ice cream on top of the fruit. Cover completely with the soufflé mixture. Bake in a preheated oven at 220°C/425°F/gas mark 7 for 3–4 minutes until lightly coloured. Sprinkle with caster sugar and serve straight away.

Chocolate Baked Alaska

SERVES 4–6

1 small chocolate-flavoured Swiss (jelly)
  roll
3 egg whites
175 g/6 oz/¾ cup caster (superfine)
  sugar
2.5 ml/½ tsp vanilla essence (extract)
8 scoops of Dark Chocolate Ice Cream
  (see page 189, or use bought)
6 whole toasted almonds

Slice the Swiss roll and lay in a single layer on an ovenproof plate. Whisk the egg whites until stiff. Whisk in half the sugar and the vanilla essence and continue whisking until stiff and glossy. Fold in the remaining sugar. Pile up the ice cream on the Swiss roll. Cover completely with the meringue mixture. Decorate with the almonds and bake in a preheated oven at 230°C/450°F/gas mark 8 for 2 minutes until turning pale golden. Serve immediately.

Spiced Lemon Block

SERVES 6

Oil, for greasing
25 g/1 oz/2 tbsp light brown sugar
75 g/3 oz/⅓ cup butter
100 g/4 oz/2 cups bran flakes, lightly
  crushed
10 ml/2 tsp ground cinnamon
Finely grated rind and juice of 2 lemons
10 ml/2 tsp powdered gelatine
2 large eggs, separated
25 g/1 oz/2 tbsp caster (superfine) sugar
200 g/7 oz/1 small can of sweetened
  condensed milk

Lightly oil a 900 g/2 lb loaf tin (pan).
Put the brown sugar and butter in a
saucepan and heat gently until the
butter has melted. Stir in the cereal and
cinnamon. Press almost half of the
mixture into the base of the prepared
tin. Put the lemon rind and juice in a
small bowl. Sprinkle the gelatine over
and leave to soften for 5 minutes. Stand
the bowl in a pan of hot water and stir
until the gelatine has dissolved
completely. Whisk the egg yolks with
the caster sugar until thick and pale.
Whisk in the condensed milk, then the
gelatine mixture. Whisk the egg whites
until stiff and fold in with a metal
spoon. Turn into the prepared tin, cover
with the remaining cereal mixture in an
even layer and press very lightly. Wrap
in clingfilm (plastic wrap) or foil and
freeze until firm. Turn out and serve
sliced.

Raspberry Vacherin

SERVES 6

4 large egg whites
225 g/8 oz/1 cup caster (superfine)
  sugar
1 litre/1¾ pt/4¼ cups Raspberry Ice
  Cream (see page 189, or use bought)
350 g/12 oz raspberries
75 g/5 tbsp double (heavy) cream

Draw two 23 cm/9 in circles on
baking parchment on baking
(cookie) sheets. Whisk the egg whites
until stiff. Whisk in the sugar a little at
a time, whisking well after each
addition until the mixture is stiff and
glossy. Use to fill a piping bag fitted
with a large plain tube (tip) and,
starting from the centre of each circle,
pipe the meringue mixture in a spiral to
fill the circles (or spread the mixture
evenly with a palette knife). Bake in a
preheated oven at 150°C/300°F/gas
mark 2 for 1 hour. Turn off the oven
and leave to cool completely in the
oven.

Carefully peel off the paper and
place one round on a freezerproof
serving plate. Quickly mash the slightly
softened ice cream with half the
raspberries and spread on the meringue
round. Press the second round on top
and re-freeze immediately before the ice
cream melts. When completely frozen
again, remove from the freezer. Whip
the cream and spread all round the side.
Decorate with the remaining raspberries
and return to the freezer. Remove from
the freezer about 45 minutes before
serving.

Strawberry Vacherin

SERVES 6

Prepare as for Raspberry Vacherin (see page 211), but substitute sliced strawberries and Fresh Strawberry Ice Cream (see page 188, or use bought) for the raspberries and Raspberry Ice Cream.

Peach Vacherin

SERVES 6

Prepare as for Raspberry Vacherin (see page 211), but substitute 3 chopped peaches and any vanilla ice cream (see page 188, or use bought) or Almond Macaroon Ice Cream (see page 190, or use bought) for the raspberries and Raspberry Cream inside. Decorate the edge with 1–2 sliced peaches.

Lemon Vacherin

SERVES 6

Prepare as for Raspberry Vacherin (see page 211), but use Lemon Ice Cream (see page 190) or any vanilla ice cream (see page 188, or use bought) in the centre and spread with a layer of lemon curd. Decorate the edge with crystallised (candied) lemon slices and angelica leaves.

Orange Vacherin

SERVES 6

Prepare as for Raspberry Vacherin (see page 211), but use Orange Ice Cream (see page 190) or any vanilla ice cream (see page 188, or use bought) in the centre and mix with 300 g/11 oz/ 1 medium can of mandarin oranges, drained, reserving a few to decorate the edge alternately with toasted whole almonds.

Chocolate Ice Cream Flan

SERVES 8

50 g/2 oz/¼ cup butter or margarine
15 ml/1 tbsp golden (light corn) syrup
15 ml/1 tbsp caster (superfine) sugar
2.5 ml/½ tsp vanilla essence (extract)
200 g/7 oz/1 small packet of chocolate
*   digestive biscuits (graham crackers),*
*   crushed*
50 g/2 oz/¼ cup raisins
Oil, for greasing
8 large scoops of Dark Chocolate Ice
*   Cream (see page 189, or use bought)*
150 ml/¼ pt/⅔ cups double (heavy)
*   cream, whipped*
50 g/2 oz/½ cup plain (semi-sweet)
*   chocolate, melted*

Melt the butter or margarine, syrup, sugar and vanilla in a saucepan. Stir in the crushed biscuits and raisins. Press into the base and sides of an oiled 20 cm/8 in flan ring set on a flat serving plate. Chill until firm. Remove the flan ring. Pile scoops of ice cream in the flan case (pie shell). Decorate with whipped cream and drizzle the melted chocolate over. Serve straight away.

Maraschino Ice Cream Gâteau

SERVES 8

100 g/4 oz/1 cup self-raising (self-rising) flour
2.5 ml/½ tsp baking powder
100 g/4 oz/½ cup caster (superfine) sugar
100 g/4 oz/½ cup soft tub margarine
2 eggs
A few drops of almond essence (extract)
Oil, for greasing
200 g/7 oz/1 small jar of maraschino cherries
10 scoops of any vanilla ice cream (see page 188, or use bought)
450 ml/¾ pt/2 cups whipping cream, whipped
Whole blanched almonds, toasted, to decorate

Put the flour, baking powder, sugar, margarine, eggs and almond essence in a food processor and run the machine until the mixture is smooth, or beat in a bowl until smooth. Turn into a greased 20 cm/8 in loose-bottomed cake tin (pan). Bake in a preheated oven at 190°C/375°F/gas mark 5 for about 25 minutes or until the centre springs back when lightly pressed. Turn out on to a wire rack and leave to cool.
    Drain the cherries, reserving the syrup. Reserve 10 cherries for decoration and chop the remainder. Split the cake in half. Put the base half back in the cake tin and sprinkle with a little of the maraschino syrup. Press the ice cream evenly on top. Cover with the chopped cherries. Press the other half of the cake on top and sprinkle with a little more of the maraschino syrup. Press down firmly. Cover the tin with foil and freeze until firm. Turn the frozen cake out on to a serving plate. Smother with whipped cream. Decorate with the reserved cherries and almonds. Freeze again until firm.

Cool Pineapple Pleasure

SERVES 6

1 ripe pineapple
30 ml/2 tbsp kirsch
6 scoops of any vanilla ice cream (see page 188, or use bought)

Cut the leafy top off the pineapple and reserve. Peel the fruit and cut the fruit into six rings, cutting out the centre core. Place in a dish. Sprinkle with the kirsch and chill for at least 30 minutes. Transfer to serving plates and fill the centre of each with a scoop of ice cream. Cut the leafy top into six slices and lay one beside each pineapple ring to decorate.

Strawberry Iced Condé

SERVES 4–6

450 g/1 lb strawberries, sliced
Finely grated rind and juice of 1 orange
15 ml/1 tbsp caster (superfine) sugar
430 g/15½ oz/1 large can of creamed
  rice pudding
8 scoops of Fresh Strawberry Ice
  Cream (see page 188, or use bought)
150 ml/¼ pt/⅔ cup whipping cream,
  whipped
Chopped pistachio nuts, to decorate

Put the sliced strawberries in a bowl with the orange juice and sugar. Leave to marinate for 30 minutes. Blend together the orange rind and rice and spoon into four to six glasses. Chill. Spoon the marinated strawberries over the rice. Top with scoops of ice cream, then a spoonful of whipped cream. Sprinkle with pistachio nuts and serve.

Peach Iced Condé

SERVES 4–6

Prepare as for Strawberry Iced Condé, but substitute 3–4 chopped, stoned (pitted) peaches for the the strawberries and use any vanilla ice cream (see page 188, or use bought). Drizzle 5–10 ml/1–2 tsp peach liqueur over each portion before topping with the cream.

Raspberry Iced Condé

SERVES 4–6

Prepare as for Strawberry Iced Condé, but substitute whole raspberries for sliced strawberries and Raspberry Ripple Ice Cream (see page 189, or use bought) for the the Strawberry Ice Cream.

Butterscotch Sundae

SERVES 4

4 scoops of any vanilla ice cream (see
  page 188, or use bought))
4 scoops of Dark Chocolate Ice Cream
  (see page 189, or use bought)
Butterscotch Sauce (see page 351), hot
Whipped cream and toasted chopped
  nuts, to decorate

Put the scoops of ice cream into four glass dishes. Pour the hot Butterscotch Sauce over and serve straight away decorated with whipped cream and chopped nuts.

Banana Butterscotch Sundae

SERVES 4

Prepare as for Butterscotch Sundae, but add 2 sliced bananas to the dishes over the ice cream before adding the sauce.

Tropical Iced Pineapple Fingers

SERVES 6

397 g/13¾ oz/1 large can of crushed pineapple
50 g/2 oz/¼ cup caster (superfine) sugar
45 ml/3 tbsp golden (light corn) syrup
Finely grated rind and juice of 1 lime
450 ml/¾ pt/2 cups coconut milk
2 egg whites
Toasted shredded coconut, to decorate

Mix together all the ingredients except the egg whites and turn into one or two fairly shallow freezerproof containers. Freeze for about 1½ hours until half-frozen. Turn into a bowl and whisk thoroughly to break up the ice crystals. Whisk the egg whites until stiff, then fold into the slushy mixture with a metal spoon. Return to the freezer containers and freeze until firm. Cut into fingers and serve decorated with toasted shredded coconut.

Figs Maria

SERVES 4

12 ripe figs, quartered
8 scoops of any vanilla ice cream (see page 188, or use bought)
30 ml/2 tbsp Marsala
3 macaroons, crushed
4 fresh cherries

Arrange the quartered figs in four glass serving dishes. Top with the scoops of ice cream. Drizzle the Marsala over and sprinkle with the crushed macaroon. Decorate each with a cherry.

Chinese Ice Cream

SERVES 4

8 scoops of any vanilla ice cream (see page 188, or use bought, but not soft-scoop)
Oil, for deep-frying
90 ml/6 tbsp plain (all-purpose) flour
2 eggs, beaten
50 g/2 oz/1 cup fresh white breadcrumbs
15 ml/1 tbsp desiccated (shredded) coconut
All-year Raspberry Sauce (see page 348), to serve

Line a baking (cookie) sheet with greaseproof (waxed) paper. Put the scoops of ice cream on it and return to the freezer immediately until very hard (preferably overnight). Heat the oil until a cube of day-old bread browns in 30 seconds. Coat each scoop of ice cream in flour, then beaten egg, then the breadcrumbs mixed with the coconut. Deep-fry for no more than 30 seconds, until golden. Serve immediately with All-year Raspberry Sauce.

Macerated Magic

Many fruits benefit from being poached, stewed or simply steeped in syrup, juice or alcohol to give subtle differences of flavour and texture. In this chapter, you will find everything from a simple fruit salad to Brandied Cherry Compôte. Hot or cold, cooked or fresh, there is a riot of colour, flavour and refreshment throughout.

Orange Flower Creation

SERVES 4

4 small sprigs of redcurrants
Caster (superfine) sugar
4 oranges (or 2 ordinary oranges and
*   2 blood oranges)*
225 g/8 oz cultivated (sweet)
*   blackberries*
90 ml/6 tbsp orange juice
10 ml/2 tsp lemon juice
60 ml/4 tbsp orange flower water
2.5 ml/½ tsp vanilla essence (extract)
30 ml/2 tbsp clear honey
60 ml/4 tbsp fromage frais, to serve

Dip the redcurrant sprigs in water, then roll gently in caster sugar to coat completely. Leave to dry on greaseproof (waxed) paper on a wire rack. Hold the oranges over a bowl to catch any juice and cut off all the rind. Slice the fruit and arrange in a circle on four individual serving plates (alternating the different types of orange, if using). Pile the blackberries in the centre of the rings. Add the orange juice to any juice in the bowl. Stir in the lemon juice, orange flower water and vanilla essence. Sweeten to taste with the honey. Spoon over the blackberries and oranges and leave at room temperature for at least 30 minutes. Put a spoonful of fromage frais on top of the blackberries and lay the redcurrant sprigs on top. Serve straight away.

Ginger Pears

SERVES 4

300 ml/½ pt/1¼ cups apple juice
50 g/2 oz/¼ cup granulated sugar
5 cm/2 in piece of cinnamon stick
Thinly pared rind of ½ lemon
2.5 cm/1 in piece of fresh root ginger,
*   peeled and lightly crushed*
4 pears, peeled, cored and halved
Atholl Brose Cream (see page 357), to
*   serve*

Put the apple juice and sugar in a saucepan and heat gently, stirring, until the sugar has dissolved. Add the cinnamon, lemon rind and ginger. Put the pears in the liquid. Bring to the boil, reduce the heat, cover and simmer very gently for 10–15 minutes until almost transparent, basting occasionally. Lift out the pears and place in a serving dish. Boil the syrup rapidly until reduced by half. Strain over the pears, leave to cool, then chill. Serve with Atholl Brose Cream.

Ginger Apples

SERVES 4

Prepare as for Ginger Pears, but substitute eating (dessert) apples for the pears. Serve with Cold Sabayon (see page 353) instead of Atholl Brose Cream.

Poirs Belle Hélène

SERVES 4

600 ml/1 pt/2½ cups water
100 g/4 oz/½ cup granulated sugar
Thinly pared rind of 1 orange
2.5 ml/½ tsp vanilla essence (extract)
4 large pears
Belgian Chocolate Sauce, (see page 351)

Put the water and sugar in a saucepan and heat gently until the sugar has dissolved. Add the orange rind and vanilla. Peel the pears and carefully cut out the cores from the base, leaving the fruit whole. Place in the syrup and simmer, covered, for 20–25 minutes, turning occasionally, until they are translucent. Remove from the heat and leave to cool in the syrup. Remove from the syrup and transfer to shallow glass serving dishes. Spoon the Belgian Chocolate Sauce over and serve cold.

Drunken Pears

SERVES 4

15 ml/1 tbsp light brown sugar
5 ml/1 tsp lemon juice
300 ml/½ pt/1¼ cups red wine
4 ripe pears, peeled

Put the sugar, lemon juice and wine in a saucepan and heat until the sugar dissolves. Cut a thin slice off the bottom of each pear so it will stand upright and carefully cut out the cores. Stand the pears in an ovenproof dish and pour the wine over. Cover with foil and bake in a preheated oven at 160°C/325°F/gas mark 3 for 30 minutes, turning once. Serve hot with the wine spooned over, or cool then chill.

Hot and Cold Pears

SERVES 4

Finely grated rind and juice of 1 lime
100 g/4 oz/½ cup granulated sugar
300 ml/½ pt/1¼ cups water
4 pears, peeled but left whole
1 egg white
150 ml/¼ pt/⅔ cup soured (dairy sour) cream

Put the lime rind and juice in a pan with the sugar and water. Heat gently, stirring, until the sugar has dissolved. Add the pears. Bring to the boil, reduce the heat and simmer gently for about 10 minutes or until just cooked. Remove from the pan with a draining spoon. Leave to cool, then chill. Boil the syrup in the pan rapidly until syrupy and reduced by half. Cover and leave until ready to serve. When ready to serve, reheat the syrup. Whisk the egg white until stiff. Stir into the syrup, then blend in the cream. Heat through. Transfer the cold pears to serving plates and spoon the hot sauce over.

Pears Margarita

SERVES 4

100 g/4 oz/²/₃ cup raisins
45 ml/3 tbsp brandy
150 ml/¼ pt/²/₃ cup double (heavy) cream
12 glacé (candied) cherries
15 ml/1 tbsp chopped angelica
15 ml/1 tbsp chopped walnuts
4 ripe pears, peeled, halved and cored

Put the raisins and brandy in a saucepan and bring just to the boil. Leave until cold. Whip the cream until peaking. Chop 10 of the glacé cherries and add to the cream with the angelica, nuts and soaked raisins. Fold in gently until well blended. Cut a tiny slice off the rounded side of each pear half so it sits steadily on the plate. Put the slices in the cavities. Place on a serving dish. Pile the cream mixture on top and decorate each with a halved glacé cherry. Chill for at least 30 minutes to allow the flavours to develop.

Pommes en Papillote

SERVES 6

6 eating (dessert) apples
50 g/2 oz/¼ cup unsalted (sweet) butter, plus extra for greasing
50 g/2 oz/¼ cup granulated sugar
25 g/1 oz/3 tbsp sultanas (golden raisins)
25 g/1 oz/¼ cup walnuts, chopped
90 ml/6 tbsp dry white wine
Chilled crème fraîche, to serve

Peel and core the apples but leave whole. Place each on a double thickness of buttered greaseproof (waxed) paper. Mix together the sugar,

sultanas and nuts and pack into the centres of the apples. Top each with a knob of butter and add 15 ml/1 tbsp wine to each parcel. Wrap tightly in the paper. Stand in a baking tin (pan) and bake in a preheated oven at 180°C/350°F/gas mark 4 for 25–30 minutes until the apples are tender. Leave to stand for 10 minutes to allow the flavours to develop then serve warm, opening the parcels at the table, and topping with chilled crème fraîche.

Apples and Oranges Bristol Fashion

SERVES 4–6

90 ml/6 tbsp granulated sugar
300 ml/½ pt/1¼ cups water
4 eating (dessert) apples, peeled, quartered and cored
4 oranges

Put the sugar and water in a saucepan and heat gently until the sugar has melted. Add the apple quarters and poach for 5 minutes until translucent. Remove from the heat and leave to cool in the syrup. Thinly pare the rind from two of the oranges. Cut the rind into very thin strips. Boil in water for 3 minutes, then drain, rinse with cold water and drain again. Cut all the pith and rind from all the oranges and slice the fruit. Add to the syrup with any juice. Leave until cold, then turn into a serving dish and chill. Serve with the orange rind scattered over.

Apples and Pears Bristol Fashion

SERVES 4–6

300 ml/½ pt/1¼ cups water
90 ml/6 tbsp granulated sugar
4 eating (dessert) apples, peeled,
    quartered and cored
4 pears, peeled, quartered and cored
Thinly pared rind and juice of 1 lemon

Put the water in a saucepan with the sugar and heat gently, stirring, until the sugar has dissolved. Add the apple and pear quarters and poach for 5 minutes until translucent. Remove from the heat and leave to cool in the syrup. Cut the lemon rind into thin strips. Boil in water for 3 minutes, then drain, rinse with cold water and drain again. Add the lemon juice to the fruit and turn into a serving dish. Chill. Sprinkle with the lemon rind before serving.

Bananas Foster

SERVES 4

40 g/1½ oz/3 tbsp butter or margarine
45 ml/3 tbsp light brown sugar
1.5 ml/¼ tsp ground cinnamon
A good pinch of grated nutmeg
4 large bananas
Any vanilla ice cream (see page 188, or
    use bought), to serve
Toasted chopped nuts, to decorate

Melt the butter or margarine with the sugar and spices in a flameproof dish. Add the bananas and turn to coat completely. Leave to stand for at least 15 minutes. Place the dish under a hot grill (broiler) for 5 minutes, turning the bananas once, until just cooked and lightly golden. Transfer to plates and top with scoops of ice cream and a sprinkling of chopped nuts.

Gingered Melon

SERVES 4

1 honeydew melon
15 ml/1 tbsp finely chopped crystallised
    (candied) ginger
5 ml/1 tsp grated fresh root ginger
250 ml/8 fl oz/1 cup dry white wine
5 ml/1 tsp ground cinnamon
15 ml/1 tbsp caster (superfine) sugar
Brandy Snaps (see page 124) and crème
    fraîche, to serve

Peel the melon, cut into eight wedges and discard the seeds. Place the remaining ingredients in a saucepan and bring to the boil. Add the melon, cover and cook for 2 minutes. Remove the melon wedges and place on warmed serving plates. Keep warm. Boil the liquid rapidly until syrupy, then spoon over the melon. Serve with Brandy Snaps and crème fraîche.

Minted Melon and Raspberries

SERVES 6

1 honeydew melon
225 g/8 oz raspberries
12 mint leaves
50 g/2 oz/¼ cup granulated sugar
A mint sprig, to decorate

Halve the melon, remove the seeds, then scoop out the flesh with a melon baller or peel and dice the flesh. Mix with the raspberries in a glass dish. Put the mint on a board with the sugar and chop finely. Sprinkle over the fruit, toss gently and chill for at least 1 hour. Decorate with a mint sprig just before serving.

Summer Melon with Strawberries

SERVES 4–6

1 small honeydew melon, balled or
*   cubed*
175 g/6 oz strawberries, sliced
Grated rind and juice of 1 lime
15 ml/2 tbsp clear honey
Smooth Strawberry Sauce (see page
*   349)*

Put the melon and strawberries in a bowl. Mix the lime rind and juice with the honey and spoon over. Toss gently and chill for at least 30 minutes. Spoon on to plates and drizzle the Smooth Strawberry Sauce over before serving.

Strawberries Marquise

SERVES 6

450 g/1 lb strawberries, thickly sliced
45 ml/3 tbsp icing (confectioners') sugar
30 ml/2 tbsp kirsch
1 small fresh pineapple
1 egg white
450 ml/¾ pt/2 cups double (heavy) cream

Put the strawberries in a shallow dish. Sprinkle with 15 ml/1 tbsp of the sugar and the kirsch. Cover and chill for 2 hours. Meanwhile, cut all the rind off the pineapple. Slice the flesh and remove the thick central core. Chop the fruit. Whisk the egg white until stiff, then whisk in the remaining sugar until stiff and glossy. Whip the cream until stiff. Fold the egg white, then the chopped pineapple into the cream and spoon into a serving dish. Spoon the macerated strawberries over and serve.

Macedoine

SERVES 6

2 nectarines, sliced
1 ripe galia melon, balled or cubed
100 g/4 oz strawberries, sliced
100 g/4 oz raspberries
100 g/4 oz/½ cup caster (superfine)
*   sugar*
30 ml/2 tbsp orange liqueur
Dry white wine
Pouring cream, to serve

Layer the fruits in a glass dish with a little of the sugar and a sprinkling of the orange liqueur between each layer. Pour over just enough wine to cover the fruit. Chill for at least 2 hours but no more than 4 hours. Serve very cold with pouring cream.

Pineapple with Kirsch

SERVES 4–6

1 ripe pineapple
150 ml/¼ pt/⅔ cup water
60 ml/4 tbsp granulated sugar
45 ml/3 tbsp kirsch
Crème fraîche, to serve

Remove all the rind from the pineapple, then cut the fruit into six or eight slices. Cut out any thick central core. Place with any juice in a shallow heatproof serving dish. Put the water and sugar in a saucepan and heat gently, stirring, until the sugar has dissolved. Bring to the boil and boil for 2 minutes. Stir in the kirsch and pour while still hot over the pineapple. Leave until cold, then chill. Serve with crème fraîche.

Sparkling Nectarines

SERVES 4

4 nectarines
10 ml/2 tsp lemon juice
½ bottle of sparkling medium-sweet white wine, chilled

Halve and slice the nectarines, discarding the stones (pits). Divide between four champagne flutes or wine goblets. Sprinkle with lemon juice and chill. When ready to serve, top up with the chilled wine. Eat the fruit with a spoon, then sip the drink.

Fresh Fruit Salad

SERVES 4–6

300 g/11 oz/1 medium can of mandarin oranges in natural juice
150 ml/¼ pt/⅔ cup pure apple or orange juice
5 ml/1 tsp lemon juice
Mixed fresh fruits, allowing about 45 ml/3 tbsp prepared fruit per person

Empty the contents of the can of mandarins, the apple or orange juice and the lemon juice into a glass bowl. Chop or slice the fruits as necessary, leaving on any edible peel (such as on apples, peaches, nectarines or plums) for colour and texture and add to the bowl. Make at least 1 hour in advance so the flavours have time to develop, except any juicy berries should be added just before serving so that the colour does not run too much. Chill until ready to serve.

Spanish Strawberry Fizz

SERVES 4

225 g/8 oz strawberries, hulled and sliced
20 ml/4 tsp caster (superfine) sugar
½ lime
½ bottle of sparkling Spanish rosé wine, chilled

Divide the strawberries between four champagne flutes. Sprinkle with the sugar and add a squeeze of lime juice to each. Chill for at least 30 minutes. When ready to serve, top up with the wine and serve straight away.

Fresh Fruit Salad with Kiwi Fruit

SERVES 4

75 g/3 oz/⅓ cup granulated sugar
300 ml/½ pt/1¼ cups water
1 red eating (dessert) apple, diced
1 green eating apple, diced
1 orange, segmented
2 kiwi fruit, sliced
1 pear, diced
1 peach, diced
*1 banana, thickly sliced and tossed in
    lemon juice*
8 fresh or maraschino cherries

Put the sugar and water in a saucepan and heat gently, stirring until the sugar has dissolved. Boil for 3 minutes, then leave to cool. Add the prepared fruits and chill for at least 2 hours to allow the flavours to develop.

Fruit Ambrosia

SERVES 4–6

Prepare as for Fresh Fruit Salad (see page 223) or Fresh Fruit Salad with Kiwi Fruit, but soak 150 g/5 oz/ 1¼ cups desiccated (shredded) coconut in 120 ml/4 fl oz/½ cup water for 30 minutes, then drain and add to the fruit salad before chilling.

Green Fruit Salad

SERVES 4–6

Prepare as for Fruit Salad with Kiwi Fruit, but use all green fruit, for example: 1 small ogen melon, balled or cubed; 2 kiwi fruit, sliced; 100 g/4 oz seedless green grapes; 2 green apples, diced; and 2 greengages, stoned (pitted) and cut into sixths. Add a dash of green chartreuse, if liked, and decorate with a few sprigs of fresh mint.

Spiced Summer Fruit Salad

SERVES 6

150 ml/¼ pt/⅔ cup water
50 g/2 oz/¼ cup granulated sugar
*1 piece of stem ginger in syrup, finely
    chopped*
45 ml/3 tbsp stem ginger syrup
12 maraschino cherries
30 ml/2 tbsp maraschino cherry syrup
Finely grated rind and juice of 1 lime
350 g/12 oz strawberries, halved
1 cantaloupe melon, balled or cubed
*225 g/8 oz seedless black grapes, halved
    if large*

Put the water and sugar in a saucepan and heat gently, stirring, until the sugar dissolves. Boil for 5 minutes. Stir in the chopped ginger, ginger syrup, maraschino cherries, cherry syrup, lime rind and juice. Leave to cool. Put all the prepared fruit in a serving bowl. Add the syrup, stir gently and chill for at least 2 hours before serving.

Fresh Fruit Platter

SERVES 6

2 star fruit
1 mango
1 pawpaw
175 g/6 oz strawberries, hulled
2 kiwi fruit
30 ml/2 tbsp kirsch or gin
Fresh Raspberry Sauce (see page 348)
Amaretti Biscuits (see page 128, or use
* bought), to serve*

Slice each star fruit into six stars. Peel the mango and cut off slices all round the stone (pit), lengthways. Halve the pawpaw, discard the seeds, peel and slice. Halve the strawberries. Peel and cut each kiwi fruit into six slices. Arrange the fruit attractively on six serving plates, leaving a space for the sauce, and drizzle the kirsch or gin over. Leave in a cool place for at least 15 minutes. Spoon the raspberry sauce on to each plate and serve with Amaretti Biscuits.

Strawberries Romanoff

SERVES 4–6

450 g/1 lb even-sized strawberries
20 ml/4 tsp icing (confectioners') sugar
Finely grated rind and juice of 1 large
* orange*
30 ml/2 tbsp Grand Marnier
Chantilly Cream (see page 358), to
* serve*

Put the strawberries in a serving dish. Blend together the remaining ingredients and pour over. Toss gently. Leave to marinate for at least 30 minutes. Serve with Chantilly Cream.

Strawberry and Peach Romanoff

SERVES 6

225 g/8 oz strawberries, hulled and
* sliced*
4 peaches, stoned (pitted) and sliced
15 ml/1 tbsp caster (superfine) sugar
30 ml/2 tbsp peach or orange liqueur
Juice of 1 large orange
Whipped cream, to serve

Put the sliced fruit in a glass bowl. Sprinkle with the sugar and add the liqueur and orange juice. Toss gently and leave to stand for 20–30 minutes. Serve topped with whipped cream.

Peach Champagne Cocktail

SERVES 4

4 peaches
20 ml/4 tsp granulated sugar
30 ml/2 tbsp brandy
½ bottle of champagne, chilled

Plunge the peaches in boiling water for 30 seconds. Drain and peel off the skins. Halve, remove the stones (pits) and dice the flesh. Place in four champagne flutes or wine goblets. Sprinkle with the sugar and add the brandy. Leave to soak for 5 minutes. Top up with chilled champagne and serve straight away.

Pêche Royale

SERVES 6

40 g/1½ oz/3 tbsp granulated sugar
150 ml/¼ pt/⅔ cup water
1 thick strip of lemon rind
30 ml/2 tbsp brandy
6 peaches, skinned, halved and stoned (pitted)
150 ml/¼ pt/⅔ cup double (heavy) cream
30 ml/2 tbsp icing (confectioners') sugar
100 g/4 oz small, ripe strawberries, sliced
30 ml/2 tbsp chopped pistachio nuts

Put the sugar and water in a saucepan with the lemon rind and heat gently, stirring, until the sugar dissolves. Bring to the boil. Add half the brandy and the peaches, reduce the heat and poach gently for 3–4 minutes until the peaches are just tender but still holding their shape. Leave to cool in the syrup.

Carefully lift the peaches out of the syrup and place cut-sides up in serving dishes. Whip the cream with the icing sugar and the remaining brandy. Fold in the strawberries and pile on the peach halves. Sprinkle with pistachio nuts and drizzle the peach syrup round the edges. Chill until ready to serve.

Pears with Passion Fruit Purée

SERVES 4

4 ripe pears, peeled, quartered and cored
4 passion fruit
300 ml/½ pt/1¼ cups sweet white wine
15 ml/1 tbsp clear honey
15 ml/1 tbsp cornflour (cornstarch)
60 ml/4 tbsp water
Juice of ½ lemon
Viennese Fingers (see page 127), to serve

Put the pear quarters in four serving dishes. Halve the passion fruit and scoop the flesh out into a small bowl. Warm the wine and honey together and bring just to the boil. Blend together the cornflour and water and pour on the hot liquid, stirring. Return to the pan, bring to the boil and cook for 2 minutes, stirring. Stir in the passion fruit pulp and simmer for a further minute. Spike with lemon juice, if necessary. Spoon the sauce over the pears and leave to cool so the flavours mingle. Chill before serving with Viennese Fingers.

Summer Pudding

SERVES 6

900 g/2 lb soft fruit such as raspberries,
*   blackberries, blackcurrants,*
*   strawberries, sliced or quartered if*
*   large*
Finely grated rind of ½ orange (optional)
45 ml/3 tbsp water
100–175 g/4–6 oz/½–¾ cup granulated
*   sugar*
8 slices of white bread, crusts removed
Classic Custard Sauce (see page 354), to
*   serve*

Put the fruit in a saucepan with the orange rind, if using, the water and 100 g/4 oz/½ cup of the sugar. Heat gently until the juices run and the fruit is soft but still holding its shape. Taste and add more sugar, if necessary.

Line a large pudding basin with some of the bread, cutting it to fit. Spoon in the fruit and juice and cover with the remaining bread, again trimming to fit and filling in any gaps. Stand the basin on a small plate and cover with a saucer or small plate. Top with weights or a couple of cans of food. Leave to cool, then chill overnight. The pudding is ready when all the juice has soaked through the bread. Turn out on to a shallow serving dish and serve with Classic Custard Sauce.

Golden Summer Pudding

SERVES 4–6

Prepare as for Summer Pudding, but use a mixture of chopped and stoned (pitted) yellow fruits such as peaches, nectarines, apricots, mangoes and segmented oranges.

Strawberry and Cherry Summer Pudding

SERVES 6

5 trifle sponges
350 g/12 oz strawberries
350 g/12 oz red or black cherries,
*   halved and stoned (pitted)*
100 g/4 oz/½ cup light brown sugar
Chantilly Cream (see page 358), to serve

Split the trifle sponges into halves and use to line a 900 ml/1½ pt/3¾ cup pudding basin, cut-sides out, trimming to fit. Reserve the trimmings and any leftover pieces. Put the strawberries and cherries in a pan with the sugar. Heat gently until the juices run. Stir gently. The fruit should still hold its shape. Spoon the fruit and juices into the basin and top with the sponge trimmings and any remaining slices. Lay a saucer on top and weigh down with weights or cans of food. Leave to cool, then chill overnight until the juices have soaked through the sponges completely. When ready to serve, loosen the edge and turn out on to a serving dish. Serve with whipped cream.

Autumn Pudding

SERVES 4–6

*5–6 slices of white bread, crusts
    removed
500 g/18 oz/1 packet of frozen forest
    fruits, thawed
75 g/3 oz/⅓ cup caster (superfine) sugar
Fromage frais, to serve*

Line a 900 ml/1½ pt/3¾ cup pudding
basin with some of the bread. Stew
the fruit in a pan with the sugar for
3 minutes. Turn into the basin. Top with
the remaining bread, cutting it to fit
completely with no gaps. Stand the
basin on a small plate, cover with a
saucer and weigh down with weights or
cans of food. Leave to cool, then chill
overnight. Turn out on to a shallow
serving dish and serve with fromage
frais.

Whisky Oranges

SERVES 6

*150 g/5 oz/⅔ cup granulated sugar
100 ml/3½ fl oz/6½ tbsp water
60 ml/4 tbsp whisky
6 oranges
Atholl Brose Cream (see page 357), to
    serve*

Put the sugar and water in a
saucepan. Heat gently until the
sugar dissolves, then boil for 2 minutes.
Stir in the whisky and remove from the
heat. Thinly pare the rind off one
orange and cut into thin strips. Boil in a
little water for 3 minutes, drain, rinse
with cold water and drain again. Pare
the rind and pith off all the oranges
over a bowl to catch any juice. Slice the

fruit and place in the bowl. Pour over
the whisky syrup and sprinkle over the
thin strips of blanched orange rind.
Leave until cold, then chill. Serve
topped with Atholl Brose Cream.

Planters' Pudding

SERVES 4

*1 fresh pineapple
8 fresh dates, quartered and stoned
    (pitted)
2 small bananas, sliced
1 passion fruit
25 g/1 oz/2 tbsp light brown sugar
45 ml/3 tbsp apple juice
45 ml/3 tbsp dark rum*

Slice the top off the pineapple about
4 cm/1½ in down from the leaves.
Reserve for a lid. Scoop out the flesh,
using a serrated knife, leaving the skin
intact. Chop the flesh, discarding any
hard core. Place in a bowl with the
dates and bananas and toss gently.
Halve the passion fruit and scoop the
seeds into the bowl. Blend together the
sugar, apple juice and rum until the
sugar dissolves. Add to the bowl and
toss gently. Chill the fruit mixture and
the pineapple shell. When ready to
serve, spoon the fruit back into the
pineapple, and replace the lid or place it
to one side of the pineapple.

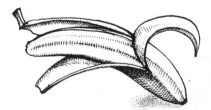

Oranges in Minted Syrup

SERVES 4

4 oranges
150 g/5 oz/⅔ cup granulated sugar
300 ml/½ pt/1¼ cups water
2 large mint sprigs
Shortbread Triangles (see page 127), to
serve

Thinly pare the rind off two of the oranges. Cut into thin strips and reserve. Discard all the pith from the pared oranges and the rind and pith from the other two. Put the sugar and water in a saucepan with the mint. Heat gently, stirring, until the sugar has dissolved. Add the oranges and the thin strips of rind. Cover and poach gently for 5 minutes. Remove the mint. Transfer to serving dishes and serve hot with Shortbread Triangles.

Orange and Chestnut Kebabs

SERVES 4

350 g/12 oz/1 large can of chestnuts,
drained if necessary
50 g/2 oz/¼ cup butter
Grated rind and juice of ½ orange
15 ml/1 tbsp light brown sugar
1 whole orange, halved and thickly
sliced
Chantilly Cream (see page 358), to
serve

Put the chestnuts in a shallow dish. Melt the butter, stir in the orange rind and juice and the sugar. Heat gently until the sugar has dissolved. Pour over the chestnuts and turn to coat completely. Leave to soak for 30 minutes. Thread on to kebab skewers, interspersing with half slices of orange. Lay on a piece of foil on a grill (broiler) rack. Grill (broil) for 4–5 minutes, turning occasionally, until golden, brushing with any remaining marinade during cooking. Serve warm with Chantilly Cream.

Eastern Oranges with Yoghurt Sauce

SERVES 4

4 oranges, peeled
Salt and freshly ground black pepper
Cumin seeds, toasted and finely
crushed
Cayenne
250 ml/8 fl oz/1 cup thick plain yoghurt
20 ml/4 tsp caster (superfine) sugar
5 ml/1 tsp finely grated fresh root
ginger

Cut each orange into six slices, then cut each slice in half. Sprinkle one side of each very lightly with salt, pepper, the crushed cumin and cayenne. Arrange overlapping in a circle on four small plates, leaving a space in the middle. Cover with clingfilm (plastic wrap) and chill.

Meanwhile, blend together the yoghurt, sugar and ginger, adding crushed cumin and cayenne to taste. Spoon into the centres of the fruit rings and serve straight away.

Caramel Oranges

SERVES 4

6 oranges
175 g/6 oz/¾ cup granulated sugar
100 ml/3½ fl oz/6½ tbsp cold water
100 ml/3½ fl oz/6½ tbsp hot water
Almond Tuiles (see page 130), to serve

Thinly pare the rind off one of the oranges and cut into very thin strips. Boil in a little water for 3 minutes, then drain, rinse with cold water and drain again. Cut off all the rind and pith from all the oranges and cut the fruit into thick slices. Place in a shallow glass dish. Place the sugar and cold water in a saucepan and stir well, then heat gently without stirring until the sugar has completely dissolved. Bring to the boil and boil until the mixture is a rich golden brown. Using oven gloves to protect from spluttering, remove from the heat and pour the hot water into the caramel, then return to the heat and stir until the caramel has dissolved. Cool slightly, then pour over the oranges and leave until cold. Sprinkle the orange shreds over and chill until ready to serve with Almond Tuiles.

Orange Raffles

SERVES 6

6 oranges
3 trifle sponges
30 ml/2 tbsp sherry
250 ml/8 fl oz/1 cup double (heavy)
*   cream*
A few drops of vanilla essence (extract)
30 ml/2 tbsp caster (superfine) sugar
Toasted flaked (slivered) almonds

Cut off and discard the rounded ends of the oranges (they will stand up better on the stalk ends) and scoop out the fruit, using a serrated knife. Chop fairly finely and place in a bowl with any juice. Crumble in the trifle sponges and add the sherry. Mix well and spoon back into the orange shells. Stand the oranges in a glass dish. Whip the cream until peaking. Whisk in the vanilla and caster sugar. Pipe or swirl on top of the oranges and sprinkle with almonds. Chill for at least 1 hour to allow the flavours to develop.

Honeyed Clementines

SERVES 4–6

6 clementines, unpeeled and thickly
*   sliced*
45 ml/3 tbsp clear honey
1.5 ml/¼ tsp ground cinnamon
Crème fraîche, to serve

Lay the clementines in a shallow dish and drizzle with the honey, then sprinkle with the cinnamon. Leave to marinate for at least 30 minutes, turning once or twice. Place a sheet of foil on the grill (broiler) rack. Arrange the slices in a single layer on the foil and brush with the marinade left in the dish. Place under a hot grill for 4–5 minutes until turning golden brown, turn over, brush with any remaining marinade and grill (broil) for a further 5 minutes. Transfer to serving plates and serve with crème fraîche.

Apples in Caramel

SERVES 6

225 g/8 oz/1 cup granulated sugar
300 ml/½ pt/1¼ cups water
6 eating (dessert) apples
Lemon juice
25 g/1 oz/¼ cup glacé (candied) cherries,
chopped
25 g/1 oz/¼ cup angelica, chopped
25 g/1 oz/¼ cup chopped mixed
(candied) peel
Crème fraîche, to serve

Put the sugar and half the water in a large heavy-based saucepan. Heat gently, stirring, until the sugar has dissolved. Bring to the boil and boil rapidly, without stirring, until a rich golden brown. Remove from the heat and place the base of the pan in cold water to cool slightly. Pour in the remaining water (be careful as it may splutter). Return to the heat and cook, stirring until the caramel has dissolved. Meanwhile, peel and core the apples but leave them whole. Coat each one in lemon juice to prevent browning. When the syrup is ready, add the apples, cover and cook gently for 5 minutes. Turn over in the syrup and cook for a further 5 minutes until just becoming tender but still holding their shape. Carefully lift out of the syrup and transfer to a serving dish. Mix together the cherries, angelica and peel and spoon into the centres of the fruit. Boil the syrup rapidly for 2–3 minutes to thicken, then pour over the apples. Leave until cold. Chill until ready to serve with crème fraîche.

Banana Trifle

SERVES 6

45 ml/3 tbsp custard powder
30 ml/2 tbsp granulated sugar
300 ml/½ pt/1¼ cups milk
300 ml/½ pt/1¼ cups single (light) cream
4 trifle sponges
60 ml/4 tbsp strawberry jam (conserve)
45 ml/3 tbsp sweet white vermouth or
sherry
45 ml/3 tbsp pineapple juice
2 large ripe bananas
300 ml/½ pt/1¼ cups whipping cream
Halved glacé (candied) cherries and
angelica leaves, to decorate

Blend the custard powder and sugar with a little of the milk in a saucepan. Stir in the remaining milk and the single cream. Bring to the boil and cook for 2 minutes, stirring all the time, until thickened and smooth. Cover with a circle of wetted greaseproof (waxed) paper and leave to cool. Split the sponges horizontally and sandwich together with the jam. Cut into pieces and place in a glass serving dish. Spoon over the vermouth or sherry and pineapple juice. Slice the bananas and stir into the cool custard. Spoon over the sponges. Chill for 1 hour to allow the flavours to develop. Whip the cream until softly peaking. Spread over the custard. Decorate with halved glacé cherries and angelica leaves.

Cidered Kiwi and Melon Bowl

SERVES 4

1 honeydew melon
4 kiwi fruit, halved and sliced
300 ml/½ pt/1¼ cups medium-sweet
 cider
Mint sprigs
Fromage frais, to serve

Halve the melon and discard the seeds. Either scoop the flesh into balls with a melon baller or peel away the skin and dice the flesh. Place all the ingredients including about 6 small mint sprigs in a glass bowl and chill for at least 1 hour to allow the flavours to develop. Remove the sprigs of mint and decorate with a few fresh sprigs before serving topped with spoonfuls of fromage frais.

Riesling Cherries

SERVES 8

175 g/6 oz/¾ cups granulated sugar
200 ml/7 fl oz/scant 1 cup water
500 ml/17 fl oz/2¼ cups Riesling or other
 fruity medium-sweet white wine
450 g/1 lb black cherries, stoned (pitted)
450 g/1 lb red cherries, stoned
Crème fraîche, to serve

Put the sugar and water in a saucepan and heat gently, stirring, until the sugar has dissolved. Bring to the boil and boil rapidly without stirring until the mixture turns a rich golden brown. Remove from the heat and pour in the wine (take care as it will splutter). Return to the heat and stir gently until the caramel has dissolved. Leave to cool slightly. Put the cherries in a serving dish and mix gently. Pour over the warm syrup and leave until cold. Chill for at least 2 hours and serve with crème fraîche.

After-Christmas Trifle

SERVES 4

8 thin slices of Christmas pudding or
 cake
30 ml/2 tbsp ground almonds
45 ml/3 tbsp port
30 ml/2 tbsp apple juice
600 ml/1 pt/2½ cups milk
60 ml/4 tbsp custard powder
45 ml/3 tbsp granulated sugar
300 ml/½ pt/1¼ cups double (heavy)
 cream
Angelica
1½ glacé (candied) cherries
15 whole blanched almonds

Put the pudding or cake in a glass serving dish. Sprinkle with the ground almonds. Drizzle the port and apple juice over and leave to soak for at least 1 hour. Meanwhile, blend a little of the milk in a saucepan with the custard powder and sugar. Blend in the remaining milk. Bring to the boil and cook for 2 minutes, stirring all the time, until thick and smooth. Cool, then pour into the dish and leave until cold.

Whip the cream until softly peaking and spread over the set custard. Cut some leaves out of angelica and three thin strips to represent flower stems. Halve the whole glacé cherry. Lay the three halves a little apart on the cream and arrange the almonds round to represent petals. Put the angelica stalks in place and arrange the leaves to look like a small cluster of flowers. Chill until ready to serve.

Victorian Trifle

SERVES 6

4 trifle sponges
Raspberry jam (conserve)
6 Almond Macaroons (see page 128, or
  use bought)
12 ratafias
75 ml/5 tbsp sweet sherry
75 ml/5 tbsp brandy
25 g/1 oz/¼ cup flaked (slivered)
  almonds
300 ml/½ pt/1¼ cups milk
2 eggs
50 g/2 oz/¼ cup caster (superfine) sugar
150 ml/¼ pt/⅔ cup double (heavy) cream
Halved glacé (candied) cherries and
  angelica leaves, to decorate

Split the trifle sponges in half and
spread with jam. Place in the base of
a glass serving dish. Roughly crush the
macaroons and sprinkle over. Crush six
of the Ratafias and sprinkle over.
Drizzle with the sherry and brandy and
leave to soak for at least 30 minutes.
Sprinkle with the almonds.

Meanwhile, to make the custard,
warm the milk in a saucepan. Separate
one of the eggs. Break the second
whole egg into the egg yolk and whisk
in half the sugar. Pour the warm milk
over and whisk well. Place the bowl
over a pan of hot water and cook,
stirring, until the custard thickens and
coats the back of a spoon. To test, lift
the spoon out of the custard and draw a
finger through the mixture adhering to
the back of the spoon: if a clear line is
left, the custard is ready. Allow to cool
slightly, then pour over the soaked
sponges. Leave until cold, then chill.

Whisk the remaining egg white until
stiff. Whisk in the remaining sugar until
stiff and glossy. Whip the cream until
peaking. Fold the egg white into the
cream. Pile on top of the trifle so it
forms soft peaks. Decorate with halved
glacé cherries and angelica leaves and
the remaining ratafias.

Mocha Orange Trifle

SERVES 6

100 g/4 oz/½ cup butter, softened
100 g/4 oz/½ cup caster (superfine) sugar
4 egg yolks
15 ml/1 tbsp instant coffee powder, plus
  extra for dusting
15 ml/1 tbsp hot water
1 chocolate Swiss (jelly) roll, sliced
15–30 ml/1–2 tbsp coffee liqueur
300 g/11 oz/1 medium can of mandarin
  oranges
300 ml/½ pt/1¼ cups double (heavy)
  cream

Beat together the butter and sugar.
Beat in the egg yolks. Blend the
coffee with the water and beat into the
mixture. Place the bowl over a pan of
hot water and whisk with an electric
beater until thick and fluffy. Arrange the
Swiss roll slices in a glass serving dish.
Drizzle with the coffee liqueur. Reserve a
few of the mandarin oranges for
decoration and spoon the remainder
over the sponge, adding enough of the
juice to moisten thoroughly. Spoon over
the coffee mixture and chill for at least 2
hours to allow the flavours to develop.

Whip the cream until softly peaking.
Spread over the surface and dust lightly
with coffee powder and the reserved
orange segments.

Old English Strawberry Trifle

SERVES 6

4 trifle sponges
30 ml/2 tbsp strawberry jam (conserve)
6 Almond Macaroons (see page 128, or
*   use bought), roughly crushed*
60 ml/4 tbsp sweet sherry or Madeira
225 g/8 oz strawberries
30 ml/2 tbsp caster (superfine) sugar
4 egg yolks
450 ml/³⁄₄ pt/2 cups milk
A few drops of vanilla essence (extract)
300 ml/¹⁄₂ pt/1¹⁄₄ cups double (heavy)
*   cream*

Split the trifle sponges in half horizontally and spread with jam. Sandwich together again and break into pieces. Place in a glass serving dish. Top with the macaroons. Spoon the sherry or Madeira over. Reserve a few strawberries for decoration and slice the remainder. Cover the macaroons with the sliced strawberries and leave to soak while preparing the custard.

Whisk together the sugar and egg yolks in a bowl. Bring the milk almost to the boil and pour over the sugar and egg yolks. Place over a pan of hot water and cook, stirring, until the custard thickens and coats the back of the spoon. To test, lift the spoon out of the mixture and draw a finger through the mixture on the back of the spoon: if a clear line is left, the custard is ready. Flavour with vanilla to taste. Allow to cool slightly. Press the strawberries gently down into the soaked sponge.

Pour the custard over and leave until cold, then chill. Whip the cream and use to cover the custard. Decorate with the reserved strawberries and serve chilled.

Italian English Pudding

SERVES 6

100 g/4 oz/1 cup plain (semi-sweet)
*   chocolate*
300 ml/¹⁄₂ pt/1¹⁄₄ cups double (heavy)
*   cream*
75 g/3 oz/1 small packet of sponge
*   (lady) fingers*
175 ml/6 fl oz/³⁄₄ cup sweet white wine
30 ml/2 tbsp brandy
25 g/1 oz/¹⁄₄ cup pistachio nuts, chopped
30 ml/2 tbsp glacé (candied) cherries,
*   chopped*
Zabaglione (see page 173), to serve
*   (optional)*

Melt the chocolate in a bowl over a pan of hot water or in the microwave. Lightly whip the cream and whisk in the melted chocolate. Place the sponge fingers in a shallow glass dish and pour over the wine and brandy. Line a 15 cm/6 in round, deep, loose-bottomed cake tin (pan) with baking parchment. Spread a layer of chocolate cream in the base. Top with a layer of the soaked sponge and sprinkle with some of the nuts and cherries. Repeat the layers until all the ingredients are used, finishing with a layer of sponge. Cover with foil and chill until firm. Turn out on to a serving plate and serve plain or with Zabaglione.

Zuppa Inglese

SERVES 8

100 g/4 oz/½ cup caster (superfine) sugar
100 g/4 oz/½ cup soft tub margarine
100 g/4 oz/1 cup self-raising (self-rising)
  flour
5 ml/1 tsp baking powder
2 eggs
Oil, for greasing
900 ml/1½ pts/3¾ cups milk
2.5 ml/½ tsp vanilla essence (extract)
5 cm/2 in piece of cinnamon stick
60 ml/4 tbsp granulated sugar
15 ml/1 tbsp cornflour (cornstarch)
8 egg yolks
90 ml/6 tbsp brandy
60 ml/4 tbsp kirsch
Thinly pared rind and juice of 1 small
  orange
60 ml/4 tbsp finely grated chocolate

Put the sugar, margarine, flour, baking powder and whole eggs in a bowl and beat until smooth (or use a food processor). Divide between two 18 cm/7 in oiled sandwich tins (pans) and level the surfaces. Bake in a preheated oven at 190°C/375°F/gas mark 5 for 20 minutes until risen, golden and the centres spring back when lightly pressed. Turn out on to a wire rack to cool.

Meanwhile, put the milk, vanilla and cinnamon stick in a saucepan and bring just to the boil. Blend together the granulated sugar and cornflour in a bowl and whisk in the egg yolks. Gradually whisk in the hot milk. Place the bowl over a pan of hot water and cook, stirring, until thick and smooth. Remove from the heat and leave to cool. Discard the cinnamon stick.

Put one cake round in a shallow glass serving dish. Sprinkle with the brandy. Pour over about two-thirds of the custard. Top with the second sponge layer and sprinkle with the kirsch and orange juice. Cover with the remaining custard and chill for at least 2 hours to allow the sponges to get completely soaked and the flavours to develop. Cut the thinly pared orange rind into very thin strips. Boil in water for 3 minutes, drain, rinse with cold water and drain again. Just before serving, sprinkle the top with the grated chocolate and decorate with the strips or orange rind.

Crimson Salad

SERVES 6

225 g/8 oz raspberries
225 g/8 oz small ripe strawberries
225 g/8 oz redcurrants, stripped from
  their stalks
60 ml/4 tbsp icing (confectioners') sugar
15 ml/1 tbsp lemon juice
Juice of 1 small orange
Amaretti Biscuits (see page 128, or use
  bought), to serve

Layer the fruit and sugar in a large glass dish. Mix together the fruit juices and drizzle over. Cover and chill for several hours before serving with Amaretti Biscuits.

Tipsy Cake

SERVES 6

100 g/4 oz/½ cup soft tub margarine
100 g/4 oz/½ cup caster (superfine)
  sugar
100 g/4 oz/1 cup self-raising (self-
  rising) flour
2.5 ml/½ tsp baking powder
2 eggs
Oil, for greasing
Apricot jam (conserve)
200 ml/7 fl oz/scant 1 cup sweet
  vermouth or port
3 Almond Macaroons (see page 128, or
  use bought), crushed
Raspberry jam (conserve)
600 ml/1 pt/2½ cups Classic Custard
  Sauce (see page 354)
Glacé (candied) cherries, whole blanched
  almonds and angelica leaves, to
  decorate

Put the margarine, sugar, flour,
baking powder and eggs in a bowl
and beat until smooth. Oil an 18 cm/
7 in cake tin (pan) and add the
mixture. Level the surface. Bake in a
preheated oven at 180°C/350°F/gas
mark 4 for about 35 minutes or until
risen, golden and the centre springs
back when lightly pressed. Allow to
cool slightly, then turn out on to a wire
rack and leave to cool completely.

Split into four layers. Put the base
slice in a serving dish and spread with
apricot jam. Sprinkle over a quarter or
the vermouth or port and scatter with a
third of the macaroons. Top with a
second layer, spread with raspberry
jam, moisten again and add more
macaroons. Repeat with the third layer,
using apricot jam again. Top with the
fourth layer and moisten with the rest
of the vermouth or port. Pour the hot
Classic Custard Sauce over the top to
coat completely. Cover with a very large
container to help prevent a skin forming
on the custard and leave until cold,
then chill. Decorate with halved glacé
cherries, whole blanched almonds and
angelica leaves before serving.

Laced Fruit Compôte

SERVES 4–5

750 g/1½ lb mixed raspberries,
  blackberries, plums and
  blackcurrants
75 g/3 oz/⅓ cup granulated sugar
100 ml/3½ fl oz/6½ tbsp water
A small piece of cinnamon stick
45 ml/3 tbsp kirsch
20 ml/4 tsp arrowroot
Classic Custard Sauce (see page 354),
  cold, to serve

Pick over the raspberries and
blackberries and discard any hulls.
Quarter and stone (pit) the plums and
remove all stalks from the blackcurrants. Place in a saucepan with the
sugar, water and cinnamon stick. Bring
to the boil, reduce the heat and cook
gently for 3 minutes until the fruit is
softening and the juices run. Mix the
kirsch with the arrowroot and stir into
the fruit. Cook, stirring gently, until the
liquid thickens and clears. Turn into a
serving bowl and leave until cold, then
chill. Remove the cinnamon stick before
serving with cold Classic Custard Sauce.

Brandied Cherry Compôte

SERVES 4–6

750 g/1½ lb red or black cherries, stoned
  (pitted)
45 ml/3 tbsp brandy
120 ml/4 fl oz/½ cup apple juice
50–75 g/2–3 oz/¼–⅓ cup granulated
  sugar

Put all the ingredients in a saucepan. Heat gently, stirring, until the sugar dissolves. Bring to the boil, reduce the heat and simmer very gently for about 5 minutes. Leave to cool, then chill before serving.

Tropical Compôte

SERVES 6

100 g/4 oz/½ cup granulated sugar
150 ml/¼ pt/⅔ cup water
2 pomegranates
1 passion fruit
2 oranges
1 mango
2 kiwi fruit
1 small pineapple

Put the sugar and water in a saucepan and heat gently until the sugar has dissolved. Bring to the boil and boil for 3 minutes. Halve the pomegranates and passion fruit and squeeze the juice as you would for a lemon. Pour into the syrup.

Hold the oranges over the saucepan to catch the juice and cut off all the rind and pith, then slice and halve the slices and add to the syrup. Peel the mango and cut all the flesh off the stone (pit) in long strips. Halve if very big and add to the syrup. Peel and slice the kiwi fruit and add to the syrup. Cut all the skin off the pineapple, slice the fruit, then cut into chunks, discarding any thick core. Add to the other fruit. Mix all together and leave until cold.

Transfer to a glass serving dish and chill for at least 2 hours to allow the flavours to develop.

Gooseberry Compôte

SERVES 6

750 g/1½ lb gooseberries, topped and
  tailed
100 g/4 oz/½ cup granulated sugar
300 ml/½ pt/1¼ cups water
30 ml/2 tbsp redcurrant jelly (clear
  conserve)
30 ml/2 tbsp grappa
Almond Tuiles (see page 130), to serve

Put the gooseberries in a pan. Cover with boiling water and bring back to the boil. Cook for 2 minutes, then drain, rinse with cold water and drain again. Put the sugar and water in a saucepan. Heat gently, stirring, until the sugar has dissolved, then boil for 5 minutes. Add the redcurrant jelly and stir until dissolved, then add the gooseberries and grappa. Bring back to the boil, reduce the heat and simmer very gently for 10 minutes until the fruit is really tender but still holds its shape. Remove the fruit with a draining spoon and transfer to a serving dish. Boil the syrup rapidly until reduced by about a third. Pour over, then leave to cool. Chill before serving with Almond Tuiles.

Rosy Three-fruit Compôte

SERVES 4–6

100 g/4 oz/½ cup granulated sugar
150 ml/¼ pt/⅔ cup water
1 wineglass of rosé wine
3 peaches, skinned, halved, stoned
  (pitted) and sliced
100 g/4 oz strawberries, halved if large
225 g/8 oz raspberries
Viennese Fingers (see page 127), to serve

Put the sugar, water and wine in a saucepan and heat gently, stirring, until the sugar dissolves. Bring to the boil and boil rapidly for 2 minutes. Add the peaches, strawberries and raspberries, bring back to the boil, then remove from the heat. Leave to cool, then turn into a serving dish and chill until ready to serve with Viennese Fingers.

Mulled Fruit Compôte

SERVES 4

225 g/8 oz/1 packet of dried fruit salad
300 ml/½ pt/1¼ cups water
½ lemon
5 cm/2 in piece of cinnamon stick
100 g/4 oz/½ cup granulated sugar
15 ml/1 tbsp brandy
Pouring cream, to serve

Soak the dried fruit in the water overnight. Place in a saucepan with the lemon, cinnamon and sugar. Bring to the boil, reduce the heat, cover and simmer gently for 20–30 minutes or until tender but not pulpy. Remove the lemon and cinnamon stick. Stir in the brandy and serve hot or chilled with cream.

Hot Winter Fruit Salad

SERVES 6

75 g/3 oz/½ cup dried figs
50 g/2 oz/⅓ cup dried, stoned (pitted)
  dates
450 ml/¾ pt/2 cups water
225 g/8 oz/1 cup granulated sugar
30 ml/2 tbsp dry sherry
1 large red eating (dessert) apple,
  quartered and sliced
1 large green eating apple, quartered
  and sliced
3 bananas, thickly sliced
15 ml/1 tbsp lemon juice
3 clementines, segmented
8 glacé (candied) cherries
2 pieces of stem ginger in syrup,
  chopped
15 ml/1 tbsp ginger syrup from the jar
Chantilly Cream (see page 358), to
  serve

Soak the figs and dates in the water for at least 6 hours or overnight. Place in a saucepan and add the sugar. Heat gently until the sugar dissolves, then simmer gently for 5 minutes. Stir in the sherry. Toss the apple and banana slices in the lemon juice. Add to the pan with the remaining ingredients. Bring to the boil again and simmer for 3 minutes. Turn into a serving dish and serve hot with Chantilly Cream.

Warm Fruit Bowl

SERVES 4–6

300 ml/½ pt/1¼ cups water
75 g/3 oz/⅓ cup granulated sugar
1 green eating (dessert) apple, diced
*   but not peeled*
1 red eating apple, diced but not peeled
1 pear, peeled and diced
2 oranges, all pith and peel removed,
*   sliced*
2 bananas, thickly sliced
15 ml/1 tbsp raisins, or halved seedless
*   grapes*
20 ml/4 tsp lemon juice

Put the water and sugar in a
saucepan and heat gently until the
sugar has dissolved, stirring
occasionally. Bring to the boil and boil
for 3–4 minutes until the syrup is
thickened but not coloured. Meanwhile,
put the prepared fruit in a serving bowl
and sprinkle with the lemon juice. Toss
gently. Pour the hot syrup over and
leave to stand for 10 minutes. Serve
warm.

Avocado Fruit Cocktails

SERVES 6

2 oranges
1 grapefruit
100 g/4 oz seedless black grapes
15 ml/1 tbsp clear honey
3 avocados
Lemon juice
90 ml/6 tbsp crème fraîche

Holding the fruit over a bowl, cut off
all the skin and pith from the
oranges and grapefruit and separate
into segments. Squeeze the membranes
to extract any remaining juice. Put the
fruit segments in the bowl. Halve the
grapes and add to the bowl with the
honey. Stir well and chill for at least
30 minutes. Halve the avocados,
remove the stones (pits) and brush with
lemon juice to prevent browning. Place
in individual serving dishes. Spoon in
the fruit cocktail and serve with
15 ml/1 tbsp of crème fraîche on each.

Creamed Fruit Cocktail

SERVES 6

2 nectarines, diced, discarding the stones
*   (pits)*
225 g/8 oz red cherries, stoned (pitted)
2 kiwi fruit, halved and sliced
50 g/2 oz/⅓ cup raisins
30 ml/2 tbsp blanched whole almonds
1 small carton of red cherry yoghurt
30 ml/2 tbsp single (light) cream
30 ml/2 tbsp apple juice

Put the prepared fruits in a bowl with
the raisins and almonds. Blend the
yoghurt with the cream and apple juice.
Mix together gently and chill for at least
1 hour to allow the flavours to develop.

Rhubarb and Honey Smoothie

SERVES 4

450 g/1 lb rhubarb, cut into short lengths
Grated rind and juice of ½ orange
90 ml/6 tbsp clear honey
Pure orange juice
15 ml/1 tbsp arrowroot
150 ml/¼ pt/⅔ cup crème fraîche

Put the rhubarb in a saucepan with the lemon rind and juice and 60 ml/4 tbsp of the honey. Cook gently until the rhubarb is tender. Leave to cool. Pour off the juice into a measuring jug. Make up to 300 ml/½ pt/1¼ cups with orange juice. Blend the arrowroot with a little of the juice in a saucepan. Stir in the remainder. Bring to the boil, stirring until thickened and clear. Spoon the rhubarb into four serving dishes. Pour the thickened juice over. Leave to cool, then chill overnight to allow the flavours to develop. Top with the crème fraîche, then drizzle the remaining honey over.

Strawberries in Balsamic Vinegar

Allow 75 g/3 oz strawberries per person. Hull and place in a bowl, halving any large ones. Sprinkle with caster (superfine) sugar, then balsamic vinegar. Leave to macerate for at least 1 hour before serving with Chantilly Cream (see page 358).

Fondant Dipped Fruits

SERVES 6

175 g/6 oz/¾ cup granulated sugar
70 ml/4½ tbsp water
25 ml/1½ tbsp orange liqueur
7.5 ml/1½ tsp sherry vinegar
Fruits for dipping, such as strawberries, peeled lychees, kumquats, Cape gooseberries (physalis), loganberries

Put the sugar and water in a saucepan with the liqueur and vinegar. Heat gently, stirring, until the sugar melts. Bring to the boil and boil rapidly to 143°C/290°F on a sugar thermometer or until the mixture forms hard threads when a little is trickled into a cup of cold water. Using a cocktail stick, dip each piece of fruit in the fondant, then immediately into cold water. Drain on a wire rack. Leave for 2–3 hours to allow the flavours to develop but eat within 12 hours.

Prunes and Almonds in Port

SERVES 6

450 g/1 lb/2⅔ cups prunes
1.2 litres/2 pts/6 cups water
Thinly pared rind of 1 orange
100 g/4 oz/1 cup blanched almonds
150 ml/¼ pt/⅔ cup port
15 ml/1 tbsp brandy
Caster (superfine) sugar
Greek-style Yoghurt (see page 359, or
  use bought), to serve

Put the prunes in a large pan. Cover with the water and leave to soak overnight. Add the orange rind. Bring to the boil, reduce the heat and simmer gently for 15 minutes until tender. Add the almonds, port and brandy and sweeten to taste with caster sugar. Bring back to the boil, reduce the heat and simmer very gently for 10 minutes. Remove the fruit and nuts with a draining spoon and place in a serving dish. Boil the syrup rapidly until reduced by half. Pour over the fruit and leave until cold, then chill. Serve with Greek-style Yoghurt.

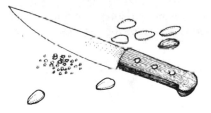

Apple and Raspberry Kissel

SERVES 4

3 cooking (tart) apples, sliced
175 g/5 oz raspberries
100 g/4 oz/½ cup caster (superfine)
  sugar
15 ml/1 tbsp cornflour (cornstarch)
150 ml/¼ pt/⅔ cup port
Grated nutmeg
Crème fraîche, to serve

Put the apple slices and raspberries in a saucepan with the sugar. Cover and cook gently until the apples are tender. Turn into a blender or food processor and purée until smooth. Pass through a sieve (strainer), if liked, to remove the seeds. Return to the saucepan. Blend the cornflour with a little of the port and stir into the purée. Add the remaining port. Bring to the boil and cook for 1 minute, stirring. Flavour with a little nutmeg. Cool slightly, then turn into individual dishes. Leave until cold, then chill for at least 2 hours to allow the flavours to develop. Serve with crème fraîche.

Apple and Blackcurrant Kissel

SERVES 4

Prepare as for Apple and Raspberry Kissel, but substitute blackcurrants for the raspberries and cinnamon for the nutmeg.

Apple and Blackberry Kissel

SERVES 4

Prepare as for Apple and Raspberry Kissel (see page 241), but substitute blackberries for the raspberries and flavour to taste with a little ground cloves instead of nutmeg.

Flaming Apples

SERVES 4

100 g/4 oz/½ cup light brown sugar
300 ml/½ pt/1¼ cups water
A pinch of ground cloves
4 eating (dessert) apples, peeled and cored but left whole
60 ml/4 tbsp dark rum
Fromage frais, to serve

Put the sugar and water in a large shallow saucepan with the cloves and heat gently until the sugar has dissolved. Add the apples and bring to the boil. Cover, reduce the heat and simmer gently for about 20 minutes, basting frequently, until the apples are translucent. Carefully lift the fruit out on to serving dishes. Boil the syrup rapidly until well reduced and syrupy. Pour over the apples. Warm the rum in a large soup ladle. Ignite and pour over the apples and serve while still flaming, with fromage frais to spoon over.

Raspberry Yoghurt Dream

SERVES 6

4 trifle sponges
350 g/12 oz frozen raspberries, thawed
30 ml/2 tbsp caster (superfine) sugar
Apple juice
300 ml/½ pt/1¼ cups vanilla yoghurt
300 ml/½ pt/1¼ cups double (heavy) cream
Demerara sugar

Break up the sponges in a glass serving bowl. Cover with the thawed raspberries and their juice. Sprinkle with the sugar and enough apple juice to moisten the sponges completely. Crush the fruit lightly. Whip together the yoghurt and cream until thick. Spread over the raspberries. Sprinkle liberally with demerara sugar and chill overnight to allow the flavours to develop and the sugar to melt.

Strawberry Yoghurt Dream

SERVES 6

Prepare as for Raspberry Yoghurt Dream, but substitute thawed frozen strawberries for the raspberries.

Summer Fruits Yoghurt Dream

SERVES 6

Prepare as for Raspberry Yoghurt Dream, but substitute thawed frozen mixed summer fruits for the raspberries.

Forest Fruits Yoghurt Dream

SERVES 6

Prepare as for Raspberry Yoghurt Dream, but substitute thawed frozen forest fruits for the raspberries.

Redcurrant Fruit Salad

SERVES 6

225 g/8 oz redcurrants, stripped from
their stalks
225 g/8 oz raspberries
1 small pineapple
45 ml/3 tbsp redcurrant jelly (clear
conserve)
150 ml/¼ tsp/⅔ cup apple juice
30 ml/2 tbsp white rum

Put the redcurrants and raspberries in a serving dish. Cut all the skin off the pineapple, cut into slices, then into cubes, discarding any thick core. Add to the other fruit. Put the redcurrant jelly and apple juice in a saucepan and heat gently, stirring, until the jelly melts. Stir in the rum. Pour over the fruit and leave until cold. Chill for several hours or overnight. Serve very cold.

Gâteau Gallery

Every dessert cake you've ever wanted to make from Devil's Food Cake to Gâteau St Honoré, and every rich, gooey, tantalising treat in between!

Gâteau St Honoré

SERVES 6

290 g/10½ oz/generous 2½ cups plain (all-purpose) flour
Salt
100 g/4 oz/½ cup butter, softened
150 g/5 oz/⅔ cup caster (superfine) sugar
A few drops of vanilla essence (extract)
9 eggs
450 ml/¾ pt/2 cups water
50 g/2 oz/¼ cup granulated sugar
300 ml/½ pt/1¼ cups milk
Glacé (candied) cherries and angelica leaves, to decorate

Sift 50 g/2 oz/½ cup of the flour and a pinch of salt into a bowl. Make a well in the centre and add 25 g/1 oz/ 2 tbsp of the butter, 25 g/1 oz/2 tbsp of the caster sugar and a few drops of vanilla essence. Separate one of the eggs, reserving the egg white covered in a separate large bowl. Add the egg yolk to the flour and butter. Work with the fingertips, drawing in the flour until the mixture forms a paste. Wrap in clingfilm (plastic wrap) and chill for 30 minutes.

Put the remaining butter in a saucepan with the water and heat until the butter melts. Meanwhile, sift all but 25 g/1 oz/¼ cup of the remaining flour with 2.5 ml/½ tsp salt on to a sheet of greaseproof (waxed) paper. When the butter has melted, add the flour all in one go and beat until the mixture is smooth and leaves the sides of the pan clean. Remove from the heat. Beat 3 eggs lightly and beat into the flour mixture a little at a time, beating well after each addition, until the mixture is smooth and glossy but still holds its shape. Use to fill a piping bag fitting with a large plain tube (tip).

Roll out the chilled pastry (paste) to a 20 cm/8 in round and place on a greased baking (cookie) sheet. Prick well with a fork. Pipe a rim of choux round the edge of the pastry round. Beat a further egg and use to brush the choux pastry. Bake in a preheated oven at 200°C/400°F/gas mark 6 for about 25 minutes until golden brown. Meanwhile, pipe about 15 small choux balls on to a separate greased baking sheet and brush with the beaten egg. Bake in the oven for about 15 minutes or until golden and crisp. Leave all the pastry to cool.

Put the granulated sugar in a small saucepan with 30 ml/2 tbsp water. Heat, stirring, until the sugar dissolves, then boil until the mixture is a pale golden brown. Use a fork to hold each choux ball and dip in the hot syrup. Place immediately round the choux pastry rim.

Separate the remaining eggs, adding the whites to the reserved white. Beat the remaining caster sugar into the egg yolks until thick and pale. Whisk in the remaining flour and a little of the milk. Bring the remaining milk just to the boil. Whisk into the egg yolk mixture. Return to the pan, slowly bring to the boil and cook for 2 minutes, stirring all the time. Flavour to taste with vanilla essence. Whisk the egg whites until stiff. Fold into the hot custard, then cook gently, stirring, for 2 minutes. Leave to cool. Spoon into the choux cake and decorate with glacé cherries and angelica leaves all round the edge. Chill until ready to serve.

Gâteau Paris-Brest

SERVES 8

*65 g/2½ oz/⅔ cup plain (all-purpose)
flour*
A pinch of salt
150 ml/¼ pt/⅔ cup water
50 g/2 oz/¼ cup butter
2 small eggs, beaten
30 ml/2 tbsp flaked (slivered) almonds
50 g/2 oz/½ cup whole almonds
50 g/2 oz/¼ cup granulated sugar
*1 quantity of Chantilly Cream (see page
358)*
Icing (confectioners') sugar, for dusting
*A few crystallised (candied) violets, to
decorate*

Sift the flour and salt twice on to a sheet of greaseproof (waxed) paper. Put the water and butter in a saucepan and heat until the butter melts. Add the flour all in one go and beat with a wooden spoon until the mixture leaves the sides of the pan clean. Remove from the heat and gradually beat in enough of the egg until the mixture is smooth and glossy but still holding its shape. Reserve the remaining egg for glazing. Use to fill a piping bag fitted with a large plain tube (tip). Pipe a 20 cm/8 in ring on a greased baking (cookie) sheet. Pipe a second ring just inside the first one. Pipe a third ring over the space between the first two. Brush with the remaining beaten egg and sprinkle with the flaked almonds. Bake in a preheated oven at 200°C/400°F/gas mark 6 for about 30 minutes or until risen, crisp and golden. Transfer to a wire rack to cool.

When cool enough to handle, split the cake in half horizontally to allow the steam to escape and leave both halves on wire racks to cool. Meanwhile, put the whole almonds and sugar in a heavy-based saucepan. Heat gently, stirring occasionally, until the sugar melts and turns a rich brown. Do not allow to burn. The almonds will pop when they are toasted. Pour into a well oiled tin and leave to set. Break up and grind in a blender or food processor to a fine powder, making sure no lumps remain. Fold the praline powder into the Chantilly Cream. Use to fill a piping bag fitted with a large star tube. Pipe some of the cream on to the base layer of the cake. Top with the second layer. Pipe whirls of the remaining cream round the top. Dust with a little icing sugar and decorate the whirls with crystallised violets. Chill until ready to serve.

Gâteau Mercédès

SERVES 8

225 g/8 oz/2 cups plain (all-purpose)
  flour
A pinch of salt
100 g/4 oz/½ cup unsalted (sweet)
  butter, softened
375 g/13 oz/1⅔ cup caster (superfine)
  sugar
A few drops of almond essence (extract)
4 eggs, separated
250 g/9 oz/2¼ cups ground almonds
Amaretto, to taste
75 g/3 oz/¾ cup crystallised (candied)
  fruits, chopped
100 g/4 oz/⅓ cup apricot jam
  (conserve)
50 g/2 oz/½ cup blanched almonds, cut
  into thin strips
Juice of ½ lemon

Sift the flour and salt into a bowl.
Make a well in the centre, add the
butter, 100 g/4 oz/½ cup of the sugar,
the almond essence and the egg yolks.
Work with the fingertips, gradually
drawing in the flour, until the mixture
forms a smooth paste. Wrap in clingfilm
(plastic wrap) and chill for 30 minutes.
  Meanwhile, beat the almonds with
the remaining caster sugar and the egg
whites. Flavour to taste with amaretto.
Mix the crystallised fruit with about
45 ml/3 tbsp of the jam. Roll out the
chilled pastry (paste) and use to line a
20 cm/8 in springform cake tin (pan).
Prick the base with a fork and spread
the fruit and jam in the base. Spoon the
almond mixture over, then scatter with
the shredded almonds. Bake in a
preheated oven at 180°C/350°F/gas
mark 4 for about 45 minutes until

golden brown and just set. Leave to
cool. Remove the tin and transfer to a
serving plate. Heat the remaining jam
with the lemon juice, adding a little
water if necessary. Brush all over the
top of the cake to glaze, then chill until
ready to serve.

Chocolate Biscuit Gâteau

SERVES 4–6

Oil, for greasing
200 g/7 oz/1 small can of sweetened
  condensed milk
50 g/2 oz/¼ cup unsalted (sweet) butter
225 g/8 oz/2 cups plain (semi-sweet)
  chocolate
2.5 ml/½ tsp vanilla essence (extract)
200 g/7 oz/1 packet of Marie or other
  plain biscuits (cookies), roughly
  crushed
50 g/2 oz/½ cup chopped walnuts
50 g/2 oz/⅓ cup raisins
A little whipped cream and walnut
  halves, to decorate

Lightly oil a 15 cm/6 in deep round
cake tin (pan). Put the milk, butter,
chocolate and vanilla in a pan and heat
gently until melted. Stir in the biscuits,
walnuts and raisins until thoroughly
coated. Turn into the prepared tin and
press down firmly. Chill until firm. Turn
out on to a serving plate. Decorate with
whipped cream and walnut halves.

Gâteau Pithiviers

SERVES 6

100 g/4 oz/1 cup ground almonds
A few drops of almond essence (extract)
100 g/4 oz/½ cup caster (superfine)
*   sugar*
40 g/1½ oz/3 tbsp unsalted (sweet)
*   butter, softened*
2 egg yolks
30 ml/2 tbsp orange flower water
225 g/8 oz puff pastry (paste), thawed
*   if frozen*
1 egg, beaten
Icing (confectioners') sugar, for dusting

Beat together the ground almonds, a few drops of almond essence, the sugar, butter, egg yolks and enough orange flower water to form a pale paste. Cut off a third of the puff pastry. Roll out to a round about 18 cm/7 in and place on a dampened baking (cookie) sheet. Roll out the larger piece of pastry to a round the same size, but twice as thick. Spread the almond paste in the centre of the thinner pastry round on the baking sheet. Brush all round the edge with water. Place the second piece of pastry on top. Brush with beaten egg to glaze and score the top with the back of a knife in a criss-cross pattern. Bake in a preheated oven at 200°C/400°F/gas mark 6 for 25 minutes. Remove from the oven and dust the top with icing sugar. Return to the oven for a further 5 minutes or until caramelised. This can be served warm or cold.

Summer Raspberry Gâteau

SERVES 4

Oil, for greasing
5 ml/1 tsp powdered gelatine
15 ml/1 tbsp water
3 trifle sponges
75 ml/5 tbsp apple juice
100 g/4 oz raspberries
150 ml/¼ pt/⅔ cup raspberry yoghurt
120 ml/4 fl oz/½ cup double (heavy)
*   cream*
A few mint leaves

Oil a 15 cm/6 in deep round cake tin (pan). Sprinkle the gelatine over the water in a small bowl and leave to soften for 5 minutes, then stand the bowl in a pan of hot water and stir until dissolved (or dissolve briefly in the microwave). Halve the trifle sponges horizontally and use some to line the base of the tin, trimming the sponges to fit and using the trimmings to fill in the gaps. Reserve the remaining sponges. Sprinkle with 30 ml/2 tbsp of the apple juice. Reserve 8 raspberries for decoration, mash the remainder and stir into the yoghurt. Stir in the dissolved gelatine. Whip the cream and fold 30 ml/2 tbsp into the yoghurt mixture. Turn into the prepared tin and smooth the surface. Put a layer of the remaining sponges over the top, again trimming and filling with the trimmings. Sprinkle with the remaining apple juice. Press down lightly. Chill until set. Turn out on to a serving plate. Decorate with the remaining whipped cream, the reserved raspberries and mint leaves.

Summer Peach or Nectarine Gâteau

SERVES 4

Prepare as for Summer Raspberry Gâteau (see page 249), but substitute peach or apricot yoghurt for the raspberry yoghurt and two peaches or nectarines for the raspberries, chopping one to add to the yoghurt and slicing the other for decoration.

Summer Strawberry Gâteau

SERVES 4

Prepare as for Summer Raspberry Gâteau (see page 249), but substitute strawberry yoghurt for the raspberry yoghurt and strawberries for the raspberries but reserving only two or three for decoration.

Summer Hazelnut Gâteau

SERVES 4

Prepare as for Summer Raspberry Gâteau (see page 249), but substitute hazelnut (filbert) yoghurt for the raspberry yoghurt and hazelnuts for the raspberries, chopping the majority and reserving a few whole ones for decoration.

Austrian Coffee Cake

SERVES 6

100 g/4 oz/½ cup butter, softened
100 g/4 oz/½ cup caster (superfine) sugar
2 eggs
100 g/4 oz/1 cup self-raising (self-rising) flour
30 ml/2 tbsp instant coffee powder or granules
45 ml/3 tbsp water
15 ml/1 tbsp schnapps or brandy
150 ml/¼ pt/⅔ cup double (heavy) cream
30 ml/2 tbsp toasted flaked (slivered) almonds

Beat together the butter and sugar until light and fluffy. Beat in the eggs, one at a time, beating well after each addition. Sift the flour over the surface and fold in with a metal spoon. Turn into a greased 900 ml/1½ pt/ 3¾ cup ring tin (pan). Bake in a preheated oven at 180°C/350°F/gas mark 4 for 25 minutes until risen and golden and the cake is beginning to shrink away from the sides of the tin. Turn out on to a wire rack to cool. Transfer to a serving plate. Blend together the coffee, water and schnapps or brandy. Spoon all over the cake, a little at a time so it all soaks in. Whip the cream and smother all over the cake. Scatter the nuts over and chill until ready to serve.

Coffee Cream Charlotte

SERVES 8

4 × 75 g/4 × 3 oz/4 small packets of
   sponge (lady) finger biscuits
45 ml/3 tbsp milk
45 ml/3 tbsp brandy
50 g/2 oz/¼ cup unsalted (sweet) butter,
   softened
100 g/4 oz/⅔ cup icing (confectioners')
   sugar, sifted
10 ml/2 tsp instant coffee powder or
   granules
10 ml/2 tsp hot water
300 ml/½ pt/1¼ cups double (heavy)
   cream
Walnut halves, to decorate

Use some of the sponge fingers to line the base and sides of a 20 cm/8 in deep, round, loose-bottomed cake tin (pan), sugared sides out. Mix together the milk and 15 ml/1 tbsp of the brandy and brush the exposed surfaces of the sponge fingers. Beat together the butter and icing sugar until smooth. Dissolve the coffee in the water and beat into the butter icing (frosting). Whip the cream until peaking. Spoon half into a separate bowl and whisk the remaining brandy into the other. Spread a layer of half the butter icing over the base of the lined tin. Top with a layer of sponge fingers, trimming to fit. Brush with some of the remaining milk and brandy mixture. Top with half the brandy-flavoured cream. Repeat the layers, finishing with a layer of brandy cream. Chill until firm.

Trim the tops of the sponge fingers level with the top of the cream. Remove the sides of the tin but leave on the base for easier serving. Place on a serving plate. Use the remaining whipped cream to fill a piping bag fitted with a large star tube (tip) and pipe rosettes of cream all round the top edge. Decorate with a few walnut halves and chill again until ready to serve. For an attractive finishing touch, tie a contrasting ribbon round the charlotte, if liked.

Orange Gingernut Log

SERVES 4–6

1 orange
450 ml/¾ pt/2 cups whipping or double
   (heavy) cream, whipped
60 ml/4 tbsp orange liqueur
200 g/7 oz/1 small packet of gingernut
   biscuits (cookies)
Toasted flaked (slivered) almonds, to
   decorate

Finely grate the rind of half the orange and thinly pare the remainder. Squeeze out the juice. Cut the pared rind into thin strips and boil in water for 3 minutes. Drain, rinse with cold water and drain again. Stir the grated rind into the cream. Mix the orange juice with the liqueur. Dip the biscuits in the liqueur mixture, then sandwich together with three-quarters of the cream. Place on a serving plate and spread the remaining cream over. Decorate with the thinly pared orange rind and a few toasted flaked almonds. Chill for at least 3 hours to allow the flavours to develop.

Jamaican Charlotte

SERVES 8–10

3 × 75 g/3 × 3 oz/3 small packets of
  sponge (lady) fingers
175 g/6 oz/¾ cup unsalted (sweet) butter,
  softened
350 g/12 oz/2 cups icing (confectioners')
  sugar
40 g/1½ oz/⅓ cup cocoa (unsweetened
  chocolate) powder
30 ml/2 tbsp rum
300 ml/½ pt/1¼ cups double (heavy) or
  whipping cream
2 bananas
15 ml/1 tbsp lemon juice
15 ml/1 tbsp caster (superfine) sugar
Toasted coconut flakes, to decorate

Use some of the sponge fingers to
line the base and sides of an
18 cm/7 in deep round, loose-bottomed
cake tin (pan). Crush the remainder.
Beat the butter until really soft. Sift the
icing sugar and cocoa over and work in
with a wooden spoon, adding the rum.
Whip the cream until peaking. Mash the
bananas with the lemon juice and sugar
and fold in half the whipped cream.
Spread half the chocolate mixture over
the biscuits (cookies) in the tin, then a
third of the crushed sponge fingers. Add
a layer of half the banana cream and
half the remaining crumbs. Repeat the
layers, finishing with a layer of banana
mixture. Chill until firm.

Trim the sponge fingers level with
the top of the banana mixture. Spoon
the remaining cream into a piping bag
fitted with a large star tube (tip) and
pipe rosettes of cream all round the top
edge. Decorate the centre with toasted
coconut flakes before serving.

Carrot and Apricot Roll

SERVES 6

4 eggs, separated
100 g/4 oz/½ cup caster (superfine)
  sugar, plus extra for sprinkling
1 large carrot, grated
50 g/2 oz/½ cup chopped almonds
100 g/4 oz/1 cup plain (all-purpose)
  flour
60 ml/4 tbsp apricot jam (conserve)
350 g/12 oz/1½ cups plain or apricot
  fromage frais

Put the egg yolks and sugar in a bowl
and whisk until thick and pale. Fold
in the carrots, nuts and flour with a
metal spoon. Whisk the egg whites until
stiff and fold in with a metal spoon.
Turn into an 18 × 28 cm/7 × 11 in
Swiss roll tin (jelly roll pan), lined with
baking parchment. Level the surface.
Bake in a preheated oven at 190°C/
375°F/gas mark 5 for about 25 minutes
until the centre springs back when
lightly pressed.

Put a sheet of baking parchment on
the work surface and sprinkle with a
little caster sugar. Turn the roulade out
on to the paper. Ease away the cooking
paper and discard. Quickly trim the
edges, if liked, then roll up with the
sugared paper inside to stop the cake
sticking together. Cover with a clean tea
towel (dish cloth) and leave to cool.
When cold, carefully unroll and discard
the paper. Spread with the jam, then the
fromage frais. Roll up and transfer to a
serving plate. Sprinkle with a little extra
sugar, if liked, and serve sliced.

Pineapple Slice

SERVES 6

---

*250 g/9 oz/1 medium can of crushed
  pineapple, drained*
*450 ml/¾ pt/2 cups double (heavy)
  cream*
Finely grated rind of 1 orange
*15 ml/1 tbsp icing (confectioners')
  sugar*
*200 g/7 oz/1 packet of digestive finger
  biscuits (graham cracker fingers)*
*Glacé (candied) cherries and angelica
  leaves, to decorate*

Put the drained pineapple on two sheets of kitchen paper (paper towels) to drain thoroughly. Whip half the cream. Take out 60 ml/4 tbsp and reserve. Fold the pineapple with the orange rind and icing sugar into the reserved whipped cream. Sandwich together half the biscuits with half the pineapple cream and lay on a serving plate. Spread with the reserved whipped cream. Sandwich the remaining biscuits and pineapple cream in the same way as before and lay on top of the first layer. Cover with foil and chill for several hours or overnight. Whip the remaining cream. Smother the cake in most of it, then pipe the remainder in swirls on top. Decorate with glacé cherries and angelica leaves and chill.

Chip Cookie Gâteau

SERVES 4–6

---

45 ml/3 tbsp port
45 ml/3 tbsp brandy
*200 g/7 oz/1 small packet of chocolate
  chip cookies*
*450 ml/¾ pt/2 cups whipping or double
  (heavy) cream, whipped*
Grated chocolate, to decorate

Mix together the port and brandy. Dip the biscuits in the mixture, then sandwich together with three-quarters of the whipped cream. Place on a serving plate and spread the remaining cream over. Sprinkle with grated chocolate. Chill for at least 3 hours to allow the flavours to develop.

Caribbean Slab

SERVES 4–8

100 g/4 oz/½ cup unsalted (sweet) butter, softened
100 g/4 oz/½ cup caster (superfine) sugar
1 large egg, separated
75 g/3 oz/¾ cup desiccated (shredded) coconut
90 ml/6 tbsp redcurrant jelly (clear conserve)
15 ml/1 tbsp lemon juice
45 ml/3 tbsp white rum
2 × 75 g/2 × 3 oz/2 small packets of sponge (lady) fingers

Beat together the butter and sugar until light and fluffy, then beat in the egg yolk. Whisk the egg white until stiff and fold into the butter mixture with 50 g/2 oz/½ cup of the coconut. Warm the redcurrant jelly and lemon juice in a saucepan. Remove from the heat. Lay eight sponge fingers in a row on a large piece of foil, sugared-sides up. Brush with a little of the rum. Spread a quarter of the coconut mixture over, then drizzle with a little of the redcurrant and lemon mixture. Repeat this process, finishing with a layer of sponge fingers. You should have a third of the coconut cream mixture left. Spread this all round the sides of the cake. Toast the remaining coconut in a frying pan (skillet) until golden, stirring all the time. Allow to cool, then press all round the sides of the cake. Using a small teaspoon, spoon the remaining redcurrant and lemon mixture between the sponge fingers along the top to decorate. Chill until firm. Serve cut into slices.

Nut Torte

SERVES 8

4 egg whites
225 g/8 oz/1 cup caster (superfine) sugar
1.5 ml/¼ tsp malt vinegar
1.5 ml/¼ tsp vanilla essence (extract)
100 g/4 oz/1 cup toasted chopped mixed nuts
45 ml/3 tbsp lemon curd
150 ml/¼ pt/⅔ cup double (heavy) cream, whipped
Crystallised (candied) lemon slices, to decorate

Whisk the egg whites until stiff. Add half the sugar and whisk again until stiff and glossy. Fold in the remaining sugar, the vinegar and vanilla, then the nuts. Spread the mixture into two 20 cm/8 in rounds on baking parchment on baking (cookie) sheets. Bake in a preheated oven at 180°C/350°F/gas mark 4 for about 45 minutes. Cool on a wire rack. Carefully lift off the baking parchment. Place one round on a serving plate. Spread with the lemon curd, then top with half the whipped cream. Top with the second nut meringue round. Decorate with the remaining whipped cream and crystallised lemon slices.

Sachertorte

SERVES 8–10

Oil, for greasing
275 g/10 oz/2½ cups plain (semi-sweet)
  chocolate
150 g/5 oz/⅔ cup unsalted (sweet)
  butter
150 g/5 oz/scant 1 cup icing
  (confectioners') sugar, sifted
5 eggs, separated
150 g/5 oz/1¼ cups self-raising (self-
  rising) flour
25 g/1 oz/¼ cup cornflour (cornstarch)
90 ml/6 tbsp apricot jam (conserve),
  sieved (strained)
150 ml/¼ pt/⅔ cup water
100 g/4 oz/½ cup caster (superfine)
  sugar
25 g/1 oz/¼ cup white chocolate

Grease and flour a 23 cm/9 in deep round cake tin (pan). Break up half the plain chocolate and place in a bowl over a pan of hot water. Stir until melted. (Or melt briefly in the microwave.) Beat together the butter and icing sugar until fluffy. Beat in the melted chocolate, then the egg yolks. Sift the flour and cornflour over the surface and fold in with a metal spoon. Whisk the egg whites until stiff. Beat a little into the chocolate mixture to soften it, then very lightly fold in the remainder with a metal spoon. Turn into the prepared tin and bake in a preheated oven at 150°C/300°F/gas mark 2 for 50 minutes or until risen and firm. Leave to cool in the tin for 10 minutes, then turn out on to a wire rack to cool completely.

When cold, split in half horizontally and sandwich together with half the jam. Leave on the wire rack. Spread the remaining jam over the top and sides of the cake. Put the water and caster sugar in a saucepan and stir well. Heat without stirring until the sugar has melted. Bring to the boil and boil until the mixture reaches the soft ball stage, when 5 ml/1 tsp of the mixture dropped into cold water forms a soft ball, or until it reaches 115°C/240°F on a sugar thermometer. Remove from the heat and immediately plunge the base of the pan briefly in cold water to prevent further cooking.

Melt the remaining plain chocolate in a bowl over a pan of hot water. Beat in the still-hot syrup. Beat thoroughly until the mixture has a smooth coating consistency. Pour over the cake and use a palette knife to spread it evenly. Work quickly before the mixture sets. Leave until firm. Melt the white chocolate in a bowl over a pan of hot water. Spoon into a small paper piping bag and snip off the very tip of the bag. Pipe the word *Sachertorte* on top and allow to set before serving.

Chocolate Hazelnut Torte

The leftover egg yolks can be used for custard (see pages 354–5), ice cream (see pages 188–94), to enrich pastry (paste) (see pages 104–20), for glazing pastry, bread or biscuits (cookies) or can be frozen for future use.

SERVES 8

For the cake:
Oil, for greasing
40 g/1½ oz/⅓ cup cornflour (cornstarch)
150 g/5 oz/1¼ cups plain (all-purpose) flour
10 egg whites
1.5 ml/¼ tsp cream of tartar
275 g/10 oz/1¼ cups caster (superfine) sugar
10 ml/2 tsp vanilla essence (extract)
For the filling and topping:
450 ml/¾ pt/2 cups double (heavy) cream
175 g/6 oz chocolate hazelnut (filbert) spread
150 ml/¼ pt/⅔ cup plain yoghurt
30 ml/2 tbsp ground hazelnuts
A small block of plain (semi-sweet) chocolate
8 toasted hazelnuts

To make the cake, grease and flour a 23 cm/9 in ring tin (pan). Sift together the cornflour and flour. Whisk the egg whites until stiff with the cream of tartar. Whisk in half the sugar and the vanilla essence. Whisk again until stiff. Add the remaining sugar and whisk again until stiff and glossy. Gently fold in the flour mixture with a metal spoon. Turn into the prepared tin and smooth the surface. Bake in a preheated oven at 180°C/350°F/gas mark 4 for about 35 minutes until risen, golden and the cake springs back when lightly pressed. Allow to cool slightly, then turn out on to a wire rack and leave to cool completely.

To make the filling and topping, whip the cream until peaking. Spoon half into a separate bowl and fold the chocolate spread into the other. Gently whisk the yoghurt into the remaining cream with the ground hazelnuts. Cut the cold cake into three equal layers. Place the base layer on a serving plate and spread half the chocolate filling over. Repeat the layers, finishing with the top layer of cake. Spread the cream and yoghurt mixture all over the cake. Scrape a potato peeler along the chocolate block to form chocolate curls and use to decorate the cake with the toasted hazelnuts. Chill for at least 1 hour before serving.

Apple and Cinnamon Torte

SERVES 6

Oil, for greasing
450 g/1 lb cooking (tart) apples, sliced
Finely grated rind and juice of 1 lemon
175 g/6 oz/¾ cup light brown sugar
175 g/6 oz/¾ cup butter
75 g/3 oz/¾ cup rolled oats
10 ml/2 tsp ground cinnamon
2 eggs
100 g/4 oz/1 cup self-raising (self-rising) flour
75 ml/5 tbsp crème fraîche
30 ml/2 tbsp toasted flaked (slivered) almonds

Grease an 18 cm/7 in deep round cake tin (pan) with a little oil and line the base with greased greaseproof (waxed) paper. Toss the apple slices in the lemon rind and juice to prevent browning. Put 50 g/2 oz/¼ cup of the sugar in a frying pan (skillet) with 50 g/2 oz/¼ cup of the butter and heat gently, stirring, until melted. Stir in the oats and half the cinnamon. Beat together the remaining butter and sugar until light and fluffy. Beat in the eggs one at a time, beating well after each addition. Sift the flour and the remaining cinnamon over the surface and fold in with a metal spoon. Fold in the apple and lemon mixture. Turn into the prepared cake tin and smooth the surface. Bake in a preheated oven at 180°C/350°F/gas mark 4 for about 50 minutes or until the centre springs back when lightly pressed. Turn out on to a sheet of greaseproof (waxed) paper on a baking (cookie) sheet and leave to cool. Slide on to a serving plate. Swirl the crème fraîche over the top, sprinkle with toasted almonds and serve.

Chestnut Gâteau

SERVES 4–6

225 g/8 oz/2 cups plain (semi-sweet) chocolate
30 ml/2 tbsp milk
430 g/15½ oz/1 large can of unsweetened chestnut purée (paste)
100 g/4 oz/1 cup flaked (slivered) almonds
15 ml/1 tbsp brandy
Oil, for greasing
150 ml/¼ pt/⅔ cup double (heavy) cream, whipped
30 ml/2 tbsp coarsely grated chocolate

Break up the chocolate and place in a pan with the milk. Heat gently, stirring, until the chocolate has melted. Whisk in the chestnut purée, flaked almonds and brandy. Spoon into an oiled 18 cm/7 in loose-bottomed cake tin (pan) and level the surface. Chill overnight until firm. Remove from the tin and smother with whipped cream. Decorate with grated chocolate before serving.

Fresh Cherry Almond Gâteau

SERVES 8

Oil, for greasing
175 g/6 oz/³/₄ cup caster (superfine) sugar
175 g/6 oz/³/₄ cup soft tub margarine
3 eggs
175 g/6 oz/1½ cups self-raising (self-
    rising) flour
2.5 ml/½ tsp almond essence (extract)
150 ml/¼ pt/²/₃ cup double (heavy) cream
175 ml/6 fl oz/³/₄ cup port
10 ml/2 tsp arrowroot
60 ml/4 tbsp toasted chopped almonds
225 g/8 oz cherries, halved and stoned
    (pitted)

Grease and flour a 20 cm/8 in deep
round cake tin (pan). Cream
together the margarine and sugar until
light and fluffy. Beat in the eggs, one at
a time, beating well after each addition.
Fold in the flour and the almond
essence. Turn into the prepared tin and
level the top. Cook in a preheated oven
at 190°C/375°F/gas mark 5 for
40 minutes or until the centre springs
back when lightly pressed. Allow to
cool slightly, then turn out on to a wire
rack and leave to cool completely.

Whip the cream. Halve the cake
horizontally and sandwich together
with the cream. Blend a little of the port
with the arrowroot in a saucepan. Stir
in the remaining port. Bring to the boil,
stirring until thickened and clear. Brush
the sides of the cake with a little of the
glaze and roll in the chopped nuts.
Place on a serving plate. Arrange the
cherries, cut-sides down, over the top of
the cake and brush with the rest of the
glaze. Chill before serving.

Angel Cake with Cherries

SERVES 6

50 g/2 oz/½ cup plain (all-purpose) flour
4 egg whites
2.5 ml/½ tsp cream of tartar
100 g/4 oz/½ cup caster (superfine) sugar
2.5 ml/½ tsp vanilla essence (extract)
25 g/1 oz/2 tbsp granulated sugar
15 ml/1 tbsp water
30 ml/2 tbsp kirsch
250 ml/8 fl oz/1 cup double (heavy) cream
225 g/8 oz red cherries, stoned (pitted)

Sift the flour on to a sheet of
greaseproof (waxed) paper. Whisk
the egg whites and cream of tartar until
stiff. Whisk in half the caster sugar until
stiff and glossy. Fold in the remaining
caster sugar and the vanilla essence.
Sprinkle the flour over and fold in
lightly with a metal spoon. Turn into an
ungreased 1.2 litre/2 pt/5 cup ring tin
(pan). Draw a knife through the
mixture to release any trapped air
bubbles. Cook in a preheated oven at
140°C/275°F/gas mark 1 for
30 minutes, then increase the heat to
160°C/325°F/gas mark 3 and cook for a
further 20–30 minutes until risen and
the centre springs back when lightly
pressed. Leave to cool for 10 minutes,
then turn out on to a wire rack to cool
completely.

Put the granulated sugar and water
in a pan and heat gently until the sugar
has dissolved. Stir in the kirsch and
leave to cool. Place the angel cake on a
serving plate. Slowly spoon the syrup
over. Whip the cream until peaking and
spread all over the cake. Arrange the
cherries in the centre and chill until
ready to serve.

Fresh Cream Gâteau

SERVES 6–8

Oil, for greasing
4 eggs
100 g/4 oz/½ cup caster (superfine)
  sugar
100 g/4 oz/1 cup plain (all-purpose)
  flour
50 g/2 oz/¼ cup unsalted (sweet) butter,
  melted
150 ml/¼ pt/⅔ cup double (heavy) cream
60 ml/4 tbsp raspberry jam (conserve)
Icing (confectioners') sugar, for dusting

Grease and line a 20 cm/8 in deep round cake tin (pan) with greased, greaseproof (waxed) paper. Whisk together the eggs and sugar in a bowl over a pan of hot water until thick and pale and the mixture leaves a trail when lifted out of the mixture. Remove the bowl from the saucepan and continue whisking until cold. Sift half the flour over the surface and very lightly fold in with a metal spoon. Sift the remaining flour over and carefully drizzle the melted butter all round the edge. Fold in lightly and gently with a metal spoon until just mixed but no more. Turn into the prepared tin and gently tap the tin on the work surface to settle the contents. Bake in a preheated oven at 180°C/350°F/gas mark 4 for 35 minutes until risen, golden and the centre springs back when lightly pressed. Allow to cool slightly, then turn out on to a wire rack, remove the paper and leave to cool completely.

When cold, halve the cake horizontally. Place one half, cut-side up, on a serving plate. Whip the cream until peaking. Spread over the cake half on the plate, then spread the jam over the cut side of the remaining half. Lay, jam-side down, on top of the cream. Dust the top with icing sugar and chill until ready to serve.

Fresh Strawberry Gâteau

SERVES 6–8

Prepare as for Fresh Cream Gâteau, but cover the cream with 100–175 g/ 4–6 oz sliced strawberries and omit the jam. Decorate the top with extra whipped cream and a few small unhulled strawberries, if liked.

Fresh Raspberry Gâteau

SERVES 6–8

Prepare as for Fresh Strawberry Gâteau, but substitute lightly crushed raspberries for the sliced strawberries.

Fresh Peach or Nectarine Gâteau

SERVES 6 8

Prepare as for Fresh Strawberry Gâteau, but substitute 2–3 ripe peaches or nectarines, sliced, for the strawberries.

Gâteau Margot

SERVES 10

Oil, for greasing
4 eggs
200 g/7 oz/scant 1 cup caster (superfine)
  sugar
100 g/4 oz/1 cup plain (all-purpose) flour
450 g/1 lb strawberries
100 g/4 oz/1 cup plain (semi-sweet)
  chocolate
300 ml/½ pt/1¼ cups double (heavy)
  cream
Finely grated rind of 1 orange

Grease and flour a 1.75 litre/3 pt/
7½ cup ring tin (pan). Whisk
together the eggs and 175 g/6 oz/¾ cup
of the sugar until thick and pale. Sift
the flour over the surface and gently
fold in with a metal spoon until just
blended but no more. Turn into the
prepared tin and bake in a preheated
oven at 190°C/375°F/gas mark 5 for
about 35 minutes or until risen and a
pale golden colour and the mixture
springs back when lightly pressed.
Turn out on to a wire rack to cool.
    Meanwhile, purée about a third of
the strawberries and sweeten to taste
with some of the remaining sugar. Melt
the chocolate in a bowl over a pan of
hot water or in the microwave. Split the
cake horizontally into three equal
layers. Spread the bottom layer and the
middle layer with the chocolate and
leave to set. Whip the cream until
peaking. Fold about a third into the
strawberry purée. Flavour the remainder
with the orange rind and sweeten to
taste with the remaining sugar.
Sandwich the three layers together with
the strawberry purée and cream
mixture. Smother the whole cake in the
orange-flavoured cream and fill the
centre with the remaining strawberries.

Gâteau Diane

SERVES 6

4 egg whites
225 g/8 oz/1 cup caster (superfine)
  sugar
350 g/12 oz/3 cups plain (semi-sweet)
  chocolate
300 ml/½ pt/1¼ cups double (heavy)
  cream
300 ml/½ pt/1¼ cups crème fraîche

Whisk the egg whites until stiff.
Add half the sugar and whisk
again until stiff and glossy. Fold in the
remaining sugar. Spread into three thin
rounds about 23 cm/9 in diameter on
baking (cookie) sheets, lined with
baking parchment. Bake in a preheated
oven at 140°C/275°F/gas mark 1 for
about 1 hour until crisp and dry. Turn
off the oven and leave there to cool.
    Melt the chocolate in a bowl over a
pan of hot water or in the microwave.
Pour about a quarter of it on to a large
plate, spread evenly and leave until set.
Whip together the cream and crème
fraîche until peaking. Whisk in the
remaining melted chocolate until thick.
Sandwich the meringue rounds together
with some of the chocolate cream. Place
on a serving plate. Spread the
remaining chocolate cream over the
sides and top. Carefully shave off long
curls of the set chocolate on the plate,
using a palette knife held almost
upright. Lay the chocolate caraque on
top of the gâteau to decorate and chill
for several hours before serving.

Devil's Food Cake

SERVES 8

175 g/6 oz/1½ cups plain (all-purpose)
  flour
1.5 ml/¼ tsp baking powder
5 ml/1 tsp bicarbonate of soda (baking
  soda)
100 g/4 oz/1 cup cocoa (unsweetened
  chocolate) powder
500 ml/17 fl oz/2¼ cups water
100 g/4 oz/½ cup white vegetable fat
  (shortening)
275 g/10 oz/1¼ cups caster (superfine)
  sugar
2 eggs, lightly beaten
Oil, for greasing
450 g/1 lb/2 cups granulated sugar
50 g/2 oz/¼ cup unsalted (sweet) butter
15 ml/1 tbsp golden (light corn) syrup
Whipped cream, to serve

Sift together the flour, baking powder
and bicarbonate of soda in a bowl.
Blend half the cocoa powder with
200 ml/7 fl oz/scant 1 cup of the water.
Beat together the vegetable fat and
caster sugar until fluffy. Beat in the
eggs a little at a time, beating well after
each addition. Fold in the flour mixture
alternately with the blended cocoa. Turn
into two greased 20 cm/8 in sandwich
tins (pans) and smooth the surfaces.
Bake in a preheated oven at 180°C/
350°F/gas mark 4 for about 30 minutes
or until a skewer inserted into the
centre of each comes out clean. Leave
to cool in the tins for 10 minutes, then
turn out on to a wire rack to cool
completely.

Put the granulated sugar and the
remaining water in a pan with the
remaining cocoa, the butter and syrup.
Heat gently, stirring, until the sugar has
dissolved. Bring to the boil and boil to
the soft ball stage, when 5 ml/1 tsp of
the mixture dropped into a cup of cold
water forms a soft ball, or to
115°C/242°F on a sugar thermometer.
Do not stir or the mixture will become
grainy. Leave to cool, then beat well
until thick and spreadable. Sandwich
the cakes together with some of the
fudge icing, then spread the remainder
over the sides and top. Chill until ready
to serve with whipped cream.

Fresh Pineapple Gâteau

SERVES 6

Oil, for greasing
100 g/4 oz/½ cup soft tub margarine
150 g/5 oz/⅔ cup caster (superfine)
*   sugar*
2 eggs
100 g/4 oz/1 cup self-raising (self-
*   rising) flour*
5 ml/1 tsp vanilla essence (extract)
1 small ripe pineapple
150 ml/¼ pt/⅔ cup double (heavy) cream
30 ml/2 tbsp kirsch
60 ml/4 tbsp apricot jam (conserve),
*   sieved (strained) if necessary*
Halved glacé (candied) cherries and
*   angelica leaves, to decorate*

Grease and flour an 18 cm/7 in loose-bottomed cake tin (pan). Beat together the margarine and 100 g/4 oz/½ cup of the sugar until light and fluffy. Beat in the eggs one at a time, beating well after each addition. Sift the flour over the surface and fold in with a metal spoon, adding the vanilla essence. Turn into the prepared tin and smooth the surface. Bake in a preheated oven at 190°C/375°F/gas mark 5 for about 30 minutes until risen and golden and the centre springs back when lightly pressed. Leave to cool slightly, then turn out on to a wire rack to cool completely.

Cut all the rind off the pineapple and cut the flesh into 1 cm/½ in slices. Cut out the thick core. Reserve three slices for the top and chop the remainder. Whip the cream and kirsch with the remaining sugar until peaking. Fold in the chopped pineapple. Sandwich the cake together with this mixture. Place on a serving plate. Warm the apricot jam in a saucepan and brush over the cake. Arrange the reserved pineapple slices on top and decorate with glacé cherries and angelica leaves. Brush any remaining jam over to glaze and chill until ready to serve.

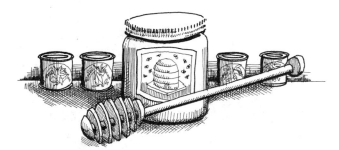

Gâteau à la Mousse au Chocolat

SERVES 8

Oil, for greasing
100 g/4 oz/1 cup plain (all-purpose)
  flour
25 g/1 oz/¼ cup cocoa (unsweetened
  chocolate) powder
2.5 ml/½ tsp baking powder
A pinch of salt
150 g/5 oz/⅔ cup unsalted (sweet)
  butter, softened
7 eggs
150 g/5 oz/⅔ cup caster (superfine)
  sugar
5 ml/1 tsp vanilla essence (extract)
250 g/9 oz/2¼ cups plain (semi-sweet)
  chocolate
15 ml/1 tbsp brandy
Chantilly Cream (see page 358)

Grease and flour a 23 cm/9 in cake tin (pan), base-lined with greased greaseproof (waxed) paper. Sift together the flour, cocoa, baking powder and salt. Melt 50 g/2 oz/¼ cup of the butter and leave to cool so the sediment settles. Whisk together four of the eggs and the sugar until thick and pale and the mixture leaves a trail when lifted out of the mixture. Whisk in the vanilla essence and continue whisking until cool. Sprinkle a third of the flour mixture over the surface and fold in with a metal spoon. Repeat with half the remaining flour. Sprinkle the remaining flour over and trickle the clarified butter over. Lightly fold both into the mixture. Turn into the prepared tin. Bake in a preheated oven at 180°C/350°F/gas mark 4 for about 40 minutes until the cake is well risen, springs back when lightly pressed and is shrinking away from the sides of the tin. Turn out on to a wire rack, remove the paper and leave to cool.

Melt 150 g/5 oz/1¼ cups of the chocolate in a bowl over a pan of hot water or in the microwave. Separate the remaining eggs. Beat the yolks into the chocolate, then beat in the remaining butter and the brandy. Whisk the egg whites until stiff and fold into the chocolate mixture. Split the cold cake into three layers. Place the base layer on a serving plate and spread with two-thirds of the chocolate mousse. Top with a second layer and spread with the Chantilly Cream. Top with the final layer. Spread the remaining mousse over the sides and top of the cake. Scrape the remaining chocolate with a potato peeler to make chocolate curls. Scatter all over the gâteau and chill until ready to serve.

Chocolate Refrigerator Gâteau

SERVES 6–8

2 × 75 g/2 × 3 oz/2 small packets of sponge (lady) fingers
15 ml/1 tbsp powdered gelatine
15 ml/1 tbsp water
175 g/6 oz/¾ cup caster (superfine) sugar
30 ml/2 tbsp custard powder
450 ml/¾ pt/2 cups milk
2 eggs, separated
300 ml/½ pt/1¼ cups double (heavy) cream
100 g/4 oz/1 cup plain (semi-sweet) chocolate
25 g/1 oz/2 tbsp unsalted (sweet) butter
1 large Mars Bar, chopped
Chopped walnuts, to decorate

L ine the base of a 900 g/2 lb loaf tin (pan) with greaseproof (waxed) paper. Line the base and sides with some of the sponge fingers. Sprinkle the gelatine over the water in a small bowl and leave to soften for 5 minutes. Stand the bowl in a pan of hot water and stir until the gelatine has dissolved completely (or heat briefly in the microwave). Blend the sugar with the custard powder, a little of the milk and the egg yolks in a saucepan. Blend in all but 15 ml/1 tbsp of the remaining milk and half the cream. Break up the chocolate and add to the pan. Bring to the boil and cook for 2 minutes, stirring, until the chocolate has melted and the mixture has thickened. Stir in the dissolved gelatine. Leave until cool and beginning to set.

Pour half the mixture into the lined tin. Cover with a layer of the remaining sponge fingers. Add the remaining chocolate mixture, then a layer of sponge. Chill overnight. Turn out on to a serving plate and remove the paper. Melt the Mars Bar in a saucepan with the reserved 15 ml/1 tbsp milk, stirring all the time. Spoon over the sponge fingers. Whisk the egg whites until stiff, then the remaining cream until peaking. Fold the egg whites into the cream. Spread all over the cake and decorate with a few chopped walnuts. Chill again before serving.

Black Forest Gâteau

SERVES 10

150 g/5 oz/⅔ cup unsalted (sweet)
butter, plus extra for greasing
50 g/2 oz/½ cup plain (all-purpose)
flour, plus extra for dusting
50 g/2 oz/½ cup cocoa (unsweetened
chocolate) powder
6 eggs
225 g/8 oz/1 cup caster (superfine)
sugar
5 ml/1 tsp vanilla essence (extract)
50 g/2 oz/¼ cup granulated sugar
425 g/15 oz/1 large can of red or black
cherries
90 ml/6 tbsp kirsch
600 ml/1 pt/2½ cups double (heavy)
cream
50 g/2 oz/⅓ cup icing (confectioners')
sugar, sifted
Coarsely grated chocolate, to decorate

Grease three 18 cm/7 in sandwich tins (pans) with a little butter and dust with flour. Sift the flour and cocoa powder twice and reserve. Melt the butter and leave so the sediment settles to the bottom. Whisk together the eggs and caster sugar until thick and pale, then whisk in the vanilla essence. Sift the flour and cocoa again over the surface, drizzle the melted butter over leaving the sediment behind and fold them all in gently with a metal spoon until just blended. Turn into the prepared tins and level the surfaces. Bake in a preheated oven at 180°C/350°F/gas mark 4 for about 15 minutes until the centres spring back when lightly pressed. Leave to cool in the tins for a few minutes, then turn out on to wire racks and leave to cool completely.

Meanwhile, drain the can of cherries, reserving the juice. Reserve a few cherries for decoration. Chop the remainder and remove the stones (pits). Put the granulated sugar in a saucepan. Add 90 ml/6 tbsp of the cherry juice. Heat gently, stirring, until the sugar has dissolved, then boil rapidly for a few minutes until syrupy. Leave to cool, then stir in half the kirsch. Put the cream in a bowl with the icing sugar and remaining kirsch. Whip until peaking. Sandwich the three cakes together with some of the cream and the chopped cherries. Spread the remaining cream all over the sides and top of the cake. Decorate the top with the reserved cherries and grated chocolate. Chill until ready to serve.

Highland Chocolate Cake

SERVES 6

Oil, for greasing
18 shortbread fingers
275 g/10 oz/2½ cups plain (semi-sweet)
    chocolate
175 g/6 oz/¾ cup unsalted (sweet)
    butter, softened
175 g/6 oz/1 cup icing (confectioners')
    sugar
Finely grated rind and juice of
    ½ grapefruit
3 egg yolks
60 ml/4 tbsp whisky
300 ml/½ pt/1¼ cups double (heavy)
    cream
Grated chocolate, to decorate

Grease an 18 cm/7 in loose-bottomed cake tin (pan) and line with greased greaseproof (waxed) paper. Arrange the shortbread fingers around the edge and base, patterned sides out.

Break up the chocolate in a bowl, place over a pan of hot water and stir until melted (or melt in the microwave). Beat together the butter and icing sugar until light and fluffy. Beat in the grapefruit rind and juice with the egg yolk, then add the melted chocolate and whisky. Turn into the prepared tin and level the surface. Chill until firm.

Carefully remove the tin and paper and place the cake on a serving plate. Whip the cream until peaking and spread all over the sides and top. Decorate with grated chocolate before serving.

Flashy Pan Desserts

Banana Flambé, Crêpes Suzette and Toffee Apple Pudding are just three of the frying pan (skillet) or chafing dish desserts you'll be able to make. There are my versions of all those classics created by master chefs over the years and many original creations too. You will also find some deep-fried specialities and a selection of sensational fondues to set your taste buds reeling.

Loukoumades

SERVES 6

For the batter:
225 g/8 oz/2 cups plain (all-purpose) flour
2.5 ml/½ tsp salt
1.5 ml/¼ tsp ground cinnamon
15 g/½ oz/1 sachet of easy-blend dried yeast
250 ml/8 fl oz/1 cup hand-hot water
Oil, for deep-frying
For the syrup:
250 ml/8 fl oz/1 cup clear honey
10 ml/2 tsp lemon juice
15 ml/1 tbsp brandy
15 ml/1 tbsp water

To make the batter, mix the flour, salt, cinnamon and yeast in a bowl. Gradually beat in the hand-hot water to form a thick, smooth batter. Cover with clingfilm (plastic wrap) and leave in a warm place for 1½ hours or until well risen and bubbling. Heat the oil to 190°C/375°F or until a cube of day-old bread browns in 30 seconds. Drop in small spoonfuls of the batter and fry until puffy and pale golden brown. They should be crisp and hollow. If the first few seem chewy, add 15 ml/1 tbsp of hot water to the batter and continue cooking the next batch. Drain on kitchen paper (paper towels).

To make the syrup, warm the ingredients together in a saucepan. Serve the fritters with the warm syrup spooned over.

Apricot Doughnuts

SERVES 6

225 g/8 oz/2 cups self-raising (self-rising) flour
50 g/2 oz/¼ cup butter or hard block margarine, diced
Milk, to mix
500 g/1 lb 2 oz/1 very large can of apricot halves, drained and dried on kitchen paper (kitchen towels)
Oil, for deep-frying
Caster (superfine) sugar, for coating

Put the flour in a bowl. Rub in the butter or margarine until the mixture resembles breadcrumbs. Mix with enough milk to form a soft but not sticky dough. Knead gently on a lightly floured surface. Divide into 12 small balls. Flatten each piece and shape around two apricot halves, paired to form a whole apricot. Pinch the edges firmly together to seal. Deep-fry in hot oil for 4–5 minutes until golden brown and cooked through. Roll the doughnuts in caster sugar and serve straight away while still hot.

Nutty Apple Doughnuts

MAKES 8–10

1 large cooking (tart) apple, grated
65 g/2½ oz/scant ⅓ cup caster
(superfine) sugar
225 g/8 oz/2 cups self-raising (self-
rising) wholemeal flour
15 ml/1 tbsp baking powder
2.5 ml/½ tsp mixed (apple-pie) spice
50 g/2 oz/¼ cup butter or margarine,
melted
60–75 ml/4–5 tbsp milk
Oil, for deep-frying

Put the apple in a bowl with 15 ml/
1 tbsp of the caster sugar and the
flour, baking powder and spice. Mix
well. Stir in the melted butter or
margarine and enough of the milk to
form a soft but not sticky dough. Knead
gently on a lightly floured surface. Roll
out thickly and cut into 8–10 rounds
using a 7.5 cm/3 in cutter. Cut out the
centres using a 3 cm/1½ in cutter.
Re-roll the cuttings and make more
rings. Deep-fry in hot oil for 3–4
minutes until golden brown and cooked
through, turning once. Drain on kitchen
paper (paper towels). Toss in the
remaining caster sugar and serve warm.

Toffee Apple Pudding

SERVES 4

50 g/2 oz/¼ cup butter
4 eating (dessert) apples, sliced
50 g/2 oz/¼ cup light brown sugar
2.5 ml/½ tsp mixed (apple pie) spice
30 ml/2 tbsp sultanas (golden raisins)
25 g/1 oz/¼ cup walnut pieces, chopped
Greek-style Yoghurt (see page 359, or
use bought), to serve

Melt the butter in a frying pan
(skillet). Add the apple slices and
sprinkle with the sugar. Fry (sauté),
tossing occasionally, for about
3 minutes until the sugar has melted
and is bubbling. Stir in the raisins and
nuts. Serve hot with Greek-style
Yoghurt.

Sticky Toffee Plum Pan

SERVES 4

50 g/2 oz/¼ cup butter
225 g/8 oz/1 cup light brown sugar
15 ml/1 tbsp lemon juice
A few drops of almond essence (extract)
4 thick slices of bread, crusts removed,
cubed
450 g/1 lb ripe plums, stoned (pitted)
and quartered
Crème fraîche, to serve

Melt the butter in a large frying pan
(skillet). Add the sugar, lemon
juice and almond essence and stir until
the sugar has melted. Fold the bread
gently through the toffee mixture until
evenly coated. Add the plums, stir
gently, then cover and cook over a
gentle heat for about 5 minutes until the
plums are soft. Serve hot, or cool then
chill before serving with crème fraîche.

Pineapple Fritters

SERVES 4

100 g/4 oz/1 cup plain (all-purpose) flour,
plus extra for dusting
2.5 ml/½ tsp baking powder
A pinch of salt
150 ml/¼ pt/⅔ cups water
8 fresh or drained canned pineapple
rings
Oil, for deep-frying
Maple or golden (light corn) syrup and
ice cream, to serve

Put the flour, baking powder and salt in a bowl. Make a well in the centre and gradually work in the water. Dry the pineapple rings on kitchen paper (paper towels), then dust with a little flour. Dip in the batter and deep-fry in hot oil until crisp and golden brown. Drain on kitchen paper (paper towels) and serve hot with syrup and ice cream.

Apple Fritters

SERVES 4

Prepare as for Pineapple Fritters, but substitute 2–3 eating (dessert) apples, peeled, cored and thickly sliced, for the pineapple.

Pear Fritters

SERVES 4

Prepare as for Pineapple Fritters, but substitute 2–3 just-ripe pears, peeled, cored and quartered, for the pineapple.

Banana Fritters

SERVES 4

Prepare as for Pineapple Fritters, but substitute 4 halved ripe bananas for the pineapple.

Rum and Apple Fritters

SERVES 4

450 g/1 lb cooking (tart) apples
30 ml/2 tbsp lemon juice
15 ml/1 tbsp rum
100 g/4 oz/1 cup plain (all-purpose)
flour
A pinch of salt
2.5 ml/½ tsp ground cloves
60 ml/4 tbsp milk
15 g/½ oz/1 tbsp butter, melted
2 egg whites
Oil, for deep-frying
Caster (superfine) sugar, for sprinkling

Peel the apples, remove the cores and cut into thick rings. Lay the apple rings on a flat plate and sprinkle on both sides with the lemon juice and rum. Leave to stand for 20 minutes.

Meanwhile, to make the batter, mix the flour, salt and cloves in a bowl. Stir in the milk and melted butter and beat until smooth. Drain off any liquid from the apples and beat in. When ready to cook, whisk the egg whites until stiff and fold into the batter with a metal spoon. Dry the apple rings on kitchen paper (paper towels). Dip in the batter and deep-fry half the batch in hot oil for 3 minutes until crisp and golden. Drain on kitchen paper (paper towels) and keep warm while cooking the remainder. Sprinkle with caster sugar and serve hot.

Tropical Banana Fritters

SERVES 4

100 g/4 oz/1 cup desiccated (shredded)
  coconut
2 bananas, mashed
75 g/3 oz/⅓ cup dark brown sugar
Finely grated rind of 1 lime
30 ml/2 tbsp dark rum
1.5 ml/¼ tsp baking powder
Oil, for deep-frying
Fluffy Boozy Cream Topping (see page
  358), to serve

Reserve 25 g/1 oz/¼ cup of the coconut and put the remainder in a bowl with the mashed bananas, sugar, lime rind, rum and baking powder. Mix thoroughly. Shape into small balls and roll in the remaining coconut. Deep-fry in hot oil for about 3 minutes until golden brown. Drain on kitchen paper (paper towels) and serve hot with Fluffy Boozy Cream Topping.

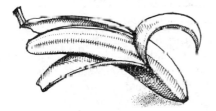

Gulab Jamun

SERVES 4

100 g/4 oz/1 cup dried milk powder
  (non-fat dry milk)
25 g/1 oz/¼ cup plain (all-purpose) flour
5 ml/1 tsp baking powder
25 g/1 oz/2 tbsp butter or hard block
  margarine, diced
1 egg, beaten
5 ml/1 tsp milk
Oil, for deep-frying
200 g/7 oz/scant 1 cup granulated sugar
750 ml/1¼ pts/3 cups water
2 green cardamom pods
30 ml/2 tbsp rose water

Put the milk powder, flour and baking powder in a bowl. Add the butter or margarine and rub in with the fingertips. Make a well in the centre and add the egg and milk. Mix to a soft but not sticky dough and knead until smooth. Divide into 16 pieces and roll into smooth balls in the palm of the hand. Deep-fry in hot oil for 5 minutes until a deep golden brown. Drain on kitchen paper (paper towels).

Put the sugar in a heavy-based pan with the water and the cardamom pods. Heat gently, stirring, until the sugar dissolves, then bring to the boil and cook for 10 minutes. Remove from the heat and add the sponge balls. Leave to cool, then add the rose water. Soak for at least 3 hours before serving.

Simple Pancakes

SERVES 4

100 g/4 oz/1 cup plain (all-purpose) flour
A pinch of salt
1 egg
300 ml/½ pt/1¼ cups milk (or milk and
    water mixed)
15 g/½ oz/1 tbsp butter, melted
    (optional)
Oil, for shallow frying

Mix the flour and salt in a bowl. Make a well in the centre and add the egg and half the milk. Beat well until thick and smooth. Stir in the remaining milk and melted butter, if using. Leave to stand, if possible for 30 minutes, before use. Heat a little oil in a frying pan (skillet) and pour off the excess into a small bowl to use for the next pancake. When very hot, pour in just enough batter to coat the base of the pan when it is tipped and swirled gently. Cook until set and the base of the pancake is golden brown. Toss or flip over with a palette knife. Cook the other side. Slide out and keep warm on a plate over a pan of hot water while cooking the remainder. Use as required.

Shrove Tuesday Pancakes

SERVES 4

1 quantity of Simple Pancakes
Caster (superfine) sugar or golden
    (light corn) syrup, warmed
Lemon juice

Make the pancakes. Sprinkle liberally with caster sugar or drizzle with warm syrup and sprinkle with lemon juice to taste. Roll up or fold into quarters and serve warm.

Crêpes Suzette

SERVES 4

1 quantity of Simple Pancakes
25 g/1 oz/2 tbsp butter
45 ml/3 tbsp light brown sugar
Grated rind and juice of 1 large orange
Grated rind and juice of ½ lemon
45 ml/3 tbsp brandy or orange liqueur

Make the pancakes. Melt the butter in the frying pan (skillet) and add the sugar. Stir until the sugar dissolves. Stir in the fruit rinds and juices. Simmer for 3–4 minutes, stirring, until the caramel dissolves and a smooth sauce is formed. Fold the pancakes into quarters and add to the pan one at a time, bathing in the sauce and pushing to one side before adding the next. Pour over the brandy or liqueur. Ignite and shake the pan gently until the flames subside. Serve straight away.

Strawberry and Banana Cheese Pancakes

SERVES 4

1 quantity of Simple Pancakes
100 g/4 oz strawberries, thinly sliced
3 small bananas, thinly sliced
Finely grated rind of 1 lime
150 ml/¼ pt/⅔ cup fromage frais
Icing (confectioners') sugar, for dusting
4 whole strawberries, to decorate

Make the pancakes. Mix together the strawberries, bananas and lime rind and divide between the pancakes. Roll up and place on serving plates. Top with a dollop of fromage frais and dust with sifted icing sugar. Decorate each plate with a whole strawberry.

Velvet Cherry Pancakes

SERVES 4

1 quantity of Simple Pancakes
200 g/7 oz/scant 1 cup low-fat soft
*   cheese*
425 g/15 oz/1 large can of cherry pie
*   filling*
30 ml/2 tbsp water
15 ml/1 tbsp lemon juice
45 ml/3 tbsp cherry brandy or kirsch

Make the pancakes. Spread each with a little of the soft cheese and fold into quarters. Turn the pie filling into the frying pan (skillet) and add the water and lemon juice. Heat until bubbling, stirring all the time. Add one pancake, bathe in sauce and push to one side of the pan before adding the next. When all the pancakes are in the pan, pour over the cherry brandy or kirsch and ignite. Shake the pan gently until the flames subside, then serve straight away.

Crêpes au Chocolat

SERVES 4 OR 8

1 quantity of Simple Pancakes
8 strawberries
60 ml/4 tbsp kirsch
300 ml/½ pt/1¼ cups whipping cream
60 ml/4 tbsp drinking (sweetened)
*   chocolate powder*
60 ml/4 tbsp grated chocolate
Icing (confectioners') sugar, for dusting

Make the pancakes. Cut the strawberries in several slices from the point to the calyx, not quite right through and gently pull so they fan out. Place in a bowl and sprinkle with the kirsch. Whip the cream with the drinking chocolate and grated chocolate. Spread on the cold crêpes, roll up and top each with a kirsch-soaked strawberry. Dust with icing sugar and serve straight away.

Strawberry and Cream Pancakes

SERVES 4

1 quantity of Simple Pancakes
515 g/1 lb 3 oz/1 very large can of
*   strawberries*
30 ml/2 tbsp cornflour (cornstarch)
Finely grated rind and juice of 1 orange
150 ml/¼ pt/⅔ cup double (heavy)
*   cream, whipped*

Make the pancakes and keep warm on a plate over a pan of hot water. Empty the strawberries and juice into a pan. Blend the cornflour with the orange rind and juice and stir into the pan. Bring to the boil and cook for 2 minutes, stirring. Divide between the pancakes, roll up and place on serving plates. Top with a large spoonful of whipped cream and serve straight away.

Christmas Pancakes

SERVES 4

*1 quantity of Simple Pancakes (see
page 272)*
350 g/12 oz/1 medium jar of mincemeat
15 ml/1 tbsp brandy
2 apples, grated
Icing (confectioners') sugar, sifted
*Greek-style Yoghurt (see page 359, or
use bought), to serve*

Make the pancakes and keep warm
on a plate over a pan of hot water.
Mix the mincemeat with the brandy
and apple. Spread over the pancakes
and roll up. Place in a flameproof dish.
Sprinkle liberally with icing sugar and
flash under a hot grill (broiler) until the
top begins to caramelise. Serve with
Greek-style Yoghurt.

Pancakes with Chocolate Hazelnut Sauce

SERVES 4

*1 quantity of Simple Pancakes (see
page 272)*
*175 g/6 oz/1½ cups plain (semi-sweet)
chocolate*
50 g/2 oz/¼ cup unsalted (sweet) butter
*75 g/3 oz/¾ cup chopped hazelnuts
(filberts)*
Toasted whole hazelnuts, to decorate

Make the pancakes and keep warm
on a plate over a pan of hot water.
Break up the chocolate and place in a
bowl with the butter and nuts. Stand
the bowl over a pan of hot water and
heat, stirring, until melted. Spoon over
the pancakes and serve sprinkled with
toasted hazelnuts.

Pancakes with Panache

SERVES 4

*1 quantity of Simple Pancakes (see
page 272)*
*500 ml/17 fl oz/2¼ cups any vanilla ice
cream (see page 188) or Dark
Chocolate Ice Cream (see page 189,
or use bought)*
*1 quantity Chocolate Caramel Sauce
(see page 346)*
Grated chocolate, to decorate

Make the pancakes and cool. Put a
scoop of ice cream in each and
fold up. Place on plates, drizzle with the
Chocolate Caramel Sauce, top with
grated chocolate and serve.

Saucy Apple Pancakes

SERVES 4

*1 quantity of Simple Pancakes (see
page 272)*
750 g/1½ lb cooking (tart) apples, sliced
75 ml/5 tbsp water
50 g/2 oz/¼ cup light brown sugar
2.5 ml/½ tsp ground cinnamon
50 g/2 oz/⅓ cup raisins
75 ml/5 tbsp lemon jelly marmalade

Make the pancakes and keep warm
on a plate over a pan of hot water.
Put the apple slices in a pan with
50 ml/3½ tbsp of the water and the
sugar. Cover and cook gently, stirring
occasionally, for about 15 minutes until
pulpy. Stir in the cinnamon and raisins.
Put the marmalade and the remaining
water in a small saucepan and heat
gently, stirring, until melted. Divide the
filling between the pancakes and roll
up. Transfer to warmed plates and
drizzle the lemon sauce over.

Trifling Pancakes

SERVES 6

1 quantity of Simple Pancakes (see
page 272)
25 g/1 oz/¼ cup cornflour (cornstarch)
25 g/1 oz/2 tbsp caster (superfine)
sugar
1 egg
300 ml/½ pt/1¼ cups milk
4 bananas
Lemon juice
45 ml/3 tbsp chopped mixed nuts
90 ml/6 tbsp strawberry jam (conserve)
Icing (confectioners') sugar, for dusting

Make the pancakes. Put the cornflour in a saucepan and blend in the sugar and egg until smooth. Stir in the milk. Bring to the boil and cook for 2 minutes, stirring all the time, until thickened and smooth. Place a circle of wet greaseproof (waxed) paper over the top to prevent a skin forming and leave until cold. Thinly slice the bananas and toss in a little lemon juice. Stir into the cold custard with the nuts. Place one pancake on a serving plate and spread with a quarter of the jam. Top with a second pancake and add a third of the banana custard. Repeat the layers, finishing with a pancake. Dust the top of the stack with icing sugar and serve cut into wedges.

Apricot Cream Pancakes

SERVES 4

1 quantity of Simple Pancakes (see
page 272)
410 g/14½ oz/1 large can of apricot
halves, drained, reserving the juice
150 ml/¼ pt/⅔ cup double (heavy) cream
20 ml/4 tsp caster (superfine) sugar
10 ml/2 tsp arrowroot
45 ml/3 tbsp kirsch

Make the pancakes. Chop the apricots. Whip the cream until peaking, then whisk in the sugar. Fold in the apricots. Fold the pancakes into sixths and spoon the cream mixture into a fold in each pancake to form filled cones. Place on serving plates. Blend the arrowroot with a little of the reserved juice in a saucepan. Stir in the remainder and add the kirsch. Bring to the boil, stirring, until thickened and clear. Spoon immediately over the pancakes and served straight away.

Strawberry and Orange Pancakes

SERVES 4

*1 quantity of Simple Pancakes (see
    page 272)*
3 oranges
100 g/4 oz strawberries, sliced
30 ml/2 tbsp sweet vermouth
45 ml/3 tbsp fromage frais
*1 quantity of Smooth Strawberry Sauce
    (see page 349)*

Make the pancakes and keep warm
on a plate over a pan of hot water.
Holding the oranges over a small
saucepan, cut off all the skin and pith,
then cut the fruit into segments both
sides of the membranes. Place the
segments in the saucepan. Add the
strawberries and vermouth. Heat
through but do not boil. Put a spoonful
of fromage frais on each pancake.
Divide the fruit mixture between them
and fold each into four. Transfer to
warmed serving plates and drizzle a
little Smooth Strawberry Sauce over
each and serve straight away.

Glazed Apple Strudel Stack

SERVES 6

*1 quantity of Simple Pancakes (see
    page 272)*
4 cooking (tart) apples, chopped
175 g/6 oz/³⁄₄ cup light brown sugar
50 g/2 oz/¹⁄₃ cup raisins
50 g/2 oz/¹⁄₂ cup chopped almonds
5 ml/1 tsp ground cinnamon
30 ml/2 tbsp orange juice

Make the pancakes and keep warm
on a plate over a pan of hot water.
Put the apples in a saucepan with
100 g/4 oz/¹⁄₂ cup of the sugar, the
raisins, nuts, cinnamon and orange
juice. Cook gently, stirring, until pulpy.
Layer the pancakes with the apple
filling on a flameproof plate. Cover the
top with the remaining sugar. Place
under a hot grill (broiler) until the sugar
caramelises. Serve straight away.

Apple and Pear Crispies

SERVES 6

*100 g/4 oz/1 cup self-raising (self-
    rising) flour, plus extra for dusting*
A pinch of salt
1 egg
*250 ml/8 fl oz/1 cup milk and water,
    mixed*
*2 cooking (tart) apples, cored and cut
    into rings*
3 small pears, quartered
Oil, for deep-frying
Caster (superfine) sugar, for sprinkling
*Hot Lemon Sauce (see page 346), to
    serve*

Sift the flour and salt into a bowl. Add
the egg and half the milk and water
and beat until smooth. Mix with
enough of the remaining liquid to form
a thick, smooth batter. Dust the pieces
of fruit with flour. Dip in the batter and
deep-fry in the hot oil for about
2–3 minutes until crisp and golden
brown. Drain on kitchen paper (paper
towels), sprinkle with caster sugar and
serve with Hot Lemon Sauce.

Quire of Paper

SERVES 8

For the batter:
100 g/4 oz/1 cup plain (all-purpose) flour
25 g/1 oz/2 tbsp caster (superfine) sugar
1.5 ml/¼ tsp grated nutmeg
3 eggs
150 ml/¼ pt/⅔ cup milk
150 ml/¼ pt/⅔ cup single (light) cream
30 ml/2 tbsp sherry
100 g/4 oz/½ cup butter
Oil, for shallow frying
For the filling:
50 g/2 oz/⅓ cup icing (confectioners')
  sugar
Finely grated rind and juice of 1 small
  lemon
Clear honey

To make the batter, sift the flour, sugar and nutmeg into a bowl. Make a well in the centre. Add the eggs and milk and beat thoroughly until smooth. Whisk in the cream and sherry. Melt half the butter and whisk into the batter. Chill for at least 30 minutes.

Meanwhile, to make the filling, beat the remaining butter until soft, then beat in the icing sugar, lemon rind and juice. Heat a little oil in a small frying pan (skillet). Add about 45 ml/3 tbsp of the batter and swirl round to coat the base. Cook until the underside is golden, then flip over and cook the other side. Slide out of the pan on to a sheet of greaseproof (waxed) paper on a plate. Cover and keep warm over a pan of hot water while cooking all the other pancakes (20 in all!). Stack the pancakes with alternate layers of the lemon filling and clear honey, finishing with clear honey drizzled over the top. Serve straight away, cut into wedges.

Swedish Raspberry Pancakes

SERVES 4–5

50 g/2 oz/½ cup plain (all-purpose) flour
10 ml/2 tsp caster (superfine) sugar
A pinch of salt
1 egg, separated
200 ml/7 fl oz/scant 1 cup milk
15 ml/1 tbsp melted butter
Oil, for shallow-frying
50 g/2 oz/¼ cup unsalted (sweet) butter,
  softened
100 g/4 oz/⅔ cup icing (confectioners')
  sugar, sifted
100 g/4 oz raspberries

Mix together the flour, caster sugar and salt in a bowl. Add the egg yolk and gradually beat in the milk to form a smooth batter. Stir in the melted butter. Leave to stand while preparing the filling. Beat together the unsalted butter and icing sugar until smooth and fluffy. Whisk the egg whites until stiff and fold into the batter with a metal spoon. Heat a little oil in a large frying pan (skillet). Drop 15 ml/1 tbsp of the batter into the pan and cook for about 1 minute on each side until golden brown and set. Keep warm while cooking the remaining pancakes. Transfer to warmed serving plates. Spoon a little of the buttercream on each and top with raspberries. Serve before all the buttercream has melted.

Pfannküchen

SERVES 6

75 g/3 oz/¾ cup plain (all-purpose) flour
45 ml/3 tbsp caster (superfine) sugar
3 eggs
300 ml/½ pt/1¼ cups milk
Oil, for shallow-frying
Unsalted (sweet) butter, softened
Black cherry jam (conserve)
5 ml/1 tsp ground cinnamon

Put the flour and sugar in a bowl. Break in the eggs and add half the milk. Beat well until smooth. Stir in the remaining milk. Leave to stand for at least 20 minutes. Heat a little oil in a large frying pan (skillet) and pour off the excess. Add 60–75 ml/4–5 tbsp of the batter and swirl the pan to coat the base. Cook until set and golden underneath. Flip over and cook the other side. Slide out of the pan and spread with a little butter and jam. Roll up and place in a serving dish. Keep warm in a low oven while cooking the remainder. Dust with the cinnamon. Serve very hot.

Orange Ginger Pancakes

SERVES 4

1 quantity of Simple Pancakes (see
page 272)
2 pieces of stem ginger in syrup,
chopped
25 g/1 oz/2 tbsp light brown sugar
150 ml/¼ pt/⅔ cup double (heavy) cream
Grated rind and juice of 1 orange

Make the pancakes. Fold each one into quarters. Put the ginger, sugar, cream and orange rind and juice in the frying pan (skillet). Heat gently, stirring, until the sugar dissolves. Add the pancakes, one at a time, turn over in the sauce, then push to one side. Repeat until all the pancakes are coated in the sauce. Serve hot.

Sweet Soufflé Omelette

SERVES 1–2

2 eggs, separated
15 ml/1 tbsp caster (superfine) sugar
15 ml/1 tbsp hot water
A knob of butter
15–30 ml/1–2 tbsp strawberry or
raspberry jam (conserve), warmed
Icing (confectioners') sugar, for dusting

Beat together the egg yolks and sugar until thick and pale. Stir in the hot water. Whisk the egg whites until stiff and fold in with a metal spoon. Heat the butter in a small omelette pan (skillet). Add the egg mixture and cook until the underside is golden brown and the mixture is almost set. Place under a hot grill (broiler) until the top is risen and golden and the mixture is just set. Remove from the grill. Quickly spread one half with the warm jam and fold over. Slide out of the pan and dust with sifted icing sugar. For a spectacular effect, heat a metal skewer in a gas flame until red hot and use to sear the top in a lattice pattern. Serve straight away.

Lemon Soufflé Omelette

SERVES 1–2

Prepare as for Sweet Soufflé Omelette, but add 5 ml/1 tsp finely grated lemon rind to the mixture and fill with lemon curd instead of jam (conserve).

Orange Soufflé Omelette

SERVES 1–2

Prepare as for Sweet Soufflé Omelette, but add 5 ml/1 tsp finely grated orange rind to the mixture and fill with orange curd or marmalade instead of jam (conserve).

Fresh Strawberry Soufflé Omelette

SERVES 1–2

Prepare as for Sweet Soufflé Omelette, but fill with 75 g/3 oz mashed strawberries, flavoured with 5 ml/1 tsp orange liqueur or orange juice. Serve with whipped cream.

Fresh Raspberry Omelette

SERVES 1–2

Prepare as for Sweet Soufflé Omelette, but fill with 75 g/3 oz lightly crushed raspberries, flavoured with 5 ml/1 tsp kirsch. Serve with crème fraîche.

Normandy Omelette

SERVES 4

6 eggs
75 ml/5 tbsp icing (confectioners')
*   sugar*
50 g/2 oz/¼ cup unsalted (sweet) butter
2 crisp green eating (dessert) apples,
*   thinly sliced*
45 ml/3 tbsp double (heavy) cream
30 ml/2 tbsp calvados

Beat the eggs with 30 ml/2 tbsp of the icing sugar. Melt 25 g/1 oz/2 tbsp of the butter in a frying pan (skillet) and fry (sauté) the apple slices for 5 minutes until golden, turning occasionally. Add the cream, calvados and 30 ml/2 tbsp of the remaining sugar and reduce the heat to very low. Melt the remaining butter in a large frying pan and add the egg mixture. Cook, lifting and stirring, until beginning to set, then cook until golden brown underneath. Spread the apple mixture over half the omelette and fold over. Slide out of the pan and sift the remaining icing sugar over.

Brandied Caramel Bananas

SERVES 6

5 cm/2 in piece of cinnamon stick
15 ml/1 tbsp orange juice
15 ml/1 tbsp light brown sugar
6 bananas
30 ml/2 tbsp orange liqueur
3 Mars Bars, roughly chopped
Milk
30 ml/2 tbsp brandy

Put the cinnamon, orange juice and sugar in a saucepan over a low heat and stir until the sugar dissolves. Thickly slice the bananas and add to the pan. Cook gently for 3 minutes. Add the liqueur and cook for a further 2 minutes.

Meanwhile, put the Mars Bars in a separate pan with 15 ml/1 tbsp milk. Heat, stirring, until the Mars Bars melt, adding a little more milk, if necessary, to keep it runny. Stir in the brandy. Spoon the bananas into serving dishes and pour over the sauce. Serve straight away.

Caribbean Bananas

SERVES 4

1 orange
45 ml/3 tbsp cocoa (unsweetened chocolate) powder
45 ml/3 tbsp light brown sugar
A pinch of ground cinnamon
45 ml/3 tbsp rum or orange liqueur
4 bananas
Fromage frais, to serve

Cut four slices from the orange for decoration. Grate the rind and squeeze the juice from the remainder into a frying pan (skillet). Add the cocoa, sugar and cinnamon and heat gently, stirring, until the sugar melts. Add the rum or orange liqueur. Peel the bananas and cut into thick chunks. Add to the pan. Baste with the sauce, cover and cook gently for 4 minutes until the bananas are just cooked but still hold their shape. Spoon into serving dishes. Top each with an orange twist and a spoonful of fromage frais and serve warm.

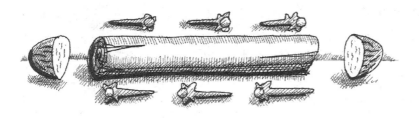

Butterscotch Bananas

SERVES 4

50 g/2 oz/¼ cup butter
75 g/3 oz/⅓ cup light brown sugar
30 ml/2 tbsp lemon juice
2.5 ml/½ tsp vanilla essence (extract)
4 bananas
300 ml/½ pt/1¼ cups Greek-style
  Yoghurt (see page 359, or use
  bought)
Toasted flaked (slivered) almonds

Put the butter, sugar, lemon juice and vanilla in a frying pan (skillet). Heat gently, stirring, until the sugar melts. Thickly slice the bananas and add to the pan. Cook for 1 minute. Divide the yoghurt between four sundae glasses. Spoon over the banana slices in their sauce, sprinkle with the almonds and serve.

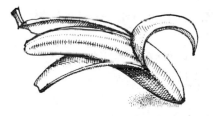

Banana Flambé

SERVES 4

40 g/1½ oz/3 tbsp unsalted (sweet)
  butter
4 large bananas, halved lengthways,
  then crossways
30 ml/2 tbsp caster (superfine) sugar
5 ml/1 tsp lemon juice
30 ml/2 tbsp brandy or rum
Chantilly Cream (see page 358), to
  serve

Melt the butter in a large frying pan (skillet) or chafing dish. Add the banana quarters and sprinkle with the sugar and lemon juice. Cook, tossing once, for 2–3 minutes until tender but still holding their shape. Add the brandy or rum. Ignite and shake the pan until the flames subside. Serve immediately straight from the pan with Chantilly Cream.

Peach Flambé

SERVES 4

Prepare as for Banana Flambé, but substitute 4 ripe peaches, skinned, stoned (pitted) and quartered for the bananas. Use orange or peach liqueur instead of brandy or rum, if preferred.

Pineapple Flambé

SERVES 4

1 ripe pineapple
50 g/2 oz/¼ cup butter
45 ml/3 tbsp kirsch
30 ml/2 tbsp caster (superfine) sugar
45 ml/3 tbsp brandy
Whipped cream, to serve

Cut all the rind off the pineapple and cut the fruit into eight thin slices. Cut out the hard core of each slice. Melt the butter in a large frying pan (skillet) or chafing dish. Add the fruit and sprinkle with the kirsch and sugar. Cook for 2 minutes, then turn over. Add the brandy, ignite and shake the pan until the flames subside. Serve immediately straight from the pan with whipped cream.

Poor Knight's Pudding

SERVES 4

8 slices of white bread, crusts removed
60 ml/4 tbsp strawberry jam (conserve)
2 eggs, beaten
150 ml/¼ pt/⅔ cup milk
75 g/3 oz/⅓ cup butter
Caster (superfine) sugar, for sprinkling
Whipped cream, to serve

Sandwich together the bread slices in pairs with the jam. Beat together the eggs and milk in a large shallow dish and add the sandwiches. Turn in the egg mixture and leave to soak for a few minutes. Melt half the butter in a frying pan (skillet) and fry (sauté) half the sandwiches until golden brown on each side. Sprinkle with caster sugar. Repeat with the remaining sandwiches. Serve hot with whipped cream.

Pain Perdu

SERVES 4

4 eggs
5 ml/1 tsp caster (superfine) sugar
8 slices of bread, crusts removed
75 g/3 oz/⅓ cup butter
100 g/4 oz strawberries, sliced
150 ml/¼ pt/⅔ cup whipping cream,
  whipped
Icing (confectioners') sugar, for dusting

Beat together the eggs and sugar. Dip in the bread slices until well soaked. Melt a little of the butter in a frying pan (skillet) and fry (sauté) one or two of the slices at a time until golden brown on both sides. Drain on kitchen paper (paper towels) and keep warm while cooking the remainder. Sandwich together in pairs with the strawberries and cream, dust with icing sugar and serve straight away.

Banana Honey Toasts

SERVES 4

4 slices of wholemeal bread, crusts
  removed
Butter
2 small bananas, sliced
75 ml/5 tbsp clear honey
30 ml/2 tbsp orange flower water
2.5 ml/½ tsp mixed (apple-pie) spice
30 ml/2 tbsp pine nuts

Spread the bread on both sides with butter and fry (sauté) on both sides to brown. Place on plates and top with the banana slices. Melt together the honey, orange flower water and spice in a saucepan. Drizzle over the banana and sprinkle with pine nuts.

Easy Chocolate Fondue

SERVES 6

350 g/12 oz/3 cups chocolate chips
40 g/1½ oz/⅓ cup dried milk powder
*   (non-fat dry milk)*
120 ml/4 fl oz/½ cup boiling water
5 ml/1 tsp vanilla essence (extract)
Cubes of plain cake, marshmallows,
*   strawberries and brazil nuts, to*
*   serve*

Put the chocolate in the fondue pot. Blend together the milk and water and add to the pot with the vanilla. Heat gently, stirring, until thickened and smooth. Do not allow to boil. Turn down the heat to very low and stir frequently to prevent burning. Arrange pieces of cake, a few marshmallows, strawberries and brazil nuts on small plates and serve with fondue forks to pierce the food and dip into the chocolate fondue.

Chocolate Orange Fondue

SERVES 4

250 g/9 oz/2¼ cups plain (semi-sweet)
*   chocolate, broken into pieces*
120 ml/4 fl oz/½ cup double (heavy)
*   cream*
Finely grated rind and juice of 1 orange
30 ml/2 tbsp orange liqueur
Orange segments, Langues de Chat
*   (see page 129), and cream-filled*
*   choux balls (see Chocolate*
*   Profiteroles, page 117), to serve*

Put the chocolate and cream in a fondue pot. Heat gently, stirring, until the chocolate has melted. Add the orange rind and liqueur and stir well. Turn down the heat to low and stir frequently. If the mixture becomes too thick, thin with a little of the orange juice. Arrange orange segments, Langues de Chats and choux balls on serving plates and serve with fondue forks to pierce the fruit and choux balls and dip into the fondue.

Buttered Rum Fondue

SERVES 6

225 g/8 oz/1 cup dark brown sugar
450 ml/¾ pt/2 cups single (light) cream
50 g/2 oz/¼ cup unsalted (sweet) butter
40 g/1½ oz/⅓ cup cornflour (cornstarch)
45 ml/3 tbsp dark rum
Almond Petits Fours (see page 112) or
*   Amaretti Biscuits (see page 128),*
*   banana chunks dipped in lemon juice,*
*   fresh pineapple chunks and pecan nut*
*   halves, to serve*

Put the sugar, cream and butter in the fondue pot and heat gently, stirring, until smooth but do not allow to boil. Blend the cornflour with the rum and stir into the pot. Cook, stirring, until thickened and bubbling. Reduce the heat to very low. Arrange the biscuits (cookies), banana and pineapple on serving plates with a few pecan halves. Serve with fondue forks.

White Chocolate Fondue

SERVES 6

*175 g/6 oz/1½ cups white chocolate,
   broken into pieces*
250 ml/8 fl oz/1 cup single (light) cream
*100 g/4 oz/⅔ cup icing (confectioners')
   sugar*
50 g/2 oz/¼ cup unsalted (sweet) butter
5 ml/1 tsp vanilla essence (extract)
*Plain or cream-filled choux balls (see
   Chocolate Profiteroles, page 117),
   Cigarettes Russes (see page 127),
   stoned (pitted) cherries and banana
   chunks dipped in lemon juice, to
   serve*

Put all the ingredients in a fondue pot
and heat gently, stirring, until
melted and smooth but do not allow to
boil. Turn down the heat to very low
and stir from time to time to prevent
burning. Arrange the choux balls,
Cigarettes Russes, cherries and banana
chunks on serving plates and serve
with fondue forks.

Mallow Fondue

SERVES 4

100 g/4 oz marshmallows
*30 ml/2 tbsp icing (confectioners')
   sugar*
150 ml/¼ pt/⅔ cup double (heavy) cream
15–30 ml/1–2 tbsp lemon juice
*Sponge (lady) fingers, sliced nectarines
   and raspberries or loganberries, to
   serve*

Snip the marshmallows with wet
scissors and place in the fondue pot
with the sugar and cream. Heat gently,
stirring, until the mixture is smooth but
do not allow to boil. Stir in the lemon
juice to taste. Turn down the heat to
very low and stir frequently. Arrange
the sponge fingers, nectarine slices and
small piles of raspberries or loganberries
on small plates and serve with fondue
forks.

After-dinner Coffee Fondue

SERVES 4

*900 ml/1½ pts/3¾ cups strong black
   coffee*
45–60 ml/3–4 tbsp brandy or whisky
20 ml/4 tsp light brown sugar
*20 American mini ring doughnuts or
   tiny plain choux balls (see Chocolate
   Profiteroles, page 117), to serve*
*300 ml/½ pt/1¼ cups double (heavy)
   cream, whipped*
*100 g/4 oz/1 cup plain (semi-sweet)
   chocolate, coarsely grated*

Put the coffee, alcohol and sugar in
the fondue pot and heat until piping
hot, stirring to dissolve the sugar.
Arrange the doughnuts or choux balls
on serving plates with fondue forks. Put
a small bowl of whipped cream and a
separate one of grated chocolate at each
place. Dip the doughnuts or choux balls
in the coffee, then in the cream and
chocolate before eating. Strain any
remaining coffee into small coffee cups
and serve at the end.

Tropical Fondue

SERVES 4

425 g/15 oz/1 large can of coconut milk
75 g/3 oz creamed coconut, chopped
50 g/2 oz/¼ cup caster (superfine) sugar
20 ml/4 tsp cornflour (cornstarch)
150 ml/¼ pt/⅔ cup single (light) cream
Banana chunks, dipped in lemon juice,
slices of mango, star fruit and/or
pawpaw, fresh pineapple cubes and
squares of gingerbread, to serve

Put the coconut milk, creamed coconut and sugar in the fondue pot and stir until smooth. Blend the cornflour with the cream and stir into the pot. Cook, stirring until the mixture thickens. Turn down the heat to very low. Arrange the tropical fruits and gingerbread on small serving plates and serve with fondue forks to spear the dippers and dip into the pot.

Raspberry Fondue

SERVES 4

350 g/12 oz raspberries
30 ml/2 tbsp icing (confectioners')
sugar
10 ml/2 tsp cornflour (cornstarch)
30 ml/2 tbsp water
Bite-sized Meringues (see page 132) and
large seedless green grapes, to serve
300 ml/½ pt/1¼ cups crème fraiche

Purée the raspberries in a blender or food processor, then pass through a sieve (strainer) to remove the seeds. Place in the fondue pot with the icing sugar. Blend together the cornflour and water and stir in. Cook until bubbling and thickened. Turn down the heat and stir from time to time. Put the meringues and piles of grapes on serving plates with a small bowl of crème fraîche on each. Serve with fondue forks.

Tequila Fondue

SERVES 4

100 g/4 oz marshmallows
170 g/6 oz/1 small can of evaporated
milk
30 ml/2 tbsp tequila
Finely grated rind of 1 lime
Fresh stoned (pitted) dates, fresh halved
and stoned apricots, fresh quartered
figs and lime wedges, to serve

Snip the marshmallows with wet scissors and place in the fondue pot with the milk. Heat gently, stirring, until smooth. Stir in the tequila to taste and flavour with the lime rind. Reduce the heat and stir frequently. Arrange the dates, apricots, figs and lime wedges on each plate. Use fondue forks to dip the sweet fruits in the fondue but suck the lime wedges in between to freshen the mouth.

Dairy Specialities

Nursery milk puddings, Crème Brûlée, Tiramisu and a vast array of cheesecakes are all here along with every other milk, cheese, yoghurt and custard dessert I've ever made!

Home-made Plain Yoghurt

MAKES 1.25 LITRES/2¼ PTS/5½ CUPS

1.2 litres/2 pts/5 cups UHT (long-life) milk
25 ml/1½ tbsp dried milk powder (non-fat dry milk) powder
150 ml/¼ pt/⅔ cup plain live yoghurt

Warm the milk until hand-hot. Blend the milk powder with the yoghurt in a bowl. Gradually whisk in the milk. Cover loosely with clingfilm (plastic wrap) and wrap in thick towels. Place in a warm place such as the airing cupboard for 2–8 hours until set. Alternatively, pour the milk and yoghurt mixture into warmed, wide-necked vacuum flasks and screw on the lids. Leave undisturbed until set. Store in airtight containers in the fridge. Serve plain, with honey or fresh fruit.

Banana Yoghurt Layer

SERVES 4

2 bananas
5 ml/1 tsp lemon juice
A pinch of ground cinnamon
300 ml/½ pt/1¼ cups Greek-style Yoghurt (see page 359, or use bought)
90 ml/6 tbsp clear honey
Sponge (lady) fingers (optional), to serve

Mash the bananas with the lemon juice and cinnamon. Beat in the yoghurt. Put a spoonful of honey in the base of four glasses. Top with half the banana yoghurt. Add a layer of the remaining honey, then top with the remaining yoghurt. Serve with sponge fingers, if liked.

Raspberry Hazelnut Yoghurt

SERVES 4

2 egg whites
50 g/2 oz/¼ cup caster (superfine) sugar
150 ml/¼ pt/⅔ cup hazelnut (filbert) yoghurt
300 g/11 oz/1 small can of raspberries, drained
30 ml/2 tbsp toasted chopped hazelnuts

Whisk the egg whites until stiff. Whisk in the sugar until stiff and glossy. Fold in the hazelnut yoghurt. Layer the yoghurt mixture and raspberries in four glasses. Sprinkle with toasted hazelnuts and chill until ready to serve.

Greek Yoghurt Dessert

SERVES 4

4 fresh ripe figs, trimmed and cut into bite-sized pieces
30 ml/2 tbsp brandy, preferably Greek
450 ml/¾ pt/2 cups Greek-style Yoghurt (see page 359, or use bought)
Clear honey

Place the figs in four glass dishes and spoon the brandy over. Cover with the yoghurt, then top with a layer of clear honey.

Apricot Greek Surprise

SERVES 4

Prepare as for Greek Yoghurt Dessert, but substitute 100 g/4 oz/⅔ cup ready-to-eat dried apricots, roughly chopped, for the figs.

Cherry Yoghurt Pots

SERVES 4

*225 g/8 oz/1 small can of cherries,
    stoned (pitted) and drained*
7.5 ml/1½ tsp cornflour (cornstarch)
150 ml/¼ pt/⅔ cup plain yoghurt
15 ml/1 tbsp clear honey
150 ml/¼ pt/⅔ cup whipping cream
*Halved glacé (candied) cherries and
    angelica leaves, to decorate*

Put a little of the cherry juice in a
saucepan and blend in the cornflour.
Add the remaining juice. Bring to the
boil and cook for 2 minutes, stirring.
Add the cherries and leave to cool.
Spoon into four clear ramekin dishes
(custard cups) or individual glass
dishes. Blend the yoghurt with the
honey. Whip the cream and fold in.
Spoon over the cherries. Decorate with
halved glacé cherries and angelica
leaves and chill until ready to serve.

Orange Yoghurt Pots

SERVES 4

Prepare as for Cherry Yoghurt Pots,
but substitute a 300 g/11 oz/
1 medium can of mandarin oranges for
the cherries and decorate with
crystallised (candied) orange slices
instead of cherries.

Prune and Orange Sundae

SERVES 4

*410 g/14½ oz/1 large can of prunes in
    natural juice, drained, reserving the
    juice*
1 small orange
A pinch of mixed (apple-pie) spice
*300 ml/½ pt/1¼ cups Greek-style Yoghurt
    (see page 359, or use bought)*
*Crystallised (candied) orange slices, to
    decorate*

Discard the stones (pits) from the
prunes and finely chop half of
them. Purée the remainder in a blender
or food processor with 30 ml/2 tbsp of
the reserved juice. Finely grate the
orange rind and add to the purée with
the mixed spice. Cut off all the rind and
pith from the orange and chop the
flesh. Mix with the chopped prunes.
Lightly fold the prune purée into the
yoghurt so it gives a marbled effect. Do
not over-mix. Spoon a little of the
chopped prunes and oranges into the
base of four sundae dishes. Top with
half the marbled yoghurt. Top with the
remaining chopped fruit, then the
remaining yoghurt mixture. Chill.
Decorate with crystallised orange slices
before serving.

Creamy Grape Dessert

SERVES 6

2 large chocolate flake bars
25 g/1 oz/2 tbsp dark brown sugar
300 ml/½ pt/1¼ cups crème fraîche
225 g/8 oz seedless black grapes, halved
225 g/8 oz seedless green grapes, halved

Crumble the flake bars and mix with the sugar. Spoon a little into the bases of six tall glasses. Top with a layer of crème fraîche. Mix the grapes together and add a layer of grapes. Repeat the layers, finishing with a layer of chocolate and sugar. Chill until ready to serve.

Creamy Mandarin Dessert

SERVES 6

Prepare as for Creamy Grape Dessert, but substitute 2 × 300 g/2 × 11 oz/ 2 medium cans of mandarin orange segments, drained, for the grapes and mix in 25 g/1 oz/¼ cup chopped pistachio nuts with the sugar and chocolate.

Strawberry Crunch Cream

SERVES 6

300 ml/½ pt/1¼ cups double (heavy) cream
25 g/1 oz/2 tbsp caster (superfine) sugar
350 g/12 oz strawberries
6 Amaretti Biscuits (see page 128, or use bought), crushed

Whip together the cream and sugar until peaking. Reserve 6 strawberries for decoration and lightly crush the remainder. Fold the crushed fruit and biscuits into the cream. Spoon into glasses, top each with a strawberry and serve.

Raspberry Crunch Cream

SERVES 6

Prepare as for Strawberry Crunch Cream, but substitute raspberries for the strawberries and crushed Brandy Snaps (see page 124) for the Amaretti Biscuits.

Whipped Raspberry Brittle

SERVES 6

Oil, for greasing
40 g/1½ oz/⅓ cup toasted hazelnuts (filberts)
100 g/4 oz/½ cup light brown sugar
75 ml/5 tbsp water
A pinch of cream of tartar
25 g/1 oz/2 tbsp butter
300 ml/½ pt/1¼ cups double (heavy) cream
150 ml/¼ pt/⅔ cup thick vanilla yoghurt
Icing (confectioners') sugar
225 g/8 oz raspberries, lightly crushed

Oil a shallow baking tin (pan) and scatter the nuts in the base. Put the brown sugar and water in a saucepan and heat gently until dissolved. Add the cream of tartar and butter. Bring to the boil and boil, without stirring, until the mixture reaches the hard crack stage (155°C/298°F on a sugar thermometer or until 5 ml/1 tsp of the mixture immediately hardens and crackles when dropped into cold water). Pour over the nuts and leave to set.

Whip together the cream and yoghurt. Fold in the crushed raspberries and sweeten to taste with icing sugar. Spoon into four glass dishes and chill until ready to serve. Turn the nut mixture into a plastic bag and crush with a rolling pin. Scatter the nut brittle over the raspberry mixture and serve straight away.

Rhubarb and Banana Yoghurt Fool

SERVES 4

450 g/1 lb rhubarb, cut into short lengths
30 ml/2 tbsp clear honey
5 ml/1 tsp ground cinnamon
45 ml/3 tbsp water
450 g/1 lb ripe bananas, roughly chopped
300 ml/½ pt/1¼ cups thick plain yoghurt
Chopped pistachio nuts, to decorate

Put the rhubarb, honey, cinnamon and water in a saucepan and bring to the boil. Reduce the heat and cook gently until the rhubarb is tender. Cool slightly, then purée with the bananas in a blender or food processor. Leave until cold. Fold in the yoghurt, turn into individual glass dishes and decorate with chopped pistachio nuts. Chill until ready to serve.

Apple and Banana Yoghurt Fool

SERVES 4

Prepare as for Rhubarb and Banana Fool, but substitute cooking (tart) apples, sliced, for the rhubarb and mixed (apple-pie) spice for the cinnamon.

All-cream Gooseberry Fool

SERVES 4

450 g/1 lb gooseberries, topped and tailed
45 ml/3 tbsp water
100 g/4 oz/½ cup granulated sugar
300 ml/½ pt/1¼ cups double (heavy)
cream

Put the gooseberries in a saucepan with the water and sugar. Heat gently, stirring, until the sugar dissolves, then cover and simmer gently until the gooseberries are very soft. Purée in a blender or food processor. Leave until cold. Whip the cream until peaking. Fold in the puréed gooseberries. Spoon into glasses and chill for 1–2 hours before serving.

All-cream Rhubarb Fool

SERVES 4

Prepare as for All-cream Gooseberry Fool, but substitute rhubarb, cut into short lengths, for the gooseberries. Flavour with the finely grated rind and juice of 1 orange, omitting the water, if liked.

All-cream Blackberry and Apple Fool

SERVES 4

Prepare as for All-cream Gooseberry Fool, but substitute 450 g/1 lb cooking (tart) apples, sliced, and 100 g/4 oz blackberries for the gooseberries, and sweeten with 75 g/3 oz/⅓ cup granulated sugar.

All-cream Damson Fool

SERVES 4

Prepare as for All-cream Gooseberry Fool, but substitute damsons for the gooseberries. Remove the stones (pits) before puréeing and sweeten with 75–100 g/3–4 oz/⅓–½ cup granulated sugar, depending on their ripeness.

All-cream Plum Fool

SERVES 4

Prepare as for All-cream Gooseberry Fool, but substitute ripe plums for the gooseberries. Remove the stones (pits) before puréeing and sweeten with 75 g/3 oz/⅓ cup granulated sugar.

All-cream Greengage Fool

SERVES 4

Prepare as for All-cream Gooseberry Fool, but substitute greengages for the gooseberries. Remove the stones (pits) before puréeing and add the finely grated rind of 1 lime. Sweeten with 75 g/3 oz/⅓ cup granulated sugar.

All-cream Apricot Fool

SERVES 4

Prepare as for All-cream Gooseberry Fool, but substitute fresh apricots for the gooseberries. Remove the stones (pits) before puréeing. Flavour with the finely grated rind and juice of 1 orange, omitting the water, if liked. Sweeten the purée to taste with the sugar.

Mango Fool

SERVES 4

1 ripe mango
45 ml/3 tbsp lemon juice
15 ml/1 tbsp caster (superfine) sugar
425 g/15 oz/1 large can of custard
150 ml/¼ pt/⅔ cup double (heavy) cream,
  whipped
Angelica leaves, to decorate

Peel the mango and cut all the flesh off the mango stone (pit). Purée in a blender or processor with the lemon juice and sugar. Fold in the custard and half the whipped cream. Spoon into four wine goblets. Decorate each with a swirl of the remaining cream and an angelica leaf. Eat within 2 hours.

Pawpaw Fool

SERVES 4

150 ml/¼ pt/⅔ cup coconut milk, home-
made (see below) or use canned
250 ml/8 fl oz/1 cup double (heavy)
  cream
25 g/1 oz/2 tbsp caster (superfine) sugar
1 pawpaw
Finely grated rind and juice of 1 lime

To make coconut milk, soak 100 g/ 4 oz/1 cup dessicated (shredded) coconut in 150 ml/¼ pt/⅔ cup boiling water until cold, then squeeze thoroughly and discard the coconut.

Put the coconut milk, cream and sugar in a bowl and whip until peaking. Peel and halve the pawpaw and discard the black seeds. Purée in a blender or food processor with the lime rind and juice. Fold into the cream mixture and spoon into glasses. Chill for at least 1 hour before serving.

Peach Fool

SERVES 4

4 small peaches, skinned, halved,
  stoned (pitted) and sliced
75 ml/5 tbsp water
45–60 ml/3–4 tbsp caster (superfine)
  sugar
5 ml/1 tsp lemon juice
15 ml/1 tbsp custard powder
300 ml/½ pt/1¼ cups milk
150 ml/¼ pt/⅔ cup whipping cream
Palmiers (see page 124), to serve

Stew the peaches in the water with 30 ml/2 tbsp of the sugar and the lemon juice until pulpy. Pass through a sieve (strainer) or purée in a blender or food processor. Blend the custard powder with 15 ml/1 tbsp of the sugar and a little of the milk in the rinsed-out saucepan. Stir in the remaining milk. Bring to the boil and cook for 2 minutes, stirring all the time, until thickened. Cover with a circle of wetted greaseproof (waxed) paper to prevent a skin forming. Leave to cool. Whip the cream until softly peaking. Fold the peach purée into the custard, then the cream. Taste and add a little more sugar, if liked. Turn into four glasses and chill until ready to serve with Palmiers.

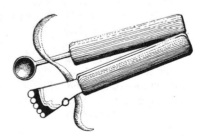

Dried Apricot and Brandy Fool

SERVES 6

350 g/12 oz dried apricots
750 ml/1¼ pts/3 cups water
75 g/3 oz/⅓ cup light brown sugar
1 egg
20 g/¾ oz/1½ tbsp caster (superfine)
    sugar
150 ml/¼ pt/⅔ cup milk
150 ml/¼ pt/⅔ cup double (heavy) cream
45 ml/3 tbsp apricot brandy
6 small mint sprigs

Put the apricots and water in a pan and leave to soak overnight. Add the brown sugar. Heat gently until the sugar dissolves. Bring to the boil, reduce the heat and simmer for 15 minutes or until the apricots are tender. Allow to cool slightly, then purée in a blender or food processor.

Beat together the egg, nearly all the caster sugar and 30 ml/2 tbsp of the milk. Bring the remaining milk almost to the boil. Pour over the egg mixture, then return to the saucepan. Heat gently, stirring, until thickened, but do not allow to boil. Sprinkle with the remaining caster sugar to prevent a skin forming, then leave to cool.

Whip the cream until softly peaking. Add half the apricot purée to the custard, then fold in the cream. Mix the apricot brandy into the remaining purée. Reserve 45 ml/3 tbsp for decoration and spoon the remaining purée into six glasses. Spoon the custard mixture over. Swirl a little of the reserved purée on top of each fool and chill until ready to serve. Decorate each with a mint sprig just before serving.

Tiger Eye Cream

SERVES 6

300 ml/½ pt/1¼ cups double (heavy)
    cream
300 ml/½ pt/1¼ cups full-cream milk
60 ml/4 tbsp caster (superfine) sugar
A few drops of almond essence (extract)
2 eggs
2 egg yolks
18 ready-to-eat dried apricots
8 whole blanched almonds
45 ml/3 tbsp water

Mix together the cream and milk with 15 ml/1 tbsp of the sugar and the almond essence to taste. Whisk in the whole eggs and egg yolks. Divide between six ramekins (custard cups). Stand the dishes in a roasting tin (pan) with enough boiling water to come half-way up the sides of the dishes. Cover with foil and bake in a preheated oven at 150°C/300°F/gas mark 2 for 30 minutes or until just set. Remove from the oven, take out of the water and leave to cool, then chill.

Meanwhile, make a slit in the side of each apricot and push an almond into each. Put the remaining sugar and the water in a heavy-based pan and stir over a gentle heat until the sugar has dissolved. Add the apricots and cook gently, stirring, until stickily coated. Do not allow to colour. Spoon, one at a time, on to a sheet of non-stick baking parchment and leave to cool. Put three apricots on top of each custard and serve.

Hot Winter Fruit Fool

SERVES 4

225 g/8 oz/1 packet of dried fruit salad
300 ml/½ pt/1¼ cups water
45 ml/3 tbsp custard powder
30 ml/2 tbsp granulated sugar
300 ml/½ pt/1¼ cups milk
Currants, to decorate

Soak the dried fruit in the water in a saucepan overnight. Bring to the boil, reduce the heat and simmer until the fruit is tender. Remove from the heat. When cool enough to handle, remove any stones (pits). Purée in a blender or food processor. Blend the custard powder with the sugar and milk in a saucepan. Bring to the boil and cook for 2 minutes, stirring all the time. Stir the fruit purée into the custard, then turn into serving dishes. Top with a few currants and serve hot.

Kiwi Quark Brûlée

SERVES 6

4 kiwi fruit, sliced
225 g/8 oz/1 cup quark
3 eggs
Finely grated rind of 1 lime
30 ml/2 tbsp caster (superfine) sugar
Granulated sugar

Put the kiwi fruit in the base of a fairly shallow flameproof dish. Whisk together the quark, eggs, lime rind and caster sugar in a basin. Stand the basin over a pan of hot water and cook, stirring, until the mixture thickens. Spoon over the kiwi fruit, leave to cool, then chill. Sprinkle a thick layer of granulated sugar over the quark custard to cover completely. Place under a hot grill (broiler) until the sugar melts and caramelises. Chill again until hard.

Victorian Cream

SERVES 8

6 trifle sponges
60 ml/4 tbsp redcurrant jelly (clear conserve)
60 ml/4 tbsp apricot jam (conserve)
100 g/4 oz Almond Macaroons (see page 128, or use bought), roughly crushed
60 ml/4 tbsp Madeira
50 g/2 oz/¼ cup caster (superfine) sugar
45 ml/3 tbsp dry white wine
45 ml/3 tbsp brandy
300 ml/½ pt/1¼ cups double (heavy) cream
150 ml/¼ pt/⅔ cup crème fraîche
Toasted flaked (slivered) almonds, to decorate

Halve the trifle sponges horizontally and sandwich six halves together with redcurrant jelly and six halves with apricot jam. Cut into halves to make 12 small sponge sandwiches. Arrange alternately in the base of a large glass dish. Scatter the macaroons over, then drizzle with the Madeira. Dissolve the sugar in the wine and brandy. Whip together the creams until softly peaking, then whisk in the wine mixture until thick. Spread over the sponges and chill. Sprinkle with toasted almonds before serving.

Crème Brûlée

SERVES 4–6

450 ml/¾ pt/2 cups double (heavy)
* cream*
2.5 ml/½ tsp vanilla essence (extract)
4 egg yolks
Caster (superfine) sugar

Bring the cream just to the boil. Stir in the vanilla. Beat together the egg yolks and 15 ml/1 tbsp caster sugar. Gradually pour the cream over, whisking all the time. Place the bowl over a pan of simmering water and cook until the mixture thickly coats the back of a spoon. Pour into four to six ramekins (custard cups). Leave to cool, then chill until set. Cover with a thick layer of caster sugar and place under a hot grill (broiler) until the sugar caramelises. Chill again before serving.

Trinity Cream

SERVES 4–6

Prepare exactly as for Crème Brûlée, but do not sweeten the custard.

Napoleon Cream

SERVES 4–6

Prepare exactly as for Crème Brûlée, but stir 15–30 ml/1–2 tbsp Napoleon brandy into the eggs and sugar before pouring on the scalded cream.

Apple and Raisin Brûlée

SERVES 6

750 g/1½ lb cooking (tart) apples, sliced
Grated rind and juice of ½ lemon
60 ml/4 tbsp water
50 g/2 oz/¼ cup caster (superfine) sugar
100 g/4 oz/⅔ cup raisins
A pinch of ground cinnamon
600 ml/1 pt/2½ cups double (heavy)
* cream, lightly whipped*
50 g/2 oz/¼ cup light brown sugar
Shortbread Triangles (see page 127), to
* serve*

Put the apple slices, lemon rind and juice, water, caster sugar, raisins and cinnamon in a large saucepan. Cover and cook gently for about 20 minutes until the apples are just tender but still hold their shape. Turn into a large shallow flameproof serving dish and leave until cold. Spoon over the cream and chill overnight. When almost ready to serve, sprinkle the top with the brown sugar and place under a hot grill (broiler) until the sugar melts and bubbles. Serve straight away with Shortbread Triangles.

Spanish Burnt Cream

SERVES 6

500 ml/17 fl oz/2¼ cups milk
1 piece of cinnamon stick
Thinly pared rind of 1 small lemon
6 egg yolks
275 g/10 oz/2¼ cups granulated sugar
25 g/1 oz/¼ cup cornflour (cornstarch)

Put the milk, cinnamon stick and lemon rind in a saucepan. Heat gently until just on the boil. Whisk the egg yolks with half the sugar and the cornflour until thick. Whisk in a little of the hot milk. Pour back into the saucepan and bring to the boil, stirring, until thick. Cook for 2 minutes. Strain into six ramekins (custard cups). Leave to cool. Cover with the remaining sugar. Stand the custards in a shallow pan of cold water. Place under a hot grill (broiler) until the sugar melts and caramelises. Leave until cold, then chill before serving.

Raspberry Brûlée

SERVES 4

225 g/8 oz raspberries
150 ml/¼ pt/⅔ cup double (heavy) cream
150 ml/¼ pt/⅔ cup thick plain yoghurt
Light brown sugar

Put the raspberries in a shallow flameproof dish. Whip together the cream and yoghurt until softly peaking. Spoon over the raspberries and chill for at least 2 hours. Sprinkle liberally with sugar to cover the top completely. Place under a hot grill (broiler) until the sugar melts and caramelises. Serve straight away.

Strawberry Brûlée

SERVES 4

Prepare as for Raspberry Brûlée, but substitute sliced strawberries for the raspberries.

Peach or Nectarine Brûlée

SERVES 4

Prepare as for Raspberry Brûlée, but substitute 4 ripe peaches or nectarines, peeled, stoned (pitted) and sliced, for the raspberries.

Apple and Orange Brûlée

SERVES 4

175 ml/6 fl oz/¾ cup crème fraîche
2 small eating (dessert) apples, diced
2 small oranges, chopped
100 g/4 oz/½ cup light brown sugar

Mix together all the ingredients except the sugar and place in a shallow flameproof dish. Chill very thoroughly. Sprinkle with the sugar and place under a hot grill (broiler) until the sugar melts. Chill again until ready to serve.

Pear and Yoghurt Brûlée

SERVES 4

425 g/15 oz/1 large can of pear quarters,
drained, reserving the juice
10 ml/2 tsp arrowroot
5 ml/1 tsp lemon juice
150 ml/¼ pt/⅔ cup plain yoghurt
1 large egg
2.5 ml/½ tsp vanilla essence (extract)
45 ml/3 tbsp granulated sugar

Chop the pears and place in a 900 ml/
1½ pt/3¾ cup ovenproof dish. Blend
a little of the pear juice with the
arrowroot in a saucepan. Stir in the
remaining pear juice and the lemon
juice. Bring to the boil and cook,
stirring, until thickened and clear. Pour
over the pears. Beat together the
yoghurt and egg until smooth, then
beat in the vanilla. Spoon over the pear
mixture and bake in a preheated oven
at 180°C/350°F/gas mark 4 for about
15–20 minutes until the custard is set.
Remove from the oven and sprinkle
liberally with the granulated sugar.
Place under a hot grill (broiler) until the
sugar melts and caramelises. Serve hot.

Rice Crème Brûlée

SERVES 6

75 g/3 oz/⅓ cup short-grain rice
600 ml/1 pt/2½ cups milk
15 ml/1 tbsp caster (superfine) sugar
4 egg yolks
250 ml/8 fl oz/1 cup double (heavy)
cream
2.5 ml/½ tsp vanilla essence (extract)
Butter, for greasing
60 ml/4 tbsp light brown sugar

Put the rice and milk in a saucepan
and bring to the boil. Reduce the
heat and simmer for 20 minutes until
tender. Whisk together the caster sugar
and egg yolks, then stir in the cream.
Stir into the rice with the vanilla
essence. Pour into a buttered shallow
ovenproof dish. Stand the dish in a
baking tin (pan) with enough hot water
to come half-way up the sides of the
dish. Cook in a preheated oven at
150°C/300°F/gas mark 2 for 1½ hours
until set. Remove from the tin. Leave to
cool, then chill. When ready to serve,
sprinkle the brown sugar liberally over
the surface of the rice. Place under a
hot grill (broiler) until the sugar melts
and caramelises. Serve straight away.

Rice Pudding

SERVES 4

50 g/2 oz/¼ cup short-grain rice
600 ml/1 pt/2½ cups milk
25 g/1 oz/2 tbsp granulated sugar
A pinch of grated nutmeg
A knob of butter or margarine

Put the rice in a flameproof dish and stir in the milk and sugar. Bring to the boil, stirring. Dust with nutmeg and dot with butter. Transfer to a preheated oven at 150°C/300°F/gas mark 2 and cook for 2 hours or until tender, creamy and golden brown on top.

Extra-creamy Rice Pudding

SERVES 4

Prepare as for Rice Pudding, but substitute 410 g/14½ oz/1 large can of evaporated milk, made up to 600 ml/1 pt/2½ cups with water, for the milk.

Fruity Rice

SERVES 4

Prepare as for Rice Pudding, but add 50 g/2 oz/⅓ cup mixed dried fruit (fruit cake mix) to the rice and sprinkle mixed (apple-pie) spice instead of nutmeg on the top.

Chocolate Rice

SERVES 4

Prepare as for Rice Pudding, but blend 30 ml/2 tbsp cocoa (unsweetened chocolate) powder with 60 ml/4 tbsp boiling water and stir into the milk before adding to the rice. Stir constantly while bringing to the boil.

Apricot Rice

SERVES 4

Prepare as for Rice Pudding, but add 50 g/2 oz/⅓ cup dried apricots, chopped, to the rice before adding the milk.

Creamy Rice with Bay

SERVES 4

750 ml/1¼ pt/3 cups whole milk
1 large bay leaf
Thinly pared rind of ½ orange
15 g/½ oz/1 tbsp unsalted (sweet) butter
50 g/2 oz/¼ cup short-grain pudding rice
25 g/1 oz/2 tbsp granulated sugar
50 g/2 oz/⅓ cup sultanas (golden raisins)

Bring the milk, bay leaf and orange rind to the boil. Leave until cold. Use half the butter to grease a 900 ml/1½ pt/3¾ cup ovenproof dish. Put the rice, sugar and sultanas in the greased dish. Strain over the milk and dot with the remaining butter. Stir gently. Cook in a preheated oven at 150°C/300°F/gas mark 2 for 2 hours or until the rice is tender and creamy. Serve hot.

Riz à l'Impératrice

SERVES 6

50 g/2 oz/¼ cup mixed crystallised
    (candied) fruits, chopped
30 ml/2 tbsp kirsch
100 g/4 oz/½ cup long-grain rice
250 ml/8 fl oz/1 cup milk
2.5 ml/½ tsp vanilla essence (extract)
10 ml/2 tsp powdered gelatine
15 ml/1 tbsp water
2 egg yolks
50 g/2 oz/¼ cup granulated sugar
250 ml/8 fl oz/1 cup single (light) cream
Thinly pared rind of ½ lemon
250 ml/8 fl oz/1 cup double (heavy)
    cream, whipped
Oil, for greasing
Halved glacé (candied) cherries and
    angelica leaves, to decorate

Soak the crystallised fruits in the
kirsch while preparing the rest of the
dessert. Cook the rice in plenty of
boiling water for 10 minutes or until
just tender. Drain and return to the
saucepan. Stir in the milk and vanilla
essence, bring to the boil, reduce the
heat and simmer for 20 minutes,
stirring occasionally. Remove from the
heat and leave to cool.

Meanwhile, sprinkle the gelatine
over the water in a small bowl. Leave
to soften for 5 minutes, then stand the
bowl in a pan of hot water and stir until
the gelatine has completely dissolved
(or dissolve briefly in the microwave).
Whisk together the egg yolks, sugar
and single cream in a bowl. Add the
lemon rind. Cook over a pan of hot
water until the custard thickens and
coats the back of the spoon. Test by
lifting the spoon out of the mixture and
drawing a finger through the mixture
adhering to the back of the spoon: if it
leaves a clear line, the custard is ready.
Remove from the heat and stir in the
gelatine. Leave until cold and on the
point of setting. Remove the lemon
rind. Stir in the rice, the soaked fruits
and the whipped cream. Turn into a
large lightly oiled mould and chill until
set. Turn out on to a serving plate and
decorate with halved glacé cherries and
angelica leaves.

Flaked Rice Refresher

SERVES 4

50 g/2 oz/¼ cup flaked rice
600 ml/1 pt/2½ cups milk
450 g/1 lb rhubarb, cut into short
    lengths
30 ml/2 tbsp water
1 piece of stem ginger in syrup, finely
    chopped
30 ml/2 tbsp ginger syrup from the jar
Clear honey
Crystallised (candied) ginger, to decorate

Put the rice and milk in a pan and
mix thoroughly. Bring to the boil
and cook for 2 minutes, stirring all the
time. Cover with a lid, remove from the
heat and leave to stand while preparing
the rhubarb. Place the pieces in a
saucepan with the water. Cover and
cook gently until soft but still holding
its shape. Add the chopped ginger and
ginger syrup and sweeten to taste with
honey. Keep warm. Return the rice to
the heat and cook for a further
5 minutes. Sweeten to taste with honey.
Spoon the rhubarb into four serving
dishes. Top with the rice, then decorate
with pieces of crystallised ginger before
serving.

Creamy Orange Rice Mallow

SERVES 4

1 orange
75 g/3 oz/⅓ cup short-grain rice
900 ml/1½ pts/3¾ cups milk
45 ml/3 tbsp granulated sugar
12 white marshmallows
45 ml/3 tbsp single (light) cream

Thinly pare the rind from the orange and cut into thin strips. Boil in a little water for 3 minutes, drain, rinse with cold water and drain again. Squeeze the juice from the orange. Put the rice and milk in a saucepan with the sugar. Bring to the boil, reduce the heat, part-cover and simmer for 30 minutes until the rice is really tender, stirring occasionally to prevent sticking. Stir in the marshmallows until dissolved. Add the strained orange juice and allow to cool slightly. Stir in the cream. Spoon into glass dishes and top with the orange rind. Leave until cold, then chill before serving.

Oeufs à la Neige

SERVES 4

3 eggs, separated
100 g/4 oz/½ cup caster (superfine) sugar
5 ml/1 tsp vanilla essence (extract)
450 ml/¾ pt/2 cups milk

Whisk the egg whites until stiff. Add half the sugar and whisk again until stiff and glossy. Fold in half the vanilla essence. Put the milk in a wide shallow pan and heat gently until very slowly simmering but not boiling. Drop spoonfuls of the meringue mixture into the milk and poach gently for 5 minutes, turning once. Carefully lift out of the milk with a draining spoon and drain on kitchen paper (paper towels.

Whisk the egg yolks with the remaining sugar until thick and pale. Gradually pour on the milk, stirring all the time. Return to the saucepan and heat gently, stirring, until the custard thickens. Do not allow to boil. Remove from the heat immediately and plunge the base of the pan in cold water. Stir in the remaining vanilla essence. Pour into a glass serving dish. Put the poached meringues on top and chill until ready to serve.

Banana Condé

SERVES 6

50 g/2 oz/¼ cup short-grain rice
30 ml/2 tbsp cornflour (cornstarch)
450 ml/¾ pt/2 cups milk
150 ml/¼ pt/⅔ cup single (light) cream
5 ml/1 tsp vanilla essence (extract)
30 ml/2 tbsp caster (superfine) sugar
4 bananas
Lemon juice
45 ml/3 tbsp redcurrant jelly (clear
  conserve), warmed
30 ml/2 tbsp rainbow coffee sugar or
  demerara sugar

Put the rice in a pan and cover with boiling water. Bring back to the boil and simmer for 15 minutes until tender. Drain. Blend the cornflour with a little of the milk in a saucepan. Blend in the remaining milk, the cream, vanilla and caster sugar. Stir in the rice. Bring to the boil and cook for 2 minutes, stirring all the time, until thickened and smooth. Leave until cold, stirring occasionally. Spoon into six glasses. Slice the bananas and toss in lemon juice. Arrange on top of the rice and brush with the redcurrant jelly. Sprinkle with rainbow coffee sugar and serve straight away.

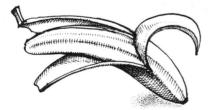

Pear Condé

SERVES 4–6

600 ml/1 pt/2½ cups milk
40 g/1½ oz/3 tbsp caster (superfine)
  sugar
75 g/3 oz/⅓ cup short-grain rice
Thinly pared rind of ½ orange
150 ml/¼ pt/⅔ cup double (heavy) cream
520 g/1 lb 3 oz/1 very large can of pear
  halves, drained, reserving the juice
90 ml/6 tbsp apricot jam (conserve)
Chopped pistachio nuts, to decorate

Put the milk in a saucepan with the sugar, rice and orange rind. Bring to the boil, reduce the heat, cover and cook over the gentlest possible heat, stirring occasionally, for about 1 hour, until the rice is tender and creamy. Remove the orange rind. Turn into a serving dish, leave until cold, then chill.

Whip the cream until peaking and spread over the rice. Top with the pear halves. Warm the jam with 15 ml/ 1 tbsp of the pear juice and brush all over the pears. Scatter with chopped pistachio nuts and chill again until ready to serve.

Peach Condé

SERVES 4–6

Prepare as for Pear Condé, but substitute peaches for the pears. Decorate with toasted flaked (slivered) almonds instead of pistachio nuts.

Semolina Pudding

SERVES 4

*50 g/2 oz/¼ cup semolina (cream of
  wheat)*
*40 g/1½ oz/3 tbsp caster (superfine)
  sugar*
600 ml/1 pt/2½ cups milk
Jam (conserve), to serve

Whisk together the semolina, sugar
and a little of the milk in a
saucepan. Whisk in the remaining milk.
Bring to the boil and cook for about
10 minutes, stirring all the time until
thick. Serve hot with jam.

Baked Semolina Pudding

SERVES 4

Prepare as for Semolina Pudding, but
once brought to the boil, turn into a
greased ovenproof dish, sprinkle with
grated nutmeg and bake in a preheated
oven at 150°C/300°F/gas mark 2 for
about 45 minutes until golden on top.

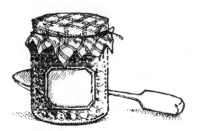

Vanilla Cornflour Pudding

SERVES 4

40 g/1½ oz/⅓ cup cornflour (cornstarch)
600 ml/1 pt/2½ cups milk
*25 g/1 oz/2 tbsp caster (superfine)
  sugar*
2.5 ml/½ tsp vanilla essence (extract)
1 egg, beaten
Butter, for greasing
*Clotted Cream (see page 359, or use
  bought), to serve*

Blend the cornflour with a little of the
milk and the sugar in a bowl. Bring
the remaining milk just to the boil. Pour
over the cornflour, stirring all the time.
Return to the saucepan and cook,
stirring, until thickened. Allow to cool
slightly, then whisk in the vanilla
essence and beaten egg. Turn into a
greased ovenproof dish. Bake in a
preheated oven at 140°C/275°F/gas
mark 1 for 45 minutes. Serve hot with
Clotted Cream.

Lemon Cornflour Pudding

SERVES 4

Prepare as for Vanilla Cornflour
Pudding, but add the thinly pared
rind of 1 lemon to the milk when
warming. Remove before turning into
the baking dish. Omit the vanilla
essence (extract).

Almond Cornflour Pudding

SERVES 4

Prepare as for Vanilla Cornflour Pudding (see page 303), but substitute almond essence (extract) for the vanilla. Scatter the top with toasted flaked (slivered) almonds before serving.

Baked Custard

SERVES 4

600 ml/1 pt/2½ cups milk
2 eggs
25 g/1 oz/2 tbsp caster (superfine) sugar
Butter, for greasing
Grated nutmeg, for dusting

Warm the milk. Lightly beat the eggs and sugar together. Pour over the hot milk, whisking all the time. Strain into an greased ovenproof dish. Dust with nutmeg. Bake in a preheated oven at 150°C/300°F/gas mark 2 for about 45 minutes or until set.

Orange Baked Custard

SERVES 4

Prepare as for Baked Custard, but add the finely grated rind of 1 orange to the milk and omit the nutmeg.

Lemon Baked Custard

SERVES 4

Prepare as for Baked Custard, but add the finely grated rind of 1 lemon to the milk and omit the nutmeg.

Macaroni Pudding

SERVES 4

50 g/2 oz short-cut macaroni
600 ml/1 pt/2½ cups milk
25 g/1 oz/2 tbsp caster (superfine) sugar
1 egg, beaten
Butter, for greasing
Grated nutmeg, for dusting

Soak the macaroni in the milk for 1 hour. Bring to the boil, reduce the heat and cook very gently until the macaroni is tender. Stir in the sugar. Allow to cool slightly, then add the egg. Turn into a buttered ovenproof dish, dust with nutmeg and bake in a preheated oven at 140°C/275°F/gas mark 1 for about 40 minutes or until set.

Extra-creamy Macaroni Pudding

SERVES 4

Prepare as for Macaroni Pudding, but use half milk and half single (light) cream instead of all milk.

Devon-style Macaroni Pudding

SERVES 4

Prepare as for Macaroni Pudding, but cook the macaroni in 300 ml/½ pt/ 1¼ cups water, then stir in 400 g/14 oz/ 1 large can of evaporated milk. Continue as above.

Sago Nursery Pudding

SERVES 4

30 ml/2 tbsp fine sago
25 g/1 oz/2 tbsp butter, plus extra for greasing
600 ml/1 pt/2½ cups milk
25 g/1 oz/2 tbsp caster (superfine) sugar
Grated nutmeg, for dusting
Clear honey, to serve

Wash the sago and place in a buttered ovenproof dish. Stir in the milk and sugar and leave to soak for 1 hour. Stir again and dot with the butter. Dust with nutmeg. Bake in a preheated oven at 140°C/275°F/gas mark 1 for 1½–2 hours or until cooked through and golden. Serve with clear honey.

Tapioca Nursery Pudding

SERVES 4

Prepare as for Sago Nursery Pudding, but substitute tapioca for the sago. Serve with jam (conserve) instead of honey, if liked.

Bread and Butter Pudding

SERVES 4

Butter, for greasing
4–6 thin slices of buttered white bread, cut into triangles
40 g/1½ oz/3 tbsp granulated sugar
60 ml/4 tbsp raisins
2 eggs
600 ml/1 pt/2½ cups milk
Grated nutmeg, for dusting

Butter a 1.2 litre/2 pt/5 cup ovenproof dish. Layer the buttered bread, sugar and raisins in the dish. Beat together the eggs and milk and strain into the dish. Dust with nutmeg. Leave to stand for 30 minutes, if possible, then bake in a preheated oven at 180°C/350°F/gas mark 4 for about 1 hour until set and golden brown.

Lemon Bread and Butter Pudding

SERVES 4

Prepare as for Bread and Butter Pudding, but add the finely grated rind of 1 lemon to the egg and milk mixture. Dust with mixed (apple-pie) spice instead of nutmeg.

Orange Bread and Butter Pudding

SERVES 4

Prepare as for Bread and Butter Pudding (see page 305), but add the finely grated rind of 1 orange to the egg and milk mixture. Dust with ground cinnamon instead of nutmeg.

Marmalade Bread and Butter Pudding

SERVES 4

6 slices of bread
50 g/2 oz/¼ cup butter
45 ml/3 tbsp orange marmalade
50 g/2 oz/¼ cup granulated sugar
450 ml/¾ pt/2 cups milk
15 ml/1 tbsp dried milk powder (non-fat dry milk)
2 eggs

Spread the bread with the butter and marmalade. Cut each slice into four triangles. Line a 1.2 litre/2 pt/5 cup ovenproof dish with half the triangles. Sprinkle with half the sugar, then top with the remaining triangles, arranged attractively. Beat together the milk, milk powder and eggs. Pour over the bread. Sprinkle with the remaining sugar. Bake in a preheated oven at 180°C/350°F/gas mark 4 for about 1 hour or until golden and set.

Pineapple Floating Islands

SERVES 4

50 g/2 oz/¼ cup butter, softened
100 g/4 oz/½ cup caster (superfine) sugar
25 g/1 oz/¼ cup cornflour (cornstarch)
2 large eggs, separated
300 ml/½ pt/1¼ cups milk
150 ml/¼ pt/⅔ cup single (light) cream
440 g/15½ oz/1 large can of crushed pineapple, drained, reserving the juice

Beat together the butter and half the sugar until light and fluffy. Blend in the cornflour and the egg yolks. Warm the milk and cream but do not boil. Pour into the butter mixture. Return to the pan and cook, stirring, until thickened. Put the pineapple in the base of a 1.5 litre/2½ pt/6 cup ovenproof dish. Pour the custard over. Whisk the egg whites until stiff, add 40 g/1½ oz/3 tbsp of the remaining sugar and whisk again until stiff and glossy. Spoon four piles of the meringue mixture on top of the custard to make 'islands' and sprinkle with the remaining sugar. Bake in a preheated oven at 150°C/300°F/gas mark 2 for 30 minutes until golden. Serve hot or cold with the reserved pineapple juice.

Peach Floating Islands

SERVES 6

4 peaches, skinned and sliced
100 g/4 oz/½ cup caster (superfine)
  sugar
30 ml/2 tbsp lemon juice
2 eggs, separated
450 ml/¾ pt/2 cups milk
A few drops of vanilla essence (extract)
15 ml/1 tbsp cornflour (cornstarch)

Put the peaches in an ovenproof dish and sprinkle with 30 ml/2 tbsp of the sugar and the lemon juice. Whisk the egg whites until stiff, then fold in 75 g/3 oz/⅓ cup of the remaining sugar. Bring the milk to the boil in a large shallow pan. Divide the egg white into six portions and drop into the simmering milk. Poach for 10 minutes, turning once. Drain on kitchen paper. Stir the vanilla essence into the milk. Whisk together the egg yolks and cornflour. Pour the milk over, whisking all the time. Return to the pan and stir in the remaining sugar. Cook gently, stirring, until the custard thickens and coats the back of a spoon. Test by lifting the spoon out of the mixture. Draw a finger across the custard on the back of the spoon: if it leaves a clear line, the custard is ready. Pour over the peaches. Put the poached whites on top. Cool, then chill for at least 2 hours.

Camembert Refresher

SERVES 6

1 cantaloupe melon
1 small honeydew melon
½ small watermelon
225 g/8 oz seedless grapes
6 individual portions of Camembert
  cheese
50 g/2 oz/½ cup toasted flaked (slivered)
  almonds

Cut the melons into wedges, discarding the seeds and peel. Arrange on serving plates. Scatter the grapes over. Put the Camembert wedges on foil on the grill (broiler) rack. Grill (broil) until warm and just beginning to run. Transfer to the plates and scatter the flaked almonds over. Serve straight away.

Soft Fruit Cheese

SERVES 4

225 g/8 oz soft fruit such as
  strawberries or raspberries
225 g/8 oz/1 cup low-fat soft cheese
15 ml/1 tbsp icing (confectioners')
  sugar
5 ml/1 tsp lemon juice
Palmiers (see page 124), to serve

Mash the fruit, then stir in the remaining ingredients with a fork until fairly smooth. Turn into a small glass bowl and chill before serving with Palmiers.

Boozy Dairy Pears

SERVES 4

4 ripe pears, halved, peeled and cored
40 g/1½ oz/3 tbsp butter, melted
100 g/4 oz/½ cup light brown sugar
225 g/8 oz/1 cup fromage frais
250 ml/8 fl oz/1 cup double (heavy)
cream, whipped
250 ml/8 fl oz/1 cup thick plain
yoghurt
90 ml/6 tbsp coffee liqueur
A pinch of ground cinnamon
Instant coffee powder, for dusting

Lay the pears on foil on a grill (broiler) rack. Mix the melted butter with 30 ml/2 tbsp of the sugar and brush over the pears. Grill (broil) for 5 minutes, turning once and brushing with more of the butter mixture during cooking.

Meanwhile, put the remaining ingredients in a bowl with the remaining sugar. Whip gently until blended and fairly stiff. Place the pears on serving plates and top with the cream mixture. Dust very lightly with coffee powder and serve straight away.

Tiramisu

SERVES 6

250 g/9 oz/generous 1 cup Mascarpone
cheese
4 eggs, separated
60 ml/4 tbsp caster (superfine) sugar
10 ml/2 tsp strong black coffee
100 g/4 oz/1 cup plain (semi-sweet)
chocolate, broken into small pieces
(optional)
120 ml/4 fl oz/½ cup weak coffee
90 ml/6 tbsp amaretto or coffee liqueur
20 sponge (lady) fingers
Drinking (sweetened) chocolate powder,
for dusting

Whisk together the cheese and egg yolks and gradually add the sugar. Pour in the strong coffee and mix thoroughly. Whisk the egg whites until stiff and fold into the cheese mixture. Gently stir in the chocolate pieces, if using. Mix the weak coffee with the liqueur and dip half the sponge fingers in it. Use to line the base of a shallow serving dish. Pour in half the cheese mixture. Dip the remaining sponge fingers in the coffee mixture and lay on top. Top with the remaining cheese mixture. Tap the dish gently on the work surface to settle the contents. Chill for at least 2 hours. Dust with chocolate powder before serving.

Chocolate Curd Cheese Torte

SERVES 8

*100 g/4 oz/1 cup plain (all-purpose)
  flour*
*200 g/7 oz/generous 1 cup icing
  (confectioners') sugar*
4 eggs
15 ml/1 tbsp milk
5 ml/1 tsp vanilla essence (extract)
*100 g/4 oz/½ cup unsalted (sweet)
  butter*
*100 g/4 oz/½ cup curd (smooth cottage)
  cheese*
150 ml/¼ pt/⅔ cup crème fraîche
15 ml/1 tbsp coffee liqueur
*100 g/4 oz/1 cup plain (semi-sweet)
  chocolate*

Line the two baking (cookie) sheets with non-stick baking parchment and mark an 18 cm/7 in circle on each. Sift the flour and 100 g/4 oz/⅔ cup of the icing sugar into a bowl. Beat in two of the eggs, the milk and vanilla until smooth. Spread a quarter of the mixture on each circle, spreading evenly with a palette knife. Bake in a preheated oven at 180°C/350°F/gas mark 4 for about 10 minutes or until lightly browned around the edges. Quickly remove from the baking paper and cool on a wire rack. Turn the paper over and spread the remaining mixture on to the other sides to make two more rounds. Bake in the same way.

Beat together the butter and remaining icing sugar until light and soft. Separate the remaining eggs. Beat the egg yolks and cheese with half the crème fraîche and the coffee liqueur into the butter mixture. Whisk the egg whites until stiff and fold into the mixture with a metal spoon. Chill.

Break up the chocolate and melt in a small bowl over a pan of hot water (or in the microwave). Spread a little over each biscuit (cookie) round, reserving a little for decoration. When the chocolate has set, place one of the biscuits chocolate-side up on a serving plate. Spread with a third of the cheese mixture. Top with a second biscuit layer, chocolate-side down. Repeat the layers, finishing with a biscuit layer, chocolate-side down. Spread the remaining crème fraîche over the top. Melt the reserved chocolate again if necessary and, using a teaspoon, drizzle it over the top. Chill until ready to serve.

Italian-style Coffee Cream Cheese

SERVES 6

*15 ml/1 tbsp instant coffee powder or
  granules*
15 ml/1 tbsp water
225 g/8 oz/1 cup Mascarpone cheese
*100 g/4 oz/⅔ cup icing (confectioners')
  sugar, sifted*
A few walnuts, chopped
*Langues de Chat (see page 129), to
  serve*

Mix together the coffee and water until dissolved. Gradually beat into the cheese with the icing sugar. Turn into a small glass dish, sprinkle with the walnuts and chill thoroughly before serving with Langues de Chat.

Mandarin and Chocolate Cheesecake

SERVES 6

50 g/2 oz/¼ cup butter, melted
*200 g/7 oz/1 small packet of chocolate
  rich tea biscuits (cookies), crushed*
*300 g/11 oz/1 medium can of mandarin
  oranges, drained, reserving the juice*
15 g/½ oz/1 tbsp powdered gelatine
225 g/8 oz/1 cup Mascarpone cheese
2 eggs, separated
75 g/3 oz/⅓ cup caster (superfine) sugar
*75 g/3 oz/⅓ cup soured (dairy sour)
  cream*
30 ml/2 tbsp orange liqueur
Grated rind and juice of 1 tangerine
Grated chocolate, to decorate

Mix together the butter and biscuit crumbs and press into the base of a 20 cm/8 in springform cake tin (pan). Chill while preparing the filling.

Chop the mandarins. Sprinkle the gelatine over the reserved juice in a small bowl and leave to soften for 5 minutes. Stand the bowl in a pan of hot water, or heat in the microwave briefly, to dissolve. Beat together the cheese, egg yolks, 50 g/2 oz/¼ cup of the sugar, the soured cream and liqueur until smooth. Stir in the dissolved gelatine. Fold in the tangerine rind and juice and the chopped mandarins. Whisk the egg whites until stiff, then whisk in the remaining sugar. Fold into the fruit mixture and spoon over the biscuit base. Chill for 3–4 hours until set before decorating with grated chocolate.

Banana Cheesecake

SERVES 6–8

*200 g/7 oz/1 small packet of digestive
  biscuits (graham crackers), crushed*
50 g/2 oz/1 cup bran flakes, crushed
75 g/3 oz/⅓ cup butter, melted
*450 g/1 lb/2 cups medium-fat soft
  cheese*
2 eggs, separated
Finely grated rind and juice of 1 lime
15 ml/1 tbsp powdered gelatine
3 bananas
50 g/2 oz/¼ cup caster (superfine) sugar
150 ml/¼ pt/⅔ cup crème fraîche
A little lemon juice

Mix together the biscuit crumbs, crushed flakes and butter and press into the base of a 20 cm/8 in springform cake tin (pan).

Beat the cheese with the egg yolks and lime rind. Sprinkle the gelatine over the lime juice in a small bowl and leave to soften for 5 minutes. Stand the bowl in a pan of hot water and stir until the gelatine has dissolved completely (or heat briefly in the microwave). Mash two of the bananas thoroughly with the sugar and stir in the gelatine mixture. Beat into the cheese mixture. Whisk the egg whites until stiff. Fold the crème fraîche, then the egg whites, into the cheese mixture, then turn into the prepared tin. Chill until set. Remove the tin and place the cheesecake on a serving plate. Slice the remaining banana thinly and dip in lemon juice to prevent browning. Use to decorate the top of the cheesecake.

Cherry Yoghurt Cheesecake

SERVES 6–8

1 large chocolate Swiss (jelly) roll, cut
   into 12 slices
350 g/12 oz/1½ cups curd (smooth
   cottage) cheese
150 ml/¼ pt/⅔ cup black cherry yoghurt
50 g/2 oz/¼ cup caster (superfine) sugar
2 eggs, separated
15 ml/1 tbsp powdered gelatine
45 ml/3 tbsp cold water
450 g/1 lb fresh black cherries, stoned
   (pitted)

Arrange some of the Swiss roll slices
around the sides of a deep 25 cm/
10 in round cake tin (pan). Reserve the
remaining slices.
   Mix together the cheese and
yoghurt in a bowl with the sugar. Beat
the egg yolks into the mixture. Sprinkle
the gelatine over the water in a small
bowl and leave to soften for 5 minutes.
Stand the bowl in a pan of hot water
and stir until completely dissolved (or
heat briefly in the microwave). Stir into
the cheese mixture with half the
cherries. Chill until on the point of
setting. Whisk the egg whites until stiff.
Fold into the cheese mixture. Turn into
the cake tin and level the surface.
Arrange the remaining cake slices over.
Chill until set. When ready to serve,
loosen all round the edge between the
sponge and the tin. Dip the base briefly
in hot water, then turn out the
cheesecake on to a serving plate.
Arrange the remaining cherries over
and serve.

Rich Raspberry Cheesecake

SERVES 8

200 g/7 oz/1 small packet of digestive
   biscuits (graham crackers), crushed
50 g/2 oz/¼ cup butter, melted
15 ml/1 tbsp light brown sugar
10 ml/2 tsp powdered gelatine
15 ml/1 tbsp water
175 g/6 oz/¾ cup medium-fat soft
   cheese
150 ml/¼ pt/⅔ cup crème fraîche
225 g/8 oz raspberries, mashed,
   reserving a few whole ones for
   decoration
50 g/2 oz/⅓ cup icing (confectioners')
   sugar
150 ml/¼ pt/⅔ cup whipping cream

Mix together the biscuit crumbs,
butter and brown sugar. Press into
the base and sides of a 20 cm/8 in flan
dish (pie pan). Chill until firm.
   Meanwhile, sprinkle the gelatine
over the water in a small bowl and
leave to soften for 5 minutes. Stand the
bowl in a pan of hot water and stir until
dissolved (or heat briefly in the
microwave). Beat the soft cheese with
the crème fraîche. Stir in the dissolved
gelatine, then fold in the mashed
raspberries and sweeten to taste with
the icing sugar. Whip the cream until
peaking. Reserve a little for decoration,
then fold the remainder into the
raspberry mixture. Turn into the
prepared flan case (pie shell) and chill
until set. Decorate with the remaining
whipped cream and reserved whole
raspberries.

Rich Strawberry Cheesecake

SERVES 6–8

Prepare as for Rich Raspberry Cheesecake (see page 311), but substitute strawberries for the raspberries and mash with 5 ml/1 tsp lemon juice to bring out the flavour.

Pineapple Cheesecake

SERVES 6

200 g/7 oz/1 small packet of thin ginger biscuits (cookies), crushed
75 g/3 oz/⅓ cup unsalted (sweet) butter, melted
225 g/8 oz/1 cup medium-fat soft cheese
1 egg, beaten
45 ml/3 tbsp caster (superfine) sugar
Finely grated rind and juice of ½ lemon
300 g/11 oz/1 medium can of pineapple chunks in natural juice, drained, reserving the juice
60 ml/4 tbsp apricot jam (conserve), sieved (strained) if necessary

Mix the crushed biscuits into the butter and press into the base and sides of a 20 cm/8 in flan dish (pie pan). Chill until firm. Meanwhile, beat together the cheese, egg, sugar, lemon rind and juice. Pour into the flan case (pie shell). Bake in a preheated oven at 160°C/325°F/gas mark 3 for about 25 minutes until set. Leave to cool. Arrange the pineapple chunks attractively on top of the cheesecake. Blend 30 ml/2 tbsp of the juice with the apricot jam in a saucepan. Stir until melted and blended. Brush all over the top and chill until ready to serve.

Walnut Cheesecake

SERVES 8

200 g/7 oz/1 small packet of shortcake biscuits (cookies), crushed
50 g/2 oz/½ cup chopped walnuts
75 g/3 oz/⅓ cup butter, melted
225 g/8 oz/1 cup curd (smooth cottage) cheese
450 g/1 lb/2 cups Mascarpone cheese
3 eggs, beaten
100 g/4 oz/½ cup caster (superfine) sugar
Finely grated rind of 1 orange
15 ml/1 tbsp orange juice
10 ml/2 tsp orange flower water
50 g/2 oz/¼ cup light brown sugar
15 ml/1 tbsp water
50 g/2 oz/½ cup walnut halves

Mix the biscuit crumbs with the chopped nuts and melted butter. Press into the base and sides of a 20 cm/8 in springform cake tin (pan). Beat together the cheeses, eggs, caster sugar, orange rind, orange juice and orange flower water and spoon into the tin. Bake in a preheated oven at 160°C/325°F/gas mark 3 for 1 hour. Turn off the oven and leave the cake to cool in the oven.

Meanwhile, stir the brown sugar and water in a heavy-based saucepan, then heat very gently until it dissolves and bubbles. Let it bubble for 1 minute, then stir in the walnut halves. Spread on an oiled baking (cookie) sheet and leave to harden. When ready to serve, remove the cheesecake from the tin and place on a serving plate. Roughly crush the walnut mixture and sprinkle over the top of the cheesecake before serving.

Coconut Cheesecake

SERVES 8

Oil, for greasing
75 g/3 oz/¾ cup desiccated (shredded)
coconut
200 g/7 oz/1 small packet of Nice or
other coconut biscuits (cookies),
crushed
50 g/2 oz/¼ cup butter or margarine,
melted
30 ml/2 tbsp light brown sugar
3 eggs, separated
100 g/4 oz/½ cup caster (superfine) sugar
225 g/8 oz/1 cup curd (smooth cottage)
cheese
225 g/8 oz/1 cup Mascarpone cheese
15 ml/1 tbsp cornflour (cornstarch)
150 ml/¼ pt/⅔ cup double (heavy) cream
Toasted coconut flakes, to decorate
Crème fraîche, to serve

Grease a 20 cm/8 in deep round loose-bottomed cake tin (pan). Toast 25 g/1 oz/¼ cup of the coconut in a frying pan (skillet) until golden brown. Mix with the biscuit crumbs, melted butter or margarine and brown sugar. Press into the base of the cake tin.

Put the egg yolks in a bowl with the caster sugar and whisk until thick and pale. Beat together the two cheeses with the remaining coconut and the cornflour. Beat in the egg and sugar mixture. Whisk the egg whites until stiff, then the cream until peaking. Fold the cream, then the egg whites into the mixture. Turn into the prepared tin and cook in a preheated oven at 160°C/325°F/gas mark 3 for about 1 hour until set. Turn off the oven and leave the cake there to cool. When cold, remove from the tin and transfer to a serving plate. Decorate with toasted flaked coconut and chill until ready to serve with crème fraîche.

Simple Lemon Cheesecake

SERVES 6

1 packet of lemon-flavoured jelly (jello)
Boiling water
200 g/7 oz/1 small packet of digestive
biscuits (graham crackers), crushed
75 g/3 oz/⅓ cup butter, melted
25 g/1 oz/2 tbsp light brown sugar
200 g/7 oz/1 small carton of low-fat
soft cheese
50 g/2 oz/¼ cup caster (superfine) sugar
Finely grated rind and juice of 1 small
lemon
150 ml/¼ pt/⅔ cup double (heavy) cream
Ground cinnamon, for dusting

Break up the jelly in a measuring jug and make up to 300 ml/½ pt/1¼ cups with boiling water. Stir until dissolved and leave to cool.

Meanwhile, mix the biscuit crumbs with the melted butter and brown sugar. Turn into a 20 cm/8 in flan tin (pie pan) and press down well. Beat together the cheese, caster sugar, lemon rind and juice. Whisk in the cold jelly. When on the point of setting, whip the cream and fold in. Turn into the flan case (pie shell) and chill until set. Decorate with a dusting of ground cinnamon.

Avocado Cheesecake

SERVES 6–8

50 g/2 oz/¼ cup butter
A pinch of ground cinnamon
200 g/7 oz/1 small packet of Nice or
*   other coconut biscuits (cookies),*
*   crushed*
Oil, for greasing
7.5 ml/1½ tsp powdered gelatine
15 ml/1 tbsp water
1 orange
1 large avocado
10 ml/2 tsp lemon juice
90 g/3½ oz/1 small packet of medium-
*   fat soft cheese*
150 ml/¼ pt/⅔ cup crème fraîche
45 ml/3 tbsp icing (confectioners')
*   sugar*
1 egg white
A mint sprig, to decorate

M elt the butter and stir in the
cinnamon and crushed biscuits.
Press into the base of a lightly oiled
18 cm/7 in flan ring set on a flat
serving plate. Chill until firm.
    Meanwhile, sprinkle the gelatine
over the water in a small bowl and
leave to soften for 5 minutes. Stand the
bowl in a pan of hot water and stir until
the gelatine has dissolved completely
(or heat briefly in the microwave).
Halve the orange widthways. Finely
grate the rind and squeeze the juice
from one half. Thinly slice the other
orange half, then halve the slices and
reserve for decoration. Peel and halve
the avocado, discard the stone (pit) and
place in a bowl. Add the lemon juice,
then mash with a fork. Beat in the
dissolved gelatine, the cheese, crème
fraîche and the orange rind and juice.

Sweeten to taste with the icing sugar.
Whisk the egg white until stiff and fold
into the mixture with a metal spoon.
Turn into the prepared flan ring and
chill until set. Remove the flan ring.
Decorate with the halved orange slices
and a sprig of mint before serving.

Rich Vanilla Cheesecake

SERVES 8–10

200 g/7 oz/1 small packet of digestive
*   biscuits (graham crackers), crushed*
75 g/3 oz/⅓ cup unsalted (sweet) butter,
*   melted, plus extra for greasing*
750 g/1½ lb/3 cups full-fat soft cheese
225 g/8 oz/1 cup caster (superfine)
*   sugar*
2 eggs
5 ml/1 tsp vanilla essence (extract)
150 ml/¼ pt/⅔ cup soured (dairy sour)
*   cream*
Grated nutmeg, to decorate

M ix the crushed biscuits into the
butter. Press into the base and a
little way up the sides of a 20 cm/8 in
deep, round, loose-bottomed cake tin
(pan).
    Beat the cheese with the sugar, eggs
and vanilla until smooth. Turn into the
prepared tin and smooth the surface.
Bake in a preheated oven at 150°C/
300°F/gas mark 2 for 1–1¼ hours or
until just set. Turn off the oven and
leave to cool in the oven. Chill for at
least 2 hours or overnight. Decorate the
top with swirls of soured cream and
dust with grated nutmeg.

Rum and Raisin Cheesecake

SERVES 8

30 ml/2 tbsp white rum
100 g/4 oz/²⁄₃ cup raisins
200 g/7 oz/1 small packet of Nice or
    other coconut biscuits (cookies),
    crushed
75 g/3 oz/¹⁄₃ cup butter, melted
50 g/2 oz/¹⁄₄ cup light brown sugar
30 ml/2 tbsp desiccated (shredded)
    coconut
45 ml/3 tbsp water
15 g/¹⁄₂ oz/1 tbsp powdered gelatine
225 g/8 oz/1 cup curd (smooth cottage)
    cheese
225 g/8 oz/1 cup medium-fat soft
    cheese
150 ml/¹⁄₄ pt/²⁄₃ cup crème fraîche
50 g/2 oz/¹⁄₃ cup icing (confectioners')
    sugar
15 ml/1 tbsp lemon juice
2.5 ml/¹⁄₂ tsp ground cinnamon
2 large eggs, separated
60 ml/4 tbsp double (heavy) cream,
    whipped
Toasted flaked (slivered) coconut, to
    decorate

Put the rum in a bowl and stir in the
raisins. Leave to soak for at least
1 hour. Mix the biscuit crumbs with the
butter, brown sugar and desiccated
coconut. Press into the base and sides
of a 20 cm/8 in springform cake tin
(pan). Chill until firm.

Put the water in a small bowl.
Sprinkle the gelatine over and leave to
soften for 5 minutes. Stand the bowl in
a pan of hot water and stir until
dissolved (or heat briefly in the
microwave). Beat the cheeses with the
crème fraîche, icing sugar, lemon juice,
cinnamon and the egg yolks. Beat in
the dissolved gelatine and the rum and
raisins. Chill until on the point of
setting. Whisk the egg whites until stiff,
then fold into the cheese mixture with a
metal spoon. Turn into the prepared flan
case (pie shell) and chill until set. Whip
the cream and spread over the top of
the cheesecake. Top with a few toasted
coconut flakes and chill again until
ready to serve.

Lime Cobweb Cheesecake

SERVES 6–8

200 g/7 oz/1 small packet of digestive
    biscuits (graham crackers), crushed
50 g/2 oz/¹⁄₂ cup chocolate chips
50 g/2 oz/¹⁄₄ cup butter, melted
500 g/1 lb 2 oz/2¹⁄₂ cups Mascarpone
    cheese
40 g/1¹⁄₂ oz/¹⁄₄ cup icing (confectioners')
    sugar, sifted
Finely grated rind and juice of 2 limes
30 ml/2 tbsp chocolate spread

Mix the crushed biscuits with the
chocolate chips and butter and
press into the base of an 18 cm/7 in
springform cake tin (pan). Beat the
cheese with the icing sugar and lime
rind and juice. Spoon into the tin and
level the surface. Chill until firm.

Remove from the tin and place on a
serving plate. Spoon the chocolate
spread into a paper piping bag and snip
off the very tip of the bag, or use an
icing syringe with a plain tube (tip),
and pipe a spiral of chocolate starting at
the centre. Using a skewer or cocktail
stick (toothpick), draw lines from the
centre to the edge all round to form a
cobweb pattern. Serve chilled.

Liquorice Cheesecake

SERVES 8

200 g/7 oz/1 small packet of rich tea
  biscuits (cookies), crushed
75 g/3 oz/⅓ cup butter, melted
50 g/2 oz black liquorice sticks, chopped
150 ml/¼ pt/⅔ cup milk
15 ml/1 tbsp powdered gelatine
45 ml/3 tbsp water
350 g/12 oz/1½ cups medium-fat soft
  cheese
1 egg, separated
50 g/2 oz/¼ cup caster (superfine) sugar
120 ml/4 fl oz/½ cup double (heavy)
  cream, whipped
1 red liquorice bootlace, cut into small
  pieces

Mix the crushed biscuits into the
butter, then press into the base of
a 23 cm/9 in loose-bottomed flan tin
(pie pan). Chill until firm.
    Put the chopped black liquorice in a
saucepan with the milk. Bring to the
boil and simmer for 5 minutes, stirring
occasionally. Meanwhile, sprinkle the
gelatine over the water in a small bowl
and leave to soften for 5 minutes. Stir
into the hot liquorice mixture until
completely dissolved. Leave to cool.
Pour into a blender or food processor
and add the cheese. Blend until smooth.
Put the egg yolk and sugar in one bowl
and the egg white in another. Whisk
the egg white until stiff, then the yolk
and sugar until thick and pale. Fold the
egg yolk mixture, then the egg white
into the cheese mixture. Pour into the
prepared flan case (pie shell) and chill
until set. Decorate the top with whipped
cream and the red liquorice pieces.

Baked Grapefruit Cheesecake

SERVES 8

200 g/7 oz/1 small packet of digestive
  biscuits (graham crackers), crushed
75 g/3 oz/⅓ cup butter, melted
450 g/1 lb/2 cups cottage cheese
150 g/5 oz/⅔ cup caster (superfine)
  sugar, plus extra for frosting
Finely grated rind and juice of
  1 grapefruit
15 ml/1 tbsp cornflour (cornstarch)
2 eggs
A few mint leaves

Mix the crushed biscuits into the
butter and press into the base of
an 18 cm/7 in loose-bottomed cake tin
(pan).
    Put the cottage cheese, sugar, the
grapefruit rind, 20 ml/4 tsp of the juice,
the cornflour and one of the eggs in a
blender or food processor and run the
machine until smooth. Separate the
remaining egg and reserve a little of the
white. Add the remaining white and the
yolk to the processor and blend again.
Turn into the prepared tin. Bake in a
preheated oven at 180°C/350°F/gas
mark 4 for about 1½ hours until set.
Turn off the oven and leave the cake
there to cool. Chill until ready to serve.
Meanwhile, brush the mint leaves with
the reserved egg white and sprinkle
liberally with caster sugar. Leave to dry
on a sheet of greaseproof (waxed)
paper. Just before serving, put a cluster
of frosted mint leaves in the centre of
the cheesecake.

Swedish Raisin Sour Cake

SERVES 8

240 g/8½ oz/generous 2 cups plain (all-purpose) flour
A pinch of salt
100 g/4 oz/½ cup unsalted (sweet) butter, diced
7.5 ml/1½ tsp vanilla essence (extract)
90 ml/6 tbsp caster (superfine) sugar
Cold water, to mix
2 eggs, beaten
250 ml/8 fl oz/1 cup soured (dairy sour) cream
225 g/8 oz/1⅓ cups raisins
60 ml/4 tbsp brandy
Finely grated rind of ½ small lemon

Sift the all but 15 g/½ oz/2 tbsp of the flour and the salt into a bowl. Add the butter and rub in with the fingertips until the mixture resembles breadcrumbs. Add 5 ml/1 tsp of the vanilla, 30 ml/2 tbsp of the sugar and enough water to form a firm dough. Knead gently on a lightly floured surface. Roll out the pastry (paste) and use to line a 23 cm/9 in flan tin (pie pan).

Beat together the remaining flour, the remaining sugar, the eggs and soured cream. Stir in the raisins, brandy, remaining vanilla essence and the lemon rind. Pour into the pastry lined tin and bake in a preheated oven at 200°C/400°F/gas mark 6 for about 20 minutes until turning golden. Reduce the heat to 180°C/350°F/gas mark 4 and continue cooking for about 15 minutes or until the filling is just set. Serve warm or cold.

Apple Cream Cheese Bake

SERVES 6

25 g/1 oz/2 tbsp unsalted (sweet) butter
900 g/2 lb sharp eating (dessert) apples, chopped
250 ml/8 fl oz/1 cup medium-sweet cider
50 g/2 oz/¼ cup granulated sugar
150 ml/¼ pt/⅔ cup double (heavy) cream
100 g/4 oz/½ cup cream cheese
2 eggs
50 g/2 oz/¼ cup icing (confectioners') sugar, plus extra for dusting
2.5 ml/½ tsp vanilla essence (extract)

Liberally grease a shallow ovenproof dish with the butter. Put the chopped apples in the prepared dish. Put the cider in a pan with the granulated sugar and heat gently until the sugar has dissolved. Pour the syrup over the apples. Cover and bake in a preheated oven at 190°C/375°F/gas mark 5 for 15 minutes. Beat together the cream, cream cheese, eggs and icing sugar with the vanilla essence. Pour over the apples and return to the oven for 20 minutes until set. Sift a little icing sugar over the surface and serve hot.

Ricotta Pudding

SERVES 6

175 g/6 oz/1½ cups plain (all-purpose)
flour
A pinch of salt
40 g/1½ oz/3 tbsp hard block
margarine, diced
40 g/1½ oz/3 tbsp white vegetable fat
(shortening), diced
Cold water, to mix
2 eggs, separated
175 g/6 oz/¾ cup caster (superfine)
sugar
175 g/6 oz/¾ cup Ricotta cheese, sieved
(strained)
40 g/1½ oz/⅓ cup ground almonds
45 ml/3 tbsp sultanas (golden raisins)
15 ml/1 tbsp chopped mixed (candied)
peel
Finely grated rind of ½ lemon

Sift the flour and salt into a bowl. Add the fats and rub in with the fingertips until the mixture resembles fine bread-crumbs. Mix with enough cold water to form a firm dough. Knead gently on a lightly floured surface. Roll out and use to line a 20 cm/8 in flan dish (pie pan). Prick the base with a fork. Fill with crumpled foil and bake in a preheated oven at 200°C/400°F/gas mark 6 for 10 minutes. Remove the foil and bake for a further 5 minutes to dry out.

Whisk together the egg yolks and 50 g/2 oz/¼ cup of the sugar until thick and pale. Beat in the cheese, almonds, sultanas, mixed peel and lemon rind. Turn into the pastry case (pie shell). Bake in the oven at 180°C/350°F/gas mark 4 for 25 minutes until firm to the touch. Whisk the egg whites until stiff. Whisk in half the remaining sugar, then fold in the remainder. Pile on top of the flan and return to the oven for a further 5 minutes until the meringue is just turning colour. Serve warm or cold.

Scottish Cream Crowdie

SERVES 6

100 g/4 oz/1 cup coarse oatmeal
600 ml/1 pt/2½ cups whipping cream
45 ml/3 tbsp sweet sherry
15 ml/1 tbsp caster (superfine) sugar
Fresh raspberries or strawberries
(optional), to decorate

Toast the oatmeal under a moderate grill (broiler), turning occasionally, until golden brown. Whip together the cream, sherry and sugar until softly peaking. When ready to serve, fold all but 15 ml/1 tbsp of the toasted oatmeal into the cream. Spoon into serving dishes and sprinkle with the remaining oatmeal. Top with a few raspberries or strawberries to decorate, if liked.

Almond Redcurrant Strata

SERVES 8

*200 g/7 oz/1 small packet of almond
    biscuits (cookies), crushed*
50 g/2 oz/¼ cup butter, melted
*225 g/8 oz redcurrants, stripped from
    their stalks*
120 ml/4 fl oz/½ cup water
30 ml/2 tbsp powdered gelatine
4 eggs, separated
350 g/12 oz/1½ cups quark
75 g/3 oz/⅓ cup caster (superfine) sugar
*300 ml/½ pt/1¼ cups double (heavy)
    cream*
Almond essence (extract)
7.5 ml/1½ tsp arrowroot

Mix the biscuit crumbs into the butter and press into the base of a 25 cm/10 in springform cake tin (pan). Chill until firm.

Place the redcurrants in a saucepan with 30 ml/2 tbsp of the water and cook gently for about 5 minutes until tender. Place 60 ml/4 tbsp of the remaining water in a small bowl and sprinkle the gelatine over. Leave to soften for 5 minutes, then stand the bowl in a pan of hot water and stir until dissolved (or dissolve briefly in the microwave). Beat the egg yolks with the quark and 50 g/2 oz/¼ cup of the sugar until smooth. Whip the cream and fold half into the quark mixture. Whisk the egg whites until stiff and fold into the quark mixture with a metal spoon. Put half the mixture in a separate bowl. Stir half the redcurrants into one of the bowls, then half the dissolved gelatine. Spread the mixture over the biscuit base. Mix the remaining gelatine into the remaining quark mixture with almond essence to taste. Spoon over the redcurrant mixture and chill until set. Blend the remaining water with the arrowroot in a saucepan with the remaining sugar and redcurrants. Heat gently, stirring, until thickened and clear. Leave until cold. Remove the springform tin and place the dessert on a serving plate. Spoon over the thickened redcurrants and decorate with the reserved whipped cream.

Butterscotch Dessert

SERVES 6

50 g/2 oz/¼ cup butter
75 g/3 oz/⅓ cup light brown sugar
90 ml/6 tbsp semolina (cream of wheat)
600 ml/1 pt/2½ cups milk
*150 ml/¼ pt/⅔ cup double (heavy)
    cream, whipped*
Walnut halves, to decorate

Put the butter and sugar in a pan and heat gently, stirring, until melted. Stir in the semolina and cook for 1 minute. Gradually stir in the milk, stirring all the time. Bring to the boil and cook for 3 minutes, stirring all the time, until thick and smooth. Allow to cool slightly, then turn into six wetted glass serving dishes. Cool, then chill. Decorate with whipped cream and walnut halves before serving.

Coffee Dairy Dessert

SERVES 6

600 ml/1 pt/2½ cups milk
2 eggs
2 egg yolks
30 ml/2 tbsp granulated sugar
15 ml/1 tbsp instant coffee powder or
granules
Icing (confectioners') sugar, for dusting

Bring the milk to the boil. Whisk together the eggs, egg yolks, sugar and coffee thoroughly. Whisk in the hot milk. Strain into six individual ovenproof dishes. Stand the dishes in a roasting tin (pan) containing 2.5 cm/ 1 in boiling water. Cover the dishes with foil. Bake in a preheated oven at 160°C/325°F/gas mark 3 for about 40 minutes until the custard is set. Remove from the heat, leave to cool, then chill. Dust with a little sifted icing sugar before serving.

Vanilla Dairy Dessert

SERVES 6

Prepare as for Coffee Dairy Dessert, but substitute 5 ml/1 tsp vanilla essence (extract) for the coffee powder or granules.

Chocolate Dairy Dessert

SERVES 6

Prepare as for Coffee Dairy Dessert, but substitute 30 ml/2 tbsp drinking (sweetened) chocolate powder for the coffee powder or granules.

Fresh Lemon Cheesecake

SERVES 6–8

200 g/7 oz/1 small packet of gingernut
biscuits (cookies), crushed
50 g/2 oz/¼ cup butter, melted
225 g/8 oz/1 cup low-fat soft cheese
100 g/4 oz/½ cup fromage frais
90 ml/6 tbsp thick plain yoghurt
50 g/2 oz/¼ cup icing (confectioners')
sugar, plus extra for dusting
Finely grated rind and juice of 1 large
lemon
Crystallised (candied) lemon slices and
angelica leaves, to decorate

Mix the crushed gingernuts into the butter and press into the base of a 20 cm/8 in flan tin (pie pan).

Beat together the cheese, fromage frais, yoghurt, icing sugar, lemon rind and 5 ml/1 tsp of the lemon juice. Turn into the flan tin and level the surface. Chill for several hours or overnight. Dredge with sifted icing sugar and decorate with crystallised lemon slices and angelica leaves before serving.

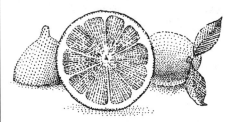

Pineapple Crowdie

SERVES 4

75 g/3 oz/¾ cup coarse oatmeal
225 g/8 oz/1 cup fromage frais
50 g/2 oz/¼ cup caster (superfine) sugar
60 ml/4 tbsp clear honey
30 ml/2 tbsp white rum
300 g/11 oz/1 medium can of crushed
  pineapple, drained thoroughly
Toasted flaked (slivered) coconut, to
  decorate

Toast the oatmeal under a moderate grill (broiler), turning occasionally, until golden brown. Beat together the fromage frais, sugar, honey and rum. Just before serving, fold in the pineapple and toasted oatmeal. Spoon into glasses and decorate with a little toasted coconut before serving.

Chocolate Custard Smoothie

SERVES 4–6

40 g/1½ oz/⅓ cup cornflour (cornstarch)
40 g/1½ oz/3 tbsp light brown sugar
600 ml/1 pt/2½ cups milk
5 ml/1 tsp vanilla essence (extract)
100 g/4 oz/1 cup plain (semi-sweet)
  chocolate
60 ml/4 tbsp double (heavy) cream

Blend the cornflour with the sugar, a little of the milk and the vanilla essence in a bowl. Put the remaining milk in a saucepan. Break up half the chocolate and add. Heat gently, stirring, until the chocolate has melted. Pour the flavoured milk over the blended cornflour, stirring. Return to the pan. Bring to the boil and cook for 2 minutes, stirring, until thickened and smooth. Allow to cool slightly, then beat in the cream. Turn into four to six glasses and cover each with a circle of wetted greaseproof (waxed) paper to prevent a skin forming. Leave until cold, then chill. Just before serving, remove the paper and grate the remaining chocolate over the surface.

Coeurs à la Crème

SERVES 4

175 g/6 oz/³⁄₄ cup full-fat soft cheese
30 ml/2 tbsp icing (confectioners')
*   sugar, sifted, plus extra for dusting*
1.5 ml/¹⁄₄ tsp vanilla essence (extract)
1.5 ml/¹⁄₄ tsp lemon juice
175 ml/6 fl oz/³⁄₄ cup double (heavy)
*   cream, whipped*
Fresh strawberries or raspberries, to
*   decorate*

To make this dish properly you must line four *coeur à la crème* moulds with rinsed and squeezed-out muslin (cheesecloth) so there is enough to fold over the top of the dessert once the moulds are filled. Beat the cheese in a bowl with the sugar, vanilla and lemon juice until fluffy. Fold in the whipped cream. Spoon into the moulds and wrap the muslin over the top of each. Place on a large plate to catch the drips and chill overnight to drain, pressing gently on top after a few hours to help the whey drain off.

When ready to serve, gently lift each heart out of its mould and remove the muslin. Place on serving plates. Dust with a little sifted icing sugar and decorate each with a few fresh strawberries or raspberries.

Peach Melba Softie

SERVES 4

60 ml/4 tbsp medium-fat soft cheese
Icing (confectioners') sugar, to taste
Finely grated rind of ¹⁄₂ orange
*   (optional)*
4 ripe peaches, skinned, halved and
*   stoned (pitted)*
300 g/11 oz/1 medium can of raspberries,
*   drained, reserving the juice*

Sweeten the cheese to taste with icing sugar and flavour with the orange rind, if liked. Sandwich the peach halves together in pairs with the cheese and place in four small glass dishes. Chill. Pass the raspberries through a sieve (strainer) to remove the seeds, then thin the purée with a little of the juice to give a smooth pouring consistency. Spoon over the peaches and serve.

Pear Melba Softie

SERVES 4

Prepare as for Peach Melba Softie, but substitute ripe pears, peeled, halved and cored, for the peaches.

Instant Cheats

You won't always have the time or the inclination to make a creative masterpiece from scratch. So here is a complete set of very quick, very easy 'cheats' from Mock Rum Babas to Almost Tiramisu, quick whips and virtually no-effort ice cream bombes. And the lovely thing is, as long as you don't tell, no one will ever know you've cheated. One tip though: if you use aerosol cream to decorate a dessert, serve it straight away as it doesn't stay aerated for very long.

Nursery Trifle

SERVES 4

1 Swiss (jelly) roll, sliced
200 g/7 oz/1 small can of fruit cocktail,
drained, reserving the juice
1 packet of raspberry-flavoured jelly
(jello)
1 sachet of peach-flavoured dessert
whip
Cold milk
Coloured sugar strands, to decorate

Put the Swiss roll slices in a glass dish. Spoon the fruit over the sponge slices. Make the juice up to 600 ml/1 pt/2½ cups with water. Use to make up the jelly according to the packet directions. Pour over the sponge and chill until set. Make up the dessert whip with milk according to the packet directions. Spread over the jelly and chill again for 1 hour. Sprinkle with sugar strands just before serving.

The Ubiquitous Trifle

SERVES 4

4 trifle sponges
300 g/11 oz/1 medium can of strawberries
30 ml/2 tbsp sherry
425 g/15 oz/1 large can of custard
170 g/6 oz/1 small can of cream
Toasted flaked (slivered) almonds, to
decorate

Crumble the sponges into the base of a glass serving dish. Empty the can of strawberries over and gently mash into the sponges. Sprinkle the sherry over. Spoon the custard over. Gently spread the cream over. Sprinkle with toasted almonds and chill until ready to serve.

Blackberry and Apple Layer

SERVES 4

5 ml/1 tsp lemon juice
400 g/14 oz/1 large can of blackberry
and apple pie filling
4 trifle sponges
30 ml/2 tbsp apple juice
300 ml/½ pt/1¼ cups vanilla yoghurt
Demerara or light brown sugar, for
sprinkling

Stir the lemon juice into the pie filling. Spoon half the mixture into the base of four glass dishes. Crumble the trifle sponges and mix with the apple juice. Spoon over the blackberry and apple. Top with the remaining pie filling. Spoon the yoghurt over and sprinkle with sugar. Chill until ready to serve.

Lovely Lemon Charlotte

SERVES 4

14–16 sponge (lady) fingers
Grated rind and juice of 1 lemon
10 ml/2 tsp gin (optional)
410 g/14½ oz/1 large can of custard

Halve the sponge fingers. Mix half the lemon juice with the gin, if using, and brush over the sponge finger halves. Arrange the halved sponge fingers around the edges of four ramekins (custard cups). Mix the lemon rind and remaining juice into the custard. Spoon into the sponge-lined ramekins. If you have any lemony sponge fingers remaining, chop them and sprinkle on the top. Chill until ready to serve.

Lemon Velvet

SERVES 4

*1 packet of lemon meringue pie filling
  mix*
300 ml/½ pt/1¼ cups water
*Grated rind and juice of 1 small lemon
  OR 20 ml/4 tsp bottled lemon juice*
150 ml/¼ pt/⅔ cup cold milk
1 sachet of Dream Topping mix
*Crystallised (candied) lemon slices, to
  decorate*

Blend the pie filling with the water in a saucepan. Bring to the boil, stirring, until thickened. Stir in the lemon rind and juice and leave until cool. Put the cold milk in a bowl and whisk in the Dream Topping until thick and fluffy. Fold into the cold lemon mixture. Spoon into four glasses and decorate each with a crystallised lemon slice.

Lemon Fluff

SERVES 4

*1 packet of lemon meringue pie filling
  mix*
200 ml/7 fl oz/scant 1 cup water
1 egg, separated
170 g/6 oz/1 small can of cream
Toasted chopped nuts, to decorate

Blend the pie filling with the water in a saucepan. Whisk in the egg yolk. Bring to the boil and cook for 2 minutes until smooth and thick. Leave to cool. When cold, fold in the cream. Whisk the egg white until stiff and fold in with a metal spoon. Turn into four glasses and chill for at least 30 minutes. Sprinkle with chopped nuts before serving.

Lemon Fluff Flan

SERVES 4–6

Prepare as for Lemon Fluff, but turn the mixture into a bought 18 cm/ 7 in sponge flan case. Chill for at least 1 hour. Decorate with aerosol cream and chopped nuts just before serving.

Rum and Raisin Flan

SERVES 4–6

100 g/4 oz/⅔ cup raisins
30 ml/2 tbsp hot water
Rum essence (extract)
*1 sachet of chocolate blancmange
  powder*
600 ml/1 pt/2½ cups milk
18 cm/7 in sponge flan case
Aerosol cream
Grated chocolate, to decorate

Put the raisins in a bowl with the hot water and add rum essence to taste. Leave to soak for 1 hour. Meanwhile, make up the blancmange with the milk according to the packet directions. Add the soaked raisins. Taste and add a little more rum essence, if liked. Place the sponge flan on a serving plate. Spoon in the blancmange mixture. Chill until set. Just before serving, add swirls of aerosol cream and sprinkle with grated chocolate. Serve immediately.

Butterscotch Maple Pecan Ice Cream

SERVES 6

1 sachet of butterscotch-flavoured
*   dessert whip*
Cold milk
300 ml/½ pt/1¼ cups UHT (long-life)
*   whipping cream*
50 g/2 oz/½ cup pecan nuts, chopped
45 ml/3 tbsp maple syrup

Make up the dessert whip with milk according to the packet directions. Whip the cream and fold into the mixture with the pecans. Turn into a plastic or metal container and freeze for 1 hour. Whisk with a fork to break up the ice crystals. Freeze for a further 1½ hours. Whisk again, then fold in the maple syrup just until you have a marbled effect, then stop mixing. Freeze until firm. Remove from the freezer 15 minutes before serving.

No-effort Chocolate Ice Cream

SERVES 6

1 sachet of chocolate-flavoured
*   dessert whip*
Cold milk
300 ml/½ pt/1¼ cups UHT (long-life)
*   whipping cream*
5 ml/1 tsp vanilla essence (extract)

Make up the dessert whip with milk according to the the packet directions. Whip the cream and fold in with the vanilla essence. Turn into a plastic or metal container and freeze for 1 hour. Whisk with a fork to break up the ice crystals. Freeze for a further 1½ hours and whisk again. Freeze until firm. Remove from the freezer 15 minutes before serving.

Chocolate Chippie

SERVES 6

Prepare as for No-effort Chocolate Ice Cream, but add 100 g/4 oz/1 cup chocolate chips with the cream.

Strawberry Ripple Ice Cream

SERVES 6

1 sachet of strawberry-flavoured
*   dessert whip*
Cold milk
300 ml/½ pt/1¼ cups UHT (long-life)
*   whipping cream*
45 ml/3 tbsp strawberry jam (conserve),
*   sieved (strained)*
5 ml/1 tsp lemon juice

Make up the dessert whip with milk according to the packet directions. Whip the cream and fold in with a metal spoon. Turn into a plastic or metal container and freeze for 1 hour. Whisk with a fork to break up the ice crystals. Freeze for a further 1½ hours and whisk again. Mix the sieved jam with the lemon juice. Fold in just until you have a marbled effect, then stop mixing. Freeze until firm. Remove from the freezer 15 minutes before serving.

Black Forest Bombe

SERVES 8–10

*350 g/12 oz/3 cups plain (semi-sweet)
  chocolate*
Oil, for greasing
*1 litre/1¾ pts/3¾ cups soft-scoop vanilla
  ice cream*
*450 g/1 lb frozen stoned (pitted) black
  cherries*
1 egg white
*50 g/2 oz/⅓ cup icing (confectioners')
  sugar*
10 ml/2 tsp lemon juice
30 ml/2 tbsp canned cream, to decorate

Melt the chocolate in a bowl over a pan of hot water or in the microwave. Lightly oil a 1.75 litre/3 pt/ 7½ cup pudding basin. Spoon a little of the melted chocolate into the basin and brush up the sides to coat completely. When set, add a little more chocolate and repeat until all the chocolate is used and the basin is evenly coated in chocolate. You need to work fast as the chocolate sets fairly quickly. Freeze for 30 minutes.

Put the ice cream in the chocolate-lined basin and smooth up the sides to form a shell of ice cream. Freeze again. Purée the frozen cherries in a blender or food processor until they form a slushy pulp. Whisk the egg white until stiff and whisk in the icing sugar. Fold in the cherries and lemon juice. Turn into the centre of the ice cream and press down well. Cover and freeze at least overnight. When ready to serve, gently loosen the top edge between the chocolate and the basin, but don't force the knife down too far or you will crack the chocolate. Stand the basin briefly in

hot water, then turn out on to a serving plate. Pour the cream over the top. It should set as it trickles down the sides. If the chocolate begins to melt a bit when you turned it out, return it to the freezer for 10 minutes to set.

Swiss Chocolate Mountain

SERVES 6–8

*2 small chocolate Swiss (jelly) rolls,
  sliced*
150 ml/¼ pt/⅔ cup double (heavy) cream
*30 ml/2 tbsp chocolate hazelnut (filbert)
  spread*
*½ × 1 litre/½ × ¾ pt/½ small block
  of chocolate ice cream, cubed*
25 g/1 oz/¼ cup chocolate chips
Icing (confectioners') sugar, for dusting

Line a 1.5 litre/2½ pt/6 cup pudding basin with the Swiss roll slices. Whip the cream and whisk in the chocolate spread. Stir in the ice cream and chocolate chips. Spoon into the sponge-lined basin. Cover and freeze until firm. Transfer to the fridge 1½ hours before serving. Turn out on to a serving plate and dust liberally with sifted icing sugar.

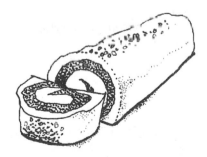

Chocolate Ripple Ring

SERVES 6

*45 ml/3 tbsp chocolate hazelnut (filbert)
spread*
30 ml/2 tbsp coffee liqueur
*1 litre/1¾ pts/4¼ cups soft-scoop
chocolate ice cream*
*Whipped or aerosol cream and grated
chocolate, to decorate*

Blend the chocolate spread with the liqueur until smooth. Turn the ice cream into a bowl. Mash with a fork, then quickly fold in the chocolate mixture to form ripples. Pack quickly into a 1 litre/1¾ pt/4¼ cup ring mould. Wrap in clingfilm (plastic wrap) and chill until firm. Dip the base of the mould in hot water briefly, then loosen round the edge with a round-bladed knife. Turn out on to a serving plate and fill the centre with whipped cream and a sprinkling of grated chocolate. Serve straight away.

Caribbean Cooler

SERVES 6

*1 litre/1¾ pts/4¼ cups soft-scoop
chocolate ice cream*
*2 bananas, mashed with a little lemon
juice*
*2 pieces of stem ginger in syrup,
chopped*
Grated chocolate, to decorate

Put the ice cream in a bowl. Quickly work in the bananas and ginger until just mixed. Do not over-mix or the ice cream will start to melt. Quickly pack into a 450 g/1 lb loaf tin (pan). Cover with clingfilm (plastic wrap) and freeze until firm. When ready to serve, dip the tin briefly in hot water, loosen the edges with a round-bladed knife and turn out on to a serving dish. Sprinkle with grated chocolate and serve straight away cut into slices.

Italian Cassata

SERVES 6

*50 g/2 oz/½ cup drained maraschino
cherries*
*1 litre/1¾ pts/4¼ cups soft-scoop vanilla
ice cream*
50 g/2 oz/½ cup grated chocolate
15 ml/1 tbsp chopped angelica

Reserve 1 cherry for decoration and chop the remainder. Put the ice cream in a bowl. Quickly mash in the chocolate, chopped cherries and angelica until just blended (don't over-mix or the ice cream will start to melt). Quickly pack into a 1 litre/1¾ pt/4¼ cup pudding basin. Cover with clingfilm (plastic wrap) and freeze until firm. When ready to serve, dip the basin briefly in hot water, loosen round the edge with a round-bladed knife and turn out on to a serving plate. Top with the reserved cherry and serve straight away.

Honey Nut Bombe

SERVES 6

*1 litre/1¾ pts/4¼ cups soft-scoop vanilla
ice cream
Grated rind and juice of 1 lemon
45 ml/3 tbsp clear honey
50 g/2 oz/½ cup toasted chopped nuts
Crystallised (candied) lemon slices, to
decorate*

Put the ice cream in a bowl. Quickly
fold in the lemon rind, juice, honey
and nuts to give a marbled effect. Don't
over-mix or the ice cream will start to
melt. Quickly pack into a 1 litre/1¾ pt/
4¼ cup pudding basin. Cover with
clingfilm (plastic wrap) and freeze until
firm. When ready to serve, dip the
basin briefly in hot water, then loosen
round the edge with a round-bladed
knife and turn out on to a serving plate.
Decorate with crystallised lemon slices
before serving.

Chocolate Cups

SERVES 6

*150 ml/¼ pt/⅔ cup whipping cream
30 ml/2 tbsp chocolate hazelnut (filbert)
spread
15 ml/1 tbsp brandy, sherry, rum or
whisky
6 ready-made chocolate cases
Toasted chopped hazelnuts or halved
glacé (candied) cherries, to decorate*

Whip the cream and fold in the
chocolate spread and alcohol.
Spoon into the chocolate cases and
swirl the tops with a teaspoon. Sprinkle
with chopped nuts or top with half a
glacé cherry. Chill until ready to serve.

Chocolate Pear Melties

SERVES 4

*4 slices of chocolate slab cake
400 g/14 oz/1 large can of pear halves,
drained, reserving the juice
20 ml/4 tsp sweet sherry (optional)
4 chocolate mint thins
Whipped or aerosol cream, to serve*

Put the slices of cake in four shallow,
individual ovenproof dishes. Spoon
10 ml/2 tsp of the pear juice over each
slice and add 5 ml/1 tsp sherry to each,
if using. Top with the pears. Lay a
chocolate mint thin on top of each and
bake in a preheated oven at 200°C/
400°F/gas mark 6 for 5 minutes until
the chocolate has melted. Serve straight
away with whipped cream.

Iced Coffee Pear Flan

SERVES 6–8

*23 cm/9 in sponge flan case
500 ml/17 fl oz/2¼ cups soft-scoop
coffee ice cream
550 g/1¼ lb/1 very large can of pear
halves, drained
Angelica leaves, to decorate
100 g/4 oz/1 cup plain (semi-sweet)
chocolate*

Put the sponge flan in a freezerproof
container. Spread the ice cream over
and freeze until firm. Top with the pear
halves, decorate with angelica leaves
and freeze again. Just before serving,
melt the chocolate in a bowl over a pan
of hot water or in the microwave.
Drizzle all over the top of the flan in a
thin stream to decorate. Serve straight
away while still frozen.

Peach Upside-down Ice Cream Cake

SERVES 8

410 g/14½ oz/1 large can of peaches, drained, reserving the juice
8 maraschino cherries, drained on kitchen paper (paper towels) and halved
1 slab of Madeira cake, cut into 1 cm/½ in slices
1 sachet of peach-flavoured dessert whip
600 ml/1 pt/2½ cups cold milk
1 sachet of Dream Topping mix

Put the peach halves, cut-side down, in the base of an 18 cm/7 in cake tin (pan) with a halved maraschino cherry in each cavity, rounded-sides out. Put the remaining cherries round the edge. Line the tin with the slices of cake. Make up the dessert whip with 450 ml/¾ pt/2 cups milk and 90 ml/ 6 tbsp of the reserved peach juice. Make up the Dream Topping according to the packet directions. Fold in together and turn into the tin. Freeze until firm. Remove from the freezer about 30 minutes before serving and turn out of the tin on to a serving plate.

Pineapple Upside-down Ice Cream Cake

SERVES 8

Prepare as for Peach Upside-down Ice Cream Cake, but substitute 350 g/ 12 oz/1 large can of pineapple rings for the peaches and vanilla- or lemon-flavoured dessert whip for the peach.

Rum and Raisin Mountain

SERVES 6

50 g/2 oz/⅓ cup raisins
30 ml/2 tbsp dark rum
1 litre/1¾ pts/4¼ cups soft-scoop vanilla ice cream
2–3 meringues, crushed
Whipped or aerosol cream, to decorate

Put the raisins in a bowl with the rum. Leave to soak for 1 hour. Turn the ice cream into a bowl and quickly mash in the soaked raisins and the crushed meringues. Do not over-mix or the ice cream will start to melt. Quickly turn into a 1 litre/1¾ pt/4¼ cup pudding basin. Cover with clingfilm (plastic wrap) and freeze until firm. When ready to serve, dip the basin briefly in hot water, loosen round the edge with a round-bladed knife and turn out on to a serving plate. Pile whipped cream on top and serve immediately.

Doughnut Ices

SERVES 4

4 ring doughnuts
4 scoops of vanilla ice cream
Chocolate dessert sauce
Toasted chopped nuts

Put the doughnuts on serving plates. Top each with a scoop of ice cream. Drizzle chocolate sauce over and sprinkle with nuts. Serve straight away.

Frozzled Trifle

SERVES 4

1 small jam- (conserve-)filled Swiss (jelly) roll, sliced
60 ml/4 tbsp sherry
300 g/11 oz/1 medium can of mandarin oranges, drained, reserving the juice
500 ml/17 fl oz/2¼ cups bought lemon sorbet
425 g/15 oz/1 large can of custard
Aerosol cream, to decorate
Crystallised (candied) orange and lemon slices and angelica leaves, to decorate

Arrange the Swiss roll slices in the base of a freezerproof serving dish. Sprinkle with the sherry. Add the drained mandarins and enough of the juice to moisten to sponge. Pile scoops of the lemon sorbet in the centre and pour the custard around. Freeze until firm. Decorate with aerosol cream, crystallised orange and lemon slices and angelica leaves just before serving.

Easy Peach Fool

SERVES 4

410 g/14½ oz/1 large can of peach slices, drained, reserving the juice
10 ml/2 tsp lemon juice
425 g/15 oz/1 large can of custard
170 g/6 oz/1 small can of cream
Halved glacé (candied) cherries, to decorate

Purée the drained peaches with the lemon juice in a blender or food processor. Fold in the custard thoroughly, then fold in the cream to give a marbled effect. Spoon into serving glasses, top each with half a glacé cherry and serve chilled with the juice handed separately to drizzle over, if liked.

Meringue Peaches

SERVES 4

4 canned peach halves, drained
Oil, for greasing
1 trifle sponge
30 ml/2 tbsp orange or peach liqueur
1 egg white
50 g/2 oz/¼ cup caster (superfine) sugar
25 g/1 oz/¼ cup flaked (slivered) almonds
Icing (confectioners') sugar, for dusting

Cut a very thin slice off the rounded side of each peach half so they will stand firm. Place on a lightly oiled baking (cookie) sheet. Finely chop the slices and place in the cavities of the peaches. Cut the trifle sponge into quarters and place a quarter in each cavity. Spoon the liqueur over. Whisk the egg white until stiff. Gradually whisk in the sugar and continue whisking until stiff and glossy. Pile the meringue mixture over the peaches and decorate with the almonds. Bake in a preheated oven at 220°C/425°F/gas mark 7 for about 5 minutes until turning lightly golden. Dust with icing sugar and serve at once.

Peach Melba Nests

SERVES 6

300 g/11 oz/1 medium can of raspberries
6 bought meringue nests
200 g/7 oz/scant 1 cup low-fat soft
cheese
410 g/14½ oz/1 large can of peach
halves, drained

Drain the raspberries, reserving the juice. Pass the fruit through a sieve (strainer) into a bowl. Thin to a pouring consistency with a little of the juice. Put the meringue nests on six serving plates. Spoon the cheese into the nests and spread out gently. Top each with a peach half, rounded-side up. Spoon the raspberry sauce over each so it runs down the sides and on to the plates. Serve straight away.

Lemon Nests

SERVES 4

4 bought meringue nests
60 ml/4 tbsp lemon curd
Aerosol cream and toasted chopped
nuts, to decorate

Put the meringue nests on serving plates. Add 15 ml/1 tbsp lemon curd to each. When ready to serve, top with aerosol cream and sprinkle with chopped nuts. Serve straight away.

Orange Nests

SERVES 4

Prepare as for Lemon Nests, but substitute orange curd for lemon and decorate with crystallised (candied) orange slices instead of nuts.

St Clement's Nests

SERVES 4

Prepare as for Lemon Nests, but put a small spoonful each of lemon and orange curd, side by side, in the nests. Decorate with aerosol cream and crystallised (candied) orange and lemon slices just before serving.

Iced Chestnut Nests

SERVES 4

245 g/8¾ oz/1 medium can of sweetened
chestnut purée (paste)
4 bought meringue nests
8 scoops of vanilla ice cream
Chocolate sprinkles, to decorate

Put the purée in a piping bag fitted with a large star tube (tip). Place the meringue nests on four serving plates. Fill each with two scoops of ice cream. Pipe swirls of the purée around the ice cream and decorate with chocolate sprinkles.

Apricot Nut Crunch

SERVES 4

*410 g/14½ oz/1 large can of apricots,
   drained, reserving the juice*
1 packet of orange-flavoured jelly (jello)
25 g/1 oz/2 tbsp butter
15 ml/1 tbsp golden (light corn) syrup
15 ml/1 tbsp chopped nuts
*50 g/2 oz/1 cup bran flakes, lightly
   crushed*
170 g/6 oz/1 small can of cream

Purée the apricots in a blender or food processor. Make the juice up to 450 ml/¾ pt/2 cups with water. Dissolve the jelly in a little of this liquid in a saucepan over a gentle heat or in the microwave. Stir in the remaining liquid. Blend in the fruit purée and turn into one large or four individual serving dishes. Chill until set. Melt the butter in a saucepan with the syrup. Stir in the nuts and bran flakes. Spread the cream over the set fruit mixture. Spoon the bran flake mixture over and chill again until ready to serve.

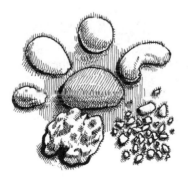

Mock Rum Babas

SERVES 6

100 g/4 oz/½ cup granulated sugar
150 ml/¼ pt/⅔ cup water
*30 ml/2 tbsp rum or water with rum
   essence (extract) to taste*
6 ring doughnuts
Whipped or aerosol cream, to decorate
Chopped pistachio nuts

Dissolve the sugar in the water. Boil for 5 minutes until syrupy. Stir in the rum. Prick the doughnuts all over with a skewer and place on a serving plate. Slowly spoon the syrup over the doughnuts and leave to soak well. Fill the centres with whipped cream and sprinkle with chopped pistachio nuts before serving.

No-effort Crumble

SERVES 4

*410 g/14½ oz/1 large can of fruit,
   drained, reserving the juice*
2 Weetabix
15 ml/1 tbsp light brown sugar
*50 g/2 oz/¼ cup butter or margarine,
   melted*
*2.5 ml/½ tsp ground ginger, cinnamon
   or mixed (apple-pie) spice*

Put the drained fruit in a 1 litre/1¾ pt/4¼ cup ovenproof dish. Crumble the cereal and mix with the sugar, butter or margarine and spice. Sprinkle over the fruit, pressing down lightly. Bake in a preheated oven at 190°C/375°F/gas mark 5 for about 15 minutes until crisp. Serve warm with the reserved juice.

Tropical Crumble

SERVES 4

*410 g/14½ oz/1 large can of fruit
    cocktail, drained, reserving the juice*
5 ml/1 tsp bottled lime juice (optional)
*100 g/4 oz/1 cup plain (all-purpose)
    flour*
2.5 ml/½ tsp ground ginger
50 g/2 oz/¼ cup butter, diced
50 g/2 oz/¼ cup light brown sugar
*50 g/2 oz/½ cup desiccated (shredded)
    coconut*
Cream, to serve

Put the fruit in the base of a shallow ovenproof dish. Sprinkle with the lime juice, if using. Sift the flour and ginger in a bowl. Add the butter and rub in with the fingertips. Stir in the sugar and coconut. Sprinkle over the fruit and press down lightly. Bake in a preheated oven at 180°C/350°F/gas mark 4 for about 25 minutes until golden brown and crisp. Serve warm with the reserved juice and cream.

Rhubarb and Ginger Crisp

SERVES 4

550 g/1¼ lb/1 very large can of rhubarb
20 g/¾ oz/3 tbsp cornflour (cornstarch)
25 g/1 oz/2 tbsp butter or margarine
8 ginger biscuits (cookies), crushed
170 g/6 oz/1 small can of cream
Light brown sugar, for sprinkling
*Crystallised (candied) ginger pieces, to
    decorate*

Drain the juice from the can of rhubarb into a saucepan. Whisk in the cornflour and add the margarine. Bring to the boil, stirring, until thickened. Cook for 2 minutes, then remove from the heat. Stir in the rhubarb and beat well until pulpy. Divide the crushed biscuits between four glass dishes. Spoon the rhubarb over and leave until cold. Spread the cream gently on top, sprinkle with sugar and chill. Decorate with crystallised ginger pieces just before serving.

Peach and Raisin Crisp

SERVES 6

*2 × 410 g/2 × 14½ oz/2 large cans of
    peach slices, drained, reserving the
    juice*
75 g/3 oz/½ cup raisins
25 g/1 oz/2 tbsp soft tub margarine
50 g/2 oz/½ cup plain (all-purpose) flour
100 g/4 oz/1 cup oat crunch cereal
*25 g/1 oz/2 tbsp caster (superfine)
    sugar*

Put the peaches in a 1.2 litre/2 pt/ 5 cup ovenproof dish. Sprinkle the raisins over. Work the margarine into the flour with a fork until the mixture resembles breadcrumbs. Stir in the cereal and sugar. Scatter over the fruit and press down lightly. Bake in a preheated oven at 190°C/375°F/gas mark 5 for about 35 minutes until crisp and golden. Serve warm with the reserved juice.

Rhubarb and Custard Charlotte

SERVES 4–5

25 g/1 oz/2 tbsp butter
4 slices of buttered bread
1 individual carton of custard
550 g/1¼ lb/1 very large can of rhubarb,
  drained, reserving the juice
30 ml/2 tbsp light brown sugar

Use a little of the butter to grease a 1.2 litre/2 pt/5 cup ovenproof dish. Line the dish with some of the bread. Spread the custard over the bread, then top with the rhubarb. Dice the remaining bread and scatter over. Sprinkle with the sugar. Bake in a preheated oven at 200°C/400°F/gas mark 6 for about 40 minutes until crisp and golden. Serve with the reserved juice.

The Canny Custard Tart

SERVES 4–6

20 cm/8 in ready-made pastry case
  (pie shell)
2 eggs
150 ml/¼ pt/⅔ cup milk
425 g/15 oz/1 large can of custard
25 g/1 oz/2 tbsp caster (superfine)
  sugar
Grated nutmeg

Put the pastry case on an ovenproof plate. Beat together the remaining ingredients except the nutmeg. Pour into the pastry case. Sprinkle with nutmeg and bake in a preheated oven at 190°C/375°F/gas mark 5 for about 40 minutes until set. Serve warm or cold.

No-fuss Bakewell-type Tart

SERVES 6

20 cm/8 in ready-made pastry case (pie
  shell)
30–45 ml/2–3 tbsp raspberry jam
  (conserve)
1 packet of sponge cake mix
Egg and water according to the packet
  directions
Almond essence (extract)
A few flaked (slivered) almonds
Cream or custard, to serve

Place the pastry case on an ovenproof plate. Spread the jam in the base. Make up the cake mix according to the packet directions and add a few drops of almond essence. Spread over the jam. Sprinkle with a few almonds. Bake in a preheated oven at 190°C/375°F/gas mark 5 for about 20–30 minutes until risen, golden brown and the centre springs back when lightly pressed. Serve warm with cream or custard.

Apricot Rice Sundae

SERVES 4

410 g/14½ oz/1 large can of apricot pie
  filling
425 g/15 oz/1 large can of rice pudding
170 g/6 oz/1 small can of cream
Toasted flaked (slivered) almonds, to
  decorate

Layer the apricot pie filling with the rice in four sundae dishes. Pipe or spoon the cream over and chill. Sprinkle with toasted flaked almonds before serving.

Coffee Nut Delight

SERVES 4

*1 packet of egg custard or crème
caramel mix*
*15 ml/1 tbsp instant coffee powder or
granules*
600 ml/1 pt/2½ cups milk
*150 ml/¼ pt/⅔ cup thick plain yoghurt
or fromage frais*
*1 small packet of peanut brittle (about
50 g/2 oz), crushed*

Whisk the egg custard or crème
caramel mix and the coffee into
the milk. Bring to the boil and boil for
2 minutes as directed. Allow to cool
slightly, then pour into a glass serving
dish. Leave to cool completely, then
chill until set. Spread the yoghurt or
fromage frais over the custard and
sprinkle with the crushed peanut brittle
just before serving.
  Note: if you use a crème caramel
mix, drizzle the caramel over the
yoghurt or fromage frais before topping
with the peanut brittle.

Black Forest Rice

SERVES 4

*410 g/14½ oz/1 large can of black
cherry pie filling*
*425 g/15 oz/1 large can of chocolate
rice pudding or plain rice pudding
with 45 ml/3 tbsp drinking
(sweetened) chocolate powder added*
170 g/6 oz/1 small can of cream
*Grated chocolate or drinking chocolate
powder, to decorate*

Layer the cherry pie filling with the
rice in four sundae dishes. Pipe or
spoon the cream over and chill. Sprinkle
with grated chocolate or dust with
drinking chocolate powder before
serving.

Apricot Yoghurt Jelly

SERVES 4

1 packet of orange-flavoured jelly (jello)
Boiling water
150 ml/¼ pt/⅔ cup apricot yoghurt
300 ml/11 oz/1 medium can of apricot
  halves, drained, reserving the juice

Break up the jelly and place in a measuring jug. Make up to 150 ml/ ¼ pt/⅔ cup with boiling water and stir until dissolved. Leave until cool, then stir in the apricot yoghurt. Make up to 600 ml/1 pt/2½ cups with the apricot juice. Turn into a wetted jelly (jello) mould or four individual glass dishes and chill until set. Turn out if in a mould. Decorate with the apricots and serve cold.

Orange Yoghurt Jelly

SERVES 4

Prepare as for Apricot Yoghurt Jelly, but substitute orange yoghurt for apricot and mandarin oranges for the apricots.

Blackcurrant Yoghurt Jelly

SERVES 4

Prepare as for Apricot Yoghurt Jelly, but substitute blackcurrant-flavoured jelly (jello) for orange, blackcurrant or blueberry yoghurt for the apricot. Use canned blackcurrants instead of apricots.

Jiffy Blackcurrant Mousse

SERVES 4

1 packet of blackcurrant-flavoured jelly
  (jello)
150 ml/¼ pt/⅔ cup boiling water
300 g/11 oz/1 medium can of
  blackcurrants, drained, reserving
  the juice
170 g/6 oz/1 small can of evaporated
  milk, chilled
170 g/6 oz/1 small can of cream

Dissolve the jelly in the boiling water. Stir in the juice from the can of blackcurrants and chill until on the point of setting. Meanwhile, whisk the chilled evaporated milk until thick and fluffy. When the jelly is the consistency of egg white, whisk in the fluffy milk. Turn into four glasses and chill until set. Spread the cream over and top with the blackcurrants.

Jiffy Mandarin Mousse

SERVES 4

Prepare as for Jiffy Blackcurrant Mousse, but use an orange- or tangerine-flavoured jelly (jello) and a can of mandarin oranges.

Dreamy Orange Mousse

SERVES 4

1 packet of orange-flavoured jelly (jello)
170 g/6 oz/1 small can of evaporated
* milk, chilled*
1 sachet of Dream Topping mix
150 ml/¼ pt/⅔ cup cold milk
1 orange, all pith and rind removed,
* sliced and chopped*

Break up the jelly and place in measuring jug. Make up to 300 ml/ ½ pt/1¼ cups with boiling water. Stir until dissolved. Leave to cool. Whisk the evaporated milk until thick and fluffy. Gradually whisk into the jelly when on the point of setting. Pour into four glasses. Chill until set. Make up the Dream Topping with the milk according to the packet directions. Fold in the chopped orange. Pile on to the mousses and serve immediately.

Marbled Mocha Delight

SERVES 6

1 chocolate Swiss (jelly) roll
450 ml/¾ pt/2 cups cold milk
10 ml/2 tsp instant coffee powder or
* granules*
1 sachet of chocolate-flavoured dessert
* whip*
150 ml/¼ pt/⅔ cup UHT (long-life)
* whipping cream*
Instant coffee or drinking chocolate
* (sweetened chocolate) powder, for*
* dusting*

Slice the Swiss roll and place in six individual glass serving dishes. Pour the milk into a cold bowl. Add the coffee and stir until dissolved. Whisk in the dessert whip until thick. Whip the cream until peaking. Fold into the dessert whip to give a marbled effect. Spoon into the dishes. Chill until set. Dust with a little coffee or drinking chocolate powder before serving.

Mandarin Custard Crunch

SERVES 4

50 g/2 oz/¼ cup butter or margarine
175 g/6 oz/3 cups fresh white or
* wholemeal breadcrumbs*
25 g/1 oz/2 tbsp light brown sugar
425 g/15 oz/1 large can of custard
170 g/6 oz/1 small can of cream
300 g/11 oz/1 medium can of mandarin
* oranges, drained*
Toasted flaked (slivered) almonds
* (optional), to decorate*

Melt the butter or margarine in a large frying pan (skillet). Stir in the breadcrumbs and sugar and cook, stirring, until golden. Turn out on to a piece of kitchen paper (paper towel). Empty the custard into a bowl and gently fold in the cream to give a marbled effect. Divide a third of the crumbs between four sundae glasses. Top with half the custard, then half the mandarins. Repeat the layers and scatter a few toasted flaked almonds over to decorate, if liked. Serve straight away.

The Easiest Strawberry Cheesecake

SERVES 6

23 cm/9 in sponge flan case
200 g/7 oz/scant 1 cup medium-fat soft
  cheese
50 g/2 oz/¼ cup caster (superfine) sugar
2.5 ml/½ tsp vanilla essence (extract)
150 ml/¼ pt/⅔ cup UHT (long-life)
  whipping cream, whipped
410 g/14½ oz/1 large can of strawberry
  pie filling

Put the flan case (pie shell) on a serving plate. Beat the cheese with the sugar and vanilla essence. Fold in the whipped cream. Turn into the flan case and chill until fairly firm. Spread the strawberry pie filling over before serving.

Luxury Blackcurrant Cheesecake

SERVES 6

Prepare as for The Easiest Strawberry Cheesecake, but spread the base of the flan case (pie shell) with blackcurrant jam and top the cheese mixture with a can of blackcurrant pie filling. Decorate with swirls of canned or aerosol cream just before serving.

Simplicity Lemon Cheesecake

SERVES 6

Prepare as for The Easiest Strawberry Cheesecake, but spread the base of the flan case (pie shell) thickly with lemon curd. Decorate the top with aerosol cream and crystallised (candied) lemon slices before serving.

Simplicity Orange Cheesecake

SERVES 6

Prepare as for The Easiest Strawberry Cheesecake, but spread the base of the flan case (pie shell) thickly with orange curd. Decorate the top with aerosol cream and crystallised (candied) orange slices just before serving.

Golden Fruit Cobbler

SERVES 4–6

410 g/14½ oz/1 large can of fruit pie
  filling
5 scones (biscuits), halved and buttered
25 g/1 oz/2 tbsp light brown sugar
Cream or custard, to serve

Put the pie filling in a 1.2 litre/2 pt/5 cup flameproof serving dish and heat gently, stirring. Arrange the halved scones, buttered-sides up, all round the top edge of the dish and sprinkle liberally with the sugar. Place under a hot grill (broiler) for about 4 minutes until the scones are golden brown and the sugar has caramelised. Serve hot with cream or custard.

Blackberry and Apple Meringue Flan

SERVES 4–6

20 cm/8 in sponge flan case
2 eggs, separated
410 g/14½ oz/1 large can of blackberry
and apple pie filling
100 g/4 oz/¼ cup caster (superfine)
sugar

Put the flan case (pie shell) on an ovenproof serving plate. Whisk the egg yolks into the pie filling and turn into the flan case. Whisk the egg whites until stiff. Whisk in half the sugar and fold in the remainder. Pile on top of the flan and bake in a preheated oven at 190°C/375°F/gas mark 5 for about 10–15 minutes until just turning colour. Serve warm.

Apricot Meringue Flan

SERVES 4–6

Prepare as for Blackberry and Apple Meringue Flan, but use apricot pie filling and decorate the meringue mixture with a few flaked (slivered) almonds, if liked, before baking.

Strawberry and Orange Meringue Flan

SERVES 4–6

Prepare as for Blackberry and Apple Meringue Flan, but mix 300 g/ 11 oz/1 medium can of mandarin oranges, drained, with a strawberry pie filling and then continue as before.

Muesli Munch

SERVES 4

410 g/14 oz/1 large can of apple pie
filling
100 g/4 oz/1 cup muesli
1.5 ml/¼ tsp mixed (apple-pie) spice
30 ml/2 tbsp clear honey
Evaporated milk, to serve

Empty the pie filling into a 900 ml/ 1½ pt/3¾ cup ovenproof dish. Mix the muesli with the mixed spice and honey. Spoon over the pie filling and bake in a preheated oven at 190°C/ 375°F/gas mark 5 for 15–20 minutes until golden and bubbling. Serve warm with evaporated milk.

Thatched Roof

SERVES 4

410 g/14 oz/1 large can of apricot pie
filling
50 g/2 oz/¼ cup butter or margarine
15 ml/1 tbsp golden (light corn) syrup
2.5 ml/½ tsp ground mace or cinnamon
3 shredded wheat cereal biscuits,
crumbled
Vanilla ice cream, to serve

Empty the pie filling into a 900 ml/ 1½ pt/3¾ cup ovenproof dish. Melt the butter or margarine in a saucepan with the syrup and mace or cinnamon. Stir in the cereal. Spoon over the pie filling and bake in a preheated oven at 200°C/400°F/gas mark 6 for about 25 minutes until golden and crisp on top. Serve hot with Vanilla Ice Cream.

Swiss Torte

SERVES 6

Oil, for greasing
4 chocolate mini Swiss (jelly) rolls
15 ml/1 tbsp powdered gelatine
30 ml/2 tbsp water
5 ml/1 tsp instant coffee powder
425 g/15 oz/1 large can of custard
45 ml/3 tbsp drinking (sweetened)
  chocolate powder
1 sachet of Dream Topping mix
150 ml/¼ pt/⅔ cup cold milk
25 g/1 oz/¼ cup plain (semi-sweet)
  chocolate, melted

Lightly oil a 15 cm/6 in deep, round loose-bottomed cake tin (pan). Cut the ends off the Swiss rolls and chop. Put to one side. Cut each roll length-ways into four slices. Arrange the slices all round the sides of the prepared tin. Sprinkle the gelatine over the water and coffee in a small bowl and leave to soften for 5 minutes. Stand the bowl in a pan of hot water and stir until completely dissolved (or heat briefly in the microwave). Remove from the pan. Stir into the custard with the drinking chocolate. Leave until on the point of setting. Make up the Dream Topping with the cold milk. Fold into the just-setting custard. Turn into the prepared tin. Scatter the chopped Swiss roll on top and drizzle with the melted chocolate. Chill until set. Remove from the tin and serve cold.

Swiss Baked Alaska

SERVES 4–6

1 small raspberry jam- (conserve-) filled
  Swiss (jelly) roll
3 egg whites
175 g/6 oz/¾ cup caster (superfine)
  sugar
8 scoops of raspberry ripple ice cream
3 glacé (candied) cherries, halved
6 angelica leaves

Slice the Swiss roll and place in a single layer on an ovenproof plate. Whisk the egg whites until stiff. Whisk in half the sugar and continue whisking until stiff and glossy. Fold in the remaining sugar. Pile the ice cream up in the centre of the Swiss roll. Cover completely with the meringue mixture and decorate with the cherries and angelica leaves. Bake immediately in a preheated oven at 230°C/450°F/gas mark 8 for 2 minutes until the meringue is turning pale golden. Serve immediately.

Rhubarb Cremolo

SERVES 6

550 g/1¼ lb/1 very large can of rhubarb, drained, reserving the syrup
1 packet of strawberry-flavoured jelly (jello)
170 g/6 oz/1 small can of evaporated milk
Whipped or aerosol cream and chopped pistachios, to decorate

Put the rhubarb syrup in a saucepan. Break up the jelly and add to the pan. Heat gently, stirring, until dissolved. (Or place the syrup and jelly in a bowl and microwave briefly, then stir to dissolve.) Pass the rhubarb through a sieve (strainer) or purée in a blender or food processor. Blend the jelly with the evaporated milk, then stir in the rhubarb. Turn into six sundae dishes and chill until set. Decorate with whipped cream and chopped pistachios before serving.

Doughnut Squares

SERVES 4–6

1 small white uncut loaf, crusts removed
300 ml/½ pt/1¼ cups apple juice
2 eggs, beaten
Oil, for deep-frying
50 g/2 oz/½ cup caster (superfine) sugar
2.5 ml/½ tsp ground cinnamon
Warmed raspberry jam (conserve), to serve

Cut the loaf into large cubes. Dip first in apple juice, then in beaten egg to coat completely. Deep-fry in hot oil until crisp and golden brown. Drain on kitchen paper (paper towels). Mix together the caster sugar and cinnamon and toss the cubes in this. Serve with warm raspberry jam drizzled over.

Ginger Mould

SERVES 4

1 packet of lemon-flavoured jelly (jello)
Boiling water
150 ml/¼ pt/1 individual carton of
*   custard*
170 g/6 oz/1 small can of cream
3 pieces of stem ginger in syrup,
*   chopped*
4 glacé (candied) cherries, chopped
1 small piece of angelica, chopped

Break up the jelly and place in a measuring jug. Add boiling water to make up to 150 ml/¼ pt/⅔ cup. Stir until dissolved. Make up to 450 ml/¾ pt/2 cups with cold water. Stir well and leave until the consistency of egg white. Whisk in the custard, cream, ginger, cherries and angelica. Turn into a wetted 750 ml/1¼ pt/3 cup jelly (jello) mould and chill until set. Turn out on to a serving plate just before serving.

Fast Sweet Pizza

SERVES 4–6

20 cm/8 in ready-made pizza base
400 g/14 oz/1 large can of custard
410 g/14½ oz/1 large can of any fruit,
*   drained, reserving the juice*
45 ml/3 tbsp apricot jam (conserve)
1 glacé (candied) cherry
Aerosol cream, to serve

Put the pizza base on a baking (cookie) sheet and spread with the custard. Bake in a preheated oven at 180°C/250°F/gas mark 4 for about 10 minutes until cooked through. Leave to cool, then decorate with the drained fruit. Melt the jam with 30 ml/2 tbsp of the reserved juice in a saucepan. Brush all over the top of the pizza and flash under a hot grill (broiler) until beginning to brown. Top with the cherry and serve straight away with aerosol cream.

Fruity Nut Dip

SERVES 4

2 large oranges
1 small carton of hazelnut (filbert)
* yoghurt*
15 ml/1 tbsp toasted chopped hazelnuts
4 fruit and nut chewy cereal bars

Halve the oranges and scoop out all the flesh, using a serrated-edged knife. Trim the bases of the shells so they stand firm. Chop the orange flesh, discarding any really tough bits of membrane. Place in a bowl and stir in the yoghurt. Spoon into the oranges, then sprinkle with the nuts. Place on four serving plates. Cut the chewy bars into cubes and arrange around with a small fork or cocktail sticks (toothpicks) to spear the bars, then use to dip into the yoghurt and orange mixture. Serve with a small spoon to eat any remaining dip.

Almost Tiramisu

SERVES 6

4 trifle sponges
150 ml/¼ pt/⅔ cup strong black coffee
1 packet of egg custard or crème
* caramel mix*
450 ml/¾ pt/2 cups milk
15–30 ml/1–2 tbsp brandy or coffee
* liqueur*
150 ml/¼ pt/⅔ cup double (heavy) or
* whipping cream, whipped*
15 ml/1 tbsp drinking (sweetened)
* chocolate powder*

Break up the sponges and place in a shallow, round dish. Add the coffee and leave to soak. Make up the egg custard or crème caramel with the milk according to the packet directions and leave to cool slightly. Stir in the brandy or liqueur. Gently pour over the sponge, leave until cold, then chill until set. Spread the whipped cream over and dust with drinking chocolate before serving.
Note: if you use a crème caramel mix, reserve the sachet of caramel. Drizzle over sliced bananas and fromage frais or plain yoghurt for another dessert.

Drizzles, Dollops and Smothers

When you're serving up such sensational puddings, you may want to add that finishing touch – a luscious sauce, flavoured cream or other suitable sweet topping such as Brandy Butter with your Christmas pud or mince pies. Many of the recipes suggest an accompaniment from this chapter but you can also use them to brighten up any plain cake or fresh or stewed fruit.

Lemon Honey Sauce

SERVES 4

60 ml/4 tbsp clear honey
Grated rind and juice of 1 lemon

Mix together and heat gently, stirring, until hot and blended. Serve hot.

Hot Honey Sauce

SERVES 4

15 g/½ oz/2 tbsp cornflour (cornstarch)
300 ml/½ pt/1¼ cups milk
15–30 ml/1–2 tbsp clear honey

Blend the cornflour with a little of the milk in a saucepan. Blend in the remaining milk. Add half the honey and bring to the boil, stirring. Cook for 2 minutes, stirring all the time. Taste and add more honey, if liked. Serve hot.

St Clement's Butter Sauce

SERVES 8

Thinly pared rind and juice of 2 oranges
Thinly pared rind and juice of 1 lemon
100 g/4 oz/½ cup granulated sugar
100 g/4 oz/½ cup unsalted (sweet) butter

Put the fruit rinds in a saucepan. Make the juice up to 600 ml/1 pt/ 2½ cups with water and add to the pan. Add the sugar and stir over a gentle heat until the sugar has dissolved completely. Bring to the boil and boil rapidly until the syrup has thickened and reduced but is not coloured. Lift out the fruit rinds with a draining spoon and discard. Whisk the butter into the sauce, a knob at a time, until thickened and smooth. Serve hot.

Hot Lemon Sauce

SERVES 4–6

15 g/½ oz/2 tbsp cornflour (cornstarch)
25 g/1 oz/2 tbsp caster (superfine) sugar
300 ml/½ pt/1¼ cups water
Juice of 2 lemons

Blend the cornflour and sugar with a little of the water in a saucepan. Add the remaining water and the lemon juice. Bring to the boil and cook for 2 minutes, stirring, until thickened and clear. Serve hot.

Peanut Butter Sauce

SERVES 6

100 g/4 oz/½ cup butter
100 g/4 oz/1 cup toasted peanuts
50 g/2 oz/¼ cup light brown sugar
90 ml/6 tbsp thick honey
Finely grated rind and juice of 1 small lemon
15 ml/1 tbsp milk

Put all the ingredients together in a saucepan. Heat gently, stirring, until well blended. Serve hot over ice cream.

Chocolate Caramel Sauce

SERVES 4–6

2 Mars Bars or similar
60 ml/4 tbsp milk
A small knob of butter

Break up the chocolate bars in a saucepan. Add the milk and butter and heat, stirring until melted and thick. Add a little more milk, if liked. Spoon over ice cream and serve immediately.

Syrup Sauce

SERVES 4

90 ml/6 tbsp golden (light corn) syrup
30 ml/2 tbsp lemon juice

Heat the syrup and lemon juice in a saucepan until hot but not boiling. Serve hot.

Maple Syrup Sauce

SERVES 4

Prepare as for Syrup Sauce, but substitute maple syrup for golden (light corn) syrup. Serve over pancakes.

Maple Pecan Sauce

SERVES 4

Prepare as for Maple Sauce, but add 30 ml/2 tbsp finely chopped pecan nuts to the mixture.

Apricot Jam Sauce

SERVES 4-6

60 ml/4 tbsp apricot jam (conserve),
  finely chopped if necessary
30 ml/2 tbsp caster (superfine) sugar
Finely grated rind and juice of ½ lemon
75 ml/5 tbsp water

Blend all the ingredients in a saucepan and heat gently, stirring, until the sugar has dissolved. Simmer for 3 minutes. Serve hot.

Strawberry Jam Sauce

SERVES 4-6

Prepare as for Apricot Jam Sauce, but substitute strawberry jam (conserve) for apricot.

Raspberry Jam Sauce

SERVES 4-6

Prepare as for Apricot Jam Sauce, but substitute sieved (strained) raspberry jam (conserve) for apricot, or use seedless raspberry jelly (clear conserve).

Blackcurrant Jam Sauce

SERVES 4-6

Prepare as for Apricot Jam Sauce, but substitute blackcurrant jam (conserve) for apricot and use the finely grated rind and juice of ½ orange instead of the lemon juice.

Marmalade Sauce

SERVES 4-6

Prepare as for Apricot Jam Sauce, but substitute marmalade for the jam (conserve) and flavour with the finely grated rind and juice of ¼ lemon and ½ orange and use only 60 ml/4 tbsp water.

Plum Jam Sauce

SERVES 4–6

Prepare as for Apricot Jam Sauce (see page 347), but substitute sieved (strained) plum jam (conserve) for apricot jam and use the finely grated rind and juice of ½ orange instead of lemon.

Fresh Raspberry Sauce

SERVES 4–6

225 g/8 oz raspberries
25 g/1 oz/3 tbsp icing (confectioners')
  sugar
15 ml/1 tbsp lemon juice

Purée the raspberries with the sugar and lemon juice in a blender or food processor. Pass through a sieve (strainer) to remove the seeds. Use as required.

Raspberry Jelly Sauce

SERVES 6

1 packet of raspberry-flavoured jelly
  (jello)
30 ml/2 tbsp redcurrant jelly (clear
  conserve)
200 ml/7 fl oz/scant 1 cup water
5 ml/1 tsp arrowroot

Break up the jelly and place in a saucepan with the redcurrant jelly and most of the water. Heat gently, stirring, until dissolved. Blend the arrowroot with the remaining water and stir into the mixture until slightly thickened and clear. Serve hot.

All-year Raspberry Sauce

SERVES 4–6

390 g/13½ oz/1 large can of raspberries
10 ml/2 tsp cornflour (cornstarch)

Purée the raspberries and their juice in a blender or food processor. Pass through a sieve (strainer), if liked, to remove the seeds. Blend a little of the purée with the cornflour in a saucepan. Stir in the remainder. Bring to the boil and cook for 2 minutes, stirring, until thickened and clear. Serve hot or cover with a circle of wetted greaseproof (waxed) paper and leave to cool.

Fresh Apricot Sauce

SERVES 4–6

450 g/1 lb ripe apricots, halved and
  stoned (pitted)
150 ml/¼ pt/⅔ cup sweet white wine
50 g/2 oz/¼ cup granulated sugar
Finely grated rind of ½ lemon
30 ml/2 tbsp kirsch

Put the apricots in a saucepan with the wine, sugar and lemon rind. Heat gently until the sugar melts, then boil for 4 minutes. Purée in a blender or food processor, then stir in the kirsch. Serve warm or cold.

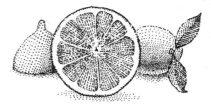

Brandied Loganberry Sauce

SERVES 4–6

225 g/8 oz fresh or frozen loganberries
45 ml/3 tbsp brandy
15 ml/1 tbsp water
Icing (confectioners') sugar

Gently stew the loganberries in the brandy and water for about 8 minutes. Purée in a blender or food processor, then pass through a sieve (strainer) to remove the seeds. Sweeten to taste with sifted icing sugar and serve cold.

Apple and Strawberry Sauce

SERVES 6

450 g/1 lb cooking (tart) apples, sliced
60 ml/4 tbsp strawberry jam (conserve)
15 ml/1 tbsp water
5 ml/1 tsp lemon juice
Caster (superfine) sugar

Simmer together all the ingredients except the sugar in a covered saucepan until the apple is pulpy. Pass through a sieve (strainer) or purée in a blender or food processor. Return to the pan and sweeten to taste with caster sugar. Serve hot.

Smooth Strawberry Sauce

SERVES 4–6

225 g/8 oz strawberries, quartered
15 ml/1 tbsp crème de cassis or
*   blackcurrant cordial*
15 ml/1 tbsp icing (confectioners')
*   sugar*
A few drops of vanilla essence (extract)

Put all the ingredients in a blender or food processor. Purée until smooth. Chill until ready to serve.

Greengage Sauce

SERVES 4

Prepare as for Fresh Apricot Sauce, but substitute greengages for the apricots and sweeten with honey instead of sugar, if preferred.

Red Plum Sauce

SERVES 4

Prepare as for Fresh Apricot Sauce, but substitute ripe red plums for the apricots.

Smooth Cherry Sauce

SERVES 4

Prepare as for Fresh Apricot Sauce, but substitute ripe cherries for the apricots and use port instead of sweet white wine.

Fudge Sauce

SERVES 4–6

75 g/3 oz/⅓ cup light brown sugar
30 ml/2 tbsp golden (light corn) syrup
300 ml/½ pt/1¼ cups single (light) cream
50 g/2 oz/¼ cup unsalted (sweet) butter
2.5 ml/½ tsp vanilla essence (extract)
10 ml/2 tsp arrowroot
15 ml/1 tbsp milk

Put the sugar and syrup in a saucepan and heat very gently until the sugar has melted. Bring to the boil and boil for 2 minutes. Put the cream and butter in a separate pan with the vanilla essence. Heat until the butter melts. Pour on to the caramel mixture, then stir until the caramel has melted. Blend the arrowroot with the milk, then stir into the cream mixture. Cook, stirring, for 1 minute until thickened. Serve straight away.

Orange Sauce

SERVES 4

Finely grated rind and juice of 1 orange
Juice of 1 lemon
15 ml/1 tbsp arrowroot
Caster (superfine) sugar

Make the fruit rind and juices up to 300 ml/½ pt/1¼ cups with water. Blend a little with the arrowroot in a saucepan, then stir in the remainder. Bring to the boil, stirring all the time, until thickened and clear. Sweeten to taste with caster sugar. Serve hot.

Pineapple and Orange Sauce

SERVES 6

300 g/11 oz/1 medium can of crushed
  pineapple
10 ml/2 tsp arrowroot
150 ml/¼ pt/⅔ cup pure orange juice

Put the contents of the can of pineapple in a saucepan. Blend the arrowroot with a little of the orange juice and add to the pan with the remaining orange juice. Bring to the boil and cook for 2 minutes, stirring until thickened and clear. Serve hot.

Jewelled Pineapple Sauce

SERVES 4–6

300 g/11 oz/1 medium can of crushed
  pineapple
25 g/1 oz/2 tbsp caster (superfine)
  sugar
25 g/1 oz/¼ cup glacé (candied) cherries,
  chopped
30 ml/2 tbsp chopped angelica
15 ml/1 tbsp currants
10 ml/2 tsp cornflour (cornstarch)
60 ml/4 tbsp water
Finely grated rind and juice of 1 lemon
  or lime

Put the contents of the can of pineapple in a saucepan and add the sugar, cherries, angelica and currants. Blend the cornflour with the water and add to the pan with the lemon or lime rind and juice. Bring to the boil and cook, stirring, for 2 minutes. Serve hot over ice cream.

Butterscotch Sauce

SERVES 4

25 g/1 oz/2 tbsp butter
100 g/4 oz/½ cup light brown sugar
15 ml/1 tbsp cornflour (cornstarch)
150 ml/¼ pt/⅔ cup milk
2.5 ml/½ tsp vanilla essence (extract)

Put the butter and sugar in a
saucepan and heat gently until the
sugar has melted. Boil for 1 minute.
Blend the cornflour with a little of the
milk. Stir the remaining milk into the
sugar and butter and bring to the boil,
stirring. Pour over the cornflour,
stirring. Return to the pan and bring to
the boil. Cook for 2 minutes, stirring all
the time. Stir in the vanilla essence.
Serve hot.

Real Caramel Sauce

SERVES 4

175 g/6 oz/¾ cup granulated sugar
65 ml/2½ oz/4½ tbsp cold water
150 ml/¼ pt/⅔ cup lukewarm water

Put the sugar and cold water in a
saucepan and heat gently, stirring,
until the sugar has dissolved. Bring to
the boil rapidly until the mixture is a
rich brown colour (but not burnt!).
Remove from the heat and pour in the
warm water (take care as it may
splutter). Return to the heat and stir
until the caramel melts, then boil
rapidly until syrupy. Leave to cool. If
the mixture is too thick when cooled,
stir in a little warm water.

Milk Chocolate Honey Sauce

SERVES 4

75 g/3 oz/¾ cup milk chocolate
45 ml/3 tbsp clear honey

Melt together in a small saucepan,
stirring. Serve hot over ice cream.

Simple Chocolate Sauce

SERVES 4

100 g/4 oz/1 cup plain (semi-sweet)
  chocolate
50 g/2 oz/¼ cup light brown sugar
150 ml/¼ pt/⅔ cup water
25 g/1 oz/2 tbsp butter

Break up the chocolate and place in a
pan with the sugar and water. Heat
gently, stirring, until the chocolate has
melted. Boil rapidly until the mixture
thickens and forms a pouring
consistency. Gradually beat in the butter
until glossy. Serve hot or cold.

Belgian Chocolate Sauce

SERVES 4-6

175 g/6 oz/1½ cups bitter Belgian
  chocolate
300 ml/½ pt/1¼ cups water
75 g/3 oz/⅓ cup granulated sugar

Break up the chocolate and put in a
saucepan with the water. Heat until
the chocolate melts, then stir in the
sugar until dissolved. Simmer until the
sauce is syrupy and coats the back of a
spoon. Serve cold.

Melting Chocolate Sauce

SERVES 4–6

175 g/6 oz/1½ cups plain (semi-sweet)
  chocolate
15 g/½ oz/1 tbsp butter
15 ml/1 tbsp golden (light corn) syrup
45 ml/3 tbsp single (light) cream

Melt the chocolate in a small bowl over a pan of hot water. Stir in the butter and syrup and stir for 2–3 minutes until the butter has melted and the mixture is thick. Do not allow the water to boil. Remove from the heat and stir in the cream. Beat well and serve hot.

Brandied Raisin Topping

SERVES 8–10

350 g/12 oz/2 cups large stoned (pitted)
  raisins (not the small seedless kind)
450 ml/¾ pt/2 cups water
120 ml/4 fl oz/½ cup brandy
50 g/2 oz/¼ cup light brown sugar
Coarsely grated rind of 1 orange
Coarsely grated rind of 1 lemon

Put the raisins in a bowl with the water and brandy. Leave to soak for 12 hours or overnight. Place in a saucepan with the sugar and orange and lemon rinds. Bring to the boil, reduce the heat and simmer for 20 minutes until syrupy. Leave until cold. Store in a screw-topped jar in the fridge for up to 3 weeks. Serve over ice cream.

Hot Banana Sauce

SERVES 4

Finely grated rind and juice of 1 lemon
25 g/1 oz/2 tbsp caster (superfine)
  sugar
1 large banana, mashed
10 ml/2 tsp arrowroot
15 ml/1 tbsp amaretto

Make the lemon rind and juice up to 250 ml/8 fl oz/1 cup with water. Place in a saucepan with the sugar. Heat gently, stirring, until the sugar dissolves, then bring to the boil and boil for 3 minutes. Stir in the banana. Purée in a blender or food processor and return to the pan. Blend the arrowroot with the amaretto and stir into the pan. Bring to the boil, stirring, until thickened. Serve hot.

White Rum Sauce

SERVES 4–6

25 g/1 oz/2 tbsp granulated sugar
120 ml/4 fl oz/½ cup water
Grated rind of ½ lemon
25 g/1 oz/2 tbsp unsalted (sweet) butter
5 ml/1 tsp cornflour (cornstarch)
120 ml/4 fl oz/½ cup white rum

Put the sugar, water and lemon rind in a saucepan. Heat gently, stirring, until the sugar dissolves. Whisk in the butter. Blend the cornflour with the rum and stir into the sauce. Boil for 2 minutes, stirring all the time. Serve hot.

Red Wine Sauce

SERVES 4

15 ml/1 tbsp caster (superfine) sugar
150 ml/¼ pt/⅔ cup water
30 ml/2 tbsp redcurrant jelly (clear
    conserve)
Thinly pared rind of ½ lemon
5 ml/1 tsp arrowroot
45 ml/3 tbsp red wine

Put the sugar, water, redcurrant jelly
and lemon rind in a saucepan.
Simmer gently for 5 minutes. Blend the
arrowroot with the wine and stir into
the sauce. Bring to the boil and cook for
1 minute, stirring all the time. Serve hot
with steamed sponge puddings or plain
poached fruit.

Amaretto Sauce

SERVES 4–6

300 ml/½ pt/1¼ cups milk
30 ml/2 tbsp cornflour (cornstarch)
25 g/1 oz/2 tbsp unsalted (sweet) butter
30 ml/2 tbsp caster (superfine) sugar
15–30 ml/1–2 tbsp amaretto

Blend a little of the milk with the
cornflour in a saucepan. Add the
remaining milk. Bring to the boil and
cook for 2 minutes, stirring. Stir in the
butter and sugar, then add the amaretto
to taste. Serve hot.

Gaelic Coffee Sauce

SERVES 4

225 g/8 oz/1 cup granulated sugar
75 ml/5 tbsp water
300 ml/½ pt/1¼ cups strong black coffee
30 ml/2 tbsp Scotch whisky
30 ml/2 tbsp double (heavy) cream

Put the sugar and water in a heavy-
based saucepan. Heat gently,
stirring, until the sugar has dissolved.
Bring to the boil and boil rapidly
without stirring until the mixture turns
pale golden brown. Remove from the
heat and pour in the coffee (be careful
as the mixture will spit). Return to the
heat and heat, stirring, until the caramel
has dissolved. Allow to cool slightly,
then stir in the cream. Serve over ice
cream.

Cold Sabayon

SERVES 4–6

50 g/2 oz/¼ cup granulated sugar
60 ml/4 tbsp water
2 egg yolks
Finely grated rind and juice of ½ lemon
15 ml/1 tbsp sherry or dry vermouth
45 ml/3 tbsp double (heavy) cream

Dissolve the sugar in the water over
a gentle heat, stirring. Bring to the
boil and boil until thickened but not
coloured. Meanwhile, whisk the egg
yolks in a bowl. Gradually pour on the
syrup in a thin stream, whisking all the
time, until foamy. Whisk in the lemon
rind and juice and the sherry or
vermouth. Whisk the cream until
peaking and fold into the mixture. Chill
until ready to serve.

Hot Sabayon

SERVES 4

3 egg yolks
15 ml/1 tbsp caster (superfine) sugar
150 ml/¼ pt/⅔ cup Marsala
1.5 ml/¼ tsp vanilla essence (extract)

Put all the ingredients in a saucepan and whisk over a gentle heat with an electric beater until thick and frothy. Do not boil. Serve immediately.

Classic Custard Sauce

SERVES 4

300 ml/½ pt/1¼ cups milk
½ vanilla pod
15 ml/1 tbsp caster (superfine) sugar
2 egg yolks

Put the milk in a saucepan with the vanilla pod. Bring to the boil and leave to infuse for 10 minutes. Remove the vanilla pod and stir in the sugar. Bring almost to the boil. Whisk the egg yolks in a basin. Whisk in the hot milk, then strain back into the saucepan. Heat gently, stirring all the time with a wooden spoon, until the mixture is thick enough to coat the back of the spoon. Test by lifting the spoon out of the custard and drawing a finger through the mixture on the spoon: if it leaves a clear line, the sauce is ready. Do not allow the mixture to boil or the custard will curdle. Serve hot or sprinkle with a little extra caster sugar to prevent a skin forming and leave until cold.

Easy Custard

SERVES 4

300 ml/½ pt/1¼ cups milk
15 ml/1 tbsp cornflour (cornstarch)
15 ml/1 tbsp caster (superfine) sugar
2.5 ml/½ tsp vanilla essence (extract)
2 egg yolks

Blend a little of the milk with the cornflour in a saucepan. Stir in the remaining milk, the sugar and vanilla essence. Bring to the boil, stirring, until thickened. Whisk in the egg yolks and cook for 1 minute, stirring. Serve hot or cover with a piece of wet greaseproof (waxed) paper and leave until cold.

Foamy Custard

SERVES 4

Prepare as for Easy Custard, but whisk the egg whites from the 2 egg yolks until stiff and fold into the made custard before serving.

Almond Foam

SERVES 4

Prepare as for Foamy Custard, but whisk 25 g/1 oz/¼ cup ground almonds into the mixture before cooking and flavour with almond essence (extract) instead of vanilla.

Sweet Orange Custard

SERVES 4–6

Prepare as for Easy Custard, but add the finely grated rind of 1 orange to the milk and omit the vanilla.

Sweet Lemon Custard

SERVES 4–6

Prepare as for Easy Custard, but add the finely grated rind of 1 lemon with the milk and omit the vanilla.

Chocolate Custard

SERVES 4–8

Prepare as for Easy Custard, but blend 15 ml/1 tbsp cocoa (unsweetened chocolate) powder with the cornflour and use only 1 egg yolk.

Coffee Custard

SERVES 4–6

Prepare as for Easy Custard, but blend 10 ml/2 tsp instant coffee powder or granules with the milk.

Mint Custard

SERVES 4–6

Prepare as for Easy Custard, but add a few drops of green food colouring and peppermint essence (extract) to taste. Omit the vanilla.

Cointreau Custard

SERVES 4–6

Prepare as for Easy Custard, but add 15–30 ml/1–2 tbsp Cointreau and the finely grated rind of ½ orange to the sauce. Omit the vanilla.

Instant Chocolate Custard

SERVES 4–6

425 g/15 oz/1 large can of custard
45 ml/3 tbsp chocolate spread

Empty the custard into a saucepan. Whisk in the chocolate spread and heat until almost boiling. Pour into a jug and serve hot.

Sweet White Sauce

SERVES 4

15 g/½ oz/2 tbsp cornflour (cornstarch)
300 ml/½ pt/1¼ cups milk
30 ml/2 tbsp caster (superfine) sugar
A few drops of vanilla essence (extract)
A knob of unsalted (sweet) butter (optional)

Blend the cornflour with a little of the milk in a saucepan. Add the remaining milk and the sugar. Bring to the boil and cook for 2 minutes, stirring all the time until thickened and smooth. Stir in the vanilla essence to taste. Beat in the butter, if using.

Dark Rum Sauce

SERVES 4–6

20 g/¾ oz/3 tbsp cornflour (cornstarch)
25 g/1 oz/2 tbsp dark brown sugar
300 ml/½ pt/1¼ cups milk
30 ml/2 tbsp dark rum

Blend the cornflour with the sugar and a little of the milk in a saucepan. Stir in the remaining milk. Bring to the boil and cook for 2 minutes, stirring. Blend in the rum. Pour into a warmed sauce boat and serve.

Brandy Sauce

SERVES 4–6

Prepare as for Dark Rum Sauce, but substitute caster (superfine) sugar for the dark brown sugar and brandy for the rum.

German Dessert Sauce

SERVES 4

1 egg
10 ml/2 tsp caster (superfine) sugar
150 ml/¼ pt/⅔ cup sweet sherry or
*   Marsala*
Thinly pared rind of ½ lemon

Put all the ingredients in a basin over a pan of hot water. Whisk with an electric beater until the sauce is foamy. Do not allow to boil. If the mixture is becoming too hot, remove the bowl from the pan and whisk to cool. Remove the lemon rind and serve straight away.

Mousseline Sauce

SERVES 4

1 egg
1 egg yolk
40 g/1½ oz/3 tbsp caster (superfine)
*   sugar*
30 ml/2 tbsp pure orange juice

Put all the ingredients in a bowl over a pan of hot water and whisk with an electric beater until thick and frothy. Serve immediately with steamed sponge puddings.

Christmas Ice Cream Topping

SERVES 4

60 ml/4 tbsp mincemeat
10 ml/2 tsp brandy

Either melt gently in a saucepan or in the microwave until just pourable. Serve immediately over vanilla ice cream.

Nut and Raisin Topping

SERVES 4

50 g/2 oz/1 small packet of mixed nuts
*   and raisins, chopped*
60 ml/4 tbsp maple syrup

Warm together in a saucepan or in a bowl in the microwave. Spoon over ice cream and serve immediately.

Lemon Topping

SERVES 4

75 ml/5 tbsp lemon curd
30 ml/2 tbsp apple juice
Crystallised (candied) lemon slices and finely chopped angelica, to serve

Warm the lemon curd with the apple juice in a saucepan or in the microwave, stirring until blended. Spoon over vanilla, coffee or chocolate ice cream and serve decorated with crystallised lemon slices and chopped angelica.

Hot Orange Topping

SERVES 4

75 ml/5 tbsp orange curd
30 ml/2 tbsp orange juice
Crystallised (candied) orange slices and chopped angelica, to serve

Warm the orange curd with the orange juice in a saucepan or in the microwave, stirring until blended. Spoon over vanilla, coffee or chocolate ice cream and serve decorated with crystallised orange slices and chopped angelica.

Atholl Brose Cream

SERVES 6

300 ml/½ pt/1¼ cups double (heavy) cream
30 ml/2 tbsp clear honey
30 ml/2 tbsp whisky

Whip the cream until softly peaking. Blend together the honey and whisky, then gradually whisk into the cream until thick. Chill until ready to serve.

Burnt Almond Cream

SERVES 6

300 ml/½ pt/1¼ cups double (heavy) cream
30 ml/2 tbsp light brown sugar
50 g/2 oz/⅓ cup flaked (slivered) almonds, well-toasted and crushed
1.5 ml/¼ tsp almond essence (extract)

Whip together the ingredients until softly peaking. Spoon into a serving bowl and chill until ready to serve.

Chocolate Cream

SERVES 4–6

75 g/3 oz/¾ cup plain (semi-sweet) chocolate (not cake covering)
15 ml/1 tbsp hot water
300 ml/½ pt/1¼ cups double (heavy) cream

Melt the chocolate in a pan over hot water. Stir in the measured hot water. Whip the cream until peaking and gently whisk in the chocolate. Chill until ready to serve.

Brandied Chocolate Cream

SERVES 4–6

Prepare as for Chocolate Cream, but substitute 15 ml/1 tbsp brandy for the water.

Coffee Cream

SERVES 4–6

*15 ml/1 tbsp instant coffee powder or
  granules*
15 ml/1 tbsp hot water
*15–30 ml/1–2 tbsp icing (confectioners')
  sugar*
*300 ml/½ pt/1¼ cups double (heavy)
  cream*

Dissolve the coffee in the water. Stir in the icing sugar to taste. Whip the cream until peaking and gently whisk in the coffee. Spoon into a serving dish and chill until ready to serve.

Brandied Coffee Cream

SERVES 4–6

Prepare as for Coffee Cream, but dissolve the coffee in 15 ml/1 tbsp brandy instead of water.

Fluffy Boozy Cream Topping

SERVES 6–8

1 egg white
*300 ml/½ pt/1¼ cups double (heavy)
  cream*
15 ml/1 tbsp brandy, rum or sherry
25 g/1 oz/2 tbsp light brown sugar

Whisk the egg white until stiff. Whip the cream with the brandy, rum or sherry and sugar until thick but not stiff. Fold the egg white into the cream mixture. Pour into a small jug and serve.

Chantilly Cream

SERVES 6–8

*300 ml/½ pt/1¼ cups double (heavy)
  cream*
*15 ml/1 tbsp icing (confectioners')
  sugar*
5 ml/1 tsp vanilla essence (extract)

Whip the cream with the icing sugar and vanilla until peaking. Turn into a serving bowl and chill for at least 30 minutes before serving.

Brandy Cream

SERVES 6–8

Prepare as for Chantilly Cream, but substitute 15–30 ml/1–2 tbsp brandy for the vanilla essence (extract).

Cointreau Cream

SERVES 6–8

Prepare as for Chantilly Cream, but omit the vanilla essence (extract) and whisk in 15–30 ml/1–2 tbsp Cointreau to taste.

Crème de Menthe Cream

SERVES 6–8

Prepare as for Chantilly Cream, but omit the vanilla essence (extract) and whisk in 15–30 ml/1–2 tbsp crème de menthe to taste.

Tia Maria Cream

SERVES 6–8

Prepare as for Chantilly Cream, but flavour with 15–30 ml/1–2 tbsp Tia Maria or other coffee liqueur.

Framboise Cream

SERVES 6–8

Prepare as for Chantilly Cream, but substitute 15–30 ml/1–2 tbsp Framboise (raspberry liqueur) for the vanilla essence (extract).

Clotted Cream

MAKES ABOUT 225 G/8 OZ/1 CUP

Clotted cream is really satisfying to make at home. Use the leftover skimmed milk for sauces or for a milk pudding.

450 ml/¾ pt/2 cups whole milk
300 ml/½ pt/1¼ cups single (light) cream

Mix together the milk and cream in a shallow heatproof bowl. Chill for at least 2 hours. Place over a pan of very gently simmering water and simmer for up to 6 hours, topping up the pan with water as necessary, until a thick golden crust forms on the surface. Gently lift the bowl off the pan and leave to cool. Chill, then skim off the clotted cream from the surface.

Greek-style Yoghurt

MAKES ABOUT 600 ML/1 PT/2½ CUPS

600 ml/1 pt/2½ cups plain yoghurt
30 ml/2 tbsp single (light) cream

Line a nylon sieve (strainer) with kitchen paper (paper towels) and place over a bowl. Tip the yoghurt into the sieve and chill overnight. The whey will drip into the bowl. Turn the thick yoghurt into a clean bowl and whisk in the cream. Chill until ready to use. Serve plain, with honey or with fresh fruit.

Brandy Butter

SERVES 6–8

100 g/4 oz/½ cup unsalted (sweet) butter, softened
225 g/8 oz/1⅓ cups icing (confectioners') sugar, sifted
30 ml/2 tbsp brandy

Beat the butter until light. Beat in the sifted icing sugar, then the brandy. Turn into a serving dish and chill until ready to serve.

Cumberland Rum Butter

SERVES 6–8

Prepare as for Brandy Butter, but substitute light brown sugar for half the icing (confectioners') sugar and dark rum for the brandy.

Jamaican Rum Butter

SERVES 6–8

Prepare as for Brandy Butter (see page 359), but substitute rum for the brandy and dark brown sugar for half the icing (confectioners') sugar. Add 5 ml/1 tsp grated fresh root ginger to the mixture.

Gaelic Butter

SERVES 6–8

Prepare as for Brandy Butter (see page 359), but substitute whisky for the brandy and add the finely grated rind of 1 small lemon to the mixture.

Cointreau Butter

SERVES 6–8

Prepare as for Brandy Butter (see page 359), but substitute Cointreau for the brandy and add the finely grated rind of 1 orange to the mixture.

Hard Sauce

SERVES 4–6

100 g/4 oz/½ cup unsalted (sweet) butter, softened
100 g/4 oz/½ cup caster (superfine) sugar
15 ml/1 tbsp brandy or sherry
50 g/2 oz/½ cup ground almonds

Beat together the butter and sugar until light and fluffy. Beat in the brandy or sherry and the almonds. Pile into a serving bowl and chill before serving.

Lemon Hard Sauce

SERVES 6

100 g/4 oz/½ cup unsalted (sweet) butter, softened
250 g/9 oz/1½ cups icing (confectioners') sugar
Finely grated rind and juice of 1 lemon

Beat together the butter and icing sugar until smooth. Beat in the lemon rind and juice. Spoon into a serving bowl and chill until ready to serve.

Orange Hard Sauce

SERVES 6

Prepare as for Lemon Hard Sauce, but substitute the finely grated rind and juice of ½ orange and 15 ml/1 tbsp orange liqueur for the lemon rind and juice.

Index